PRIMAL DRIVES

Primal Drives

Lore Book II: The Warrior

MATT STURM

Published by Living Kosmos

COPYRIGHT

Primal Drives

Edited by Taylor Plimpton. Yoga illustrations by Jurre Blom.

Published by Living Kosmos, LLC
30 N Gould St | Suite R | Sheridan, WY 82801 | USA www.livingkosmos.com
ISBN-13: 979-8-9904819-4-7

ADVANCED PRAISE

A total game-changer! These practices profoundly transformed my relationship with sex and pleasure. The trajectory of my life has dramatically shifted as a result. Men: Get the book. Work with Matt. Uplevel your life!

Matt Mochary
author of *The Great CEO Within*

Sturm's book is one of the wisest—and most important—I've ever read. The breadth of his knowledge when it comes to human nature, psychology, and spirituality is astounding. Still, what's most remarkable is that he not only traces how we got here, but where we can go. In the end, Sturm offers a vision of what's possible—a path of growth, health, and well-being—and through reading his book, we find ourselves well on our way.

Taylor Plimpton
Book editor

Book II: The Warrior is a lucid and clear pointer to what's needed now, on the very edge of authentic masculinity becoming adopted and applied or rejected and distorted, again. This is a deeply insightful examination into where and how humanity can re-empower its genuine Warrior. It's also a widely comprehensive multi-dimensional map of humanity's evolution itself. Strongly recommended for those who are deeply committed to creatively materializing the fullness of true human potential, now.

Adam Gainsburg
MarsGates.com

Primal Drives offers the map for men to redefine one of the darkest archetypes in human history, the warrior. In Matt's thorough invitation, he delineates the path for men to redirect aggression and sexuality to serve a higher purpose. Aggressive instincts become channeled into life building and generative action. Sexual energy enters into service to sovereignty, purpose, and realization. Matt asserts that the redefinition of these two essential components of the warrior archetype only emerges through a man's willingness to be intimate with where he holds their distortion within. As he honestly meets this darkness with the courage and vulnerability of his heart, he discovers a subsuming compassion for himself and for others. This is the direct connection between the warrior and the Bodhisattva, the Saint, the King who serves his domain for the benefit of all. This is a must read for all men hungry to rewire and upgrade their primal nature and authentic power in service to NOW times.

Katherine Zorensky
Catalyst for New Paradigm Leaders
www.beingkatherinez.com

The consequences of male violence—against women, children, nature, and each other—are undeniable, rooted in the generational momentum of exploitation and the violation of the feminine in all her forms. At the heart of this crisis is the archetype of the Warrior—a foundational aspect of the male psyche. When unmoored & unmentored, the Warrior is destructive, perpetuating harm rather than protecting life. In *Primal Drives*, Matt Sturm offers a bold and practical approach to transmuting the destructive aspects of war & sexual violence into pathways of justice and sexual self-mastery. Through illuminating insights, reflective practices, archetypal maps, and actionable exercises, this phenomenal workbook supports men to reclaim their primal power as a force for creation, connection, and integrity. *Primal Drives* is a call to action for men ready to transform themselves—and the world.

Ian MacKenzie
The Mythic Masculine
themythicmasculine.com

In this time of great initiation, Sturm offers a timely invitation and alchemical yet practical guide to orient and exercise our identities as men by challenging our destructive impulses and assumptions about the future while providing a nuanced path toward generative possibilities. There is a warrior in each of us, and how well we understand and embody each of his facets will determine how victorious we are at transmuting today's impossible challenges into life-sustaining opportunities. Primal Drives meets the Men's Movement where it's at, and calls it one big leap forward from its focus on the empowered individual towards inspired collective responsibility and liberation.

Justin Hartery LMFT
Founder of Source Embodiment

CONTENTS

PART III - SEX

INTRODUCTION

Have you met your inner Warrior? This archetype is an essential part of the masculine psyche. Throughout human history, men have been called into Warriorship, often as a matter of survival. We fought to protect what we held dear. Sometimes, the Warrior fights for a cause like glory or an ideal. But what does becoming a Warrior mean in today's context? Are you still dressing up like the knight, Don Quixote, chasing windmills and figments of past battles? Has your Warrior gone to sleep, leaving you a simple pawn in your own life? Or is your Warrior a liability, prone to lashing out in unpredictable ways? Men: It is time to get our Warriors online in a healthy, integrated way. You owe it to your loved ones and to the world. Most of all, you owe it to yourself. Your inner Warrior wants to get you in shape, clean up your messes, and clarify your priorities so you can start living your best life.

Within men's work to date, the Warrior archetype has largely focused on physical prowess and engaging responsibly with one's life. When I feel good in my body, I bring a joyful energy to everything I do. Stepping into integrity changed my whole life. But this is only the beginning. The next generation of Warriorship—the organic masculine expression of Warriorship—includes the discipline and purpose of the traditional approach, and transcends it. The monumental task for Warriors today is to make the world sustainable for all humans.

The vision and practices I'm presenting here invite the men's movement beyond its current focus on personal growth to include social transformation. For this reason, *Lore Book II* is not only for men looking to awaken their inner Warriors—this text is also for the current and future leaders of the men's movement. Get the download offered here, internalize it, make it your own, and use these resources in your men's groups, trainings, and organizations. This text outlines a bold new vision for men's work, offering a roadmap for how we can materially change society for the better.

Of course, this is not the final answer—it's simply the next iteration. As your brother, I want to invite you to continue innovating and iterating with me on what the Warrior can be. We hold an incredible amount of potential here. It is time to channel this vitality into *right work*.

As a Warrior embodying the organic masculine, I am called to own and take responsibility for the ways my unintegrated Warrior has caused harm in the past—and perhaps continues to inflict harm today. Collectively, we have inherited an expression of Warriorship that has misused *aggression* and *sex* as weapons against the flourishing of life. In significant segments of our culture, the Warrior is immature and wounded.

When my Warrior is not actively causing harm, I frequently find him checked-out, complacent, apathetic, and uninspired. It is far easier to choose comfort over fighting for truth. Far too often, I have suppressed my Warrior in favor of carefree relaxation. This is the collective legacy we are grappling with. Unless I consciously evolve my Warrior, he remains mired in these cultural distortions.

Once I activate my Warrior, he will guide me into the core of my being to discover my role in the transformation that humanity desperately needs.

Here are the two Herculean tasks of the organic Warrior:

1. Bring an end to male violence; and
2. Enact a sexual revolution in masculinity.

This work promises to reshape our civilization to bring us into sustainability with our planet. Each task is monumental. In these pages you will find my visions to move from violence to peace and to fundamentally change sexuality for men. My real goal is to offer you the tools to make these changes within yourself. You can fundamentally change your relationship with violence and find peace within yourself, and you can step into sovereign choice around ejaculation, unleashing your own personal sexual renaissance. With these audacious goals in mind, it is my pleasure to welcome you to the second workbook in the *Organic Masculine* series!

In *Lore Book I*, we undertook initiation into the archetype of the Magician, focusing on the foundational question for men's work today: *What is masculinity?* There, I provided the following definition:

Here is my understanding of masculinity through the integral lens. My holistic self has a natural and innate capacity to recognize masculinity, which provides the true and trustable experience of the masculine. The masculinities that proliferate throughout gender identity and expression are one layer of the masculine morphic field. This field imbues all realms of the kosmos below unity consciousness, including biology, subtle energy, causal archetypes, and the high-archetypes. At the high causal layer, the primal, divine, sacred masculine forms a trinity together with the primal, divine, sacred feminine and the primal, divine, sacred androgyne. The masculine and feminine fields define themselves contextually through polarity with each other. Thus there is no *singular* or *universal* masculine trait, only specific instances of polarity. Definition only happens contextually. And yet, my heart feels and recognizes the masculine, beyond theories or concepts, in the immediacy of experience. Whatever traits or context the masculine is wearing in that moment *is* the true masculine here and now. I know the masculine when I feel him. The morphic field of masculinity is simultaneously singular and infinitely diverse. This field manifests uniquely within each individual and is continuously evolving throughout individuals, cultures, and humanity.[1]

With this basis, my next question is: *What is a man's job today?* As an integral man embodying the organic masculine, what am I here to do? What constitutes right action? To answer these questions, I must turn to the archetype of the Warrior, whose core trait is *action*. In this workbook, I will share my perspectives on the evolving roles of the organic masculine within contemporary society.

In *Lore Book I*, I claimed that it is no longer a man's job to fight, to rule, and to provide. These roles have been passed down to men since the birth of Western civilization, but they no longer hold true today. The deconstruction of these roles in postmodern society has left many men feeling lost, purposeless, or alienated. If I'm not fulfilling these roles, then what is my purpose and where is my value? But from another perspective, today's man is blessed with a liberation from the confines of these roles. Our generation of men has unprecedented access to spiritual technologies, healing modalities, and developmental resources that allow us to forge a new path. Utilizing these new tools, together with the courage and discipline of the Warrior, we stand on the brink of profound transformation. We have an incredible opportunity today to step into our integrity, purpose, and service as men. We will bring these online, not by adopting a culturally defined role, but by redefining masculinity within the wholeness of our beings.

The male version of the Warrior archetype touches the darkest corners of human history, including murder, war, rape, torture, pillage, and enslavement. Like it or not, this is my heritage as a man. Warriorship is not about distancing myself from these shadows. On the contrary, I am tasked to become intimate with them. The capacity for such atrocities exists within me, as it does within all men. Acknowledging this fact is crucial. Without ownership, these wounds remain exiled, preventing genuine integration, healing, and maturation.

The first step on the path of the Warrior is to not be afraid of myself. Yes, the dark masculine lives within me, but that does not mean it defines me. By facing my fears head-on, I illuminate these shadowy parts. I learn that when I come into relationship with these shadows, they lose their power over me, and in turn, I gain a deeper trust in myself.

There are two overarching ways that masculinity is causing harm in the world today. The first is hegemonic masculinity:

> I define hegemonic masculinities as those masculinities that legitimate an unequal relationship (locally, regionally, and globally) between men and women, masculinity and femininity, and among masculinities.
>
> —Messerschmidt[2]

Men hold the vast majority of power and resources. Men make up 87 percent of world leaders,[3] 90 percent of fortune 500 CEOs,[4] and 87 percent of the world's billionaires.[5] Often we hear this inequality referred to as *patriarchy*, but I prefer to use the term *hegemonic masculinity*. Hegemony means dominant power. So this term describes a system where a small number of men wield power over everyone else in society. Just the fact that political and economic power is so overwhelmingly imbalanced is harmful for humanity and the earth.

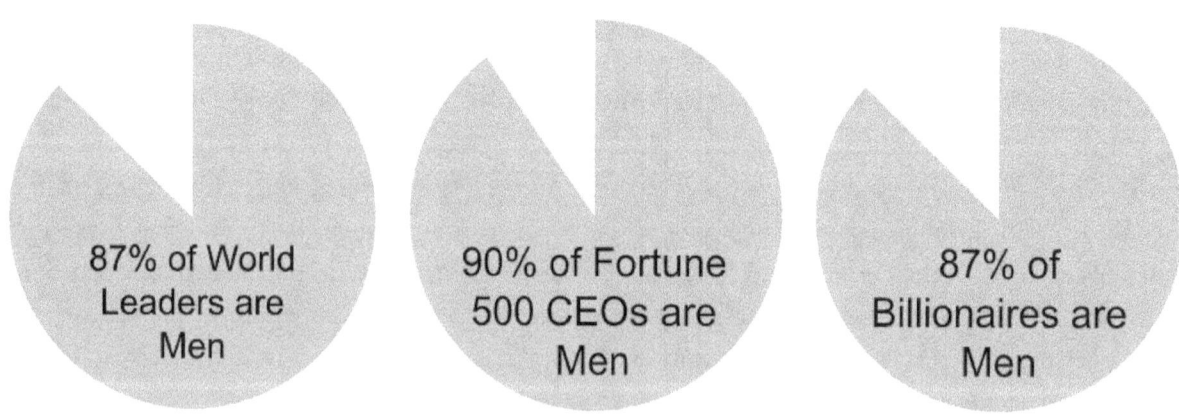

Figure i. Hegemonic Masculinity

The second way that masculinity is causing harm is through violence. Men perpetrate a staggering amount of violence: 98% of sexual assaults[6] and 90% of homicides are committed by men.[7] These figures are for individual acts so do not include war, genocide, or institutional violence—

all of which are also overwhelmingly male-enacted. Often we hear the term *toxic masculinity*, but I prefer the term *male violence*. I'm highlighting my language because both hegemonic masculinity and male violence are specific, well-defined terms, and I think all of us can agree that these are two pretty big problems.

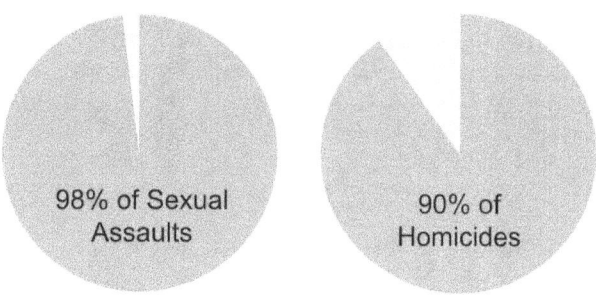

Figure ii. Male violence

In our exploration of the Warrior, we'll focus on the topics of sex and violence, which are perhaps the two strongest motivating forces of masculinity. Testosterone influences both sex and aggression. It is nature's version of hot sauce for the male body. But to truly integrate my impulses for sex and aggression, I need to go beyond hormones. These primal drives form the core of my most wild and instinctual nature. Personally, the two most dangerous parts of my psyche, which I have been most invested in repressing, are my *killer* and my *sexual ravager*. My pathologies of sex and aggression are exactly what the Warrior archetype must come to terms with.

The primal nature of sex and aggression makes them incredibly strong motivators. Robert Moore refers to unintegrated sexuality as a *universal solvent*, capable of dissolving family, career, and anything else it touches when it goes unchecked. Paul Gilbert suggests that male violence might be the world's single greatest cause of suffering. Because of the strength of these drives within me, I need to dedicate a significant amount of my vitality to their regulation. Ironically, suppressing my own aggression creates further inner conflict within my psyche.

I have respect for men's work that accesses the Warrior archetype through primal skills like archery and physical sparring. These approaches have helped me to access my aggression. They have helped get me out of my head. Yet, these approaches have been only partial solutions on my path. If the solution to male violence were as simple as wrestling or going into the woods and screaming, the men's movement would have solved these issues in the 1970s.

I do not pretend to understand every martial art and primal skill out there, but broadly speaking, practicing combative techniques in the name of nonviolence is a fallacy. As Einstein observed, "You cannot simultaneously prevent and prepare for war." While this type of men's work helped me confront my fear of violence, I was not able to become less violent or more compassionate through it. Often, I've observed that these practices either subtly or overtly promote hegemonic masculinity. What I offer in this workbook is a different approach.

My mission as a Warrior is to *integrate* these primal parts of myself by owning my capacities for physical and sexual violence. Embracing these powerful forces, I become intimate with them—how they function, what needs they serve in me, and where in my history they source from. My practice is to feel myself in the spaces of hatred, insecurity, disgust, dark pleasure, shame, and humiliation. As I learn to stay present in my body, all of these emotions unlock a tremendous amount of life force.

Most importantly, my goal is to integrate my pathologies of sex and aggression into the wholeness of my adult, organic self. By bringing these shadow parts into the light of consciousness, fully feeling them, and then loving them from my centered, sovereign core, they transform. I transform. When I offer my shadows a seat at my inner council, they bring profound gifts: my inner killer teaches me total dedication to the truth, and my sexual ravager unleashes my erotic potency. When I no longer need to suppress these parts, I become free to channel this primal power toward life-affirming causes. Moreover, it is only by experiencing the root of my violence that I can begin to move beyond it. This is the path of the organic Warrior.

Here in *Lore Book II,* I share my field notes in exploring the archetype of the Warrior. As always, I hope you will receive these words as a kind of provisional guidance to inspire your personal process of discovery. Take what works and leave what doesn't. Part I contains an invocation of the Warrior's archetype and mythology, as well as my investigations into the themes of integrity and purpose.

Part II ventures into the realms of individual and collective forms of violence. Along the way, I offer a vision for adopting a nonviolent life and I explore frameworks to engage in social activism. Nearly all of the ills in the world today can be understood as forms of violence: mass extinction and climate change, income inequality and poverty, and social systems of oppression and war—just to name a few. As the dismantling power of postmodernity picks up momentum and the self-actualization of the integral paradigm emerges, these *givens* of violence in our world will not only be called into question—I believe we will begin to move beyond them. The shift to world peace—not in wishful idealism, but in actuality—can only happen to the extent that we as individuals commit ourselves to nonviolence. When the majority of humans reach the level of development where we are able to practice nonviolence in our own lives, then world peace will naturally follow. This journey begins by acknowledging the possibility of a nonviolent life. These themes form the core of Part II.

My focus in Part III is sex, where I will share the techniques and practices that I used to learn sexual self-mastery and non-ejaculatory orgasms. These practices not only promise more fulfilling sex, they address the many sexual pathologies that stem from our agendas to ejaculate. As a man who is attracted to women, I have instinctual urges to compete with other men for access to sexually desirable women and to seduce women into sex. My core motive is ejaculation, which drives a whole host of undesirable behaviors.

By learning how to withhold ejaculation, a number of life-changing experiences simultaneously unlocked for me. First, I began having orgasm after orgasm during sex. This alone was pretty epic. I stopped pressuring myself or my partner to achieve ejaculation. With this shift, the vast majority of my sexual agendas and seduction strategies immediately became irrelevant. Through these practices, I began to unlock deeper layers of authenticity and nonattachment in my romantic and sexual relationships. All of the energy I was expending by spilling my seed reintegrated in the form of vitality, focus, and drive in my life. And perhaps most profoundly, sexual intercourse shifted into a playground for self-discovery, healing, intimacy, and spiritual realization. For me, this has been nothing short of a revolution in sexuality. In Part III, I will share with you everything I've learned over the last decade—not only through my personal practice but also through coaching other men on their journeys to sexual self-mastery.

At the end of this workbook are five appendices covering the metaphysics I laid out in *The Organic Masculine*. I highly recommend you work your way through that book before diving into this one. In Appendix I, I give an overview of Integral Theory, largely inspired by Ken Wilber. Integral Theory is a cutting-edge, comprehensive approach to understanding reality. Weaving together science, spirituality, and philosophy, Integral Theory attempts to synthesize a grand theory of everything. The integral approach looks across many theories and disciplines to find commonalities which are assembled into a theory of theories, or a *metatheory*.[8] In Appendix I, I outline the developmental journey that individuals and cultures make through paradigms of consciousness. Appendix II covers the states of consciousness, which are the present-moment experiential realms from waking consciousness up to nondual suchness. Appendix III outlines my approach to archetypes, the process of initiation, and character theory. Finally, Appendix IV pulls paradigms, states, and archetypes together into a unified framework for human growth, awakening, and maturation. My recommendation is to read through these appendices after this introduction and before starting in on Chapter One with *The Archetype of the Warrior*. The material I cover throughout this workbook assumes you understand the topics in the appendices. That said, the material in the appendices is dense, and you're welcome to simply dive into the Warrior and pick up the philosophy along the way.

Now that we have an outline of this workbook, let's take a moment to look at the big picture. Imagine a version of you where instead of stuffing your aggression down or lashing out with it, you have the tools to stay centered while you welcome the power of that energy to flow through you. Imagine you are able to channel that energy into building a better life for yourself. Now imagine that the same is true of your sexual energy—you are able to welcome it to flow through you, so that it can contribute to your creativity in healthy, satisfying, and respectful ways. Imagine how much different your life could be with these two forces working on your behalf. Now imagine that most of the men you know also have this realignment active in their lives. How much safer will everyone in society be when we, as men, have integrated our sex and aggression in a healthy, life-affirming way? Imagine what then becomes possible for humanity...

I want to close by sharing two perspectives. First, the Warrior accomplishes what initially seems impossible. Not only is the shift to a nonviolent life possible, it is a natural outcome of our evolutionary trajectory. Similarly, not only is it possible to have multiple, full-body orgasms without ejaculating, you are now holding a step-by-step process to guide you into mastery. My first point is that these shifts are possible for you in the foreseeable future.

My second point can be illustrated by Mahatma Gandhi, who was perhaps the greatest Warrior the world has ever known. During the final 35 years of his work as a political activist, Gandhi walked an equivalent distance to circling the earth twice. The Warrior acts. It is through dedication and perseverance that massive transformation becomes a reality. My call in this workbook is for us to integrate our primal drives of aggression and sex in service to the organic masculine. These two feats are no less monumental than Gandhi's achievement of liberating India from British rule through nonviolence. They are possible. What they will ask, however, is that we be willing to walk around the circumference of the earth twice.

Notes

[1] *The Organic Masculine, Lore Book I: The Magician*, Sturm.

[2] "Multiple Masculinities" in *Handbook of the Sociology of Gender, 2nd ed*, Risman et al.

[3] "Facts and figures: Women's leadership and political participation," unwomen.org

[4] "Women CEOs run 10.4% of Fortune 500 companies. A quarter of the 52 leaders became CEO in the last year" Hinchliffe, Fortune.com

[5] "The World's Richest Self-Made Women In 2024," Wu, Forbes.com

[6] "National Intimate Partner and Sexual Violence Survey," Basile et al. CDC.

[7] "Global Study on Homicide," United Nations Office on Drugs and Crime.

[8] "Instead of postulating a theory that competes against other theories for a singular truth, integral looks across all theories, compares and contrasts them, to create a comprehensive theory of theories." Excerpt B, Wilber.

PART I - THE WARRIOR

| 1 |

The Archetype of the Warrior

Figure 1.1 Strength, Rider-Waite Tarot

The key to warriorship and the first principle of Shambhala vision is not being afraid of who you are. Ultimately, that is the definition of bravery: not being afraid of yourself. Shambhala vision teaches that in the face of the world's great problems, we can be heroic and kind at the same time. Shambhala vision is the opposite of selfishness. When we are afraid of ourselves and afraid of the seeming threat the world presents, then we become extremely selfish. We want to build our own little nests, our own cocoons, so that we can live by ourselves in a secure way.

–Chögyam Trungpa[1]

My relationship with the archetypal Warrior begins with discomfort. This is not an easy archetype. If I am to make any trustworthy connection with the Warrior it will require that I be willing to sit in my discomfort. Warriorship deals with topics like anger, aggression, conflict, and boundaries—evoking emotions that are challenging to feel and tasks that are daunting to undertake. On one hand, we need Warriors in the world; on the other hand, Warriors are causing great harm in the world. While the Warrior can be joyful, even that can slip into fundamentalism or bloodlust. Engaging with the Warrior is like learning to work with fire. It is a bright and powerful energy. When guided properly, it can accomplish great work—but it demands respect. Without skillful use the Warrior can burn us or cause a blaze that can level whole nations. But the Warrior is universal. Everyone has a Warrior within. And therefore, we must be willing to roll up our sleeves and welcome the discomfort of exploring this dynamic archetype.

The Warrior is the motivating force for action in the psyche. His drive, passion, and inspiration provide a major source of energy and an impetus for change. He is focused, practical, and dedicated to follow-through. Words are wind; it is action that matters to the Warrior. In his light, the Warrior is a devoted servant of truth, a protector of beauty, empowered by his own innate goodness. In his shadow—well, there's a lot of shadow. We'll get to that.

On the mandala, the Warrior is associated with the South direction and the attributes of dedication and action. His element is fire: the element of purification, cleansing, and transformation through heat. The Warrior burns away all falsity and obscuration so that only what is true remains.

In my opinion, the Warrior is the most important archetype in men's work today. Since the mythopoetic movement began in the 1980s, the reclamation of the *male-warrior* has been a primary focus of men's work. Connecting with the Warrior is a major draw, or sometimes even *the* draw for men to engage in men's work. Speaking very broadly on behalf of men, I believe this is because we don't have a healthy relationship in our culture with Warrior energy. More precisely, we are lacking Warrior initiation. For many men, our Warriors are either violent bullies or repressed beneath the facade of the nice guy. Few and far between are contemporary men who have truly integrated their Warrior.

But, as I will explain below, *Warrior* initiation is not *manhood* initiation. This is a major misunderstanding throughout contemporary men's work. Many men's retreats claim to be creating mature men, when in actuality they are awakening archetypal Warriors. Initiation into Warriorhood is a powerful and beautiful thing. But by claiming "this" is what it means to be a man, men's work as a movement has confused its members, alarmed postmodernists and feminists alike, and stunted the organizations whose stated aim is to bring realized *men* into the world. Clarifying the archetype of the Warrior—what he is and what he is not—and integrating him into his proper place in the male psyche is crucial for the future of men's work.

In addition, the Warrior archetype carries an incredible amount of shadow, baggage, wounding, obscuration, and misappropriation. This also stems from the fact that our culture lacks proper Warrior initiation. The West has been missing Warrior initiation as a core aspect of our culture since feudal knights were overtaken by the Age of Reason. But we desperately need Warriors in our society to show up, to advocate, to stand in integrity, and to remake the world. It's impossible to say which is worse: the harm caused by our wounded shadow-Warriors, or the good work left unfulfilled by our lack of integrated light-Warriors. This is why the Warrior archetype is so important.

In this chapter, I will examine several shadows of the Warrior: the *tough/generous* and *burdened/enduring* character strategies, the *sadist* and the *masochist*, and the *killer* and the *sexual ravager*. I'll then examine the transcendent version of the Warrior, known as the Peacemaker. But first, why is Warrior initiation different from manhood initiation and why does this matter? My intention is to provide a clear understanding of the Warrior archetype. By answering this question, I will also address the postmodern critique which asks whether men's work should continue to include the archetype of the Warrior at all today.

Iron John

Robert Bly's book *Iron John* became the foundation of the mythopoetic men's movement after its publication in 1991. For me, what is remarkable is not the depth of Bly's analysis about the deep masculine, nor the accuracy of his conclusions about men, women, and society. What is truly remarkable is just how popular the book became. It spent 62 weeks on the New York Times best seller list and continues to be a top 25 book in men's studies today, 35 years later. Clearly, *Iron John* touched something real for men.

Bly's perspective is that the counterculture revolution of the 1960s produced the "soft male." In the language of Integral Theory, the postmodern paradigm enacts sensitive men.

There's something wonderful about this development—I mean the practice of men welcoming their own "feminine" consciousness and nurturing it—this is important—and yet I have the sense that there is something wrong. The male in the past twenty years has become more thoughtful, more gentle. But by this process he has not become more free. He's a nice boy who pleases not only his mother but also the young woman he is living with. In the seventies I began to see all over the country a phenomenon that we might call the "soft male."... The "soft" male was able to say, "I can feel your pain, and I consider your life as important as mine, and I will take care of you and comfort you." But he could not say what he wanted, and stick by it. *Resolve* of that kind was a different matter.

—Robert Bly[2]

The soft male is unhappy, is unattractive to women, and is a dutiful follower in society, destined to live a life of mediocrity. This is the insight that Robert Bly got brilliantly right. Men feel disempowered, disconnected from their sexual potency, and unvalued by society. Bly's formulation of the masculine problem resonates with an overwhelming number of men. In fact, it defined the zeitgeist of the mythopoetic movement in the 1990s and continues to inspire men's work today.

Bly's solution to the soft male problem gets some things right and other things confused. Perhaps the biggest confusion is his mixup between the Warrior and the King. Bly claims we are lacking Zeus energy—by which he means the assertive authority of the King archetype. He claims, "the inner King is connected with our fire of purpose and passion."[3] In my view, resolve, fire, purpose, and passion are the domains of the Warrior. The King makes decisions, yes, but it is the Warrior who carries them out. In my mandala, the King holds the element of earth with the quality of being, while the Warrior holds the element of fire and the quality of action. I agree that the issues of the soft male require more resolve, but the Warrior addresses this, not the King. Bly is not alone in this confusion though. It traces back to the beginning of western civilization:

The Lord is a man of war: the Lord is his name.

—Exodus 15:3

Who is this King of glory? The Lord strong and mighty, the Lord mighty in battle.

—Psalms 24:8

It's an unfortunate misunderstanding that explains why we don't see more Kings emerging from men's work and why outsiders observing men's retreats raise concerns: We've been doing Warrior initiation and calling it manhood initiation.

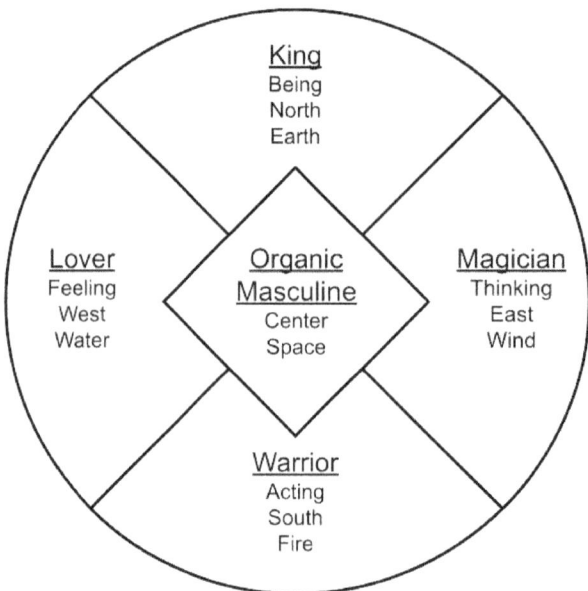

Figure 1.2 The archetypal masculine psyche

Among the gems that Bly got right: Men have become disconnected from their fathers through modernity. "The love unit most damaged by the Industrial Revolution has been the father-son bond."[4] Fathers once taught their sons a trade and worked side by side. Today fathers are emotionally and physically absent from adolescent sons. Fathers no longer take their sons out into the world and away from their mothers. Therefore the attachment bond between boys and mothers never breaks and men become soft. They dissociate from the masculine capacity for penetration, or never develop the skill to wield it well. This mother-son bond needs to be severed in early adolescence for healthy masculine development. Enter the tale of Iron John.

Once upon a time, there was a king with a forest near his castle. Hunter after hunter would venture into the forest and never return, so the king declared the woods dangerous and made it off-limits to all. Some years later, to win favor with the king a new huntsman decided to find out what danger lurked in the forest.

> The huntsman therefore set forth with his dog into the woods. It was not long before the dog picked up a scent and wanted to follow it, but the dog had run only a few steps when it came to a deep pool, and could go no further. Then a naked arm reached out of the water, seized the dog, and pulled it under.[5]

The huntsman fled and returned with a group of men and buckets who proceeded to empty out the pool of water. At the bottom of the pool, they found a hairy man with iron-like skin. They subdued and bound this Wild Man and brought him to the king. He was given the name Iron John (or in some versions, Iron Hans). The king locked him in a cage and gave the only key to the queen to safeguard.

Figure 1.3 The fight in the forest[6]

Let's pause our story here. In Jungian symbolism, the pool of water is the unconscious. This pool holds the parts of ourselves that have been neglected, exiled, and disallowed by the ego and super-ego/self-image. The unconscious is where the archetypes live, and it is here that we find the *Wild Man*. When exiled in the unconscious, he acts out to get his needs met: killing hunters, snatching dogs, and so forth. He becomes an unruly killer. Once in contact with the Wild Man, our waking consciousness would hope to control and contain him, just like the king locking him in a cage. But as his name suggests, the Wild Man is not easily tamed. Continuing now with the tale.

The king had a son of eight years. One day he was playing in the courtyard, and during his game his golden ball fell into the cage.

The boy ran to the cage and said, "Give me my ball."

"Not until you have opened the door for me," answered the man.[7]

Figure 1.4 Eisenhans in the cage[8]

Iron John tells the boy that the key to the cage is hidden under his mother's pillow. The boy eventually agrees to steal the key. When he opens the lock of the cage, he cuts his finger. Iron John returns the golden ball to the boy and departs the city. As he is leaving, the boy cries, "My parents will beat me if they find out I released you, take me with you!" Iron John agrees and they escape into the forest.

As boys grow into teenagers, the archetype of the Wild Man emerges in the psyche. The golden ball of the boy represents his innocence and vitality. We lose that ball into the shadowy parts of our psyche and must liberate it again by giving sovereignty to the Wild Man. Returning to Robert Bly's problem statement for the soft male: We are boys who have never liberated our Wild Man. He's the one holding that *special something* that we're lacking.

Liberating the Wild Man is a rite of passage. In order to undertake this initiation, we must steal the key from beneath our mother's pillow. Bluntly, we must stop being momma's boys, stop following the rules, and start following our own desires. Personally, when I undertook this initiation using the Iron John myth at a men's retreat, I was given a leather medicine pouch shaped like a pair of testicles at the end. This is what we gain. Bly calls it *resolve.*

This rite of passage, which I will refer to as *unchaining the wild man,* is a real and necessary step in the maturation of the masculine psyche. This step is what so many men are missing today. It's why the book, *Iron John,* is so immensely popular. In one way or another, unchaining the wild man is a core focus of the vast majority of contemporary men's work. This initiation is very much needed.

However, the mythopoetics got confused about what this rite of passage actually represents. In the story, the little boy frees the Wild Man. The Golden Boy undergoes initiation to become the adolescent Heroic Warrior. But this is not what transforms a boy into a *man*. From my perspective, this is how a boy becomes an *adolescent*.

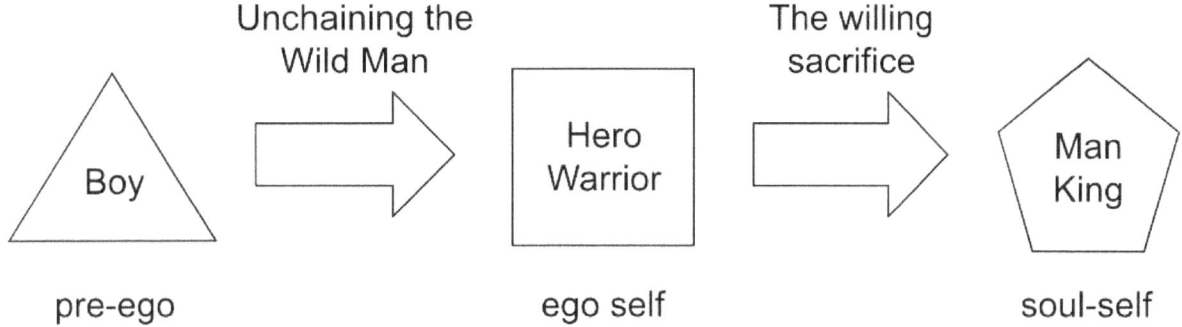

Figure 1.5 Initiations from boy to hero to man

In *The Organic Masculine*, I made the observation that we live in an adolescent culture: one based on achievement and self-glorification. Part of the pathology of our culture is that we have forgotten what adulthood entails and think superheroes are the pinnacle of our development. The myth of Iron John describes the masculine rite of passage into the Heroic Warrior. It is a *boy* becoming an *adolescent*—not an *adolescent* becoming a *man*. The brave huntsman and the Wild Man are two aspects of the Heroic Warrior. The tale of Iron John says nothing about the rite of passage into manhood, called *the willing sacrifice*.

At this point in the story, the boy and Wild Man now leave the familiar territory of the parents and adventure into the wilderness.

> The man took the boy to a spring and said, "Look, this golden spring is as bright and clear as crystal. You shall sit beside it, and take care that nothing falls into it, otherwise it will be polluted. I shall come every evening to see if you have obeyed my order."[9]

The boy eventually breaks his agreement. First his finger and then his hair fall into the pool, becoming golden each time. Gold is an important symbol in this myth. The boy loses his golden ball. Now his hair becomes gold. Gold is the lifeforce of the archetype. Now in adolescence, his vitality is no longer through play with his ball, it is in growing his lion's mane. The erotic vitality of a man's hair is paralleled in the Biblical myth of Samson, whose super-human strength was dependent on the length of his hair. In the Iron John story, the teenage hero now unleashes his animal nature, his Wild Man. When Iron John finds out the boy broke his agreement, he sends him away. The boy was once a prince, and now he travels as a stranger to a new kingdom where he finds lowly work as a garden boy.

War comes to the kingdom and the boy, seeking glory, calls on Iron John who magically supplies him with a horse and armor. The boy wins the battle on behalf of the kingdom. Desiring to know the identity of the mysterious knight, the king offers his daughter's hand in marriage to whoever catches a golden apple. Wearing red armor supplied by Iron John, the boy catches the apple but does not reveal himself. The next day, there's another golden apple toss, and this time Iron John gives the boy white armor. Again the boy catches the apple, but does not reveal himself. During the third apple-toss, the boy wears black armor. This time, when he catches the golden apple and gallops away, the king's men pursue him, wounding his leg, and knocking off his helmet to uncover his golden hair.

Figure 1.6 The mysterious knight[10]

The simple gardener's boy is revealed as the heroic knight. He wins the king's daughter in marriage, is reunited with his parents, and reconnects with Iron John who had been cursed with shaggy hair and iron skin until someone pure of heart could set him free. It turns out Iron John is also a king and offers all his treasures to the boy, who lives happily ever after.

The boy's first wound is in separation from his mother when he unlocks the gate. In the story, he cuts his finger. The first wound marks the initiation of *unchaining the Wild Man*. The boy's second wound happens while he is wearing the black armor of the knight. This wound marks the Warrior initiation. At first, the Warrior wears red armor. This symbolizes the unbridled passion and sexual drive of new Warriors. As he matures, the Warrior advances to white armor and he begins to fight for the sake of his ideals. The Warrior becomes a protector. Finally, the Warrior wearing black armor becomes wounded. He discovers his mortality and encounters his own shadows. It is through this wound that the Warrior becomes trustable and receives his full initiation. The mature, integrated Warrior in black armor is not motivated by his red passions or white ideals. The Warrior in black is slow to fight and does so out of compassion.

> The Black Knight wields his sword reluctantly and only when he has reached the sober realization that it is necessary. The man who has integrated the White with Red Knights, and accepted Black Knighthood has confronted his own Warrior Shadow and moved toward taking moral and spiritual responsibility for his own aggression.
>
> —Moore and Gillette[11]

Whereas the feminine progression of alchemical colors are white (virginity), red (menstruation), and black (crone), the masculine Warrior's series is red (passion), white (idealism), and black (compassion/mortality). Lesser known is the androgyne's series, which is black (pain and alienation), white (new light and community), and red (joy and power).[12]

The full initiation into Warriorhood marks the culmination of the Hero. In the story, the boy marries the girl, achieves fame and wealth, and integrates the Wild Man. This is what Heroes are supposed to do. The Hero and the Warrior are blurred together in the tale of Iron John, and in my model, this enmeshment is exactly how the adolescent masculine psyche forms. We become Heroic-Warriors in the developmentally appropriate phase of adolescence.

However, the Hero of Iron John does not become a King, a father, or a man. I do not want to imply that there is anything wrong with the Iron John initiations. In fact, the boys living in adult bodies among us are in dire need of it. But this is not a story about what it means to be a man. That requires yet another initiation in which the sovereign center of the self passes from the ego to the soul-self. During this initiation, the King comes online as the fourth part of the psyche, and the Warrior differentiates from the Heroic ego. Refer to Figure 1.5 above and check out Figure A3.3 in Appendix III. The manhood initiation is called *the willing sacrifice*, in which the man's priorities broaden beyond his personal self-improvement and he takes on both responsibility and service toward the larger web of life.

The Warrior's initiation has been misinterpreted as the manhood initiation in much of men's work. For sure, the Warrior is *part* of being a man. He is an indispensable quarter of the adult mandala. However, let us not mistake him as the *whole* of being a man.

In the last section of the Iron John fairy tale, we see the king and the king's daughter working together to come into connection with the nameless hero. In the Jungian interpretation of this myth, all the characters are archetypal parts of the psyche. The adult king and the inner feminine are both *others* for the heroic warrior. But they are coaxing him to reveal himself. And once that connection is made, the boy's mother, father, and Wild Man all show up. This *other nexus* of the psyche is the Self. It is the intelligence that is looking to integrate all parts into wholeness. However, the hero is playing warrior games and generally being avoidant. (Personally, I wouldn't know anything about that type of behavior.) So the latent king and inner feminine offer him an apple. Again the color gold is significant. These apples symbolize the lifeforce of adulthood. They represent nourishment and are offered by the feminine. The Self is calling the lost hero back home. Another biblical parallel is the parable of the prodigal son, who leaves his father with his inheritance, but once the son spends it in the world, he returns back to be reunited with his father as the source of life-giving wealth.

At the climax of the fairy tale, the hero reveals himself, marries the girl, is reunited with his estranged parents, and lifts the curse from Iron John who turns out to be a king himself. This *happily ever after* note is where the tale ends. But let me ask you what you think would realistically happen next for our nameless hero. He just rushed into marrying a woman he's barely spoken to. His new father-in-law, the story notes, has already felt offended by the boy's pride. The parents that he stole from and ran away from now re-enter his life. Does this sound like a recipe for happiness?

Tapping into another Biblical parallel, we have a simple garden boy accepting an apple from a woman. What happens next is *the fall*. The hero's carefree days of playing in the garden and riding horses in the woods come to a close. This is the next chapter that our adolescent culture hasn't yet fully learned, and it remains unwritten in this tale. The fruition of the hero's journey is a glorified exaltation of the hero, yes, but that is immediately followed by *the willing sacrifice* where the hero offers his life for the greater good. The hero dies to become the king. The ego offers its service to the larger soul-self. The symbolic death here does not mean gone forever. It means the Hero part is no longer the sovereign center, but is now a member of the council. The Warrior takes his seat in service to the King, and the ego braids its will into the large soul-self. The Iron John tale takes us up to the culmination of the Hero, but does not narrate the next step, which is initiation into manhood, the King, and the sacred marriage. And so, while this tale powerfully and marvelously initiates boys into heroes and turns red Warriors into black Warriors, it does not offer initiation into the masculine adult. When men reenact this myth today, we are initiating our inner boys into adolescent Hero-Warriors.

Meanwhile, as the mythopoetic men's movement was gaining popularity in the 1990s, observers began to raise some very relevant questions about both the intentions and outcomes of this type of men's work. The focus on awakening the *male-warrior* and on a return to a *deep masculine* that we lost during industrialization aroused concerns. Viewed through the postmodern feminist lens, the mythopoetic men's movement seems regressive. It smells distressingly similar to the mythic/ traditional paradigm with its patriarchy and dominator hierarchies. And in fact, Promise Keepers, which is an Evangelical Christian men's movement, is exactly that.

But the mythopoetics were Jungians. Jung was a medical doctor and firmly inhabited the mental/modern paradigm. The mythopoetics recognize the ills of toxic masculinity, stemming from the mythic/traditional paradigm, and capitalism, from the mental/modern paradigm. They advocate for becoming a spiritual man, for grieving, and engaging in shadow work through the sacred wound. They want you to find your authentic masculinity. Their retreats function through intergenerational rituals that foster brotherhood. This movement incorporates sophisticated and highly transformational inner work and is not focused on in-group belonging or dominant power structures characteristic of the traditional paradigm. So although the name "mythopoetic" would seem to imply that it resides in the mythic/traditional paradigm, I place this movement squarely within the plural/postmodern paradigm, which is appropriate for a movement arising in the 1980s. Just as the Romantics of the 19th century were a faction of modernity that idealized the past, the mythopoetics are a faction of postmodernity that idealizes the masculinity of the past. Just as the Goddess hypothesis places the feminine of pre-civilization Europe on a pedestal for women,[13] the mythopoetics do the same for pre-industrial masculinity, called the *deep masculine*.

We can even contextualize the mythopoetic and similar male therapy movements as a natural response against the gender deconstruction project of postmodernism. Let's trace the evolution of mainstream masculine identities. Men in the traditional paradigm share a vision of the values-driven strong man.[14] Masculine strength creates safety through authority. Men in the modern paradigm share a vision of the principle-driven achieving man.[15] Masculine strength creates value through achievement. In postmodernity, strength, achievement, masculinity, and maleness *are* the problems. These are identities to be deconstructed. But that begs the question: deconstructed into what?

Dismantling identity is often a confusing process, and men attempting to undertake liberation from masculinity often hold no coherent answer for *then what?*. The Effeminate Movement posited that men should become like women.[16] Psychological androgyny proposed that men should carry both masculine and feminine traits.[17] And rounding out the space of logical alternatives, some men went for "the annihilation of masculinity."[18] None of these positions, by design, held a clear, compelling identity for men to rally around, and thus, none became a mainstream movement. Through the process of deconstruction, the *sensitive new-age guy* has emerged as postmodernism's ideal man. While the emotional awareness and sensitivity of the postmodern man is a much-needed step beyond the dominating tendencies of traditional and modern masculinities, the *soft male* remains largely ridiculed and abhorred. bell hooks summarized the whole situation like this:

> Once the 'new man' that is the man changed by feminism was represented as a wimp, as overcooked broccoli dominated by powerful females who were secretly longing for his macho counterpart, masses of men lost interest.[19]

In the vacuum left by postmodernity's masculine deconstruction, the mythopoetics found some solid masculine ground in Jungian archetypes and myths: the Wild Man and the *deep masculine*. The mythopoetic movement has largely emerged, whether intentionally or unintentionally, as a response against the anti-male sentiment of postmodern feminism and the demasculinization of men.

Given this context, it makes sense that the mythopoetic movement has resisted integrating the postmodern feminist critique of new-age men's work. This critique, which centers upon the Warrior archetype, holds true for much of men's work today. Here it is:

> But in focusing on how myth and ritual can reconnect men with each other, and ultimately with their own deep masculine essences as a means of dealing with men's pain, mythopoetic discourse and practice manage to sidestep the central point of the feminist critique—that men, as a group, benefit from a structure of power that oppresses women, as a group.

> When we look at nonindustrial societies, we see that the more rape-prone societies tend to be those that have high levels of male-dominated sex segregation in public spaces and those that celebrate war (Sanday, 1981). Thus, I concluded, it seemed dangerous that the mythopoetic men were celebrating the image of 'the male warrior,' within the context of their expressed need to create homosocial rituals that emphasized and reinforced men's separation from women.
>
> —Connell[20]

This applies to men's groups far beyond the mythopoetics. By creating men's-only spaces, where men connect with their power through the archetype of the Warrior, men's work is prone to reinforcing a culture of hegemonic masculinity. When systemic oppression and male privilege are not acknowledged in men's work, these well-meaning personal growth organizations contribute to gender inequality and may even further entrench domestic violence.

Notice that there are two women in the Iron John story, the queen/mother and the king's daughter/maiden. The boy's mother never speaks a line. For having such an important role, she has no voice of her own. While the mother is a zero-dimension character, the maiden has one dimension: She is interested in the hero because of his golden hair.[21] The portrayal of women as symbolic foils for the active male hero is one way that mythology has perpetuated hegemonic masculinity.

> As flesh, Woman loses her agency and it is the male who retains it, as well as the ability to act as hero. Woman disappears and is replaced by symbol because she is not fully allowed her subjectivity. Thus it becomes starkly clear why mythological figures of Woman are marked as non-heroic. Woman has been positioned as the purely phylogenetic source material (ripe, passive flesh) that has silently enabled the 'dazzling exploits' of the ontogenic male.
>
> —Dr. Sarah Nicholson[22]

Even though it may be invisible to men, and even though it is not our intent, reenacting this myth in men's work objectifies women as wicked stepmothers on one hand, and *ripe, passive flesh* to be won by the hero on the other hand. The masculine and feminine are not in active relationship with each other in this myth. There is no true intimacy. The women simply play a role for the hero. *She is not fully allowed her subjectivity.*

The two occasions when the hero is wounded both happen when he is running away from the feminine. The first wound is after he has stolen the key and is unlocking Iron John. He has transgressed against his mother and disobeyed his parents' orders. The second wound is while galloping away after catching the third golden apple from the maiden. Again the hero is distancing from the feminine. When I disconnect, blame, or degrade the feminine, my masculine is disempowered in the process. In contrast, when I connect, uplift, and celebrate the feminine, my masculine is uplifted in equal measure. Unfortunately, this myth does not portray a harmonious mutual support between the sexes. We are all wounded as a result.

This antagonism toward mothers in particular has been amplified by Robert Bly. In his view, mothers want to civilize their boys—to maintain them as good boys through possessiveness. Mothers teach their sons a female attitude of mistrust toward masculinity, and often shame them out of their power. Mothers are prone to a type of emotional incest with their sons, using them for emotional satisfaction and soul-companionship needs that are no longer fulfilled by the father. Bly sees this as an unconscious enactment by women of the dark side of the Great Mother archetype. It is not so much that mothers are malicious toward their sons as that a primitive form of the Great Mother archetype is blocking the maturation of young men. This is a feature of a society that has lost rites of passage and mature gender relationships.

Therefore, according to Bly, mothers in Western culture are either unwilling or unable to support their boys in becoming Wild Men. Our task as boyhood initiates is to steal the key from our mother.

> And the key has to be *stolen*. I recall talking to an audience of men and women once about this problem of stealing the key. A young man, obviously well trained in New Age modes of operation, said, "Robert, I'm disturbed by this idea of stealing the key. Stealing isn't right. Couldn't a group of us just go to the mother and say, 'Mom, could I have the key back?'?" His model was probably consensus, the way the staff at the health food store settles things. I felt the souls of all the women in the room rise up in the air to kill him. Men like that are as dangerous to women as they are to men. No mother worth her salt would give the key anyway. If a son can't steal it, he doesn't deserve it.
>
> —Robert Bly[23]

In order to embody the Wild Man, I need to choose my own desires over the path laid out by my mother. However, this message can equally be interpreted as: *men need to take what is theirs from women.* I can't imagine Bly's quote above inspiring confidence in anti-patriarchy feminists.

But there is an even deeper point that I'd like to illuminate, which is that I believe this passage about the key has been grossly mis-read and mis-interpreted by the mythopoetics. All of the life-force-carrying power objects for the hero are golden. The child plays with his golden ball and the hero's hair turns golden. On each step of his Warrior initiation, he catches a golden apple. But the key is not golden. It's just a regular key. And in fact, the key is not the boy's key. It's the father's key. The father locks up his Wild Man and gives the key to his wife. The symbolism is pretty clear: As a man, I domesticate myself in relationship. Stepping into true ownership means acknowledging that my mother is not to blame for the man I am today. Nor is she withholding my power from me. I'm the one who has locked up my Wild Man and given away my key. The disempowerment that I suffer is nobody's fault but my own. By characterizing the mother as withholding power from her son, Bly is positioning himself as an innocent victim to the overbearing mother. She has left him with two options: continue to be a soft male or forcibly take back what's his. Again, not an interpretation that inspires gender healing.

> It is easy to blame women and to project our anger onto them. We might feel they've caused our pain and hurt. Women, we must recognize, don't have this kind of power in our lives. Not blaming them, and not blaming ourselves as well, are part of dealing with anger and recognizing where its roots lie.
>
> —Paul Kivel[24]

Connell goes on to observe that pro-feminist activism is fundamentally at odds with men's work focused on empowering and connecting men. For those of us actively engaging in men's work, it is worth allowing this perspective to sink in a bit:

> The familiar forms of radical politics rely on mobilizing solidarity around a shared interest. That is common to working-class politics, national liberation movements, feminism and gay liberation. This *cannot* be the main form of counter-sexist politics among men, because the project of social justice in gender relations is directed *against* the interests they share. Broadly speaking, anti-sexist politics must be a source of disunity among men, not a source of solidarity. There is a rigorous logic to the trends of the 1980's: The more men's groups and their gurus emphasized solidarity among men (being 'positive about men,' seeking the 'deep masculine,' etc.), the more willing they became to abandon issues of social justice.
>
> —Connell[25]

This is why the large men's work organizations today are not making big waves in anti-oppression activism. They are helping men become empowered, for sure. But they are not engaging in gender liberation work. This is also why you've probably never heard of any of the men's movements that are specifically doing gender activism work. They rarely attract many men, and certainly don't publish best-sellers like *Iron John*.

> Any men's movement that does not directly address male violence, racism, class issues, and homophobia can only remain exclusive and superficial. We are not all the same, and our differences matter—sometimes in life-threatening ways—in this society.
>
> —Paul Kivel[26]

On the one hand, reclaiming the male warrior is undeniably of ample interest for men. This work is real. It is good work with tangible benefits. On the other hand, the postmodern project of dismantling hegemonic masculinity appears to be disconnected from men's work at best, and in direct conflict with men's work that focuses on the two Iron John initiations (or the like) at worst. This is a bind not just for men's work or academic gender studies, but for our society as a whole. How do we reconcile postmodern feminism with the Warrior archetype? How can we realistically engage men in both personal and social transformation, especially considering that men as a group hold the dominant social power?

I believe this bind has multiple solutions. The answer is not, "Stop doing male-warrior initiations." Whatever we condemn and suppress moves into the collective shadow and eventually returns in distorted form. (By the way, this is largely where the Warrior is now in our culture: relegated to the shadows and wreaking havoc through violence). Like it or not, the Warrior archetype is here to stay. It does no good to leave Iron John at the bottom of the pool or to lock him in the cage. So the first step is to embrace the Warrior. All of us, of all sexes and genders, have Warriors inside of us. When I give my Warrior a seat in my council, he doesn't need to act out to get his needs met. And when I value my Warrior, he offers incredible gifts in return.

The next step in men's work is to understand how the Warrior and his initiation fits into the masculine psyche. The Warrior's initiation (red to white to black) is simultaneously empowering and humbling. In a healthy society, it is a passage that all men would undertake. And importantly, this is *not* the initiation into manhood. Warrior initiation is an archetypally adolescent initiation (which can be undertaken as early as biological adolescence but is relevant for biological adults of any age, as archetypal maturity is distinct from biological age). Having received the Warrior's initiation, I still have more work to do to become an archetypal man.

Boys should be taken into a group of mature men to become Heroic Warriors. There is both wisdom and tradition backing this up.[27] However, the next step for men's work is to re-engage and re-integrate with folks of all genders. Becoming a man happens in society in connection with family, community, and kingdom. So if the goal of men's work is to shepherd realized men into the world, then we need to bring the *manhood* aspect of men's work into mixed-gender ritual spaces. While we're here, let's acknowledge that concentrating power, privilege, and authority in all-men's circles does, by definition, contribute to hegemonic masculinity. We also need to stop blaming women and mothers for the lack of Wild Men and Warriors in the world. It's not their fault, and as long as we hold ourselves as victims to our mothers, we will never truly find our power.

Finally, stepping into the integral paradigm radically changes these crossed incentives. The bind between the Warrior and postmodern feminism is only a bind from within the postmodern worldview. The key trait for the postmodern paradigm is sensitivity within an ethno-centric context. Some folks at this level become sensitive to gender oppression. In contrast, the men engaging in men's work become sensitive to masculine grief, pain, and anger. In the quoted passage above, Connell deftly identifies that men's solidarity groups will not advocate against their own self-interests.

The integral paradigm transcends this apparent gridlock by offering a new view with new tools. The key trait in the integral paradigm is evolution. The integral prime directive is to support all people—across all paradigms, religions, nationalities, and *genders*—to become self-actualized. Men looking through the integral paradigm see anti-oppression work in their best interest. So even though the developmentally appropriate focus within the postmodern paradigm is to heal my individual wounds and my group's collective wounds, now in the integral paradigm my developmentally appropriate tasks are to become self-actualized and to empower *everyone* to self-actualize.

Furthermore, whereas postmodernity conceptualizes nonviolence, integral embodies it. What has been most disturbing for me attending organized men's retreats is the promotion of the Warrior archetype without also teaching nonviolence. Here's what men's work gets right: I understand that I bring my Warrior out of the shadows by coming into direct contact with my own violence. This process is volatile and it's why we use a strong ritual container in nature. Symbolically, we empty out the pool of the unconscious to bring Iron John into full awareness. Men's work understands that if you leave him in the pool, he will kill people. Men's work also understands that locking him in a cage imprisons our vitality along with him. We need the Wild Man as an ally. But where men's work has largely fallen short is in taking the next step, which is nonviolence. The integral paradigm *groks* nonviolence through and through. In the pages below, I will explore nonviolence and the transcendent Peacemaker archetype in depth.

Here is the claim I am making: As the integral worldview begins to permeate more men's work, those men will be motivated through their own self-interest to engage in social liberation work. Integral synthesizes the Warrior archetype and postmodern feminism into a coherent, internally valid, mutually aligned vision for social actualization. The task of the Warrior within the first-tier stages of development is to protect his family, his people, and his values. The second-tier task of the Warrior IS social justice, and he brings an incredible vitality of disciplined action to the project with him. This represents an incredible transformation for the Warrior! This synthesis between the Warrior and social justice is a core thesis of this book. Warriorship, when properly integrated, becomes the motivating force to reshape the world. My intention is to provide you with the understanding, tools, and inner work necessary to passionately embody this integral approach to Warriorship.

Prompts for Journaling and Discussion

Have you undertaken the *unchaining the Wild Man* initiation into the archetypal Hero, formally or informally? If so, when and how?

Have you undertaken the red to white to black initiations into your archetypal Warrior? If so, when and how? What color is your Warrior today?

How do you experience the Warrior within?

Which people in your life have modeled integrated Warriorship for you?

What famous Warriors from pop culture and mythology do you admire or identify with?

Draw a self-portrait of the Warrior within you.

Shadow Elements and Character Strategies

The warrior's way wounds boys and men; it has been the arrow shot through the heart of their humanity. The warrior's way has led men in the direction of an impoverishment of spirit so profound that it threatens all life on planet Earth.

—bell hooks[28]

Having offered a clearer vision for the Warrior and his role in the masculine psyche, now I'd like to turn my attention to the shadows of the Warrior, which loom large across human history and the world today. Violence, aggression, rage, entitlement, bullying, and grasping for power are all symptoms of the hyper-active, out-of-control Warrior. War, genocide, rape, torture, and pillaging have cost untold human lives and potential. The first step in understanding (and ultimately transforming) these collective-level shadows is to examine the individual pathologies of the Warrior, and then to pinpoint the places within myself where those capacities exist.

Any outward act of violence brings with it an inward numbing or disconnection. Masculine systems of oppression—whether they dominate over women, children, other men, or the earth—are maintained by outward aggression and inward disconnection. This internal gap forms a barrier around the vital, feeling heart, creating isolation and species disidentification for those in "privilege" at the top of the oppressive system. All beings suffer at the hands of the shadow Warrior.

Character strategies are immature personality traits that generally form during childhood. I give an overview of these in Appendix III (see figures A3.4 and A3.5). Each of the four archetypal parts of the psyche is associated with an outward and an inward character strategy. The two strategies of the unintegrated Warrior are *tough/generous* and *burdened/enduring*.

The healing journey is not about eliminating these strategies, but bringing them into balance under the guidance of the adult self. When integrated, these character strategies form the foundations of the Warrior and offer us gifts. Finally, when the maturation process advances to the transpersonal Self, the transcendent form of the Peacemaker comes online (more on this below).

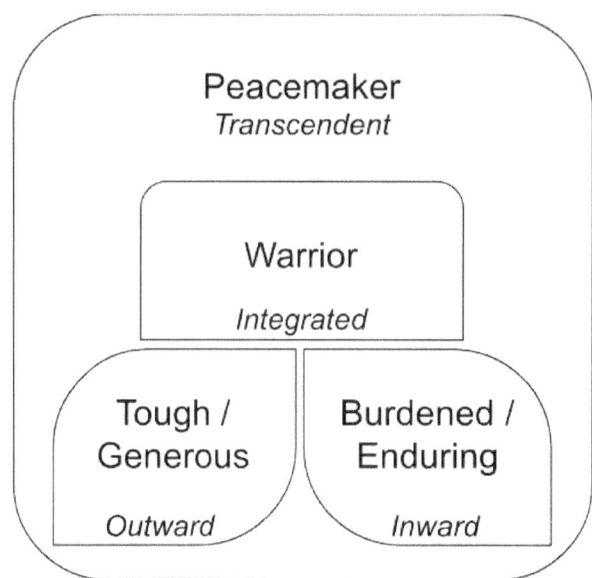

Figure 1.7 Archetypal structures of the Warrior

In character theory, the Warrior's hyper-active outward expression is the tough/generous strategy. This immature strategy arises for a young Warrior who must be strategic in order to meet his needs in a hostile environment. In particular, this strategy is a response to experiences of receiving violence, neglect, or abandonment. As the tough/generous character, I assume a false air of power and confidence to get what I want. I will bully or push proactively, and then reward those who are loyal and subservient in order to maintain my powerful status. At core, I employ this strategy because I believe I will not be loved and taken care of just as I am. I have learned that my vulnerability and weakness will be taken advantage of by others, so I proactively project my toughness outward. I develop a charismatic persona that is attractive, but ultimately overpowering for relationships. Deep down, I believe that everyone will eventually leave me. I compensate with my behavior pattern, which becomes a self-fulfilling cycle: I act big to secure love, but that act is what eventually pushes others away.

Figure 1.8 John Wayne as the tough/generous hero[29]

Limiting beliefs typical of the tough/generous character include, "I must dominate or I will be dominated," "My real feelings will be used against me," "I cannot be weak," and "You are only using me for my value and someday you will leave me."

The path of becoming integrated in the Warrior involves taking risks. As the tough/generous character, I must learn to risk being authentically me, being vulnerable, and being woundable by those I love. This also entails attracting loving, attuned partners and community who will meet my vulnerability with kindness. With repeated positive outcomes of risking my vulnerability and being loved in return, I am able to learn a new pattern. My core fears of abandonment and being alone become less believable as I center more fully in my vulnerable self and am met with greater depths of intimacy through relationships.

If not hyper-active, the unintegrated Warrior can polarize the opposite direction into impotent rage, self-abuse, and helpless self-pity. This is the nice guy who is afraid to assert his own desires, care-takes others, and conforms to other strong personalities. In this character, I do not have a solid sense of myself. Here, the Warrior is suppressed and the gifts of setting boundaries, taking strong action, and living a passionate life are blocked along with it. Beneath my very agreeable exterior is impotent rage.

This inward character strategy is called burdened/enduring, in which I view connection and relationship coming at the cost of my freedom. I assume the needs of others, which become the burden that I carry. I compulsively make myself responsible for everything and everyone. As a result, I feel both victimized by and secret resentment toward those I am close to. I have learned that my one powerful tool is to resist. I will stubbornly resist taking action or making changes. Although I feel responsible for the world, I will resist assuming real responsibility and avoid taking the decisive action that my responsibilities would entail. Most of my behavior is slow, persistent, and made out of obligation. As a child developing this strategy, my playfulness and spontaneity were likely suppressed. I learned that love was conditional on my obedience.

Figure 1.9 Eeyore the donkey from Winnie the Pooh as the burdened/enduring character[30]

Limiting beliefs typical of the burdened/enduring character include, "I need to suppress my opinions, aliveness, or self in order to be loved," "It's my job to take care of you/everyone," "Connection comes at the cost of freedom," and "I will never get what I really need." In addition, this character carries the sentiments, "You can't make me do anything," and "My only option is to resist."

To integrate the burdened/enduring strategy, I need to own what is mine and release that which is not mine. In particular, I need to own that the freedom I long for is being withheld by no one but me. It is up to me to find my truth and live my life. In addition, I need to identify the patterns of codependency, merging, and conforming in my relationships. All parties need to actively work to notice when these unhealthy systems emerge, to name them in the moment, and to make new, empowered choices. Caretaking others is always a choice that I make, and I am always free to make a new choice.

Here is another lens on the shadows of the Warrior. The hyper-active pathology can be called *sadism*, which means taking pleasure in inflicting pain on others. The hypo-active pathology can be called *masochism*, taking pleasure in inflicting pain on self. The masochist is the part that Bly was speaking out against:

We see more and more passivity in men, but also more and more naïveté. The naïve man feels a pride in being attacked. If his wife or girlfriend, furious, shouts that he is "chauvinist," a "sexist," a "man," he doesn't fight back, but just takes it. He opens his shirt so that she can see more clearly where to put the lances. He ends with three or four javelins sticking out of his body, and blood running all over the floor. If he were a bullfighter, he would remain where he was when the bull charges, would not even wave his shirt or turn his body, and the horn would go directly in. After each fight friends have to carry him on their shoulders to the hospital.

—Robert Bly[31]

Wherever one of these pathologies is externally enacted, it means the other pathology is internally working in my unconscious. Every outward masochist (every passive, naïve man) has a sadist on the inside taking cruel pleasure in his suffering. When I am outwardly collapsed into masochism, then my inner sadist has assumed my disowned power and is delighted in torturing my weaker pleasing self.

Conversely, if I am acting out in sadistic violence, that means my self-flagellating masochist is inside me levying guilt, shame, and judgments on my transgressions and perceived hidden weaknesses. When my natural wholeness fragments, I often create a bi-polar split: inward masochist plus outward sadist, or inward sadist plus outward masochist.

In either case, the wars and conflicts that I manifest outwardly in the world are most often a symptom of the ferocious inner battles within my divided psyche. The Warrior is the part of me that fights. When my inner or outer conflicts flare up, it is a sign that my Warrior is either unintegrated or under-developed. Paradoxically, the solution to inner or outer conflict is to cultivate more of the healthy Warrior. Suppressing my Warrior (which is what "civilization" generally does to its citizens) only strengthens my unconscious need for aggression to vent, and creates more violence in the long-run. The healthy Warrior is able to meet conflict honestly, set appropriate boundaries, and take action to bring the system, internal or external, back into harmonious alignment.

In the table below, I map some emotions and characters of the shadow Warrior in a progression of increasing nervous-system stress. On the right side, I list the three states of activation according to polyvagal theory, and on the left are the masochist and the sadist.[32] Between each state is a barrier that must be crossed which functions in both directions: up-regulating into more stress and down-regulating into relaxation. The masochist lives in the calm, nervous, pleasing state of ventral vagal; the Sadist lives in the fight-or-flight intensity of sympathetic activation; and beyond the sadist is the shut-down and dissociation of the dorsal vagal state.

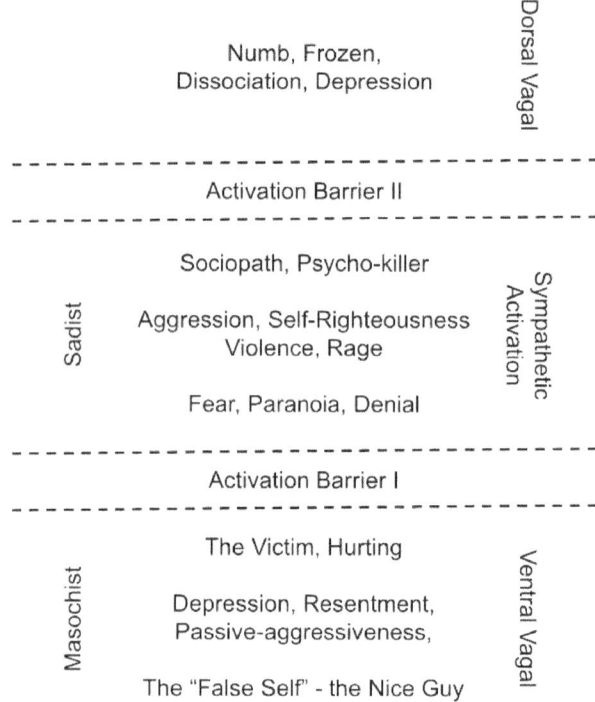

Figure 1.10 Levels of aggression and nervous system states

I can use *parts psychology* for yet another lens on the distortions of the Warrior. I have a part inside of me that is a *killer*. This part is deadly serious, completely uncompromising, and will do whatever it takes to accomplish his task, including taking a life. This is my Killer. For many men, he is the most challenging and confronting part to connect with. In equal measure, he generally holds a good deal of vitality that has been partitioned off from the ego.

When I was twelve years old, I got into a fight with one of my friends during volleyball practice after school. What began as a verbal argument escalated to shoving which escalated to punching. I threw a single punch which caught my friend right across the nose, breaking it in four places and sending blood gushing across the locker room. What had begun as frustration between friends had quickly become a serious incident. Not only was I now in big trouble, but more importantly, my aggression had inflicted significant damage to my friend's face. My friend had to undergo surgery and a lengthy recovery process. I was horrified.

What I learned from this episode is that my Killer is a liability. I learned to lock him away and never let him out. I became afraid of my own power, and so I shut myself down. Over a decade later in a psychedelic journey, I rediscovered my Killer. He had been neglected for a very long time. In my teens and twenties, I honestly thought, "I just don't have a killer instinct. It's not a part of me." Not only did I disown him, I then thoroughly forgot where and how I lost him. In order to integrate the killer, I needed to admit to myself that I could take a life—indeed, that in certain circumstances I *might* do so—and make space for the fear, anger, and dark pleasure that I felt around this part.

When integrated, the Killer becomes an incredibly powerful aspect of the Warrior, and adds his gifts of focus, commitment, and grit into service of the larger Self. My Killer is the one who is going to keep me alive in a life-or-death situation. He's the one who is not afraid to speak the uncomfortable truth. He's the one who is willing to deal with the ugly, messy, neurotic, pathological parts of myself. He gets his hands dirty when the rest of me is unwilling.

In my life, he's the part who quits my dead-end job, ends my toxic relationship, and kicks me out of my addictive habits. On multiple occasions, my Killer has destroyed my life in total love. He finds the truth and is willing to stand by it, even if it costs his life. This uncompromising dedication to truth is terrifying to the comfort-orientation of my ego. The first thing I learned on the path of the Warrior is it's not going to be comfortable.

The internal parts for each person are unique. Some people have a Destroyer separate from their Killer. I have a sexual Ravager who is a distinct part. My sexual Ravager fully embodies my desires and turn-ons. He is not ashamed of his strong erotic energy. He is not bound by social conditioning and is unconcerned if someone gets offended. At first, I labeled this part the Rapist. I was afraid of him and I was afraid to hurt someone with my sexuality. After befriending this part, I learned that he'd rather be called the Ravager than the Rapist. He's clear he won't intentionally harm anyone. In fact, if the other person isn't a full yes to an encounter, he loses interest. What a pleasant surprise to discover that my most primal sexual part is turned on by consent. (For some folks, non-consent is a turn-on. I have seen this navigated in the kink community with skill and care to create a scene of "consensual non-consent," meaning all parties agree on the parameters where non-consent takes place.) But for me, my Ravager gets turned on by my partner's turn-on. My Ravager connects me to my primal, wild sexuality. He opens me to more of my pleasure, and he knows how to play and have fun.

Before I learned how to integrate this part, he was my shadow Rapist. I knew he was with me, but I refused to engage with him. Other people could feel that psychic split in me. I'm presenting as a nice guy, but somewhere else in me, there is a sexual hunger that I'm in denial about. That dissonance is what makes me feel unsafe. When I am integrated and owning my Ravager, my sexuality is both present and trustable.

In addition to my Killer and Ravager, I've inherited aggressive and ferocious instincts through evolution. On the path to becoming an integrated Warrior, I must reckon with all these wild internal parts. This is the deeper meaning of the Tarot card, Strength, pictured at the opening of this chapter. On the card, the Warrior is the woman in white. She has learned to tame the ferocious beast within, not through suppression, but through kindness.

The woman tames the lion… When we assimilate the hostile, destructive, dangerous, wild forces in nature to the uses of mankind, we add to those forces the quality of human consciousness.

—Paul Foster Case[33]

This reckoning is the task of the Warrior. It is a path of courage—*cour* meaning *of the heart.* The Warrior calls me to love all of the *hostile, destructive, dangerous, wild forces* within me. My task is to make friends with these powerful forces and to harness them with kindness so they become docile like the lion with his mouth held open. It is through this process of unrelenting love that I discover my Strength, and the integrated Warrior assumes sovereignty in his quadrant of my psyche.

Integrating these shadow elements is no small feat. It requires total dedication and fearlessness in an ongoing way. But the rewards are monumental. I want this for you as your brother. When others feel this integration in you, they will find you both safe and attractive. And the world needs this from you. We are dying from a lack of integrated Warriors who are able to show up in ruthless kindness, in furious compassion, in blazing truth.

Prompts for Journaling and Discussion

How has the shadow Warrior affected your behavior in your life?

What experiences have you had as the recipient of the shadow Warrior in other men?

Do you identify as Tough/Generous? Burdened/Enduring? The Sadist? The Masochist?

What is your relationship with your Killer, Destroyer, Ravager, or similar parts?

The Warrior's Sword

Figure 1.11 Arthur drawing the sword from a stone[34]

Each man carries a sword. Whether I admit it or not, whether I own it or not, the sword is part of who I am. This sword cuts two ways: I can use it to take a life and I can use it to protect a life. Coming to terms with this sword and learning how to wield it is part of the initiation into the integrated, adult Warrior.

Masculine aggression is real. While it is true that all humans have shadow Warriors, it is also true that the vast majority of physical violence committed today and throughout human history has been at the hands of men. Acknowledging this aggression is the first step. It exists in the world and it exists within me.

It is my responsibility to integrate my masculine aggression. Dismissal, repression, avoidance, and otherwise making-nice have the effect of pushing this aggression more deeply into the shadow. Labeling this aggression as wrong, demonizing it, and blaming others for it have similar results. This approach creates a ticking time-bomb where the repressed aggression builds up toward an explosive release. In addition, it locks away my life-force and potency. This aggression is not something I will process into resolution, evolve beyond, or heal my way out of. Each man carries a sword. It is a fundamental part of our psyches. It is my task to learn how to use it.

My masculine aggression includes anger, self-righteousness, urges to kill others, urges to kill myself, the capacity to mercilessly torture, victimization, rage, bloodlust, apocalypse fantasies, rape fantasies, and apotheosis fantasies. When I have disowned these parts from my waking consciousness, it means they own me. If I become provoked, any of these parts has the power to take over my system and rule my behavior. This is the Dr. Jekyll and Mr. Hyde phenomenon, the Hulk's black-out rage, and the explosive violence of the alcoholic.

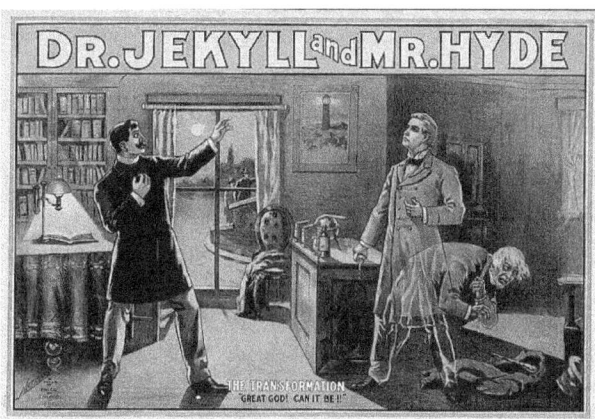

Figure 1.12 Dr. Jekyll and Mr. Hyde[35]

On the path of becoming an integrated Warrior, I must meet all of these dark parts of myself. When I grasp the sword, I must understand the potential for harm and destruction that is possible through the power I wield. Nevertheless, I must grasp the sword and learn how to use it.

In one version of the King Arthur legend, the boy pulls the sword from the stone. He is a humble page looking for a sword for the knight he serves. Many other knights have attempted to pull the sword from the stone in hopes of becoming King and failed. They were led by their agendas for power and personal gain. The sword, who would serve only the true King, did not yield to these knights. The sword released for Arthur, the simple boy, coming from humility in service to his knight. When I approach my sword from humility and service, then my power is trustable. I become a conduit for the archetype of the King, the Self, and Life to move through me. The integrated Warrior is a servant.

Learning to wield the sword brings me to the immediacy and inevitability of death. The power of the sword includes the power to take a life and it becomes my responsibility to choose how I use it. In addition, the sword makes a claim on me. Because I have this power, I am called to act. Action is the quality of the Warrior. It is no longer acceptable to stand idly by while injustice and harm are being perpetrated. I must be willing to stand for what is true with total conviction, even if it means my own death. From Jesus, to Gandhi, to Martin Luther King, Jr., the price of fighting for peace was death. The understanding that total commitment includes one's own death is a concept that each of these men knowingly faced well before their final hours.

The red knight fights for his own glory. In this stage, my passion and desire to prove myself leads me into battle. For me, the sword is a tool to gain power.

The white knight fights for his ideals. As a white knight, I fight on behalf of chivalry, justice, and honor. Women, children, and the elderly must be protected and my realm must be defended. My sword is a shining beacon of the purity of my just cause.

The black knight fights sparingly in kindness. Now, I've learned to tame my red passions, and my ego is no longer running the show. I understand that the purity of idealism brings its own form of self-deceptive blindness. Honor cloaks pride and idealism harbors fundamentalism. Every white sword turns red when used on another. Every act of violence in self-protection provokes an equal response of self-protective violence in an unending cycle of retribution. The symbolic wound of the black knight is his willing recognition of the suffering of the world. We are all acting out our wounds and fantasies, including me. Most importantly me, because I'm the only one I can truly work on. As the black knight, I wield the sword because I see that to not wield the sword would cause more suffering. The sword is my responsibility as an agent of compassion in the world.

The Warrior's sword brings with it gifts in equal measure to its shadows. Inspiration, energy, dedication, and integrity are just a few of the gifts of the Warrior. Wielding the sword cultivates courage—the courage to face my fears and the courage to know myself: *"not being afraid of who you are,"* in Trungpa Rinpoche's words. Through facing my demons and fears, I discover my innate goodness. This goodness is pure and simple. It becomes the solid ground of every action, my *basic sanity*. I learn to trust myself (or, more accurately, my Self). I learn to trust the powerful energies of Life that I channel through my sword, both in destruction and in creation. Life is organic—it naturally works to create more life—and as the Warrior, I become the active agent of this organic force.

The Peacemaker

The transpersonal form of the Warrior that emerges together with the sovereignty of the Self is called the *Peacemaker*. The primary trait of the Warrior is action. At the level of the Peacemaker, action is an expression of compassion. The Peacemaker is the fruition of the Warrior.

The Peacemaker could also be called the bodhisattva or the saint. He works tirelessly for the benefit of all. He recognizes that all beings are interdependent. When he looks into another's eyes, he sees himself.

Figure 1.13 Guanyin, bodhisattva of compassion[36]

This begins with the recognition of suffering, the first noble truth of Buddhism. Life is hard. It hurts. I carry all sorts of pain, trauma, wounds, and delusions. I think I can maybe fix my situation, but the more I try, I realize that "I" can't actually fix anything. My suffering is inescapable. As I become grounded in the reality of my suffering, I gain a certain degree of hopelessness.

From this place, I can see that whenever I harm or cause suffering for others, it is due to my own suffering. My pain, my limiting beliefs, my darkness, etc., are the distortions that I react to when I am causing suffering. From this comes the determination to work on myself. Working on myself does not entail becoming "healed" or "enlightened." Those are my ego's agendas for self-perfection to transcend suffering. I see that striving in this way only creates more suffering for myself. Every ambition creates more attachment. Working on myself means acceptance. I am allowing me, exactly as I am.

The same logic about the root of suffering applies to everyone who has ever caused me harm— they are suffering too. They are hurting me out of their reactivity or ignorance because they have been hurt. Seeing this is compassion. We are all suffering together. If I attempt to pull myself upward at the cost of someone else, that is only my delusion. It will inevitably cause more suffering for me. When I hurt someone because they hurt me, I am only causing more suffering for both of us.

What can I do with so much suffering? I can work on myself by loving each and every part of me. I learn mindfulness—how to be present and observe the powerful feelings and urges within me. I learn to listen—becoming calm and receptive without agenda or defense. This brings me into stillness. I practice silence. Paradoxically, by welcoming my suffering, I discover peace.

Peace does not mean no waves of emotions or no challenges. Peace means that my emotions and stories are welcomed from an internal place of balance and resource. The Peacemaker does not eliminate strong emotions; instead, he penetrates into the core of them with total kindness. I willingly allow these waves to arise and join with them without a struggle. When I am available to hold it, my anger is pure aliveness and represents one of my most powerful and direct expressions of love. Similarly, I become fearless by stepping boldly into the center of my fear. Fearlessness is not the absence of fear, it is total commitment to being present to fear. This internal process of embracing my experience is how I open to peace.

The Peacemaker practices nonviolence. As we will explore in Chapter 6, the first step in nonviolence is to understand violence. Without an understanding of violence—and indeed, without becoming intimate with violence—true nonviolence is impossible. At its core, every act of violence, whether physical, emotional, psychological, or spiritual, diminishes or destroys the capacity of an entity to meet their needs. Because most acts of violence stem from an unmet need in the first place, violence forms a self-reinforcing cycle of pain and need. Recognizing the cycle, I become empowered to step outside of it. I learn how to choose peace. Often, this means willingly receiving the pain and suffering of others.

> When you have reconciled internally, peace and love become possible. When you embody peace and love, you can change a difficult situation more easily. Disarmament can be done unilaterally. If you disarm yourself, it means you've decided not to attack or inflict injury; you have become peaceful. Even if the other person is not aware of it yet, the moment you disarm yourself, give up the fight, and practice beginning anew in yourself, healing begins and you undergo a transformation that very soon will have an effect on the other person. They may then also decide to disarm and succeed in transforming their wrong perceptions, anger, and violence, too. We can do this as individuals and also as a nation.
>
> —Thich Nhat Hanh[37]

The Peacemaker transcends and includes the Warrior. This means the Peacemaker builds upon the action, dedication, and passion of the Warrior. But whereas the Warrior would kill to protect himself or those he loves, the Peacemaker chooses to lay down his sword in love.

In our culture, we tend to confuse the Peacemaker, who actively advocates for justice, with the Pacifist who avoids conflict. Pacifism without advocacy is a form of avoidance. As we shall see with the Mythos of the Peacemaker in Chapter 2, the role of the Peacemaker demands an incredible amount of action.

> Peacemaking doesn't mean passivity. It is the act of interrupting injustice without mirroring injustice, the act of disarming evil without destroying the evildoer, the act of finding a third way that is neither fight nor flight but the careful, arduous pursuit of reconciliation and justice. It is about a revolution of love that is big enough to set both the oppressed and the oppressors free.
>
> —Claiborne, Wilson-Hartgrove, and Okoro[38]

Practicing compassion awakens my vital heart to the universal love of all that is. It tenderizes my heart to the grief of human suffering. And it opens me to know my Self as a universal expression contained wholly within each individual. The Peacemaker is a radical force of love, capable of transforming the entire world.

Prompts for Journaling and Discussion

What does it mean to you to wield the Warrior's sword?

How do you relate to being a Peacemaker?

What is compassion?

Notes

[1] *Shambhala: The Sacred Path of the Warrior.*

[2] *Iron John: A Book about Men.*

[3] *Ibid.*

[4] *Ibid.*

[5] Iron Hans, Jacob and Wilhelm Grimm.

[6] Hans Burgkmair.

[7] Iron Hans, Jacob and Wilhelm Grimm.

[8] Gordon Browne.

[9] Iron Hans, Jacob and Wilhelm Grimm.

[10] Robert Leinweber.

[11] *The Warrior Within.*

[12] See: *Hermaphrodieties,* by Raven Kaldera.

[13] "[Marija Gimbutas'] work presents the thesis that the [Neolithic period] reveals pre-patriarchal forms of representations of the female divine and was witness to events that led to the fall from matricentric to patriarchal social structures... She developed the hypothesis that a widespread agrarian culture had flourished throughout Neolithic Europe between 6500 and 3500 years BCE, venerating a singular Great Goddess (Gimbutas 1989, xix)." *The Evolutionary Journey of Woman,* Nicholson.

[14] "Hard times create strong men, strong men create good times, good times create weak men, weak men create hard times." *Those Who Remain,* Hopf.

[15] "We choose to go to the moon. We choose to go to the moon in this decade and do the other things, not because they are easy, but because they are hard, because that goal will serve to organize and measure the best of our energies and skills, because that challenge is one that we are willing to accept, one we are unwilling to postpone, and one which we intend to win, and the others, too." JFK, Rice University, 1962

[16] "As effeminate men oppressed by masculinist standards, we ourselves have a stake in the destruction of the patriarch, and thus we must struggle with the dilemma of being partisans (as effeminists) of a revolution opposed to us (as men)." "The Effeminist Manifesto," Dansky et al.

[17] "Defined in these terms of a combination of stereotypically masculine and feminine qualities, the liberated man approaches the model of a psychological androgyny proposed by Bem (1974) and others (Heilbrun, Spence, Helmreich, and Stapp, 1974) as a new paradigm of mental health and a new 'model of perfection, free from culturally imposed models of masculinity and femininity.' (Bem, 1975, p. 53)." "Changing men: the rationale, theory, and design of a men's consciousness raising program," Schapiro.

[18] "The annihilation of masculinity was both a goal and a fear for these men. Oedipal masculinization structured the world and the self for them in gendered terms, as it does for most men. To undo masculinity is to court a loss of personality structure that may be quite terrifying: a kind of gender vertigo." *Masculinities*, Connell.

[19] *The Will to Change.*

[20] *Masculinities, 2nd ed.*

[21] Thus, this story fails the Bechdel Test, usually applied to movies, which asks, 1) does this story have at least two women in it, who 2) talk to each other, about 3) something besides a man. For *Iron John*, the answer is no.

[22] *The Evolutionary Journey of Woman.*

[23] *Iron John: A Book about Men.*

[24] *Men's Work: How to Stop the Violence that Tears Our Lives Apart.*

[25] *Masculinities, 2nd ed.*

[26] *Men's Work: How to Stop the Violence that Tears Our Lives Apart.*

[27] "We accept the tradition that women must work with women in order to build a feminine identity and that men must work with men in order to build a masculine identity." *The Spirit of Intimacy*, Somé.

[28] *The Will to Change: Men, Masculinity, and Love.*

[29] *The Telegraph Trail*, Marceline Day, John Wayne, 1933. Image by: IMAGO / Everett Collection.

[30] Image by Lozzer22 CCA 3.0

[31] *Iron John: A Book about Men.*

[32] I'll delve more deeply into polyvagal theory in *Lore Book III, The Lover.*

[33] *The Tarot: A Key to the Wisdom of the Ages.*

[34] *The Story of King Arthur and His Knights,* Pyle.

[35] Image by the National Printing & Engraving Company, public domain.

[36] Guanyin Shrine on Mount Putuo in Zhejiang Province, China. Photo by Nyarlathotep1001, CC BY-SA 4.0

[37] *How to Fight.*

[38] *Common Prayer: A Liturgy for Ordinary Radicals.*

| 2 |

Mythos of the Warrior - Gandhi

Figure 2.1 Mahatma Gandhi, London, 1931

Truth is like a vast tree, which yields more and more fruit, the more you nurture it. The deeper the search in the mine of truth the richer the discovery of the gems buried there, in the shape of openings for an ever greater variety of service.

—Mahatma Gandhi[1]

Once there was a shy, unremarkable Indian boy named Mohandas. He was short and thin, not particularly academic, and not particularly athletic. He grew up in a small town in India to a prosperous family. At the age of thirteen, he married his wife in an arranged marriage. She was also thirteen at the time. They would remain married for the next 75 years. At the age of eighteen, Mohandas sailed to London for school to become a lawyer. Three years later, he was called to the bar in London. It was 1891.

MOHANDAS KARAMCHAND GANDHI,
Barrister-at-Law.

Figure 2.2 Gandhi graduating from law school, age 21, London

This marks Gandhi's entry as a knight of the red armor. Some Warriors wield the sword, others wield a pen. Gandhi returned to India and began his career awkwardly.

As a lawyer he failed both in Rajkot and Bombay. In the latter city he had a ten-dollar case but was literally too shy to open his mouth in court and gave the brief to a colleague.

—Louis Fischer[2]

Gandhi picked up odd jobs to make ends meet. The local politics and drama disgusted him. So, when a firm offered to send him to South Africa for a year, he gladly accepted. At the age of 23, the young hero traveled to a new land to seek his fortune.

Early during his stay in South Africa, Gandhi was traveling by train for a case. During the journey, he was told by the railway officer that he must move from first class to third class for being "colored." He resisted and as a result, he was kicked off the train and his belongings were confiscated. He spent a night shivering in the cold until another train arrived the following day.

This was a pivotal incident for Gandhi. The wound of discrimination awakened his idealism. Within a week of the train incident, Gandhi organized a meeting of local Indians and gave his first public speech on racism. Undeterred by this and many other acts of discrimination, this young lawyer only resolved more deeply to make things right:

The hardship to which I was subjected was superficial, only a symptom of the deep disease of colour prejudice. I should try, if possible, to root out the disease and suffer hardships in the process.

—Gandhi[3]

This moment marks Gandhi's growth from the red Warrior as a young lawyer out to make his name to the white Warrior as a public servant fighting for what he believed in. His priorities and actions both began to shift from this point forward.

After several months, Gandhi completed the legal case he had been employed for in South Africa. He made plans to sail back to India to return to his wife and children. On the day of his goodbye party, he chanced to read an article in the newspaper about a bill to "deprive Indians of the right to elect members of the Natal Legislative Assembly." As he discussed this blatantly racist bill with his friends at the party, he came to the realization that if he didn't organize to stop this bill, no one would. Now, these were not people who Gandhi had any expectation to ever see again, nor was this his home community or country. But seeing the situation, there was no question for this young Indian lawyer that his calling was to stay and organize.

He canceled his ticket home and relinquished his comfort and self-interest for the sake of others. Further, he refused payment because of the public nature of the work. "Fees are out of the question. There can be no fees for public work. I can stay as a servant."

This is the full expression of the white Warrior taking on the mantle of service to a cause. Some Warriors serve a code, some serve a King, and some serve the Divine. Gandhi was in service to Truth: "My uniform experience has convinced me that there is no other God than Truth."

After three years of anti-racism advocacy, Gandhi realized that his work would keep him much longer in South Africa, so he sailed back to India to retrieve his wife and two children. While in India, Gandhi published a pamphlet on the plight of Indians in South Africa. This pamphlet was picked up by newspapers and media across India, London, and eventually made its way back to South Africa.

Upon his return to South Africa, his ship and another ship arrived at the same time, full of about 800 Indians. Both ships were blocked from entry by an angry mob of white men. Incensed by Gandhi's publication, their intent was to force Gandhi and these Indians to return to India. After twenty three days of embargo, the ships were permitted to enter the harbor and disembark. Gandhi was spotted and soon the angry mob attacked him.

> They pelted me with stones, brickbats and rotten eggs. Someone snatched away my turban, whilst others began to batter and kick me. I fainted and caught hold of the front railings of a house and stood there to get my breath. But it was impossible. They came upon me boxing and battering. The wife of the Police Superintendent, who knew me, happened to be passing by. The brave lady came up, opened her parasol though there was no sun then, and stood between the crowd and me. This checked the fury of the mob, as it was difficult for them to deliver blows on me without harming Mrs. Alexander.
>
> —Gandhi[4]

This episode marks Gandhi's archetypal entry into the black Warrior. It would not be his last physical hardship during his career, but at this juncture, Gandhi first came face to face with the very real possibility that his public advocacy work might get him killed. Before departing the boat, the captain asked Gandhi whether he would stick to his principle of nonviolence if attacked, to which Gandhi answered, "I hope God will give me the courage and the sense to forgive them and to refrain from bringing them to law."[5] After the incident, Gandhi decided to press no charges against his assailants. It is only by going through such an ordeal that we find out what we are truly made of.

Figure 2.3 Gandhi in South Africa, 1909

Gandhi was by no means perfect. He fought with his wife. In his early years, he was openly racist toward black people and placed Europeans on a pedestal. He began as a product of his culture, inheriting all the prejudices and vices of his time. The most inspiring aspect of Gandhi, for me personally, is his transformation from an unremarkable Indian lawyer into a great saint. He wasn't born a *mahatma*, he became one. Gandhi made this change quite simply through an outstanding dedication to his self-work.

> [Gandhi] had a violent nature and his subsequent mahatma-calm was the product of long training in temperament-control. He did not easily become an even-minded, desire-less yogi. He had to remold himself. Recognizing his deficiencies, he made a conscious effort to grow and change and restrain his bad impulses. He turned himself into a different person.
>
> —Louis Fischer[6]

Like Warriors across all times and cultures, Gandhi took a number of vows in order to strengthen his service. He vowed to be vegetarian. He vowed to live a simple life without gathering possessions or wealth. He vowed to spend one day each week in silence. After his fourth child, he resolved that sex and child-rearing were negatively impacting his work as a servant. So he took a vow of celibacy, called *brahmacharya*.

Every day of the [celibacy] vow has taken me nearer the knowledge that in brahmacharya lies the protection of the body, the mind, and the soul. For brahmacharya was now no process of hard penance, it was a matter of consolation and joy. Every day revealed a fresh beauty in it. But if it was a matter of ever-increasing joy, let no one believe that it was an easy thing for me. Even when I am past fifty-six years, I realize how hard a thing it is. Every day I realize more and more that it is like walking on the sword's edge, and I see every moment the necessity for eternal vigilance.

—Gandhi[7]

But the culmination of his life's work, and what he is most remembered for, is the vow of nonviolence, or *ahimsa*. For Gandhi, "Ahimsa is the basis of the search for truth." Gandhi was not the first to practice non-violence, but he was the first to bring it into large-scale politics as a mechanism for social change.

Gandhi also coined the term *Satyagraha* which translates to *firmness in truth*. With these two principles, nonviolence and Satyagraha, Gandhi laid the foundation for a fundamentally new expression of the Warrior archetype. This shift began with Henry David Thoreau's *Civil Disobedience* and was later carried forward by Dr. Martin Luther King, Jr., but the man who cast the mold for the Warrior's exalted archetype of the Peacemaker is undoubtedly Gandhi. The shift from violence as a remedy to total commitment to nonviolence in service to truth marks the passage from the Warrior into the Peacemaker.

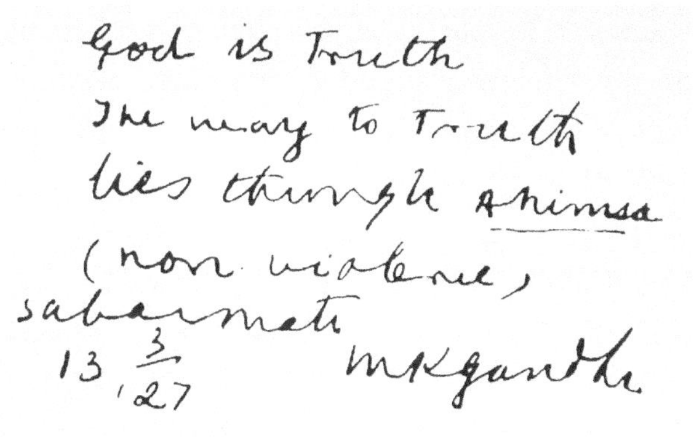

Figure 2.4 Gandhi's handwriting: "God is Truth. The way to Truth lies through Ahimsa (non-violence)"[8]

The immature Warrior uses violence for his narrow self-interest. The full Warrior uses violence as a means of protection. The Peacemaker goes beyond the Warrior by committing to nonviolence. He is willing to stake his life for the sake of what is true.

A nation that wants to come into its own ought to know all the ways and means to freedom. Usually they include violence as the last remedy. Satyagraha, on the other hand, is an absolutely non-violent weapon. I regard it as my duty to explain its practice and its limitations. I have no doubt that the British Government is a powerful Government, but I have no doubt also that Satyagraha is a sovereign remedy.

—Gandhi[9]

Gandhi began with small injustices at the local level. He fought discriminatory legislation. He organized peasant farmers to stand up for fair wages. With success after success, his renown and position grew, and his faith in nonviolent non-cooperation strengthened. For Gandhi, there was no truth too small and no injustice below his station. His dedication was total. For example, one day while attending a big meeting of the Indian Congress...

There were only a few latrines, and the recollection of their stink still oppresses me. I pointed it out to the volunteers. They said pointblank: 'That is not our work, it is the scavenger's work.' I asked for a broom. The man stared at me in wonder. I procured one and cleaned the latrine.

—Gandhi[10]

Here is how the humble Indian lawyer changed the world through Satyagraha. He willingly chose to disobey laws that were unjust. In his disobedience, he committed absolutely to do no harm and willingly received insult, assault, imprisonment, and suffering for the sake of his cause. This commitment to truth and willingness to suffer, for Gandhi, was a form of self-purification. It was an active choice to stand in the holy fire that burns away all impurities. Gandhi stood in total dedication to the belief that truth and justice will prevail.

The Gandhian theory of Satyagraha or dynamic soul-force, thus, is based on the acceptance of the concept of suffering for the vindication of truth and justice. Satyagraha is, in its innermost essence, an attempt at self-purification through suffering. It signifies a genuine, intense and sincere quest for the vindication of Truth, which is God, through suffering. It is, hence, based on an invincible belief in the ultimate triumph of divine justice.

—Jai Narain Sharma[11]

Through nonviolent non-cooperation, the heart of the Peacemaker opens with compassion for the oppressor. In addition, the willingness to take on suffering for the sake of truth opens the heart of the "oppressor" into our shared humanity. The entire paradigm of *might makes right* via conflict is subverted. In addition, deliberate suffering for the sake of a just cause rouses public support. It lights a fire under people to act.

With enough action, enough publicity, and in service to the cause of truth, the most powerful empire on the planet was made to yield. Winston Churchill has every right to be considered among the greatest Warriors of the twentieth century. He was truly an integrated Warrior who understood the cost of violence. When confronted by Gandhi the Peacemaker, Churchill rightly understood the threat:

> It is alarming and nauseating to see Mr Gandhi, a seditious Middle Temple lawyer, now posing as a fakir of a type well known in the east, striding half naked up the steps of the viceregal palace, while he is still organising and conducting a campaign of civil disobedience, to parlay on equal terms with the representative of the Emperor-King.
>
> —Winston Churchill[12]

In the end, Churchill, together with the mighty British Empire, were forced to yield to Gandhi's non-violent commitment to truth. The emancipation of India and Pakistan through non-violent resistance stands today among the most noble and powerful political changes humanity has ever undertaken. This is the profound power of the realized Peacemaker.

Figure 2.5 Quit India Stamp

> I believe that in the history of the world, there has not been a more genuinely demo-cratic struggle for freedom than ours. I read Carlyle's French Revolution while I was in prison, and Pandit Jawaharlal has told me something about the Russian revolution. But it is my conviction that inasmuch as these struggles were fought with the weapon of violence they failed to realize the democratic ideal. In the democracy which I have envisaged, a democracy established by non-violence, there will be equal freedom for all. Everybody will be his own master. It is to join a struggle for such democracy that I invite you today. Once you realize this you will forget the differences between the Hindus and Muslims, and think of yourselves as Indians only, engaged in the common struggle for independence.
>
> —Gandhi, Quit India Speech, August 8, 1942

In 1942, Gandhi led a large-scale movement calling for Indian sovereignty. The Indian congress passed a resolution calling for the immediate withdrawal of British forces and Indian self-governance. Nationwide non-violent protests ensued. Britain responded by arresting over 100,000 political activists, levying fines, and publicly flogging demonstrators. Five years later, with the close of WWII, the British government ceded control. India and Pakistan became sovereign nations. The death toll between British officials and Indian protestors attributed to this emancipation movement counted in the mere thousands—a staggering accomplishment.[13]

And so, an Indian lawyer demonstrated that on a global scale, humans have the capacity to politically self-emancipate by non-violent means. It happens through dedicated service to truth—an ideal which is "hard as adamant and tender as a blossom."[14] Beyond the gift of democratic self-governance for Indians and Pakistanis, Gandhi has given humanity the imprint of the Peacemaker as the transcendent version of the Warrior.

In the wake of emancipation from British colonization, India saw wide-scale fighting and riots between Hindus, Muslims, and Sikhs. In response to the violence, Gandhi staged a fast. He declared that he would fast until the fighting stopped, even if it caused his death. "But death for me would be a glorious deliverance rather than that I should be a helpless witness to the destruction of India, Hinduism, Sikhism, and Islam."[15] For five days, he neither ate nor drank. His already thin body lost two pounds per day, dropping to 107 pounds. Despite kidney failure and bouts of losing consciousness, Gandhi negotiated with the Indian government to pay Pakistan $125 million. He issued daily prayers and when he was too weak to leave his bed, he received thousands of supplicants who passed by. From the fighting factions, Gandhi asked for pledges for peace plus detailed plans for their implementation. When he received written guarantees for the restoration of Mosques, the evacuation of refugee camps, and the mutual protection of "life, property, and faith," he broke his fast.

Gandhi was willing to suffer to the point of death, not only for the sake of Hindus like himself, but on behalf of all faiths and all people. His courageous act opened the hearts and minds of men in the midst of blood feuds and religious war. Gandhi interrupted the cycle of violence for an entire nation. This is the power of the Peacemaker.

Prompts for Journaling and Discussion

Where do you see injustice in your life, community, society, and world?

For each case of injustice you identified, what is your ideal vision of truth?

In what ways are you willing to dedicate yourself to stand for truth?

What suffering are you willing to undertake for the sake of your cause?

Notes

[1] *Mahatma Gandhi Autobiography: The Story Of My Experiments With Truth.*

[2] *Gandhi: His Life and Message for the World.*

[3] *Mahatma Gandhi Autobiography: The Story Of My Experiments With Truth.*

[4] *Ibid.*

[5] *Ibid.*

[6] *Gandhi: His Life and Message for the World.*

[7] *Mahatma Gandhi Autobiography: The Story Of My Experiments With Truth.*

[8] March 13th, 1927.

[9] *Mahatma Gandhi Autobiography: The Story Of My Experiments With Truth.*

[10] *Ibid.*

[11] *Rediscovering Gandhi.*

[12] Address to the Council of the West Essex Unionist Association on February 23, 1931.

[13] However, it's worth noting that Winston Churchill, in his disdain for Gandhi and Indians, diverted food supplies from Bengal in 1943, causing an estimated 4 million deaths. Also worth noting, during the partition of Pakistan and India, an estimated million deaths were incurred between Hindus and Muslims as 10-20 million people became displaced.

[14] *Mahatma Gandhi Autobiography: The Story Of My Experiments With Truth.*

[15] *Gandhi: His Life and Message for the World.*

| 3 |

Paradigms of Integrity

Figure 3.1 Code of Hammurabi[1]

Integrity is the first task of the Warrior. One meaning of the word *integrity* is "the capacity to stay together." Consider the term *structural integrity*. Integrity imparts the qualities of *soundness, coherence,* and *definition*. Without integrity, the unified whole disintegrates into a heap. When I am in integrity, I'm grounded and I have access to my center. When I am out of integrity, I am lost in the wasteland.

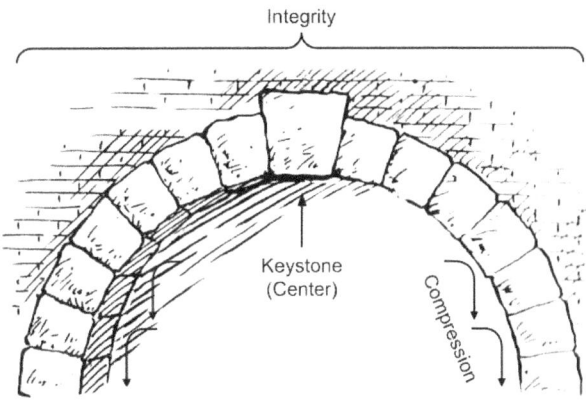

Figure 3.2 Structural integrity of an arch

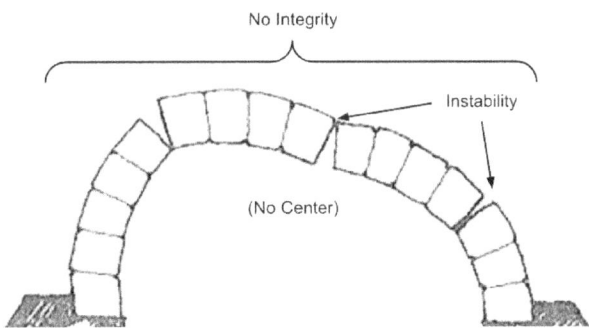

Figure 3.3 Arch without integrity

In my messy life, it is my Warrior who cuts through all falsity and distraction to find the core of truth. His dedicated action brings me to my center. Once I have found my center, I can come into integrity. Here, integrity means wholeness. Just as an *integer* is a whole number, when I am in integrity, I am whole. I become undivided and complete. Without integrity, I am incoherent and scattered. In integrity, I am united and capable.

Integrity happens through agreement. I make a commitment to myself to live in integrity. Here in *Lore Book II: The Warrior*, integrity is the first step of growth because it is the necessary foundation for all subsequent transformation. Integrity calls me to be clear and honest about my life. It's uncomfortable. I have to really want it. And once I've stepped into integrity, I need to stay dedicated to it.

For me, the benefits of committing to integrity have been profound. I used to tell little white lies. And then I would forget what I said to whom. It took real energy to remember and perpetuate these un-truths. They allowed me to hide myself from others. When I decided to stop lying and I chose integrity, I was amazed by how liberated I felt. My friends and loved ones began to see more of the real me. Deeper intimacy became possible. They began to trust me more too. And perhaps most importantly, I began to trust myself. Building trust with myself has led to more confidence and agency to live the life I want. Having found my integrity, I use it as the trustworthy foundation for everything I do in my life.

Now, let's slow down a bit and take a breath together. If you read through the material here, you will likely find some useful information. But if you *engage* with this material, you might meaningfully change your life. This is my invitation. Perhaps the concept of integrity is new to you. If so, ask yourself: Are you ready to commit to coming into integrity? Or perhaps you've explored enough growth work to have a relationship with integrity already. If so, are you willing to use this opportunity to learn more about integrity and recommit yourself?

We are going to explore what integrity means throughout the next two chapters. But before we get into the details, my suggestion is for you to take a few moments, explore what integrity means for you, and decide for yourself what you want your relationship with it to be. Once you are clear with yourself, the rest of the information in this chapter will become personally relevant for you, and therefore far more useful. Here we go:

What integrity means to me:

My commitment to live *in integrity*, in my own words:

My full given name:

Figure 3.4 Personal integrity commitment

I know I will not be perfect, and that's ok. This knowledge requires me to make one more commitment:

When I fall out of integrity, I commit to doing whatever is required for me to come back into integrity as I have defined it for myself, and to do so with self-kindness.

Put your initials here: _____

* * *

Now let's explore what integrity means and how to apply it. Each paradigm of consciousness understands the self-world according to its lens, so each paradigm will have a unique perspective on the meaning of integrity. I offer a tour of these paradigms in Appendix I. By using the paradigmatic lenses to provide multiple definitions of this concept, I gain a more holistic, integral understanding of integrity. In addition, I can see where I may have unintegrated layers in myself, which I am then able to update. Finally, by using the concept of integrity to trace the paradigms, I am bringing myself deeper into my understanding of these structures of consciousness–I'm working on my personal evolution.

Paradigm	Integrity means
Integral	Wholeness and actualization
Plural/postmodern	Systemic harmony
Mental/modern	Principles and inalienable rights
Mythic/traditional	Honor and loyalty

Figure 3.5 How paradigms interpret integrity

Integrity at Mythic/Traditional

Figure 3.6 The samurai Onikojima Yatarō[2]

The mythic/traditional paradigm developed to enable humans to organize into large groups. In the prior paradigm, magic/tribal, the size of a cohesive group is limited by the number of people we can remember and recognize, which is around 150. In a tribal organization, everyone knows everyone personally. This creates safety and cohesion. In order for a larger group to establish that same safety and cohesion, we move to a more complex social paradigm. The mythic/traditional paradigm uses myths and traditions to unify a group. If you believe what we believe, then you're one of us. The myths are held by a singular authority. In addition to providing cultural identifiers for in-group and out-group membership, the myths provide a set of morals to follow. Codes of ethics and laws that are handed down through tradition and enforced by the centralized authority ensure the smooth functioning of civilization.

Integrity in this paradigm means following the code of ethics. If I disobey the code, I'm a sinner or criminal and I am subjected to punishment, damnation, exiling, or death. By following the code, I secure my salvation and contribute to the power and glory of my central authority and chosen group.

The warrior is pre-eminently a 'man of honour'; he keeps his word, is loyal to his leader and to his comrades, and fights honourably without resorting to illegitimate, underhand tricks or ruses; he defends and protects the wounded, the aged and women and children, even the helpless prisoners of the enemy.

–Barry McCarthy[3]

Admission according to the liturgical mode.

Figure 3.7 Ceremony bestowing knighthood in the twelfth century[4]

In the Warrior archetype, this is known as a *code of honor*. It is the set of rules, handed down by society or religion, that moralize the Warrior. Adherence to this code is what constitutes integrity. In medieval Japan, the samurai warriors followed the bushido code. In Europe, the knights followed the code of chivalry. In both cases, the codes evolved over time and varied from clan to clan. These were considered to be the Warrior's way of life, which included loyalty to one's lord, protecting the weak, and fighting against evil. The Warrior lives by this code and the Warrior dies by this code.[5]

The Ten Commandments of the code of chivalry:[6]

1. Thou shalt believe all that the Church teaches, and shalt observe all its directions.
2. Thou shalt defend the Church.
3. Thou shalt respect all weaknesses, and shalt constitute thyself the defender of them.
4. Thou shalt love the country in which thou wast born.
5. Thou shalt not recoil before thine enemy.
6. Thou shalt make war against the Infidel without cessation, and without mercy.
7. Thou shalt perform scrupulously thy feudal duties, if they be not contrary to the laws of God.
8. Thou shalt never lie, and shalt remain faithful to thy pledged word.
9. Thou shalt be generous, and give *largesse* to everyone.
10. Thou shalt be everywhere and always the champion of the Right and the Good against Injustice and Evil.

I can feel the place in myself that loves these images and myths. I'm excited about the romantic ideal of living a life of honor. It's a deep, powerful, passionate part of me. It's the place that connects to the Warrior and King archetypes—my mythic self. At the same time, when I read the ten commandments of chivalry, I can feel my rebellious teenager rise up in opposition to the Church and any external authority trying to run my life. Both internal parts, the honorable knight and the rebellious teen, are very committed to integrity. Each has a different relationship with authority. On my path to owning the full spectrum of integrity, it's important for me to understand my relationships to codes of honor in the mythic/traditional paradigm.

Prompts for Journaling and Discussion

What code do you live by?

When you consider mythic images of the warriors of old—knights, samurai, braves, vikings, and so on—what do you find exciting or compelling? What do you find off-putting or discordant?

When in your life were you most enthralled by this type of warriorship?

Integrity at Mental/Modern

This above all: to thine own self be true,
And it must follow, as the night the day,
Thou canst not then be false to any man.

–Hamlet, Shakespeare

When I step into the mental/modern paradigm, my rational mind is central. I understand the world through science and logic. I understand myself through reason. I no longer need an external authority to tell me what is morally true. The truth is *logical* and *universal.*

In 1785, Immanuel Kant laid out the philosophical framework for integrity in the mental/modern paradigm. He begins with the observation that if I take an action out of adherence to some moral code, out of *duty*, then my motivation for the action is to be *judged positively* by society. Duty always carries an external agenda and so any action made out of duty cannot be good in itself. The motivating reason why I take the action is what makes it good or bad, moral or immoral. Even the outcome of the action is less important than the intention I hold in making it. So, according to Kant, the goodness of an action can only be judged by the principle that motivates it. He then provides a principle. Integrity means to act as if the maxim governing my action were a universal law for all humans. This is known as the *categorical imperative.* If I act only in the way I would want every human to behave, then I will choose the greatest moral good. Here it is in Kant's words:

> An action from duty has its moral worth not in the purpose to be attained by it but in the maxim in accordance with which it is decided upon, and therefore does not depend upon the realization of the object of the action but merely upon the principle of volition in accordance with which the action is done… Hence nothing other than the representation of the law in itself, which can of course occur only in a rational being, insofar as it and not the hoped-for effect is the determining ground of the will, can constitute the preeminent good we call moral… Since I have deprived the will of every impulse that could arise for it from obeying some law, nothing is left but the conformity of actions as such with universal law, which alone is to serve the will as its principle, that is, I ought never to act except in such a way that I could also will that my maxim should become a universal law.

> —Immanuel Kant[7]

The shift that we are making is beyond any specific code or system and takes us into the realm of universal rights. All humans are rational, therefore we all hold the same inalienable human rights. These universal rights were articulated by Thomas Paine in 1791, six years after Kant's categorical imperative. Here's an excerpt:

For these reasons the National Assembly doth recognise and declare, in the presence of the Supreme Being, and with the hope of his blessing and favour, the following sacred rights of men and of citizens:

I. Men are born, and always continue, free and equal in respect of their rights. Civil distinctions, therefore, can be founded only on public utility.

II. The end of all political associations is the preservation of the natural and imprescriptible rights of man; and these rights are Liberty, Property, Security, and Resistance of Oppression.

III. The Nation is essentially the source of all sovereignty; nor can any individual, or any body of men, be entitled to any authority which is not expressly derived from it.

IV. Political Liberty consists in the power of doing whatever does not injure another. The exercise of the natural rights of every man, has no other limits than those which are necessary to secure to every other man the free exercise of the same rights; and these limits are determinable only by the law.

–Thomas Paine[8]

Our current rendition of these rights is known as the Universal Declaration of Human Rights, which was proclaimed by the United Nations in 1948. Here are the first three articles out of thirty:

I. All human beings are born free and equal in dignity and rights. They are endowed with reason and conscience and should act towards one another in a spirit of brotherhood.

II. Everyone is entitled to all the rights and freedoms set forth in this Declaration, without distinction of any kind, such as race, colour, sex, language, religion, political or other opinion, national or social origin, property, birth or other status. Furthermore, no distinction shall be made on the basis of the political, jurisdictional or international status of the country or territory to which a person belongs, whether it be independent, trust, non-self-governing or under any other limitation of sovereignty.

III. Everyone has the right to life, liberty and security of person.

–Universal Declaration of Human Rights

Now, an important distinction here is that these rights are not universal because some document or organization claims them to be so. Rather, each principle reveals itself as logically true, *"which can occur only in a rational being,"* and is then universalized. From the viewpoint of the rational mind in the mental/modern paradigm, *these truths are self-evident.* Integrity means I am treating all humans according to the universal rights that I am able to deduce. Furthermore, to act from a place of integrity, I must be able to free myself of the moralizing of any outside system. I cannot be parroting other thinkers. I must be able to logically examine my actions and self-determine what is morally true. Emerson calls this *self-reliance*:

> To believe our own thought, to believe that what is true for you in your private heart is true for all men, -- that is genius… There is a time in every man's education when he arrives at the conviction that envy is ignorance; that imitation is suicide; that he must take himself for better, for worse, as his portion; that though the wide universe is full of good, no kernel of nourishing corn can come to him but through his toil bestowed on that plot of ground which is given to him to till… Whoso would be a man must be a nonconformist. He who would gather immortal palms must not be hindered by the name of goodness, but must explore if it be goodness. Nothing is at last sacred but the integrity of your own mind. Absolve you to yourself, and you shall have the suffrage of the world.
>
> —Ralph Waldo Emerson[9]

And so, in the mental/modern paradigm, it is by trusting myself that I come into integrity. By trusting in my capacity for reason, which is a universal human gift, I am able to access the truest form of integrity. As Emerson put it: "*Nothing is at last sacred but the integrity of your own mind.*"

I remember being introduced to Emereson's "Self-Reliance" in high school. Along with other Transcendentalist writings, this essay inspired my first steps beyond the membership-identities I had been holding as a teenager and from my Catholic upbringing. At the time, I felt how those affiliations no longer fit, but I didn't know where to turn next. "Trust thyself: every heart vibrates to that iron string." This essay helped set in motion my ongoing commitment to finding myself. Returning to these words today, I feel every bit as inspired. How can I be in integrity, if I don't know myself? The only truth that I need is the one arising from within. Aligning to my inner knowing and living fearlessly from that place is the expression of integrity in the mental/modern paradigm.

Prompts for Journaling and Discussion

What principles do you live by? How are these different from a Warrior's code?

Have you let go of society's concepts of right and wrong to find your own inner knowing? What was that process like?

Integrity at Plural/Postmodern

One superpower that comes online in the plural/postmodern paradigm is *systems thinking*. Instead of perceiving self and world as discrete entities governed by discernable rules, as in the modern paradigm, I now see systems which are governed by emergent patterns. My psyche is a system of parts. Society is a system of social actors. Integrity now applies to the harmonious functioning of the networks that I participate in.

Let's use the human body as an example. The modern paradigm sees discrete units governed by laws. Each body is a collection of molecules which individually are coherent and integrous. But unless these molecules work together in a coherent pattern, they do not produce a cell. This is what the plural/postmodern paradigm is able to understand. The organization and interactions of the molecules (i.e., the system) must be in integrity to produce the next higher level of complexity. For a living system, this is known as autopoiesis. Similarly, the cells must coordinate their interactions for the organ to be coherent. And the organs must work together as a system for the body to function. At each level, the harmonious networking of the parts enables the integrity of the higher-level, emergent system.

The integrity of the network's pattern applies to my interpersonal relationships, my cultural ties, my connection to nature, and on and on. In plural/postmodern, I see systems.

A second superpower is *sensitivity*. Beyond using logic as the final arbiter of morality and truth, I now begin to include feeling. My emotions and nervous-system regulation become embedded in a richer understanding of *my truth*. I recognize that my psyche consists of a collective of parts, or an *internal family*. Each part has their own agenda. My inner child, my critic, and my protectors are *parts* of the psychological *system* of me. Each part needs my love and acceptance. Each part needs me to be *sensitive* to their needs. When all of my parts are working together, my system comes into integrity.

> The family therapy movement, which viewed extreme individual behaviors in the context of a larger system, liberated the field of mental health to focus on context and relationships. Internal Family Systems (IFS) takes this perspective further by viewing the psyche as a relational milieu that is populated by independent entities. IFS guides us to be curious about the motives and interactions of this inner populace, who have their own stories to tell… The IFS model brings systems thinking into the intrapsychic realm. In psychotherapy it works well to conceptualize and relate to individuals as *psychic systems*.
>
> —Richard Schwartz and Martha Sweezy[10]

In addition to becoming increasingly internally sensitive, I become aware of a plurality of social actors. Integrity calls me to move beyond the self-reliance of the modern paradigm where each individual is trusted to care for themselves. In plural/postmodern, I recognize that some people are not capable of caring for themselves but still hold universal rights—for example, children. I also recognize that certain groups of people have been marginalized or oppressed by social systems, and this compels me to ensure equal rights for all members of society.

> All human rights are universal, indivisible, interrelated, interdependent and mutually reinforcing and must be treated in a fair and equal manner, on the same footing and with the same emphasis, and recalling that the promotion and protection of one category of rights should never exempt States from the promotion and protection of the other rights.
>
> —United Nations Declaration on the Rights of Peasants

In the prior section, I referenced the United Nations Universal Declaration of Human Rights as modernity's definition of universal rights. Since publishing that declaration, the United Nations has further made the following proclamations and treaties:

- Convention on the Elimination of All Forms of Racial Discrimination
- Covenant on Economic, Social and Cultural Rights
- Covenant on Civil and Political Rights
- Convention on the Elimination of All Forms of Discrimination against Women
- Convention on the Rights of the Child
- Convention on the Rights of Persons with Disabilities
- Convention on the Rights of Migrants
- Declaration on the Right to Development
- Declaration on the Rights of Indigenous Peoples
- Declaration on the Rights of Peasants and Other People Working in Rural Areas

This plurality of declarations is sensitive to the harmonious functioning of our interdependent global system. The United Nations today is thoroughly building out the plural/postmodern governance structures for society.

As an individual in the plural/postmodern paradigm, integrity means not simply acting according to moral truths as discerned by my rational mind. I must additionally place my actions within the cultural contexts where they are held and interpreted. I become increasingly aware of my cultural biases, self-defensive mechanisms, and privileges. This represents postmodernism's healthy, proper development for social integrity.

Where I do not agree with the plural/postmodern paradigm is the position of *moral relativism,* which can be stated as follows:

> The truth or falsity of moral judgments, or their justification, is not absolute or universal, but is relative to the traditions, convictions, or practices of a group of persons.[11]

Now this metaethical position is itself an absolute statement of truth, albeit not a moral one. But the relativist position rests on an objectivist foundation, which seemingly contradicts the spirit of the position. "All moral truths are relative" is stated as an absolute truth.

The real issue I see with the claim, "moral judgements are *not universal,*" is its direct opposition to the declarations of rights: "All human rights are universal, indivisible, interrelated, interdependent and mutually reinforcing." The incompatibility between these two positions is direct, unambiguous, and stark. To take just one example, if we hold that it is universally true that all humans deserve the right to access to education, then a culture or religion that denies education to women is in breach of this basic human right. The moral relativist position would instead argue that denying education can be morally justified within a given culture, that it is a relative moral truth. In my view, the moral relativist position is unconscionable.

When I make the giant leap from plural/postmodern into the integral paradigm, the discrepancies with relativism become glaringly obvious. I will include a few arguments against relativism from integral authors in the endnotes here,[12] here,[13] and here.[14]

Prompts for Journaling and Discussion

What does it feel like to be part of a group or team that is not working well together?

What does it feel like when the system is functioning harmoniously?

Make a list of your inner parts. For each part, ask them what name they would like to be called, and ask how you (adult self) can support this part.

Examine the patterns in your life, including relational systems and behavior routines. Which patterns need your attention to come into greater integrity?

Integrity at Integral

Because the word *integrity* shares the same root as *integral,* it is no surprise that the integral paradigm highly values this concept. The core experience of integral is wholeness. From the integral paradigm I inhabit a holistic self, embedded in a holistic humanity, interconnected within a holistic ecosystem. I see wholes within wholes, or more accurately, holons within holons. A holon is an entity that is simultaneously both a whole and a part - see Appendix I for a full discussion. Integrity is the property that coheres a holon.

In addition to wholeness, the primary value of the integral paradigm is evolution. I recognize that I live in an evolving universe, that human culture is evolving, and that my personal journey is one of development. Holons across all scales are self-becoming. I want this evolution to be virtuous, meaning I want to create more wholeness, more freedom, and more well-being. Enabling virtuous evolution brings my focus onto the *process.*

Process is a third layer of complexity that comes into view at integral. The modern paradigm sees material. Substance and structure follow scientific laws. The postmodern paradigm sees patterns. Structures interact in relational systems with emergent properties that can only be understood by looking at their organization: patterns. Integral sees an even deeper layer of complexity: *process.* The process is what is happening right now, inclusive of both structure and pattern. Process governs how the structure changes the pattern, and how the pattern changes the structure. The process level is where I can observe the evolution of the system over time. Structures are visible, measurable components. Pattern is the invisible, discernable organization. Process is the experiential unfolding—the creative advance into novelty.

> This striking property of living systems suggests process as a third perspective for a comprehensive description of the nature of life. The process of life is the activity involved in the continual embodiment of the system's pattern of organization. Thus the process perspective is the link between organization and structure…Drawn from autopoiesis, the three perspectives of organization, structure, and process provide an integrative conceptual framework for the understanding of biological life. All three are totally interdependent. The pattern of organization can be recognized only if it is embodied in a physical structure, and in living systems this embodiment is an ongoing process.
>
> —Capra & Luisi[15]

Within an evolving kosmos, integrity means that the process is unfolding virtuously. *Eros* is the drive of parts to reach upward toward greater wholeness. This is an integrous process. The opposite process is a drive toward death, or *Thanatos.* Interestingly, the two core themes of this workbook, sex and aggression, have also been characterized as Eros and Thanatos. In virtuous equilibrium with Eros is *Agape*. Just as parts naturally self-transcend upward (Eros), in equal measure, wholes reach downward to embrace parts (Agape). The compassion of the larger for the smaller is Agape. Instead of a downward *embrace*, the process could alternately be one of *fear*, termed *Phobos*. Eros and Agape are the virtuous processes of love in action. They are integrity-generating processes. Thanatos and Phobos are the discordant processes of dissolution and dissociation. They degrade integrity.

> It was a doctrine [ie: the philosophy of the Cambridge Platonists] in which love played a central part; not only the ascending love of the lower for the higher, Plato's *eros*, but also a love of the higher which expressed itself in care for the lower, which could easily be identified with Christian *agape*. The two together make a vast circle of love through the universe.
>
> —Taylor[16]

If I have a virtuous process, then the results will take care of themselves. Integrity in the integral paradigm is about getting the process right. When this happens, the holon evolves upward on the developmental ladder. Life naturally advances into greater wholeness and complexity, following the cosmogenetic principle. Human consciousness naturally moves toward greater freedom, *eleutheropoiesis*.

When I'm in integrity—meaning the process by which I'm living my life is working well—I will inherently move into a state of well-being. The virtuous process will also lead to increasing degrees of self-actualization.

> This integrity, this unity beyond fragmentation, this incorruptible character, this synergy, gives a person an ability, a capacity, a mental, emotional, physical and spiritual strength to lead their life with ever-increasing levels of well-being and development of their potential. Integrity in this broader sense is the basis of what can be called personal power or authentic power. It is the source of what we refer to as true empowerment that may become authentic or transformative leadership.
>
> —Raúl Rosado[17]

At integral, integrity means cohering into wholeness and aligning with virtuous processes, Eros and Agape, for personal transformation and empowerment.

Prompts for Journaling and Discussion

What does wholeness mean to you?

Where in your life are you reaching upwards to grow into something bigger (Eros)?

Where are you reaching downward to embrace smaller parts (Agape)?

How have you experienced a drive toward dissolution (Thanatos)?

Where do you experience fear, Phobos, and how does it hold you back?

Some other terms for integrity at integral include, *self-actualization, self-authorship,* and *personal empowerment.* How do you connect these terms with the concept of *integrity*?

Notes

[1] Mbzt cc by-sa.

[2] Painting by Utagawa Kuniyoshi, 19th century.

[3] "Warrior Values, a socio-historical survey" in *Male Violence*, Archer.

[4] *Chivalry*, Gautier.

[5] "Generally speaking, the Way of the warrior is resolute acceptance of death. Although not only warriors but priests, women, peasants and lowlier folk have been known to die readily in the cause of duty or out of shame, this is a different thing. The warrior is different in that studying the Way of Strategy is based on overcoming men. By victory gained in crossing swords with individuals, or enjoining battle with large numbers, we can attain power and fame for ourselves or our lord. This is the virtue of strategy." *The Book of Five Rings*, Musashi.

[6] *Chivalry*, Gautier.

[7] *Groundwork of the Metaphysics of Morals*.

[8] *The Rights of Man*.

[9] *Self-Reliance*.

[10] *Internal Family Systems Therapy*.

[11] "Moral Relativism," Stanford Encyclopedia of Philosophy Archive.

[12] "One of the downsides of the postmodern stage is found in its 'value relativism.' Examples of the 'anything goes' inclusiveness of value relativism can be seen in many areas of contemporary society such as New Age spirituality, alternative medicine, multiculturalism, and victim politics. And value relativism is especially prevalent at elite universities. Within academia and much of our education system there are many postmodernists who firmly believe that all social hierarchies are essentially subjective, and that modernism is in no way superior to what came before it. This is not to say that every one of these expressions of the postmodern worldview are necessarily pathological, but in these areas of our culture the values of comparative excellence and the hierarchy of achievement are generally subordinated to the preferred values of equality and inclusiveness. However, in an evolutionary universe organized by hierarchical development at every level, to attempt to eliminate hierarchy is to deny what is real." *Integral Consciousness and the Future of Evolution*, McIntosh.

[13] "This is called a 'performative contradiction,' because you yourself are doing what you claim you cannot or should not do. This view ranks ranking as being bad; judges judging as being oppressive; gives a very Big Picture about why Big Pictures are not possible; claims it is universally

true that there are no universal truths; places hierarchies on the lowest level of its particular hierarchy; and claims its view is superior in a world where nothing is supposed to be superior." *The Religion of Tomorrow*, Wilber.

[14] "A special case of pluralism is the academic discipline of *deconstructive postmodernism*. It believes that it is impossible to defend any belief by proclaiming that all views are subjective and therefore legitimate since everything is relative. When relativism is carried to its logical extreme no view or interpretation is better than any other. All are equal. Postmodernists believe that any metanarrative succumbs to the same subjective arbitrariness. They deny the legitimacy of all hierarchies and all hierarchical ordering. When Pluralists adopt this belief, they may be hypersensitive to perceived instances of judgment as 'better' or 'valuable' in human terms... In the extreme case, postmodernists assert with absolute certainty that there is no position from which to judge anything. They do not yet recognize the inherent self-contradiction in their assertion. It is, of course, a form of judgment and hierarchical ordering of values as those who disagree clearly have a less evolved view from theirs." "Ego Development: A Full-Spectrum Theory Of Vertical Growth And Meaning Making," Cook-Greuter.

[15] *The Systems View of Life: A Unifying Vision.*

[16] *Sources of the Self.*

[17] *Consciousness-in-Action.*

| 4 |

The Integrity Arch

Figure 4.1 Archway[1]

In the prior chapter, I put forward a theory for integrity from the integral paradigm. Now, I want to take action to make integrity real in my life. The integrity process that I will be presenting here is inspired by one of my teachers, Francoise Bourzat. She and her partner created their Holistic Model for a Balanced Life to support experiences of expanded states of consciousness, drawing on indigenous wisdom traditions and somatic psychotherapy.[2] In my adaptation, the Integrity Arch, I examine each element through the three perspectives of complexity introduced in the prior chapter: structure, pattern, and process.

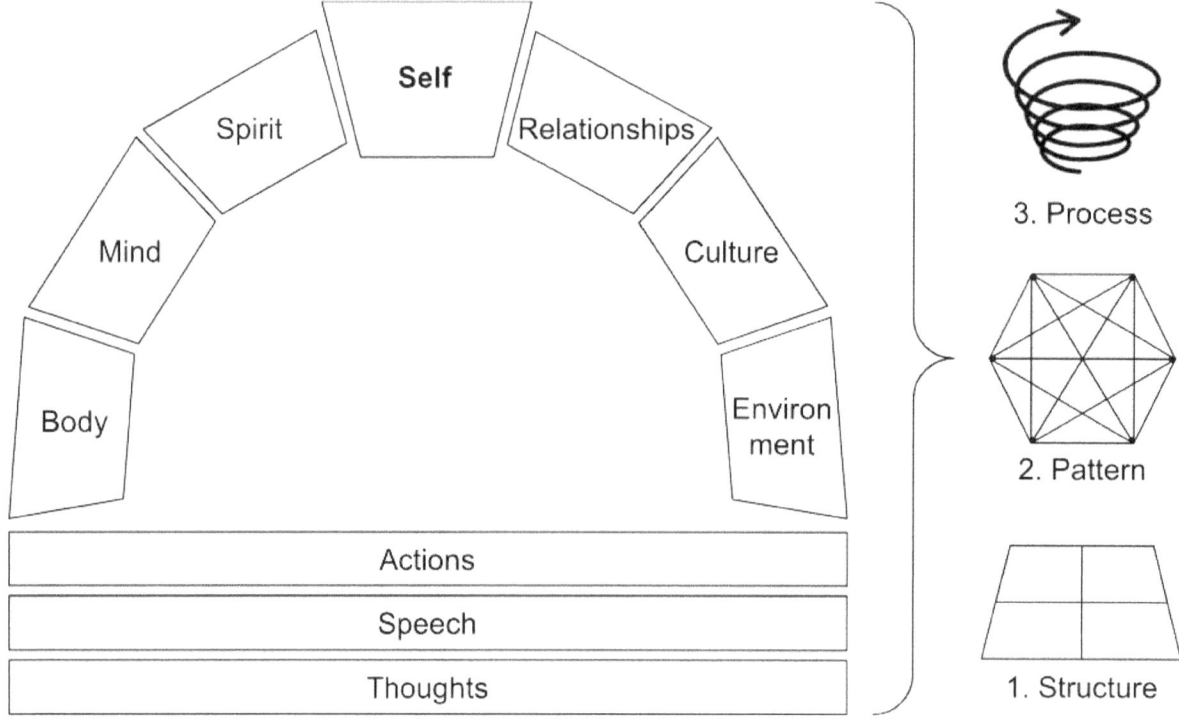

Figure 4.2 The Integrity Arch

First an overview, and then I'll dive into individual categories. I use the arch as a symbol for integrity. Each brick balances the forces of the entire arch, so each brick needs to be whole in order for the arch to be whole. The center brick, known as the keystone, is my self. I am inhabiting the center of my life, around which everything else is balanced. The left three bricks are personal categories and the right three bricks are interpersonal categories. The entire arch rests on the foundations of my thoughts, speech, and actions. Without a solid foundation, the arch is prone to collapse. When the foundation and all the bricks are coherent, then the whole arch becomes structurally integral. It becomes weight-bearing, strong, and resilient. Every brick can be examined through three perspectives of increasing levels of complexity: structure, pattern, and process.

I use this approach to take inventory of where I am in integrity and where I am ready to make a change in my life. One could make the argument that there are layers beneath thinking. Emotions and the experiences arising from the body are more primary than thoughts. Nature is more fundamental than either thinking or emotions. But in terms of using this model for *integrity*, I find that aligning my thinking is the first step. Moving downward from thinking into the causes of my thinking shifts the focus from integrity to psychotherapy. That said, this model is surprisingly deep. Let's take a look!

Foundation: Thoughts, Speech, and Actions

> We are what we think.
> All that we are arises with our thoughts.
> With our thoughts we make the world.
> Speak or act with an impure mind
> And trouble will follow you
> As the wheel follows the ox that draws the cart.
>
> We are what we think.
> All that we are arises with our thoughts.
> With our thoughts we make the world.
> Speak or act with a pure mind
> And happiness will follow you
> As your shadow, unshakable.
>
> –The Dhammapada[3]

The foundation of integrity has three levels: thoughts, speech, and action. The first level is my thoughts. Whatever I'm thinking becomes the basis for the second level, my speech. And what I speak becomes the basis for my actions. All of the other bricks in the arch are types of relationships. My thoughts, speech, and actions determine how I show up in any of these relationships. This is why I begin to work on integrity through these three categories.

I'll first examine my thoughts, speech, and actions through the structure view. Then, I'll look at patterns, and finally processes. These three levels of complexity provide a thorough framework for understanding myself. Examining my structures, patterns, and processes produces a meta-process synergy where I am engaging with a process which itself creates more integrity. Simply put, exploring the integrity arch is an integrity-creating process.

I want to begin by setting an intention to come into integrity—we did this at the beginning of Chapter Three in Figure 3.4. Take a moment to revisit this intention now. I align my thinking toward integrity. Without this, nothing else matters.

In the structural view, I examine the contents of my thoughts. The structural level of my thoughts are the actual thoughts themselves. In particular, I want to pay attention to the types of thoughts I'm having, including judgments, beliefs, and ideas.

Judgments usually have a value attached to them like good or bad, positive or negative, or pleasurable or painful. They also include thoughts with the word "should" in them. "I *should* be waking up earlier." "You *should* be respecting my boundaries."

Beliefs interpret reality to make meaning out of it. Limiting beliefs are statements that keep me small based on a hurtful experience from my past that I've internalized. *I'm not worthy of love* and *The world is hostile toward my needs* are two examples.

Ideas are something new coming to mind. They might take the form of creative brainstorms, daydreams, future plans, and critical analysis.

Use the Thoughts column of the table below to record your inventory. Do not feel compelled to put something in each box. This framework is simply here to help bring awareness to each of these places within yourself. Take an inventory of your thoughts and then reflect. What are the beliefs and messages that you are telling yourself? Are these the thoughts that you would choose to have for your well-being?

Contents	Thoughts	Speech	Actions
Positive, honest, aligned			
Neutral			
Negative, dishonest, distorted			

Figure 4.3 Content inventory of thoughts, speech, and actions

Speech comes next. This is where most conversations about integrity primarily focus. The contents of my thoughts are directly related to the contents of my speech. Because I'm giving voice to the thought and speaking something into the world, it is a stronger form of manifestation. Integrity of speech means I say what is true–and whatever I *say* I will do, I actually follow through and *do.* This is why I put speech as the layer between thoughts and actions. My word carries an immense amount of power. By speaking my truth, I align more fully to my inner truth. When I follow through on my spoken commitments, I build trust in myself and in my relationships. Use the table above to take inventory of what you are saying. When am I speaking honestly, with positive intent? When am I telling lies, withholding information, gossiping, or speaking negatively?

Next are my actions. The content of my actions covers what I am doing and how I am spending my time. Integrity means my actions are healthy and aligned with my thoughts and speech. When I am not in integrity, my actions are not supporting my well-being or they are not aligned with my thoughts and speech. If I'm saying one thing but doing something else, I'm out of integrity. Use the table above to take an inventory of your actions.

This is the first perspective on my thoughts, speech, and actions: the structural perspective. I now have awareness of the contents of what I'm thinking, saying, and doing.

Now I'm going to examine the same three categories through the perspective of *patterns.* At the thinking level, instead of examining the contents of my thoughts, I shift to look at the qualities and organization of my thinking. Am I looping on a topic? Is my thinking clear, logical, and focused? At the top of the spectrum are mental states of creativity, flow, and connection. These patterns increase my overall well-being. At the bottom of the spectrum are patterns of repetitive thinking, obsessing, dullness, dissociation, anxiety, or stress. These patterns of thinking reduce the integrity of my mental state. Use the table below to list your patterns of thinking.

Patterns	Thoughts	Speech	Actions
Impeccable, creative, engaging			
Clear, simple			
Repetitive, checked-out, frenzied			

Figure 4.4 Pattern inventory of thoughts, speech, and actions

My thought patterns become the basis for my speech patterns. Similarly, I want to examine the qualities of my speech. Am I always rushing through what I have to say? Do I chatter or digress so I'm speaking without connection to my thoughts? Is my speech clear and simple? At the high end of the spectrum, my speech is impeccable, meaning honestly aligned with both thoughts and actions. Impeccability of speech is a pattern of showing up and continuing to say what's true.

In his book *The Four Agreements*, Don Miguel Ruiz's first agreement is, "Be impeccable with your word." This is the single most important step in his body of work to move from a life of suffering to a life of mastery.

Now let us see what the word impeccability means. *Impeccability* means "without sin." Impeccable comes from the Latin *pecatus*, which means "sin." The *im* in impeccable means "without," so *impeccable* means "without sin." Religions talk about sin and sinners, but let's understand what it really means to sin. A sin is anything that you do which goes against yourself. Everything you feel or believe or say that goes against yourself is a sin. You go against yourself when you judge or blame yourself for anything. Being without sin is exactly the opposite. Being impeccable is not going against yourself. When you are impeccable, you take responsibility for your actions, but you do not judge or blame yourself. From this point of view, the whole concept of sin changes from something moral or religious to something commonsense. Sin begins with rejection of yourself. Self-rejection is the biggest sin that you commit. In religious terms self-rejection is a "mortal sin," which leads to death. Impeccability, on the other hand, leads to life.

—Don Miguel Ruiz[4]

The third layer is my actions. The pattern of my actions includes my behaviors and habits. An example of a positive pattern would be regular hygiene and exercise. An example of a negative pattern would be procrastinating on a project, staying up late cramming, and then crashing after the project is over. I want to look for whether my overall well-being is supported by my behaviors or eroded by them. Write out your patterns of action in the table above.

This is the second perspective: patterns of thoughts, speech, and actions. Now, I'll move on to the process perspective, which is the deepest level of complexity. The process-level is where the magic happens.

The thoughts I am choosing right now will change both the contents and patterns of my thinking moving forward. I can use my thinking to reach upward to embrace greater forms of understanding (Eros). I can use my thinking to reach downward to embrace the fragmented parts of myself (Agape). Alternatively, my thinking may be in a self-destructive process (Thanatos) or ruled by fear (Phobos). I have some degree of choice in my thinking, and I can choose to shift my state so that my thinking supports my well-being. I can use specific thoughts, like affirmations, to create positive mind-states. This is how the process engages the structure to change the pattern. Similarly, I can create patterns like flow states to create positive thoughts. Here, the process engages the pattern to produce the structure. "I'm going to get myself into a creative brainstorm state in order to be effective on this project" is an example of the upward-reaching process of Eros. "I am slowing my mental state down so my inner child isn't overwhelmed" is an example of the downward-embracing process of Agape.

The first vicious process is Thanatos. Death and dissolution are part of the natural processes of life, so these are not always negative or "bad." I want to contextualize the process I'm in to see whether it supports my overall well-being. Is a psychic death most in service to me right now? Or am I either fixating or avoiding the natural death process? Where are limiting beliefs, harsh judgments, or negative self-talk leading me into a spiral downward?

The second vicious process is Phobos. Fear and skepticism serve very important purposes in the psyche. They provide discernment and protection. Again, I want to look at the process that is unfolding with my fear. Is fear ruling my life? Or am I able to hear the message that fear has to give me, adjust my course, and then release my fear?

Finally, in some areas of my thinking I notice that there is no active process unfolding. This can be either positive or negative. If I'm in a good structure and pattern, then this aspect may not need any change at this time. Once I get into the habit of thinking positively, for example, the wise choice is probably to stabilize this new structure and pattern. Realistically, I only have capacity to engage a few areas in meaningful change at any given time. So stabilizing my non-focus areas is a very useful skill. Trying to evolve all aspects of my life simultaneously is not likely to be successful.

An unchanging process may also be negative. I might be avoiding or resisting this aspect of my life. I may be fixated or stuck in this area when a change appears scary or painful. In these cases, no change is actually Thanatos or Phobos freezing me into my situation. Life wants to breathe and move. Change wants to happen. So if I'm stuck and there is *no process*, I might more accurately categorize that as a death or fear process that has a hold on me. Use your discernment and utilize this model in the way that makes sense for you as you fill out the table below.

Process	Thoughts	Speech	Actions
Eros (Evolution, Growth) & Agape (Compassion, Healing)			
Unchanging, stable, stuck, stagnant			
Thanatos (Death) & Phobos (Fear)			

Figure 4.5 Process inventory of thoughts, speech, and actions

For the processes of my speaking, integrity means my speech is either uplifting and growth-oriented or compassionate and healing. When I bring conscious intention to my speech, I can use it for the well-being and wholeness of myself and anyone who hears me. At the bottom end of this spectrum is hate-speech and fear-mongering. These processes create negative patterns and structures.

Finally, the process of my actions is an opportunity to consider how my behaviors are changing over time. Am I creating more and more positive habits for myself? Have I been coasting recently? Is my behavior slipping into either dissolution or fear? By cultivating a positive process in my thinking and speech, I will see a positive outcome in my actions.

This is where accountability can be incredibly helpful. Having a friend, a mentor, or a men's group to share my thoughts, speak my truth, and report back on my actions supports a positive process. I do not have to carry all of my personal growth work alone. And by working on my process in a group I create more integrity for the group as a whole.

Look back over the previous three tables. Having taken this inventory, now ask: Where do I want to be? And what process will get me there? Engaging the processes of Eros and Agape will shift the contents and patterns of my thoughts, speech, and actions. This is how the process-level permeates the two shallower perspectives. Begin with thoughts. If I get my thinking right, my speech will follow. And if I get my speech right, my actions will follow.

Now that I've explored integrity in these three foundational layers, I'm ready to look at specific relational areas in my life. Any changes to integrity in the upper bricks of the arch will be supported by the integrity of my thoughts, speech, and actions.

Body

I am choosing to come into integrity in my relationship with my body. My body is both the vessel that carries me through this life, and my greatest teacher on my path. Integrity means I am caring for my body in the same way I would for any animal that is dependent on me. At the same time, integrity means I am listening to my body and honoring its messages as if it were my own personal guru.

I relate with my body through diet, exercise, rest, physical health, and sexuality. I'll examine each of these aspects through the three perspectives of structure, pattern, and process.

Beginning with the structural view, I examine the content of my body's phenomena:

- The structure of my diet is the food that I eat. Is the food I eat healthy or unhealthy? Do I eat too much or too little food? Do I feel connected to my food? Do I grow food and prepare food? Do I enjoy eating? Ask yourself, "What does integrity look like in regards to the food I eat?"
- What exercises I am performing? Exercise can be used to burn fat and carbs, to build endurance, flexibility, strength, or dexterity. I can use exercise as part of a sport or skilled activity. Am I exercising too much or too little? Is my exercise right for my body and do I enjoy it? What other physical practices would I like to explore? What does integrity look like in regards to my exercises?
- How is the quality and quantity of my rest? Am I sleeping too much or too little? Am I sleeping well? Outside of sleep, do I make space for leisure and rest? Am I nourished and recharged by my rest? Do I enjoy it?
- For physical health, I want to consider the ailments I have and the treatment that I'm able to access. Do I get regular check-ups? Do I seek treatment and follow through to address any health conditions? How do I take care of myself when I feel sick?
- Sexuality includes how I engage with other partners and my own self-pleasure. Am I using sex in an unhealthy or addictive way? Am I repressing my sexuality? Do I enjoy sex and self-pleasure?

Use the table below to create your own body inventory at the level of structure.

Body Aspect	Integrity of Structure and Content
Diet	
Exercise	
Rest	
Physical Health	
Sexuality	

Figure 4.6 Structures of relationship with aspects of the body

Now I examine each of these aspects through the ongoing patterns in my life:

- What is the pattern in my diet? Do I go through cycles of binge and purge? Do I eat the same food or am I creative with my diet?
- What is my exercise routine? Is this routine too much or too little? Is it consistent or inconsistent? What do I want my exercise routine to be?
- Is my rest consistent or variable? Do I go through cycles of manic activity and depression? Do I burn myself out? Is my pattern of resting supporting me to live an active and creative life?
- How does my physical health change over time? Do I have chronic illnesses? Do I have recurring injuries? Is my health trending upward or downward? What can I do to support the patterns of my physical health?
- What frequency do I engage in sex and self-pleasure? How long is each session? Is there a pattern for how I'm using sex: stress relief, self-validation, boredom, or routine habit? When was the best period of my sex life and when was the hardest?

Fill out your inventory for the patterns in relating with your body:

Body Aspect	Integrity of Pattern
Diet	
Exercise	
Rest	
Physical Health	
Sexuality	

Figure 4.7 Patterns of relationship with aspects of the body

Finally, I want to examine the process that I'm taking with each aspect of my body. Am I actively engaging in change? Is no change happening? Am I in a positive or negative process? More specifically, is my process virtuously reaching up through Eros or embracing down through Agape? Or is my process moving towards death or ruled by fear? With awareness of my current process, what process would I like to choose for myself and how can I transition to this new process? What structures and patterns need to shift to support a different process? What support and resources do I need to make these changes?

Body Aspect	Integrity of Process (Eros, Agape, static, Thanatos, Phobos)
Diet	
Exercise	
Rest	
Physical Health	
Sexuality	

Figure 4.8 Process with aspects of the body

As an example, imagine that I identify feeling out of integrity in my use of pornography. This lands in the sexuality aspect of my body. To work on integrity here, I first want to identify the structure and content of my porn use: what am I watching, how often, and for how long? Where is this out of integrity and what amount, if any, feels *in integrity*.

Next, I want to look at the pattern of my usage. How do I feel immediately before I engage in porn? How do I feel immediately afterward? Is my use consistent or do I binge with it? What else is happening in my life (stress, work, relationship, big emotions) that may be contributing to this use? What pattern of use, if any, do I want to have with porn?

Third, I want to examine the process view. Is my current use supporting me evolving into my best self (Eros)? Is it helping me heal fragmented or wounded aspects of my sexuality (Agape)? Is my porn use killing or destroying aspects of me (Thanatos)? How is fear influencing my use of porn—am I afraid to express my desires in a real relationship, for example (Phobos)?

Now, what process do I want to have and how do I get there? Is going cold-turkey the right approach or should I wean myself down? What other support might I need in terms of therapy, human connection, hobbies, or rest to make this change? How can I ensure that I really shift to the new process, pattern, and structure? What might get in the way of this?

For any changes to structure, pattern, and process, I want to be sure to choose goals for myself that are S.M.A.R.T. Each goal needs to be *specific, measurable, achievable, relevant,* and *time-bound.* When I set a goal for myself and complete it, I create a positive reinforcement loop that increases my capacity for change. When I set an unrealistic goal, that's a signal to myself that I am not fully committed to making this change. Missing a goal erodes my inner integrity. That said, setting achievable baseline goals together with stretch goals helps me achieve what I set for myself while giving me room to expand beyond what I think is possible.

Once I have a clear plan, I return to my foundations of thought, speech, and action. I align my thoughts to the new relationship I want to create with porn. I create mental clarity for what I want. I can see myself taking the steps to be successful. Then I put these thoughts into words. I journal. I speak my intentions aloud to other humans in my life, including partners, therapists or coaches, friends, or members of my men's group. I ask them to hold me accountable to my new goals. Then I take action. I choose new structures and patterns to engage a new process. Over time, I revisit my inventory to assess whether I'm ready to iterate a new structure, pattern, and process in this area of my life.

Mind

I am choosing to come into integrity with my mind. Integrity of mind applies to the aspects of my intellect, emotions, and unconscious. Again, I'll be examining these through the perspectives of structure, pattern, and process. Here we go, beginning with structure:

The capacities of my intellect include discursive thinking, logic, scientific reasoning, prioritizing and planning, communication, access to memories, and identity. Am I supporting my intellect to be clear and focused? Am I hampering my intellect through substance use, social media, or other distractions? Is my personality flexible and humble? Am I prone to narcissism or self-doubt? Ask yourself, "What does it mean to be in integrity with my intellect?"

For the structural level of emotions, consider these five primary emotions: fear, grief, anger, pain, and joy. Each one is a primordial feeling state. These emotions require no logical trigger and need no rational content for why they arise. In addition to the primary emotions, I have *affects,* which are automatic responses to my environment. These are: disgust, surprise, interest, and embarrassment. For each of these emotions and affects, I am able to subdivide them into more refined labels for my feelings (see Figure 4.9, below). Emotions and affects arise in my body and must then be received and interpreted by my mind. Am I aware of my emotions and am I available to feel them? Do I repress my emotions? Am I overpowered by strong emotions? Do I have a healthy relationship with each emotion and affect? Do I fixate, fabricate, or obsess on an emotional state? Can I separate my narratives (i.e., the story of what's happening) from my feelings? Integrity means I am available to feel my full spectrum of emotions and affects. When they arise, I make space to feel them, receive any messages they have for me, and then allow them to flow through me.

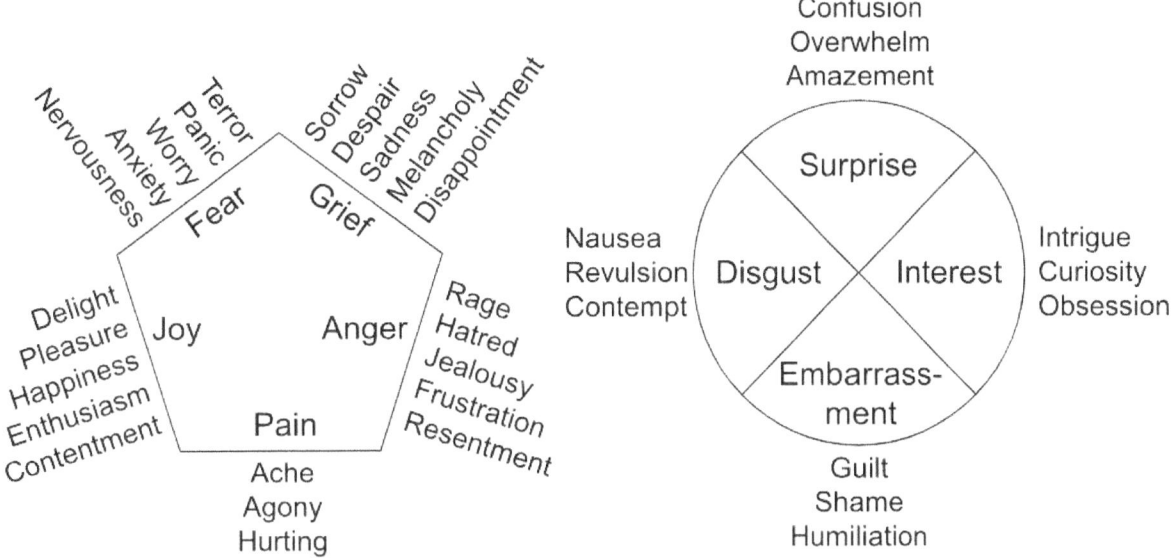

Figure 4.9 Feelings and Affects

The unconscious includes all aspects of my psyche that lie outside my waking consciousness. I access the contents of my unconscious through dreams, fantasies, shadow work, and altered states of consciousness (eg: yoga nidra, meditation, psychedelics, shamanic practices, and so on). Integrity at the structural level of my unconscious means I am paying attention to receive these messages. I may keep a dream journal, undertake psychotherapy, or seek honest reflections from loved ones about my blind spots. Being out of integrity here means ignoring, avoiding, or repressing the positive or negative parts of myself that are looking to come into awareness. What is showing up in my life that I haven't wanted to look at? What am I in denial about?

Record your inventory of the structure of intellect, emotion, and unconscious in the table below:

Mind Aspect	Integrity of Structure and Content
Intellect	
Emotion	
Unconscious	

Figure 4.10 Structures of relationship with aspects of the mind

Now the pattern perspective.

My intellectual patterns are my ongoing habits and behaviors across the same areas: discursive thinking, logic, reasoning, prioritization and planning, communication, memory, and identity. For each area, am I learning or growing here? Am I utilizing this part of my intellect effectively? Does this area move through cycles of high function followed by low function, rise and crash, mania and depression? Integrity here means creating patterns of consistent function and increasing capacity. In other words, a healthy pattern includes effective utilization of my intellect together with on-going learning.

Emotional patterns are particularly powerful for me to examine. It's easy to get caught in my emotional content, but the pattern reveals the underlying systems driving my emotions. For each primary emotion and affect in Figure 4.9, above, I want to consider how often these show up in my life. What is happening for me when these emotions arise? What purpose are they serving for me? What part of my psyche (inner child, inner teenager, judge, skeptic, victim, etc.) is the emotion being utilized by? Or which character strategy (tough/generous, burdened/enduring, etc.) is showing up with these emotions? One way to understand the concept of becoming *emotionally triggered* is my adult self who is usually in charge is *taken over* by a fragmented part using strong emotions. An internal part is a pattern of my psyche. Where are my parts running my life? How is my adult's relationship with each of my parts? If I judge, dislike, or even hate my other parts, this is an opportunity to come into greater integrity. My adult has the option to love and accept each of my other parts, and thus create a harmonious relationship in my inner tribe.

In addition, I want to notice which emotions or affects I do not regularly feel. If I never feel anger, for example, that is likely an indication that I am suppressing this emotion. I want to be in relationship with each of these emotions. Each one serves a useful purpose and is part of the full spectrum of human experience. Why do I not feel a given emotion or affect? Was there a time in my life when this emotion cost me something, or did it feel unsafe at some point? How can I reestablish a connection with this emotion today?

In the pattern level of my unconscious, I want to examine my inner parts that I've repressed: my exiles, shadows, and complexes. An exile is a part of me that my consciousness has deemed unsafe or unacceptable and then repressed from conscious awareness. My shadow is all the aspects of myself, positive and negative, that I cannot see because I have not yet learned to fully love myself there. A complex is a sub-personality with its own agenda. These are three ways of explaining essentially the same phenomena, which is that my unconscious holds aspects of my psyche that act differently than my adult self would choose. It's one thing to have a substance binge under pressure (food, alcohol, drugs, etc.)—in this case I would look at the content of what triggered that. It's another thing to have a recurring behavior of binging, a pattern. What are my unconscious patterns? Who is controlling that pattern? What part, shadow-element, or complex is taking over? Consider behaviors of addiction, depression, binging, sabotaging, or rupturing relationships. What services are my shadow parts providing that my adult self is not currently supplying? One example is they help me set boundaries when I am avoiding conflict.

Fill out your inventory on integrity of mind-patterns here:

Mind Aspect	Integrity of Pattern
Intellect	
Emotion	
Unconscious	

Figure 4.11 Patterns of relationship with aspects of the mind

Finally, I turn to the process perspective.

There are two types of intellectual learning. The first is learning a new skill, subject area, or content. These are intellectual *patterns* of learning. The second is learning to see the self and world in a new way. This is a *process* at the intellectual level because it is working on the structures and patterns of the intellect itself. The *pattern of my intellect* is another way to describe my *paradigm of consciousness* (traditional, modern, postmodern, or integral). My paradigm is the pattern through which I filter and make sense of my reality. The *process of my intellect* is how my paradigm is changing over time. Eros is growing into a higher paradigm. Agape is embracing and integrating lower developmental aspects of self. Thanatos is regression and Phobos is dissociation. Phobos results in the creation of new shadow material. Here's some good news: By engaging in the material in these workbooks, including undertaking the Integrity Arch, you are powerfully growing and embracing your psyche.

So consider: How is my understanding of self and world changing? When and where does my self-world regress? What aspects of my self-world am I disconnected or dissociated from? How is my self-world growing?

Process at the emotional level means identifying patterns of behavior that are driven by triggered younger parts, and then learning to step out of the familiar system into something new. First I learn to see my pattern, then I become aware of new options in the heat of the moment, then I access the vitality to make a new choice in that moment. In other words, first I recognize when I'm *blended* with a fragmented part (meaning that part has taken over my internal system), then I separate my adult self from the fragmented part and get centered in my adult self. Then my adult gains agency to choose my behavior and give love to the fragmented part. This process includes both Eros and Agape. I am stepping into greater sovereignty and agency, and I am bringing compassion to my fragmented parts. As I become more resilient and stronger in my adult self, I open my capacity to feel powerful emotions without being taken over by them. This is the virtuous process. Emotional regression, often in the wake of trauma, emotional abuse, or severely adverse experiences, is the vicious process. This takes the form of dissolution of my adult's sovereignty, Thanatos, or dissociation from threatening emotions, Phobos.

The process of integrating my unconscious into the wholeness of my psyche is called *individuation*. This process is undertaken primarily by the Self, which is the psychic center of my consciousness. Importantly, the Self is not my egoic waking consciousness. My ego works toward its own egoic ends. My Self works toward the integration of the whole psyche. This process largely happens as my personality and waking consciousness allow and attune to the naturally unfolding individuation process. The archetypes are universal patterns of consciousness (characters and personalities) that influence me. *Individuation* refers to the Self's disentanglement from the unconscious influence of the archetypes. My Self becomes an individual. I can support my individuation process through therapy, dream-work, altered states of consciousness, and so on. Archetypes have the potential to take over my psyche. My shadow can act out. Sometimes these seemingly regressive episodes are what the psyche needs to bring the shadows into light to be integrated. Integrity here largely means making space for the process to unfold itself. In addition, I need to develop a strong foundation in my psyche in order to relate with the archetypes. This is known as strengthening the ego-archetype axis.

Take inventory of your integrity at the mind-process level:

Mind Aspect	Integrity of Process
Intellect	
Emotion	
Subconscious	

Figure 4.12 Process with aspects of the mind

The nature of the Integrity Arch is that it shines a light directly on my growth edges. These are the places where I am available to change. Finding my edges is uncomfortable. I meet my resistance, avoidance, and distraction patterns on the journey to my edges. This is Warrior's work. My egoic self naturally selects for what is familiar, and my growth edges are by definition where I am changing. Sometimes, I engage my growth edge (Eros) or embrace my edge (Agape). Most of the time, I can see my edge, but I'm not able to make a change. It's important to stress that integrity is not about perfection. Rather, integrity is a process. I choose to engage with my process to whatever extent I can. In the places I'm stuck or regressing, I love myself there. I choose kindness. I recognize that I will still judge or punish myself for not meeting my edges, meaning I'll choose cruelty instead of kindness. And then I have the option to feel my pattern of being cruel to myself. This allows me to take a step back and bring kindness to the place in me that has learned self-cruelty as my best option right now. In each moment, I am choosing how I meet my experience. This recognition and ownership of choice is another aspect of integrity at the mind level. Whenever I choose kindness, that automatically re-aligns me with Agape, love's compassionate embrace.

Spirit

Spirit includes my relationship with the unseen world, expanded states of consciousness, and connection with spiritual lineages, traditions, and religions.

From the structure perspective, I examine the content of my spiritual experiences and relations. What spiritual practices am I engaging in? These might include meditation, yoga, prayer, chanting, or charity work. Are these practices the right fit for me at this time? Am I engaging with them enough, too much, or too little? What states of consciousness are opening for me (i.e., gross, subtle, causal, witness, nondual). Am I in connection with my guides, ancestors, spirits of the land, deities, or other beings from the unseen world? What spiritual reading or study am I undertaking? Am I connected to spiritual lineages, traditions, or religions? What are my spiritual beliefs, including faith, afterlife, divine power, and morality? Integrity at this level means consciously deciding which spiritual practices to undertake and then following through.

Use this table to record your inventory for the integrity of your spiritual life, starting with structure in the top row. I've provided two columns, one to examine the specific spiritual practices, and the second for relationships with spiritual communities.

Spirit	Practices	Lineage, Organization, or Teacher
Structure/Content		
Pattern		
Process		

Figure 4.13 Integrity of spirit

From the pattern perspective, I look at the ongoing role of spirituality and my relationship with it. Did I have a religious upbringing? Was that a positive or negative experience for me? How has my upbringing informed my spirituality today? What was the most significant spiritual experience of my life? How have I changed and what does that experience mean to me today? How much time and energy do I currently devote to spiritual study, practice, and worship? Is this the right level of engagement for me? How often do I go on spiritual, personal, or nature retreats? Integrity at this level means finding the right amount of space to dedicate to spirituality. What do I want my practice to look like on a daily, weekly, and even yearly basis?

Finally, in the process perspective, I look at how my spiritual path is changing over time. Am I becoming more involved or less involved with spiritual practice or religion? Are the states of consciousness that I'm accessing becoming more expansive? Am I developing spiritual qualities? In the table below, I've listed spiritual qualities from three spiritual traditions.

Buddhism		Yoga		Christianity	
Eightfold Path	Right view	Yamas (disciplines)	Nonviolence	Beatitudes	Poor in spirit
	Right resolve		Truth		Mourning
	Right speech		Non-stealing		Meek
	Right conduct		Right use of energy		Pursuit of righteousness
	Right livelihood		Non-greed		
	Right effort	Niyamas (duties)	Cleanliness		Merciful
	Right mindfulness		Contentment		Pure of heart
	Right samadhi		Discipline		Peacemaking
Immeasur-ables	Loving kindness		Study		Persecuted for righteousness' sake
	Compassion		Devotion to the divine		
	Sympathetic joy				
	Equanimity				

Figure 4.14 Spiritual qualities in Buddhism, Yoga, and Christianity

Developing on the spiritual path requires discipline and dedication. However, if it arises from an agenda to achieve a particular level of realization, that is a form of spiritual materialism. It is my ego co-opting my spiritual path and represents a step backwards. If I look at the list of spiritual qualities above and make a determination to become more like that, I'm engaging in a form of spiritual materialism. Rather, as I deepen in my practice, I will naturally become interested in these qualities as they begin to arise within me. Because my ego tends to become invested in my spiritual progression, judging the process of my spiritual path is a tricky thing.

Spiritual bypassing is another pitfall, in which I dissociate from the realities of messy human life by coasting in spiritual bliss realms or using spiritual platitudes. In addition, Chogyam Trungpa coined the term *psychological materialism* which refers to an attachment to identity, social position, or opinions as "the real you."

At the end of the day, none of these spiritual pitfalls are problems so much as they present opportunities. Awareness around these patterns is the first step in changing them. When I blindly engage in any of these processes, it stems from a core of not believing I'm safe enough to open into a more expansive experience of self and reality. The spiritual path is not linear either. Dark nights, depression, existential fear, and death-like experiences are all part of the natural unfolding of the journey. For me, it's mainly about continuing to create space for my soul to make the journey and then following my authentic desires for practice and worship.

Relationships

My interpersonal relationships include romantic partnership(s), friends, coworkers, and family.

From the structural perspective, I take inventory of my current relationships, specifically: Who are the most important people in my life? Who triggers me the most? Who in my life do I have unprocessed emotional material with? For each of these relationships, I want to consider how my thoughts, speech, and actions shape this relationship. Then, I find clarity in my vision for an aligned relationship with each of these people. I consider what the most beneficial and exciting version of this relationship could be. Then I consider what I can do to help shift this relationship. What do I need to communicate, and where have I not been transparent or honest? How do I want to show up? Record your inventory in the table below.

	Person(s)	Vision for aligned relationship	Changes to my thoughts, speech, and actions
Most important people			
People who trigger me			
People I have unprocessed material with			

Figure 4.15 Structure and content of relationship

In the pattern view of relationships, I consider each connection as a relational system. Instead of looking at the *content* of the relationship, I examine *how* relating happens. Let's use the analogy of partner dancing. Instead of focusing on the dance technique, I look at how the dancers move together. How are we dancing together? Is it harmonious, creative, push-and-pull, or ruptured?

Here is one of my Hakomi teachers explaining relational systems:

> Systems in human relationships are repetitive, patterned sets of behaviors, feelings, and attitudes that are self-perpetuating and self-reinforcing. Systems are predictable. People can be counted to act in certain characteristic ways in response to each other. Thus, if you get angry, I can be relied on to withdraw, which predictably increases your anger and predictably exacerbates my withdrawal. There is a circularity to them in which one person's behavior tends to evoke the other's defense which in turn tends to evoke more of the first person's unwanted behavior.
>
> —Rob Fisher[5]

In the table below, I list some common relationship patterns. This table is by no means exhaustive.

Pursuer / Distancer	Attacker / Withdrawer	Pusher / Resister
Leader / Follower	Talker / Listener	Rational / Emotional
Conservative / Impulsive	Homebody / Adventurous	Introvert / Extrovert
Giver / Taker	Overfunctioning / Underfunctioning	Caretaker / Wounded or Addicted

Figure 4.16 Examples of role-based patterns in relational systems

Now I return to the relationships that I listed in the *structure* table above. For each of these relationships, what is the pattern? I want to consider whether habitual roles show up, whether the same conversation or argument repeats itself without resolution, whether responses become automatic or predictable, and whether our interactions create vicious or self-reinforcing cycles.

Once I understand the dynamic, I ask myself, what role do I play in this system? How do my thoughts, speech, and actions maintain this system?

Relationship	Name the system	My role in the system

Figure 4.17 Systemic patterns in relationships

In my work as a therapist, I have counseled many clients who can easily identify the dysfunctional relational systems they are in, but are unable to move beyond them. Awareness of the system is the first step, but in order to change, I need to move from the system to the process perspective.

In order to shift a relational system, it is tremendously helpful if all members of the system agree to participate in the process of changing. If I'm trying to shift the system while my partner is reinforcing the system, then change is both slower and more conflict-prone.

I start by describing the pattern together with the other person. Can we name this pattern together? What can we both agree is happening here? What is the experience like on my side and what is it like on your side? Get specific: what physical, emotional, and verbal cues contribute to the system? Name the component parts (structure) and operational patterns (system) without judgment or blame.

Now that we both have a shared understanding of what's happening, can we agree to work together to shift this pattern? If so, can we agree that either one of us can name the system in real time when we notice it? We agree to be in a process of change together.

After becoming aware of the pattern in real time, I next learn to *step outside of the system* in the moment it becomes activated. This means I take a pause from my behavior in the role and bring my curiosity. Then, I name what is happening in concrete terms without judgment. Here are the behaviors, body-languages, and emotions that come together to form the pattern. I detach myself from the pattern so I can study it. By analogy, in order to understand a game of soccer, I need to take in both teams at once rather than focusing on a single player.

Stepping outside of the system frees me to make a new choice in terms of structure and pattern. What would a healthy response in this situation look like? How would I like to be showing up? Working at the process level allows me to reach down into both the content and the roles to adjust and grow.

Codependence, enabling, and abuse are destructive patterns in relationships. These systems keep people small and hurting. They prevent the flourishing and growth of each individual and are therefore rooted in Thanatos and Phobos.

> Codependence occurs when your behavior is determined by someone else's, when others rely on you to maintain their destructive behaviors and addictions, and when you are subordinate to others and thereby not true to your own feelings… When we are codependent we do not have relationships, we have entanglements.
> —Gay and Kathlyn Hendricks[6]

Ultimately, integrity from the process perspective of relationship means that all parties involved are relating in a way that supports both their individual well-being and the well-being of the relational system. Mutually uplifting relationships form virtuous processes.

Culture

Integrity at the level of culture has a distinctly different feel from the bricks of the arch that we've considered so far. In order to work on cultural integrity, I will need to understand how culture is created. Focusing on cultural integrity will necessarily lead us into a conversation about systemic oppression.

The structural components of culture are *cultural identity groups*. These groups of people hold distinct definitions of identity with which I share membership. I simultaneously belong to many cultural identity groups. Some are given to me by society. These include race, nation of origin, sex, and gender-assignment. Some identity groups I choose through participation in social institutions. These include religion, education, profession, and hobbies. Each cultural identity group holds its own idiosyncratic language, norms, traditions, mythology, art, literature, clothing, and historical figures of import. All these factors come together in a shared experience of identity to create culture.

Use the table below to take an inventory of the cultural identity groups you belong to. For each group, list the cultural markers that distinguish this identity from other identities. These are the shared cultural elements (language, norms, appearance, etc.) that demarcate this cultural group.

Identity Category	My Affiliation	Cultural markers
Race[7]		
Nationality[8]		
Ethnicity / Ancestry[9]		
Political Party[10]		
Generation / Age[11]		
Sex[12]		
Gender[13]		
Sexual Orientation[14]		
Body Ability[15]		
Mental Ability[16]		
Class[17]		
Education Level[18]		
Education Focus / Major		
Professional Role		
Professional Industry		
Community		
Hobby		

Figure 4.18 Inventory of social identity groups and cultural markers

Integrity at the structural level of culture means I am engaging in the cultural practices of my identity groups with respect. I am embracing the cultural practices and expressions that are healthy and promote well-being, while eschewing the practices that are intolerant or unhealthy.

In addition, I am honoring the cultural expressions of other identity groups in my society. I engage in *cultural appreciation* instead of *cultural appropriation*. Appropriation means profiting from another culture's practice without permission, attribution, or sharing the proceeds. I don't need to look far to find examples of this type of exploitation.[19] Appreciation means learning the cultural meaning and context of a practice, receiving permission to use or adapt it, attributing that practice to its source, and sharing any of the benefits I receive. When done with reciprocity, all cultures become richer through the sharing, remixing, and adapting of cultural practices.

In order to understand cultural patterns at the systems level, I first need to understand how culture is held and transmitted by society. Individual people *produce* culture through use of cultural tools like language, clothing, traditions, art, music, and pastimes. In addition, individuals *receive* culture from other humans. These cultural practices and markers are held in collective identities and impressed upon each individual who subscribes to that identity. The practices are further established and maintained by institutions like religions, governments, businesses, museums, schools, etc. Institutions influence both individuals and identity groups while simultaneously being shaped by them. All three categories interact to create, maintain, and transmit culture. The table below illustrates the interplay of these three social actors. Within Integral's four-quadrant matrix, the individual psyche occupies the upper left quadrant, identity groups are located in the lower left quadrant, and social institutions occupy the lower right quadrant.

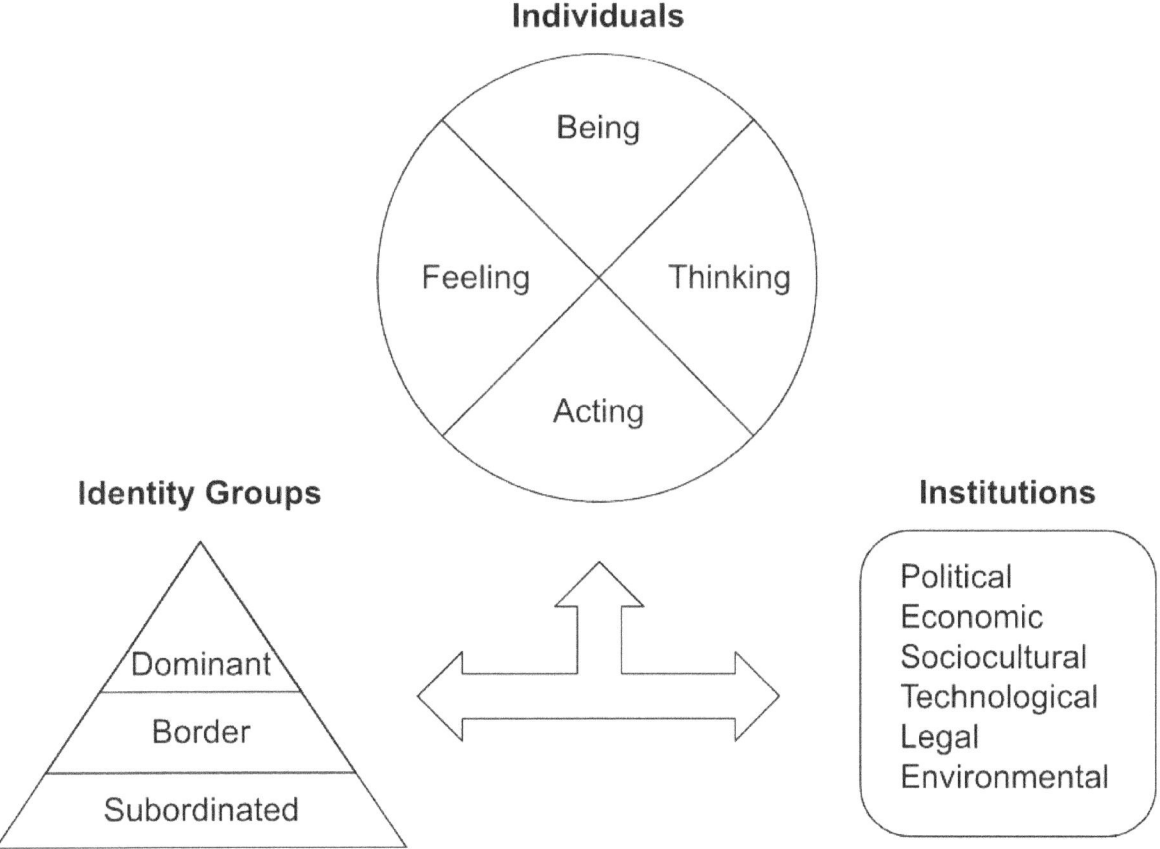

Figure 4.19 Social actors that hold culture

Individuals are personal actors who interpret culture through the four parts of the psyche: thinking, acting, feeling, and being.

Identity groups are the cultural memberships that I belong to that tell me who I am within society.[20] Identity groups hold attitudes, beliefs, behavior patterns and meanings. Within systems of oppression, these are often delineated into two categories, dominant or subordinated. Dominant groups are also called *privileged* or *agent* groups. Subordinated groups are also called *marginalized* or *target* groups. The dominant group holds more power and influence in society, receives benefits, and defines the norms and preferred modes of expression. Dominant groups create and determine the mainstream culture of a society. Subordinated groups hold less power, experience discrimination, may exist outside the mainstream cultural norms, and may be exploited by the mainstream. Dominant groups generally suppress the cultures of subordinated groups and impose their own culture upon them.

Identity groups are the social entities that determine the dominant/subordinated power structures, which are then operationalized by both individuals and institutions.

Identity groups do not fit neatly into two categories however. Dominant and subordinated group identities operate within specific contexts. These power dynamics may shift or even reverse in different contexts. In addition, these identity groups are not necessarily binary. Border identities do not fit neatly into either dominant or subordinated power dynamics. One example is children adopted and raised by parents of a different race than their own. Another personal example: I identify as queer in my sexual preference, but I am able to *pass* as heterosexual, accruing the privileges that come with this identity, and I am able to *code switch* to belong with gay male culture and other bisexual or pansexual humans. Border identities blur the lines or jump between dominant and subordinated power positions.

Institutions are the long-term structural components of a society that are enacted in the outer world. The standard economic categorization of institutions follows the PESTEL acronym: political, economic, sociocultural, technological, environmental, and legal. Institutions instill and enforce the norms of a culture through policies and practices. Individuals who hold power often use institutions as the vehicle for the dissemination of cultural attitudes and beliefs.

Now that we have this framework, I can move to the pattern level of culture. Here, I examine how the identity groups I listed in Figure 4.18 above interact with other identity groups within each category of my culture. I want to understand whether identity groups across a category are mutually uplifting, or if there is a power dynamic between these groups that would cause a social system of oppression. For example, men as dominant group members earned 18 percent higher wages on average than women in the United States in 2022.[21] This reveals the power relationship between men and women in the economy.

I'm not responsible for the power structures of collective identity groups, but I am responsible for how I hold my identities and how I interact with individuals who hold other identities. Using this framework, I can examine whether I am treating people differently based on in-group or out-group affiliations. Am I choosing to affiliate with identity groups that alleviate suffering in the world?

Similarly, I'm not responsible for how institutions function in my society, but I am responsible for how I engage with those institutions. Am I supporting institutions that are aligned with my values?

Use the table below to take inventory of how your group identities are positioned within society. For each identity, indicate whether yours occupies the dominant or a subordinated position, and then list any specific privileges or discrimination that you experience by holding this identity. One of the tricky things about privileges for dominant group members is that they are often initially invisible because they are assumed to be the norm.[22] If you can't identify any privileges from an identity you hold in the dominant position of society, that's a clue that your privileges are invisible and require deeper investigation to bring into awareness.

Identity Category	Am I Dominant, Subordinated, or Border?	Specific privileges bestowed or discrimination imposed
Race		
Nationality		
Ethnicity / Ancestry		
Political Party		
Generation / Age		
Sex		
Gender		
Sexual Orientation		
Body Ability		
Mental Ability		
Class		
Education Level		
Education Focus / Major		
Professional Role		
Professional Industry		
Community		
Hobby		

Figure 4.20 Inventory of cultural privilege or discrimination

Here are two personal examples of how a chosen community and chosen hobby bestow privilege and contribute to social hierarchy.

For a number of years, I was deeply involved with the Burning Man festival. Founded on ethics including radical-self expression, community, participation, and radical inclusion, Burning Man has its own subculture (or, more accurately, several subcultures). By participating in this community, I learned a particular ethic, language, style of dress, and so on. I became a member of *burner culture.* Outside of the festival, I was living in San Francisco where burners worked in innovative start-up, tech, and entrepreneurial roles. My affiliation with the culture and institution of Burning Man present me with job opportunities and social capital that non-burners do not have access to. Belonging to this community has bestowed numerous privileges in my life. I use this example to illustrate how a community with a counter-cultural aesthetic, *radical inclusion* as a principle, and positive cultural intent can still be co-opted by social systems of privilege.

Another example is the hobby of golf. Growing up, my dad played golf and taught me how to play. This is an expensive sport with a high learning curve. The institutions of country clubs and golf courses are often membership organizations with selective criteria to join. Because golf is a pastime of upper- and middle-class Americans, the fact that I know how to play golf means I have access to these privileged people and their culture. I can comfortably speak the language and wear the clothing. I understand not to step on someone's line and I laugh at the joke about "putting from the rough." I'm hip to the lingo. The only reason I know these things is because of the social position of the family I happened to be born into. Because I hold this skillset, I may strike a business deal or earn a promotion over a game of golf. At the surface level, it's easy to think, "Golf is just a sport," but when I examine the social systems that golf is embedded within, it becomes apparent that this hobby is a privilege-bestowing skillset in certain contexts.

For the cultural identities I hold that are subordinated, I want to bring awareness to how I may have *internalized* the system of oppression. These are the attitudes and behaviors from society that I have consciously or unconsciously agreed to.

> Oppression depends on the internalization and acceptance of advantaged and dis-advantaged social group relationships within the social hierarchy of the larger society. Disadvantaged social groups can live within a system of oppression that injures them or deprives them of certain rights without having the language or consciousness (Freire used the term "conscientizgao") to name the oppression or to understand their situation as an effect of oppression, rather than the natural order of things. Memmi described this as "psychological colonization," whereby disadvantaged groups internalize their oppressed condition and collude with the oppressive ideology and social system, a process Freire referred to as "playing host to the oppressor."
>
> —Adams & Zúñiga[23]

In addition to looking at the interplay of social identity groups *within* each category, I also want to examine the ways social identities interact *across* categories. Each social category is defined and influenced, in part, by the other categories in my society. This is known as *intersectionality.*[24] The dominant and subordinated groups cluster into super-affiliations across categories.

Institutions are created, organized, and directed by people who are *simultaneously members of multiple dominant groups* within their society. In the US, for example, virtually all major economic, political, cultural, and social institutions created during its founding years (and since) were established by and for the benefit of white, owning class, heterosexual, Christian, pro-American, men of European descent.

—Raúl Rosado[25]

Integrity at the pattern level of culture means I am aware of the benefits and stigmas conveyed by my culture based on the group identities that I hold. Awareness of the systems is an important first step. However, in order to change these patterns, I need to move to the process level of engagement.

Changing systems of oppression is notoriously hard. It requires a combination of individual work, culture shifting, and institutional reform. Fortunately, over the past 50 years, some incredible groundwork has been done on anti-oppression processes. In Figure 4.21 below, I have graphed simplified versions of three processes for social change. Each model addresses a different aspect of the social change process.

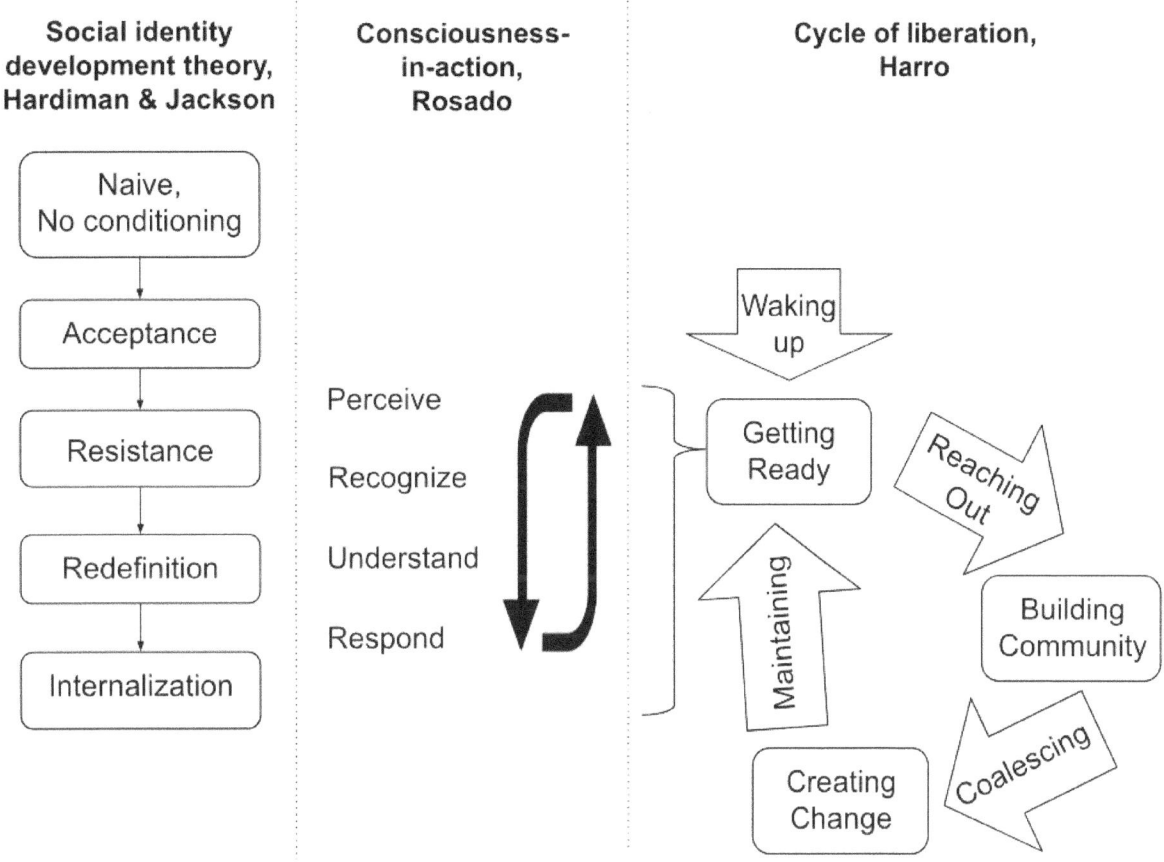

Figure 4.21 Three anti-oppression change processes[26]

Let's begin on the left of the chart with Hardiman and Jackson's social identity development theory. This theory presents a ladder of progression that individual members of both dominant and subordinated groups traverse on their journeys. Every human begins at the *naive phase* with no social conditioning. Through socialization over the first few years of life, we are each taught the attitudes and behaviors for systemic oppression. Both dominant and subordinated identity groups learn the rules for how their category functions. These become *accepted* as the norm. Sometimes the acceptance phase is passive, meaning social hierarchy is implicitly learned by behavior patterns. Sometimes acceptance is actively taught, for example, "Those people are like *that* and our people are like *this*."

The third phase in this model is *resistance*. At a certain point, individuals in both dominant and subordinated groups question the way things are. Dominant group members shift their narrative from blaming subordinated groups for their low position to understanding their own group as the source of oppression. This stage usually begins with guilt for colluding in an oppressive system. Subordinated group members at the resistance stage question the dogma about how things work and become aware of the attitudes and behaviors that create oppression. For subordinated members, this phase is often characterized by anger or backlash against dominant group members, subordinated group members who collude with dominant groups, and institutions that perpetuate oppressive practices. In general, this phase is characterized by a reaction against the status quo.

The fourth phase is *redefinition*, where both dominant and subordinated group members focus on creating new identities that are authentic, aligned with their values, and do not contribute to oppressive systems. Individuals in this step are less reactive and more responsive. There is a return of personal agency and a rediscovery of one's identity after the distancing of the resistance step. Re-definition, by the way, is the sweet spot for these Organic Masculine workbooks: We are working on redefining masculinity outside of hegemonic structures.

The fifth phase is *internalization* where the redefined identity is then integrated into all aspects of one's life. This is an ongoing process where old conditioning is discovered and then updated. The new identity becomes more automatic and natural.

This model, *the social identity development theory*, outlines the phases that individuals generally move through. The next model, *consciousness-in-action*, addresses the question of *how* one moves through the phases (middle column on the graph). Each stage begins with *perception* (for example, "I can see the attitudes and behaviors of oppression," or "I become aware of my reactive emotions toward oppressive institutions.") Perception leads to *recognition*, the second step. Here, I name and acknowledge the oppressive act. Recognition of the pervasiveness of systemic oppression leads me to want to understand these systems. *Understanding* is the third step. Critical analysis, exploring models (like these), and taking classes on social justice are examples of the understanding step. Understanding alone is not enough to create social change, however. The fourth step is *responding*. We choose how to act to bring about positive change. These four steps are recursive, meaning individuals tend to cycle through them multiple times as they progress along the phases in social identity development.

The third model is *the cycle of liberation*, which examines how social change happens across individuals, identity groups, and institutions (right column on the chart). The cycle begins with me *waking up*. An incident disrupts my assumptions of the way things are. This is parallel to moving from the *acceptance* to *resistance* phase and entering the *perceive* step in the other models. This leads me to *get ready* by doing the internal work of empowering myself, deconditioning my socialization, and becoming inspired to create a change. Getting ready accounts for all of the individual work covered by the other two models. Next I *reach out* to other change makers, use my voice against injustice, and take a stand for what I believe is right. This leads me to *build community*. Here I connect with other people (both "like me" and "not like me") who are also in the redefinition phases, building coalitions and creating new collective identity dynamics. The next step is *coalescing*, where

I organize groups, educate others, and become a leader for this new way of being. *Creating change* focuses on the dissemination of culture and institutional practices and policies. Finally these new changes must be actively *maintained* by integrating the changes and fostering opportunities for others to make the journey in the cycle of liberation.

In summary, the process is to work on myself and move through the phases of acceptance, resistance, redefinition, and internalization. I do this by becoming aware of my current phase, recognizing and naming the dynamics of this phase, understanding the larger systems, and then responding by taking appropriate action. Once I have moved far enough along on my own journey, I then become an agent for social change by connecting with other change agents, building coalitions, and enacting cultural and institutional change. All three of these models offer guidance for the unfolding of the process. In reality, I will often be straddling multiple phases simultaneously, and I may advance in a nonlinear fashion.

Culture can also be caught in a vicious cycle of fear or spiraling toward collapse (Phobos and Thanatos). I see plenty of examples of this in Western civilization today. As an individual within a dysfunctional culture, there will always be some dissonance as I work toward greater personal integrity. I both receive from culture and contribute to culture—the inner work that I do on social justice is bound to feel uncomfortable as I move against the mainstream, but it is also simultaneously creating greater momentum for a more equitable society to emerge.

Now, for each identity category that we've been working with, use the table below to identify where you are in the change process. In the middle column, you can track your location along the *social identity development theory*, and in the right column, track your position in the *cycle of liberation.*

Identity Category	Social identity: Naive, Acceptance, Resistance, Redefinition, Internalization	Liberation cycle: Waking up, Getting ready, Reaching out, Building community, Coalescing, Creating change, Maintenance
Race		
Nationality		
Ethnicity / Ancestry		
Political Party		
Generation / Age		
Sex		
Gender		
Sexual Orientation		
Body Ability		
Mental Ability		
Class		
Education Level		
Education Focus / Major		
Professional Role		
Professional Industry		
Community		
Hobby		

Figure 4.22 Inventory of cultural change processes

Integrity at the process level of culture means I am aligned with the values of my chosen identity groups, I am redefining the dominant or subordinated aspects of my identity groups, and I am engaging with communities and institutions to create a more equitable culture. To re-cap: The structural level means identifying my cultural identity groups; the pattern level entails understanding the power dynamics between these identity groups and how that affects my behaviors and attitudes; the process level means actively undertaking individual and social anti-oppression work.

I'll return to these concepts in Chapter Seven, where I'll use the paradigms to understand cultural identity, justice, and power-wielding social holons. In Chapter Eight, I will dive more fully into systems of oppression in my exploration of collective forms of violence. There will be much more to come on socio-cultural dynamics.

Environment

For the environmental aspect of integrity, I will consider two categories: the natural world, and my home and work spaces in the built environment.

In the structural perspective of the natural world, I begin by considering which lands I am in relationship with. What is the ecosystem like around my home? Even if I'm in an urban environment there are likely numerous plants and animals in my neighborhood. In addition to the land where I live, what other places am I connected to? These may include hiking trails, ski hills, the ocean, and retreat venues. I also want to consider places that have been meaningful in my life, for example the home I was raised in or the town where I attended college. For each one of these places, what makes it meaningful for me and which aspects of the place am I in relationship with?

For example, in my native state of Colorado, the Aspen trees change colors over the course of two weeks in the fall. During this magical time, swaths of yellow, orange, and red reach across the dark green canvas of pine trees throughout the high country. I used to go to Rocky Mountain National Park in the fall to listen to the bugling mating call of the wild moose. Recounting these facts today from my current home on Kaua'i connects me to the natural environment of Colorado.

Place	What is meaningful? What aspects am I in relationship with?

Figure 4.23 Inventory of connections with the natural world

Staying in the structural perspective, I now want to consider the built environment that I inhabit for home, work, and social time. Are these places messy or clean, beautiful or run-down? How is my living space a reflection of my internal life? Kurt Vonnegut tells a story about his brother, who when asked about the messy state of his laboratory, tapped his head and quipped, "If you think this laboratory is bad, you should see what it's like in here."[27] Is my space clean or cluttered? Do I have an altar? What kinds of plants, art, or precious objects do I have in my home?

Spaces where I spend time (home, work, etc...)	What does this space say about me?

Figure 4.24 Inventory of built spaces I inhabit

At the pattern level, I am looking at the relational exchange between me and the places I listed above. What am I contributing to these spaces, positive or negative? What am I receiving from these spaces? How am I consuming from my environment, and what waste am I emitting?

For example, in my garden, I contribute my time and effort. I receive peace of mind and connection with the earth. I am consuming fresh vegetables and I am composting my food scraps back into the soil. This is an optimal pattern of relationship with land.

As a global citizen, I am contributing perhaps a little to picking up litter on hiking trails. I am receiving food, shelter, and all the accoutrement of my modern life-style. I am consuming foods sourced from around the world, my home runs on solar but my car runs on gas, and I regularly purchase electronics, clothing, and airfare. My waste includes carbon dioxide from my car, plastics, aluminum, glass and food scraps from meals, and used consumer goods that I either donate or trash. In contrast to the gardening example, this is not a balanced pattern of reciprocity with the earth.

Place or Space	Contributing	Receiving	Consuming	Emitting

Figure 4.25 Inventory of relational exchange with my spaces

Integrity at the process level for the environment means I am growing toward a more sustainable future and embracing aspects of the natural world that have been damaged or polluted. Additionally, I am limiting my engagement with a social system that is gripped in fear and driving toward death. Looking back at the previous two tables, how can I grow and embrace the spaces I inhabit (process applied to structure) and how can I improve the flows of resources with my environments (process applied to pattern)?

At the process level, I can use the same approach that I outlined for the cultural integrity process in the prior section. In this case, my affiliation with modern humans is the dominant social group and all natural life is the subordinated group.

> An interior dominator hierarchy remains in place for most modern people with regard to nonhuman beings. Until a critical mass of people evolve to postmodern levels of interiority, in which heedless domination of human and nonhuman beings becomes unacceptable and immoral, environmentalism will remain a reform movement within technological modernity. When this developmental transformation occurs, but not before, we will see the widespread adoption of what Hans Jonas called "the imperative of responsibility." Then and only then will we feel responsible to this world and other species.
>
> —Esbjorn-Hargens and Zimmerman[28]

Interestingly, humans are also the subordinated group for environmental oppression. Today's generation and wealthy individuals are reaping the privileges, while tomorrow's generation and impoverished individuals will feel the hardest impact. But we all suffer due to ecosystem degradation.

In this process, instead of my *cultural identity*, I want to examine my *environmental identity* in order to liberate myself from the system of oppression. Who am I in relationship with the environment? Am I an eco-adventurer, activist, scientist, eco-shaman, policy advocate, or green businessperson? Am I in passive acceptance of the status quo, enjoying the comfort of consumerism? Am I resisting? Am I redefining my eco-identity? Have I begun to engage in collective action, and if so where am I within the *cycle of liberation*? Use the table below to record your inventory.

Environmental Identity	**Social development:** Naive, Acceptance, Resistance, Redefinition, Internalization	**Liberation cycle:** Waking up, Getting ready, Reaching out, Building community, Coalescing, Creating change, Maintenance

Figure 4.26 Inventory of environmental change processes

I'll use my personal journey through the environmental identity change process as an illustration. Following *social identity development theory*, I was born naive in total integration with the natural world. Over the first few years of my life, I learned the norms of attitudes and behaviors of humans and I learned to separate myself in a position of power over the natural world. Sometime in my late teens, I entered the resistance phase and became both guilty and adversarial toward the way humans were treating the earth. In my early 20s, thanks to books like *Cradle to Cradle* and *Natural Capitalism*, I entered the redefinition phase where I began to respond to the oppressive system instead of reacting against it. Redefinition has been a long journey that continues to evolve for me as I break down ever more barriers between myself and the natural world. This underlines my understanding that integrity is a process, not a destination.

As I did more of my inner work around the impact of humanity on the globe, I decided to dedicate my career to using business as a tool to solve climate change. Following the *cycle of liberation*, I reached out to other thought-leaders. I earned a master's degree and entered a community of like-minded humans attempting to redefine our relational system with the planet. I spent my next eight years after grad school focusing on climate—in the *creating change* category. While I have worked in some amazing jobs on climate change and renewable energy, I cannot claim to have meaningfully made a dent in this massive issue. Burnout is real, and I've been there on multiple occasions.

In my early thirties, I began to see that the business world was no longer the right place for me to focus. I needed to turn inside. For one thing, my own psychological baggage needed my attention. And in the bigger picture, I recontextualized climate change as a spiritual problem, not a business or policy problem. At core, we humans need to change our relationship with the earth.

This begins with me. As I transitioned into a different career, I moved through the *consciousness-in-action* steps of perceiving, recognizing, understanding, and responding. I exited the corporate world and entered into my studies of somatics, spirituality, and consciousness, which has brought me where I am today. On *the cycle of liberation*, I then returned to the *getting ready* stage, and now I'm re-entering collective action from a fuller sense of self and a more holistic understanding of the issues.

Humanity's impact on the environment is a complicated topic, one which is heavily influenced by the paradigm of consciousness that we inhabit. I'll give a more comprehensive understanding of the environment through the Integral lens in Chapter 7 and frame some solutions in Chapter 8.

The Self

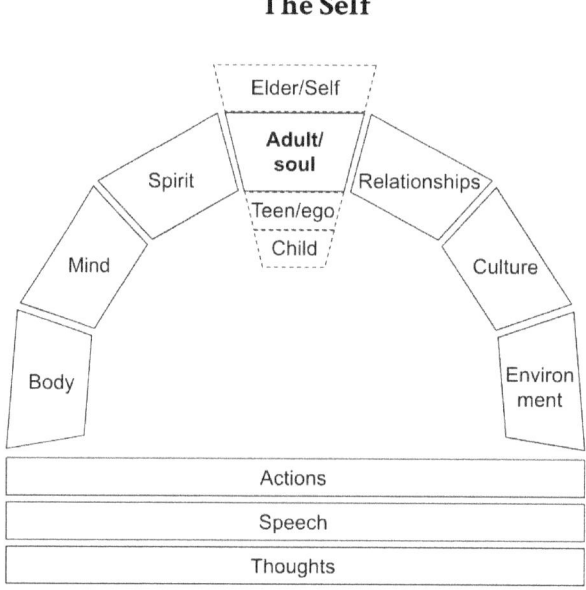

Figure 4.27 Adult self as keystone of the Integrity Arch

The final brick in the Integrity Arch is also the most important: the self. As the keystone, the self is the center of the entire structure. The self balances all other aspects and in turn is supported by each of them. The focal point of integrity is choosing myself. I am choosing to take care of myself and do what is right for me. I am choosing to be the center of my world. I'm not hiding. I'm not giving myself away to job, relationships, or distractions. I'm not abandoning myself to the needs of others. Nor am I losing myself to addictions or astral realms of consciousness. I'm choosing Matt first: simple, ordinary me. I am the center of my life and my universe. I am choosing to inhabit this center and live from it.

Personally, I am a student of the Hakomi Method of psychotherapy. The word Hakomi was channeled in a dream by a student of the system's creator. With some research, they discovered that Hakomi is a Hopi word which can be translated as "How do you stand in relation to these many realms?"[29] Integrity means I understand my place. I am showing up in a good way across the realms of mind, body, spirit, relationships, culture, and environment. I am aligning my thoughts, speech, and actions to support my engagement with these many realms.

As human beings, each of us have incredible access to experience the sacred kosmos. I can explore psychic realms and the farthest reaches of consciousness. I can explore shamanic and elemental realms. These are our birthright and our privilege to experience if we wish. I even have the option to live in one of those realms. Integrity means being what I am. On my path, this has meant choosing to be human first. I am prioritizing my human life. I am choosing to center my life in the ordinary, mundane, physical world of taxes and messy relationships. The more deeply I choose to inhabit my humanness, the more trustably all the other realms of existence naturally arise in my experience. I don't need to leave to go find more. I can center and receive the entire kosmos in my heart. Integrity means staying to be present for what is here in my life now.

The locus of my "self" grows through a progression of developmentally-appropriate stages. First I am a child, then an adolescent, then an adult, and finally an elder. There are gendered archetypes associated with each stage, and for men these are boy, hero, man, and elder (see Figure A3.3 in Appendix III). At the center of the adolescent self is the ego who learns skills and works to become an able human in the world. At the center of the adult self is the soul, who knows my work and my path in this lifetime. The adult soul-self is oriented toward service. Finally, the elder accesses the higher Self (also called atma, buddha-mind, or Christ consciousness). The Self is a transpersonal experience of the unity of all beings.

When I become an adult, the child and adolescent selves do not disappear. They remain in my inner council. They may take over my system and run the show when they feel hurt or neglected. My responsibility as an adult is to be the driver of the bus full of my internal parts. Integrity means each part is valued and has a seat. But I, as the adult, am sitting at the wheel deciding where we go. Integrity of self means my adult is sovereign and responding to my life. My adult is loving and approving of my younger parts. I am responsible for ensuring we are all working together in a harmonious system. In addition, my adult self is able to receive guidance and wisdom from my Self.

There is a common misconception that I transition upward spiritually by killing the ego. More accurately, each successive layer of self transcends and includes the younger more limited selves. My adolescent is supported by a healthy child. My adult is able to follow my soul's guidance with the help of a healthy, integrated adolescent ego. And my Self emerges to the extent that I fill out into a healthy adult and then learn to put my soul in service to the larger consciousness. Each aspect of self is vital. Each one needs my love, respect, and nurturance.

How do I know I'm in my adult self? The Internal Family Systems theory has identified a number of qualities (known as the 8 C's) that are present when I am acting from my adult self:

Our core Self, the soul that is revered in spiritual traditions, encompasses curiosity, compassion, calm, confidence, courage, clarity, creativity, connectedness, and kindness.
—Schwartz & Sweezy[30]

When I am experiencing these qualities, that is a good sign I'm in my adult self. When I'm not experiencing them, or especially when I'm in the opposite states, that's a sign that one of my fragmented parts has become triggered and has taken over my psyche. Integrity doesn't mean I never get triggered. It means I am working to recognize when I lose my center, and I am learning to come back to my center: to live and respond from my adult self. I am creating resilience in my capacity to *self*-organize.

In addition to mediating between the aspects of self, the role of my adult is to balance my arch. Each brick is important to the wholeness of my being. Each aspect requires my time and attention in a way that provides equilibrium for the arch as a whole. There have been periods where I really needed to focus on a relationship or when I was passionately absorbed in spiritual practice to the neglect of the other realms, and this is fine for a limited time. But in the long run, I want to be engaging and growing through all of these aspects in my life. My adult self is responsible for the interplay of my arch as a system. Centered in my adult, I know *how I stand in relation to all these realms.*

Summary

Over the course of this chapter and the prior one, I've explored what integrity means through the holarchy of paradigms. I then provided a very thorough tool, the Integrity Arch, to take inventory of integrity in my life. My goal is to open possibilities for you with the processes that I've outlined for each element of the arch. Attempting to radically transform every element simultaneously is a recipe for failure, so the final aspect of working with the Integrity Arch is *kindness.* I only want to engage with the amount of material that I can realistically handle. This is how I am kind to myself. I recognize that the change process is often slow and nonlinear. I want to do my best to show up and then meet every step I make with kindness.

At this point, I would encourage you to flip back to Figure 3.4 and your personal integrity commitment. We began with your definition of integrity because that is what truly matters. Now that you've read what I have to say, go back and update what integrity means for you. Then make a plan for yourself on which areas you want to focus on, and journal some realistic, measurable, time-bound goals for yourself. Finally, share your integrity commitment with a friend, men's group, or mentor to help hold you accountable. Remember that any goal you set is a step along a path that is always unfolding. Integrity means choosing to make the journey.

Notes

[1] Image by Flux

[2] "Drawing on my experience with Julieta and the Mazatec tradition, as well as the other indigenous, earth-based communities I have spent time with over the years, I developed the Holistic Model for a Balanced Life. By using the Holistic Model for a Balanced Life as a tool for self-inquiry, one can thoroughly examine the many aspects of their life and determine whether they are in balance or not. This model also helps those who live in the modern industrialized world prepare for a journey into an expanded state of consciousness—including the formulation of an intention—as well as navigate the integration phase that follows." *Consciousness Medicine*, Bourzat.

[3] Translated by Thomas Byrom.

[4] *The Four Agreements.*

[5] *Experiential Psychotherapy with Couples: A Guide for the Creative Pragmatist.*

[6] *Conscious Loving.*

[7] Asian, Black, indigenous, Latino/Hispanic, White, etc.

[8] US American, Mexican, Canadian, British, Japanese, etc.

[9] African-American, Asian-American, European-American, Latino, Native American, etc.

[10] Mainstream (Republican or Democrat), Radical (Socialist, green, communist, pro-independence ethnonational).

[11] Child, adolescent, adult, elder. Boomer, Gen X, Millennial, Gen Z.

[12] Male, female, intersex, transsexual.

[13] Man, woman, genderqueer, transgender, third gender, agender…

[14] Heterosexual, gay, lesbian, bisexual, queer, multisexual…

[15] Able or disabled.

[16] Neurotypical or neurodivergent.

[17] Upper/owning class, middle/professional class, lower/working class, low-income/poverty class.

[18] Primary school, high school, community college or associate, college, masters, Ph.D.

[19] For example: "In 1939, Solomon Linda, a Zulu musician who grew up herding cattle in drought-prone Msinga in South Africa, improvised a few notes at what was then Johannesburg's (and sub-Saharan Africa's and possibly the continent's) lone recording studio…[Linda] uttered into being the musical phrase that would soon make its way to every corner of the world, albeit with lyrics he never wrote: "In the jungle, the quiet jungle, the lion sleeps tonight."… In the United States, the song was rejiggered for white singers who couldn't quite manage the beat but saw their perky doo-wop arrangements climb the charts nevertheless. Eventually, Disney took notice; Linda's lilting lullaby is arguably the heart of 'The Lion King.' Record executives interviewed by Malan estimated that, as of 2000, Linda could've earned $15 million in revenues and royalties. Instead, when he died of kidney failure at age 53 in 1962, he was buried a pauper in an unmarked grave." "What Does Cultural Appropriation Really Mean?", Mishan.

[20] "I would like to reserve the expression *collective identity* for reference groups that are essential to the identity of their members, which are in a certain way 'ascribed' to individuals, cannot be freely chosen by them, and which have a continuity that extends beyond the life-historical perspectives of their members." *Communication and Evolution of Society*, Habermas.

[21] "In 2022, American women typically earned 82 cents for every dollar earned by men." "The Enduring Grip of the Gender Pay Gap," Kochhar.

[22] "People are often unaware of privileges accorded to them based on dominant social group memberships, because those privileges have been normalized to be expected. By contrast, people who are denied the same privileges are often painfully aware of them. Advantaged groups sometimes oppose social justice change efforts because they fear losing privileges that they assume to be their "rights" even though those so-called rights are not enjoyed by everyone." "Core Concepts for Social Justice Education," Adams & Zúñiga in *Teaching for Diversity and Social Justice*, Adams et al.

[23] "Core Concepts for Social Justice Education," in *Teaching for Diversity and Social Justice*. 3rd Ed., Adams et al.

[24] "Intersectionality suggests that our various advantaged and disadvantaged social group memberships do not act independent of one another, or in a simply additive way. Rather, they interrelate to create specific experiences of oppression that are not reducible to one or another identity (Crenshaw, 2003; Hankivsky, 2014). For example, people of color who experience racial microaggressions are complicated by gender (for women and for men alike, as well as those whose gender expression is outside the norm), by religion (given the ways that religions associated with the Arab or Asian diaspora are racialized or the Black Church historically kept outside of white Christianity), by class (given the ways in which economic advantage or disadvantage are linked to racial classification), and so on (Cross, 2012; Wijeyesinghe & Jackson, 2012)." "Core Concepts for Social Justice Education," Adams & Zúñiga in *Teaching for Diversity and Social Justice*. 3rd Ed., Adams et al.

[25] *Consciousness-in-Action, Toward an Integral Psychology of Liberation and Transformation.*

[26] Adapted from: "Conceptual Foundations for Social Justice Courses," Hardiman & Jackson in *Teaching for Social Justice and Diversity 1st ed.* Adams; *Consciousness-in-Action,* Rosado; and "The Cycle of Socialization," Harro in *Readings in diversity and social justice,* Adams.

[27] *Slapstick,* Vonnegut.

[28] *Integral Ecology.*

[29] "David Winter had a dream in which I [ie, Ron Kurtz] handed him a piece of paper with the words 'Hakomi Therapy' on it. The word was meaningless then to all of us, though David thought it might be an Amerindian word. David went home, an eight-hour trip, and looked the word up in some reference books he had back there. He discovered it was a Hopi Indian word (sometimes spelled hakimi) with two related meanings. Its current usage is 'Who are you?' Its archaic meaning is 'how do you stand in relation to these many realms?'" *Body-Centered Psychotherapy: The Hakomi Method,* Kurtz.

[30] *Internal Family Systems Therapy.*

| 5 |

Purpose

Figure 5.1 Book jacket of *A Treatise on Navigation and Nautical Astronomy*[1]

If you have your *why* for life, you can get by with almost any *how.*

–Friedrich Nietzsche[2]

My purpose describes the best and highest way that I can engage in my life. It is the North Star that I use to guide my journey. Without a purpose, I am lost. Following my purpose, I have meaning. Accomplishing my purpose, I find fulfillment. Within the process view, my purpose enables me to understand if my actions are virtuous expressions of Eros and Agape, or if I am in Phobos or Thanatos. It is the principle against which I measure the employment of my time and energy.

As we shall presently explore, the Warrior does not give me my purpose. However, it is the Warrior who takes responsibility for keeping me connected to my purpose. He sets boundaries, keeps me disciplined, and creates clarity for my priorities. Living a purpose-driven life is Warrior's work.

The purpose for every human is unique, like your own personal fingerprint for the unfolding of your life. We often discuss it as if there is one immutable purpose, but in reality, we have multiple selves with multiple purposes. At different times and in different phases, my priorities need to shift. My psyche is a collection of different subpersonalities, or parts. Each part has its own function, its own purpose. For some parts, the purpose is simple. Protectors protect, judges judge, and skeptics doubt.

However, my archetypal roles (boy, hero, man, and elder) each carry a purpose that is unique to me. By dialoguing with these inner parts, I can understand the purpose of each one. Then, it's up to my adult self to balance these different priorities and to bring fulfillment to the purpose of each part. This is known as leading a purpose-driven life, which leads to the experience of self-actualization (or perhaps more accurately, selves-actualization). When my parts become fulfilled, they enter into communion in my psyche and I become whole.

In this chapter, I will explore the parts of my inner child (actually inner children), my inner teenager, my adult soul-self, and my Self. Each of these parts has a message for me about my purpose. We left off in the prior chapter discussing integrity of the selves as the keystone of the Integrity Arch. Integrity arises when each aspect of self is fulfilling its purpose.

Child Parts

The inner child can be interpreted in a number of ways. Because this workbook series is interested in archetypal maturation, I often discuss the child as an archetypal role of the self. But as a therapist working with clients, I usually treat the inner child as a part of the psyche. This part has their own needs and personality that contributes to the internal system. With this approach, I am careful not to attach to "my inner child" as a singular concrete entity. It is more accurate to conceptualize the *child state* as a regressed state of consciousness. Often the regression is tied to a particular age, memory, and emotion. Because I experienced many ages, memories, and emotions throughout my childhood, I have access to many distinct child states. The inner child is important because they are the map maker. This is where our core beliefs, personality traits, character strategies, and orientations to self and reality are formed and held. The good news is that by engaging with our inner children, we can update our limiting beliefs and immature character strategies.

In the Hakomi method, we work with three distinct inner children: the organic child, the strategic child, and the wounded child. The organic child is natural, happy, playful, curious, and available for connection. This is the child who has all their needs met. In response to situations where my needs were not met as a child, I had to find a strategy to get by. This is my strategic child. This part is an intelligent adaptation to an imperfect world by a child who is not able to fully take care of themself. The wounded child is the young part of me that feels hurt, unlovable, isolated, or unworthy.

Each of these inner children offers essential input for my purpose. My organic child tells me who I'm here to be. My strategic child shows me what I'm here to learn. And my wounded child shows me how I'm here to love. These three aspects (being, learning, and loving) form the foundational layers of my multifaceted purpose.

Child Part	Qualities	Purpose
Organic child	Natural, playful, curious	Who I am here to be
Strategic child	Working to get needs met	What I'm here to learn
Wounded child	Hurt, unlovable, unworthy	How I'm here to love

Figure 5.2 Child parts and purpose

In order to access these parts and receive their wisdom, I must go back and become that child again.

The core beliefs of the child are held in state-specific consciousness and are usually not available in ordinary awareness. They are available in the state in which they were first learned.

—Marilyn Morgan[3]

A few words of caution here. As I work with my child parts, I want to go slow and stay resourced. I may encounter some big emotions that have been locked away since my childhood. We call this *core material*. If core material surfaces, that's a good sign. It means my body and my unconscious feel safe enough to open. If this happens, I simply stay in my body and feel whatever arises. It's important not to overwhelm myself or take on too much. I want to stay within my window of tolerance. If I start to approach my limit, I just make a decision to come back into my adult and ground myself. If you know you have childhood trauma, you may want to undertake this exploration together with a trained therapist. And if you're like me when I started this work, you may find that certain childhood parts are not accessible. I would hit a psychic wall and just go numb. That's simply the larger intelligence of my psyche keeping me safe. I'm not here to push. Instead I want to honor my blocks and resistance. Curiosity and safety enable me to explore my child parts.

The Organic Child

We'll begin with the organic child. To do this exercise, you'll need a quiet, comfortable space, a large sheet of paper and something to color with like crayons or markers.

Come into mindful awareness.

> Take a few breaths and allow your system to slow down. Bring your awareness inside. Notice what's happening in your internal landscape. Find your inner witness. Just observe your thoughts, emotions, and sensations for a few breaths until you feel calm and centered. For the duration of this exercise, I want my mindful observer to be with me.

Immerse yourself in a happy memory from childhood.

> Allow your mind to relax and open. Go back to a happy memory from your childhood. Find one specific memory. Whichever memory comes to mind, trust it and use it here. Take yourself back to that moment. How old are you? Where is this memory taking place? What are you doing? Who else is with you? Really go back. Bring all the details to life. Be there again.

Draw a picture of yourself in this memory.

> Give yourself at least ten minutes. Draw a representation of you as a child in the picture. Draw whatever scene is happening. You can include symbolic elements to represent emotions or important themes.

Give your picture a caption.

Complete this sentence to describe your picture:

I am (__descriptive qualities__), living a life of (__action or experience__).

For the first part of the sentence, which qualities describe you as a child in this memory? Use descriptive words like: playful, creative, adventurous, brave, calm, friendly, artistic, funny, gentle, or mischievous. Hone in on the one or two most important words to describe yourself.

For the second part of the sentence, describe what's happening. Make the description universal instead of specific. So instead of "swimming with grandpa," I would go with "spending quality time with loved ones in nature."

Take your time and hone in on exactly the right language to describe your scene.

Review the purpose from your organic child!

Thank your organic child and come back to your adult self. Your picture and your caption describe the purpose of who you came here to be. Consider this your first draft. You may need to adjust it or go back and do it again.

Here is my example:

I am joyful and creative, living a life of adventure.

This is *who I am here to be.* Your job as an adult is to put yourself in situations where you get to be these qualities, having this experience. This is how you fulfill your organic child's purpose.

The Strategic Child

Now let's do a similar exploration of the strategic child. I'll need a cozy space and a fresh piece of paper with my coloring tools.

Come into mindful awareness (as above).

Immerse yourself in a childhood memory where you had an unmet need.

Allow your mind to relax and open. Keeping your observer on board, go back to a time in your childhood when something hard was happening. You weren't getting your needs met. Maybe your need was for connection, or approval, or attention, or love. Maybe you had a need for dignity, or a boundary wasn't being respected. Find one specific memory from your childhood. Once you find a memory, be curious. What is your need in this memory? How old are you? Where are you? Who else is present? Be there in the scene again.

What did you do to get your need met?

What happens in this memory? How do you react? What behavior did you employ in order to take care of yourself? What actions did you take? Here are a few examples: fighting, resisting, collapsing, hiding, sneaking, seeking attention, pleasing, or working extra hard.

Draw a picture of yourself in this scene.

Give yourself at least ten minutes. Draw yourself as a child in the picture. Draw whatever scene is happening. You can include symbolic elements to represent emotions or important themes. Draw the strategy that you are using to get your need met.

Give your picture a caption.

Complete this sentence to describe your picture:

I am (__descriptive qualities__), using (__strategy__) to meet my needs.

For the first part of the sentence, which qualities describe you as a child in this memory? Use descriptive words like: upset, lonely, resentful, angry, anxious, insecure, sad, hurt, shocked, protective, confused, fussy, or scared. Hone in on the one or two most important words to describe yourself.

For the second part of the sentence, describe the strategy you learned to use. Make the description universal instead of specific. So instead of "refusing to take a nap," I would go with "resisting." Referencing the Hakomi character strategies is a good place to look to identify your strategy if it's not immediately clear. They are listed in Figures A3.4 and A3.5 in Appendix III.

Take your time and hone in on exactly the right language to describe your scene.

Review your purpose from your strategic child.

Thank your strategic child and come back to your adult self. Your picture and your caption describe the purpose of what you are here to learn.

Here is my example:

I am resentful, using resistance to meet my needs.

When I get triggered, this is who I become and what I do. Granted, I may have a number of different strategies for different situations. But this is my strategic child's automatic reaction to challenging situations. It's my default program.

Now ask yourself: If I were the adult I am today in this childhood memory, what other options would be available to me for my behavior? What could I do to take care of myself? How could I meet that child's needs? And most importantly, if I were able to choose a new option, would I still need to use this strategy? For most people, in most adult situations, we now have more options. In fact, I can begin to see that my childhood strategy is usually no longer a very effective way to get my needs met today.

Working with my strategy opens many avenues for learning. For one thing, I learn that my adult is capable of meeting my needs. My strategic child can learn to bring his needs to my adult and trust him to follow through. While it's ok for me to be upset, I don't need to get all worked up. My strategic child can just tell my adult what he needs. And I don't need to follow the same strategy I figured out as a three-year-old anymore. I can learn new behaviors to take care of myself when I'm triggered.

The purpose statement from my strategic child shows me which limiting beliefs and young behavior patterns are ready to change and grow. This is my purpose for learning. Feel free to repeat this process a few times with different memories to uncover different strategies.

The Wounded Child

Moving now to the wounded child. Again, get yourself situated in a supportive space and grab a blank sheet of paper.

Come into mindful awareness (as above).

Immerse yourself in a childhood memory where you were feeling hurt.

> Go slow and proceed with care. I don't need to open up anything that's going to overwhelm me. With your mindful observer present, go back to a time from childhood where you were hurt, wounded, or upset. Relax and allow the memory to arise without effort. Find one specific experience. Take yourself back into that place. Be curious. What are you feeling? How old are you? Where are you and who else is around? What caused you to feel hurt?

Draw a picture of yourself in this memory.

> Take ten minutes. Draw yourself and the emotions you are feeling. Draw the world around you. Perhaps include the event that triggered the hurt and then the aftermath of what

happened in your inner world in reaction. As you draw, allow yourself to immerse in your wounded child.

Give your picture a caption.

> *I am (__descriptive qualities__) in a world that is (__descriptive qualities__).*

> Here are a few examples: *I am in pain in a world that is dangerous. I am lonely and my parents are uncaring. I am humiliated and adults are aggressive.*

> Take your time to find the right words for the essence of who you are in this memory.

Ask your wounded child what kind of support they needed in this memory.

> Imagine that your adult self is there with your wounded child in your memory. This is a magical scene where you can step in and help in real time. What does your child need right now? For example, someone to be their friend, someone strong to create boundaries, someone to listen or to explain what's happening, or just a hug. Usually our wounded children could use a hug. Have a little conversation and find out what they need.

Review your purpose from your wounded child.

> Come back to your adult self and thank your wounded child. Take a few breaths. Your picture and the caption describe the place where you feel most disconnected from love. The purpose arising from your wounded child is to love yourself in this place. In order to do that, you need to create a relationship with this little one. They need to be able to tell you *how* they want to be loved. Sometimes it's as simple as sitting with them in silence. Other times it's very specific: When someone starts yelling at me, I need to know that you'll take me to safety.

The practice is to discover how my wounded child wants to be loved and then love myself exquisitely in this way. This is my purpose for love. Again, you are free to repeat this exercise multiple times for different needs and situations.

Now review your three purposes from these inner child-parts.

Organic child	Who I'm here to be	I am _____, living a life of _____.
Strategic child	What I'm here to learn	I am _____, using _____ to meet my needs.
Wounded child	How I'm here to love	I am _____ in a world that is _____.

Figure 5.3 Purpose statements of child parts

These statements from my inner children form the foundational level of my purpose. As a child, I created my first maps for reality and created my belief system to go with it. These beliefs remain in the substrate of my consciousness (in implicit memory) and color my interpretations of the world. By clarifying these beliefs and actively engaging with my inner-child parts, I can update my operating system with adult consciousness. My core motivations arise from these younger parts, and by fulfilling them, I am able to be, learn, and love in my purpose-driven life.

> The child and its experiences built the world view and the self-image. The child was the map maker. So, in contacting and working with the child, you have the possibility of changing those maps and the person who is now using them. By working with that child. By just being there with that child, by talking to it and holding it and explaining things, by being careful and concerned and patient, just by doing that, you change the way that child feels about itself and the world. And in doing that, you change the adult, too.
>
> —Ron Kurtz[4]

The Inner Teenager

The next aspect of selfhood is the inner teenager who marks the emergence of the independent ego. At this stage, I can think for myself, manage my priorities, and determine my path in life. In order for my ego to become independent, I needed to individuate from the authority figures and rules that governed my childhood. Teenagers rebel. The developmental tasks of my teenage self are to learn, to achieve, and to belong. These capacities are still relevant for me today and they represent purpose for my inner teenager.

The learning of the teenage self is focused on building skills and honing a craft. Broadly, learning happens for all aspects of self. Specific to the teenager is learning the skill set to come out of the parents' nest and into the world. It is learning in service to making a living.

In past times, humans would find a single profession or career and stick with it for life. If you're like me, you've already had multiple careers and more are likely coming your way. So today, the question is not, "What is the one right career choice for my life?". The question is, "What is the right career for this phase in my life?".

In order to answer that, I return to the purpose statement from my organic child: *who I'm here to be*. The highest alignment for my profession is a role that allows me to fulfill my organic child's purpose while also paying my rent. Again, the specifics of what that role is may evolve over time, but I want the qualities of that purpose statement to be included.

So in my example—*I am joyful and creative, living a life of adventure*—there are a million roles that this could apply to. It's a very open-ended prompt. This is great news, because it means I can make myself available for opportunities as they present themselves and I can actively work to co-create the career I want to have. For me personally, I know that when my routine gets stale, that's a sign the job is no longer a fit for me. With a purpose statement like mine, it's no wonder I've explored a few careers already. The exploration is part of what makes me feel fulfilled.

If my career isn't fitting my organic child's purpose statement, what training do I need to do to prepare myself for a role that is a fit? Once I have found the career fit, the next question is what skill-building do I need to do in order to continue to be successful in this role? Skills have the quality of stacking on each other.

On my path, I first learned mathematics and coding. I became really good at analysis and structured thinking. Then, in order to apply that within a green business context, I needed to learn management skills. Business school was my next step. Then, because my career was taking me into the energy industry, I needed to learn about electricity production, transmission, and distribution. With each successive step, the next learning objective comes into view. My ego and my inner teen are the ones who kept me on track with my skill-building.

Take a few moments now to assess:

- Is my current professional role a fit for my organic child's purpose statement?
- If no, what needs to change, or where do I need to look next?
- If yes, what learning, training, or skill-building do I need to undertake to thrive in this position?

In addition to learning, my inner teen thrives in competition. Now, there are two orientations toward competition. The first is to compete against someone else, where one person wins and the other person loses. The competition is decided by the relative comparison of who did better and who did worse. The second orientation is competition undertaken for its own sake. Here, I want to see how far I am able to excel. In this orientation, I am mainly competing against myself, and the other competitors are there as allies to help me strive toward glory. The competition is decided by how far each of us is able to embody our ideal performance. This second orientation is what I would call *competition in excellence*.

My inner teen wants to achieve. He wants to excel. He wants to become all he can be. This requires motivation and discipline. It is easy to become complacent, comfortable, and lazy. My inner teenage achievement consciousness combats my inertia. I discover both dignity and self-respect when I really show up to work toward my goals.

Ask yourself:

- What goals do I want to set for myself?
- What practice regimen will I need in order to accomplish my goals?
- Where am I succumbing to laziness?

Finally, the inner teenager is responsible for keeping me engaged with friends, family, and peers. Humans participate in incredibly complex social interactions which contribute to our mental, emotional, and physical health. We need to have meaningful engagement with other humans and we need to belong. As children, we don't choose who we belong with. Generally, children belong with their family and whatever other children they happen to be in contact with. Teenagers, however, form cliques. Teens create social hierarchy and select their friend group. This capacity continues to operate when we are adults.

My inner teen is responsible for keeping me engaged with the people who matter in my life. In addition, this part is responsible for finding the friends and community that really meet me. I need friends who are on my level, learning and achieving along with me.

Ask yourself:

- Do I belong with my family of origin?
- Do I have friends who I belong with?
- Do I have a community where I belong?
- What do I need to do to bring these relationships more into alignment?

In summary, purpose for my inner teenager means utilizing the managing and relational features of my egoic self to craft my life in the world. My inner teen helps me continue to learn the skillset that is aligned with my organic child's purpose, reach toward my goals and achieve them, and find connection with family, friends, and community.

The Adult Self

The adult is the soul-self. This is the trans-egoic aspect of me that knows my path in this life. It is the me that was here before I was born, and it is the me that will be here after I die. Whereas my ego self is centered in the head, my soul-self is centered in the heart. By coming out of my head and into my heart, I learn to listen to the direct and immediate knowing of my soul.

In order to find my soul's purpose, I need to move beyond my ego's self-centeredness and the pictures of success from society. This act of surrender is terrifying for my ego. I resist, subvert, and distract from allowing my feeling heart to hold me and guide me. But the truth of my heart is visceral and trustable in a way that the truth of my head can never be. Once I discovered the passageway into my heart, I slowly learned to live more and more of my life from this place: my soul-self.

> A man has not really begun to be alive until he has lost himself, until he has released the anxious grasp which he normally holds upon his life, his property, his reputation, and his position.
>
> —Alan Watts[5]

As we just saw, the inner teenager plays the role of a shepherd for the purpose of the organic child. His role is to ensure that I'm in my happy place while I'm making a living in the world. The adult self plays a similar role for the strategic child and the wounded child.

There is a metaphor about the wound we each receive when we are little. The wound goes deep into my young psyche and profoundly shapes my relationship with the world. That wound stays with me and replays itself in a million different situations as I age. Even though I try to get rid of the wound, it continues to return. But there is more to this wound than pain. It serves a deeper purpose in the development of the human soul.

> The original wound cellularly enforces duality onto and into the child's being. For some little ones, the wound literalizes into experiences of abuse and trauma, while for others it is a much more subtle occurrence. Regardless of the specific experience, the *sacred wound* marks the first time the self directly experiences that it is not the same as its source. This paves the way for its lifelong journey of rediscovering that source (God, truth, purpose, oneness, etc.) through its own evolutionary make-up.
>
> —Adam Gainsburg[6]

Eventually, I learn to embrace my wound, transforming it into a *sacred wound*. By turning toward my wound, tending to it, allowing it, and listening to it, the wound begins to teach me. This cut that refuses to close provides the opening for wisdom to enter. My wound becomes my medicine. Through this mysterious process of embracing my pain, I learn how to heal. As I progress on this journey, I become a healer.

> In the process of refusing to go cold in my heart, deciding to stay with myself through the pain and the reality, and titrating the flow of intense emotions, I found strange medicine being made right in my mind and body, by my pain.
>
> —Pixie Lighthorse[7]

My *sacred wound as medicine* becomes my gift back to the world. It paves my life path and shows me how to be of service. This is where I find my dharma, my soul's purpose.

Go back to your purpose statements for your strategic child and your wounded child. Here are my examples:

> Strategic: *I am resentful, using resistance to meet my needs.*

> Wounded: *I am alone in an uncaring world.*

For these two statements, ask yourself, "What was the *missing experience* that I needed in that moment as a child?" As children we have an innate knowing of how love is supposed to feel. When it's not present, we know that it's missing. My strategic child and wounded child are still waiting for that missing experience. So today as an adult, I can look back and see what that missing experience would be. If it's not immediately clear, I can simply ask my inner child, and once we have enough trust, he will be eager to tell me.

In my examples here, the missing experience is connection. Not just someone being close-by, but someone caring, who understands what's happening for me. My missing experience is *intimacy*. For you, the missing experience might be: being supported, being seen, being held, feeling safe, having dignity, holding a boundary, trusting myself, or trusting a loved one. Fill out your answer in the table below.

Part	Purpose from Fig 5.3	Missing Experience
Strategic Child		
Wounded Child		

Figure 5.4 Missing Experiences

Once you have your missing experiences, take a step back and check these out. In the times in your life when you've felt the most triggered or hurt, would this missing experience have been helpful? We are looking for the wound and missing experience that has surfaced again and again in a variety of ways.

Once I feel the resonance in naming my wound, I make it sacred by embracing it. We began this process with *what I'm here to learn* and *how I'm here to love* for child's purposes. Now it's my adult's job to create situations where I'm able to receive these missing experiences.

As I learn and love through my sacred wounds, I step into my soul-gifts for the world. Pixie Lighthorse says, "Heartache births healers,"[8] and Rumi said, "God's treasures are buried in ruined hearts… If you become a helper of hearts, springs of wisdom will flow from your heart." My sacred wound creates the medicine that my soul is here to offer. This becomes my path of service, my dharma. Insert your missing experiences from the table above into this sentence:

My soul's service is to offer (__missing experiences__) to myself and the world.

So, in my example, *my soul's service is to invite intimacy for myself and for others.* This is my soul-work. Of course, it is possible to have many medicines and many soul-purposes, and my focus may change through different phases of my life. But I find that every time I engage in this process, it reliably brings my current purpose into focus.

The Self

The Self is the transpersonal aspect of consciousness that is woven through all sentient beings. Because the Self recognizes the Self in all, it works in service to the benefit of all beings. This is the purpose of the Self. It is the same for me as it is for you because there is only one Self. In Buddhism, this is exemplified by the Bodhisattva who works tirelessly to generate immeasurable loving kindness, compassion, sympathetic joy, and equanimity. In the Christian tradition, the prayer of St. Francis begins, "Lord, make me an instrument of your peace." In the Bhagavad Gita, Krishna describes karma yoga as "selfless action performed for the benefit of others." Every mystical tradition will arrive at a similar formulation when the practitioner reaches the level of the Self.

I am here in support of life.

I am choosing life.

I am here to be ALIVE.

I offer my gifts in service to the flourishing of all life.

I dedicate my practice to the eternal aliveness of love.

The good news is that my egoic self is not the one who needs to figure out what service at this level looks like. The bad news, at least from my ego's perspective, is that both my egoic self and my soul-self are required to surrender to this all-embracing path of compassion in order to realize the

Self. Purpose at the level of the Self unfolds naturally, moment-by-moment. The Self's purpose is Self-evident.

Summary

Each aspect of selfhood has its own purpose and mission. My three inner-child parts, the organic child, the strategic child, and the wounded child, provide the foundational level of my purposes: who I'm here to be, what I'm here to learn, and how I'm here to love. My inner teen shows me the skill-development, achievement, and belonging that I need to take care of myself in the world. His job is to bring my organic child into my career. My soul-self shows me my path of service. My blessing and my medicine are created by first giving myself the missing experiences I never received as a hurt child, and then by learning to offer that missing experience to others. Finally, at the level of the Self, my purpose is to love all beings including myself and to generate compassion to end all suffering.

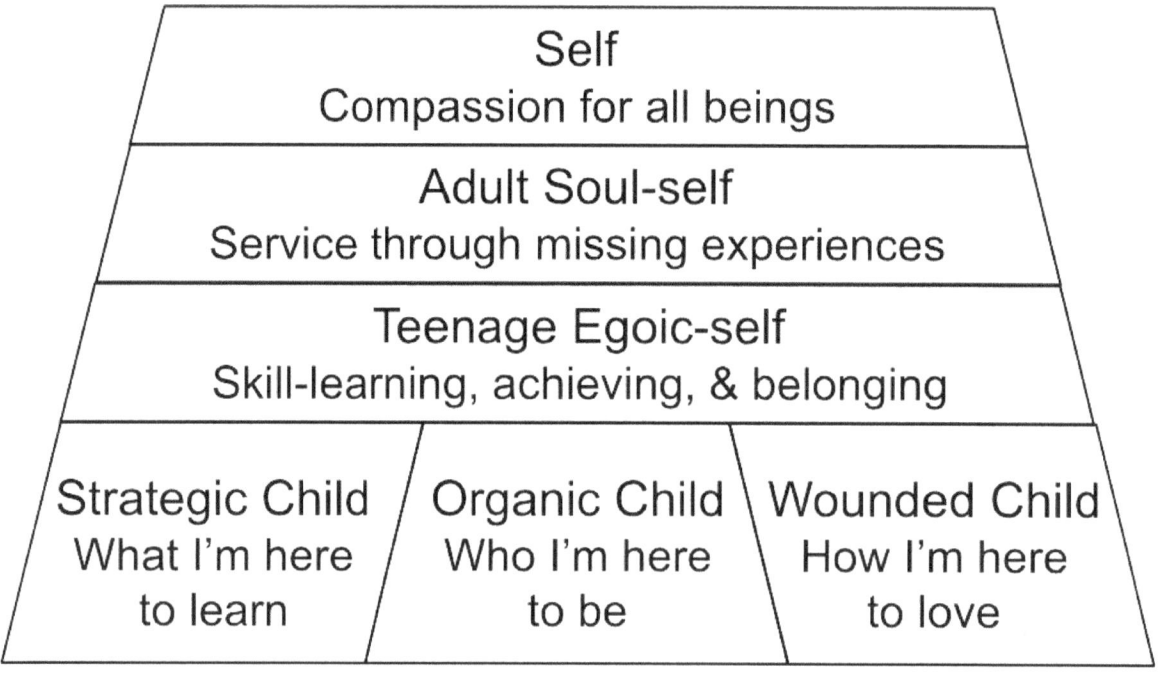

Figure 5.5 The purpose for each aspect of selfhood

The level of purpose that I am aligning to in a given moment depends on my internal and external circumstances. My focus may shift over the course of a day or a month or a year. As long as I am listening to my internal parts, the most important purpose will naturally reveal itself to me. My job as an ego is to pay attention and then to take action to fulfill all these purposes in my life.

Notes

[1] NOAA Photo Library, CCA 2.0

[2] *Twilight of the Idols.*

[3] "Child States and Therapeutic Regression," from *Hakomi Mindfulness-Centered Somatic Psychotherapy*, Weiss et al.

[4] *Body-Centered Psychotherapy: The Hakomi Method.*

[5] *Become What You Are.*

[6] *Chiron, The Wisdom of a Deeply Open Heart.*

[7] *The Wound Makes the Medicine: Elemental Remediations for Transforming Heartache.*

[8] *Ibid.*

PART II - VIOLENCE

| 6 |

Individual Violence

Figure 6.1 Laocoön and His Sons[1]

A cursory look at history shows the enormity of suffering caused by male violence; in the wars, rapes, tortures and beatings that men have perpetrated on their fellow men, women and children. Indeed, male violence may even outrank disease and famine as the major source of human suffering.

—Paul Gilbert[2]

The claim I make with the term, *the organic masculine,* is that there is a core of masculinity that is life-affirming. There exists a healthy expression of masculinity that is valuable, sacred, and beneficial for all of us. I include the archetype of the Warrior in my picture of the organic masculine. By extension, I believe there is a sacred, life-honoring aspect of the Warrior archetype. In order to find this core and have it be trustable and true, I need to bring the shadows of the Warrior to light. In this chapter, I'll share my understanding of violence at the level of the individual. Then, in Chapters 7 and 8, I'll explore collective violence.

What is violence?

The definition used by the World Health Organization is:

Violence is the intentional use of physical force or power, threatened or actual, against oneself, or against a group or community that either results in or has a high likelihood of resulting in injury, death, psychological harm, maldevelopment or deprivation.[3]

I want to use this definition as a starting point. I list it here not because I think it's particularly accurate or insightful, but rather because this is what most of us have in mind for the concept of violence. To paraphrase: Violence is the use of physical force to cause harm. One distinction that sociologists make is between *aggression* and *violence.* Aggression is the physical act. Violence is the harm caused, including physical, emotional, and psychological aspects.[4] Aggression may or may not result in violence.

This is an important distinction because our aggression is an innate feature of being human. It is a primal drive and it carries a tremendous amount of life-force along with it. I do not want to eliminate my aggression. Rather, I want to integrate my aggression so it flows through me organically. The Wild Man archetype is in healthy relationship with his aggression. Violence, on the other hand, causes harm by definition. Coming to terms with my violent behavior is the requirement for true non-violence, and that is our focus.

Now, here's the reason why it is imperative for men's work to address the topic of violence. According to a United Nations study:

Ninety per cent of the suspects brought into formal contact with the police for intentional homicides in 2021 were men… In 2021, most global homicides (81 per cent) targeted men and boys, with women and girls comprising a significantly smaller share (19 per cent). However, women and girls are disproportionately affected by homicide perpetrated by intimate partners or family members, which accounts for 56 per cent of all female homicide victims.[5]

Physical violence is overwhelmingly perpetrated by men. Mostly, men kill other men. However, the recipients of non-lethal violence are largely children, women, and the elderly.[6] And the consequences of physical violence go far beyond bodily injury. Violence contributes to ongoing issues with mental health, sexual and reproductive health, and chronic diseases, all of which disproportionately affect women and children.[7] In addition, over 98% of sexual assaults are perpetrated by men.[8]

It is no stretch to say that violence is a pathology of the masculine Warrior archetype. It is able-bodied men and teens who perpetrate the vast majority of violence—and everyone else in society who suffers the bulk of the consequences. Violence is a men's issue. In order to change violence, men need to change. In order for society to heal from violence, men need to heal the causes of violence within. This is Warrior's work.

Every violent death is preventable, and it is our collective moral responsibility to achieve this goal.

—United Nations Secretary-General Antonio Guterres

How Paradigms Understand Violence

In the *Magician's Lore Book*, I examined how masculinity is interpreted and experienced through the developmental paradigms of consciousness. The mythic/traditional paradigm uses gender essentialism to argue for male and female traits based on biology and instinct. The mental/modern paradigm sees the genders as essentially equal rational minds with inherent human rights—i.e., *liberal feminism*. The plural/postmodern paradigm views gender as a social construction that intersects with other social identity categories, exemplified by post-structuralism and queer theory. From the integral paradigm, I can see that each paradigm brings a partial truth to the complex topic of gender. I can welcome each of those truths and weave them into a more holistic integral gender theory.

In this chapter, I want to use the same process to understand male violence. The mythic/ traditional paradigm explains violence through the lens of male physiology and instincts. The mental/modern paradigm examines violence behaviorally, and the plural/postmodern paradigm is able to place violence within systemic power dynamics. Each view offers its own truth, outlined in the table below. By examining these diverse theories together, I gain a more comprehensive understanding, which opens new possibilities to address male violence.

Paradigm	Interpretive Lens	Cause of Male Violence
Plural/postmodern	Social-construction	Power-relations and hegemonic masculinity
Mental/modern	Rational ego	Learned behavior and social norms
Mythic/traditional	Mythic or natural order	Testosterone and male instincts

Figure 6.2 First-tier interpretations of male violence

Violence through the Mythic/Traditional Paradigm

Why males? We know that testosterone plays a role in male aggression. Testosterone measurably increases behaviors associated with mating, competition, and aggression. But testosterone alone does not fully determine aggressive behavior.

There is evidence to support the *challenge theory*, which posits that aggressive behavior for males is most likely when (1) testosterone is heightened and (2) social uncertainty or challenges are present.[9] Challenge plus testosterone leads to aggression.

Taken a step farther, the *Male-Warrior Hypothesis* postulates that males have inherited distinct psychological and behavioral patterns that make us prone to fighting and domination.[10]

> The Male Warrior Hypothesis (MWH) establishes that men's psychology has been shaped by inter-group competition to acquire and protect reproductive resources. In this context, sex-specific selective pressures would have favored cooperation with the members of one's group in combination with hostility towards outsiders.[11]

Why are 90 percent of homicides committed by men? Because in circumstances of challenge, both testosterone and evolutionary psychology lead men to be violent.

This is the mythic/traditional interpretation of male violence. Male physiology and instincts have evolved along with group dynamics such that male violence serves individual and collective purposes. Individually, violence is utilized by males to compete for social position, resources, and access to women. Collectively, violence is utilized to compete for and maintain a group's access to resources and political power.

Another evolutionary theory posits that male violence is a natural result of species where males mate with multiple females, known as *polygyny*. Humans are one such species.

> Our species-typical sex difference in violent aggression is one which we share with other effectively polygynous mammals, and its link with effective polygyny is well understood. By 'effective polygyny', we refer to a breeding system in which the variance in fitness amongst males exceeds that amongst females. Diverse threads of morphological, physiological, developmental and psychological evidence are consistent in indicating that hominid evolution has been characterized by a moderate degree of effective polygyny. Effective polygyny is a circumstance conducive to the evolution of a male psychology more combative and risk-prone than that of females.
>
> —Daly and Wilson[12]

The link between polygyny and male violence is evident in the countries today in which this practice is prevalent.[13] Polygyny has the effect of concentrating access to resources and women in the hands of the strongest, most powerful men. Thus, young men are incentivized to aggressively compete for these scarce resources. Because all humans have shared in a polygynous past, this theory holds that the propensity for violence has become part of the instinctual programming for males.

To summarize the evolutionary biological stance on male violence, centered in the mythic/traditional paradigm: Males have an innate predisposition toward physical violence. We have evidence linking male violence to situations of heightened testosterone together with social challenge, and a hypothesis suggesting that the masculine psyche has evolved to include a propensity for aggression. While useful for understanding some of the causes of violence, this perspective does not offer any solutions to the issue of male violence. Rather, it views males as inherently violent, stemming from a complex adaptation to social-evolutionary pressures.[14] From this perspective, it seems we should just come to terms with the reality of male violence in our world. But perhaps we can see more by shifting paradigms.

Violence through the Mental/Modern Paradigm

The mental/modern paradigm places the ego as the sovereign center of the self. This paradigm's theory of male violence needs to explain how the rational mind, recognizing the inalienable rights of all humans, would nevertheless be capable of violence. In this paradigm, violence is understood behaviorally as a release of primal energy from the unconscious by an ego which is either uncontrolled or poorly socialized.

Ego development is considered the primary controlling mechanism over natural impulses such as aggression... According to this approach, impaired ego development occurs with inadequate socialization. This is supported by studies of violent criminal offenders which indicate that they tend to come from cruel, harsh, conflict-ridden homes.

—Hoffman, Ireland, and Widom[15]

In this view, violent behavior is learned. The learning happens primarily during childhood when the ego is still forming and highly impressionable. Violent behavior is passed down by interactions with family, peers, and culture.[16] First, physical violence is either witnessed or experienced. Then it is normalized and in some cases rewarded and reinforced. Finally, as the child becomes an adult, that learned behavior is then reenacted toward others.

Children, for example, will imitate adults who punch dolls especially when the observers are angry and when the aggression appears justified. Adults who as children observed hitting between their parents are more likely to be involved in severe marital aggression, even more so than those who were hit as teenagers by parents.

—Hoffman, Ireland, and Widom[17]

When children are exposed to violent behavior in this way, they will tend to assume hostile motives in others, and view violence as either normal or positive. This learned socialization carries forward into adulthood.[18] Learned behavior thus creates a cycle of violence where aggression is passed down through successive generations of children.

Childhood violence has far-reaching impacts beyond the physical or sexual injuries sustained. Trauma impairs healthy maturation by keeping one *frozen* in the traumatized state. Traumatized children become hypervigilant to threats and are prone to reenactments in an unconscious attempt to release the stuck trauma.[19] In addition, childhood trauma arrests healthy development and causes a whole host of impairments.[20]

One result of early trauma is that the archetypal child-self is frequently unable to create a psychological foundation that is strong enough to initiate into the archetypal roles of adolescent, adult, and elder. The healthy archetypal life-cycle, illustrated in Figure 6.3, becomes impaired for a given family or culture. Instead, biological adults remain children on the inside and perpetuate a cycle of violence upon future generations (Figure 6.4).

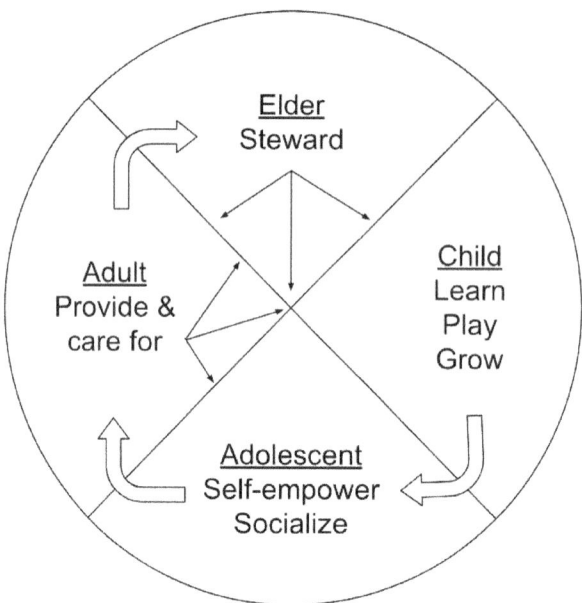

Figure 6.3 Healthy interrelationships of archetypal roles

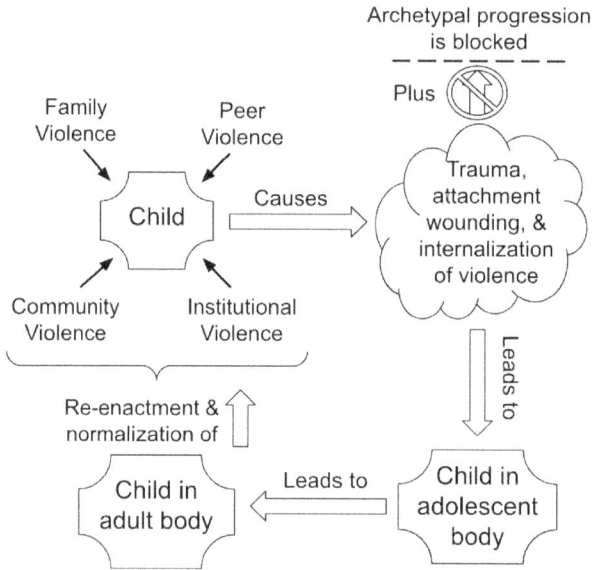

Figure 6.4 Intergenerational cycle of violence

In my view, the two pathologies of untreated trauma and our inability to mature through the archetypal life-cycle are mutually reinforcing core causes of our broken society. If we are ever going to address the looming crises of ecosystem degradation, wealth disparity, and political instability, we will first need to heal these two underlying wounds.

The mental/modern paradigm's approach to addressing violence is cognitive behavioral therapy, which targets the primary agent of the ego. Just to note, addressing violence through *trauma healing* is a postmodern-level approach and through *archetypal initiations* is integral-level working hand-in-hand with magic/tribal social technologies. I'm including these higher-level perspectives and solutions here because they address the modern-level view that violence is learned behavior.

One of the shortcomings of the behavioral view is the inability to explain why violence is overwhelmingly perpetrated by males, given that children of all sexes are recipients of violent behavior. The mental/modern explanation posits that because we each are governed by a rational ego, it is some deficiency to our ego's functioning that allows for violent behavior. Somewhat mysteriously from this worldview, males are staggeringly more prone to violence than females.

> Occasionally explicit, but more often implied, is the proposition that women and men would behave identically if treated identically. The common practice of invoking 'sex roles in our society' when discussing sex differences carries the additional implication, whether intended or unwitting, that the differences under consideration are absent or reversed in other societies. In the case of violence, neither of these propositions has an evidentiary basis or coherent theoretical rationale.
>
> —Daly and Wilson[21]

The main point from this quote above is that males uniformly commit the vast majority of physical violence irrespective of their culturally learned behavior. The best explanation the behavioral approach can muster is that boys are socialized to be aggressive.[22] While this may have threads of truth, it does not explain *why* males are socialized to be aggressive or offer any solutions on how to shift these cultural biases. Although this view offers valuable perspectives, we are still stuck in a violent world without a viable solution.

Violence through the Plural/Postmodern Paradigm

Individuals within the plural/postmodern paradigm are understood as conditioned subjects acting within socially constructed systems. In order to understand violence, I need to understand both my conditioning and the social systems in which my reality is defined.

By way of comparison, the modern paradigm studies the behavioral patterning that the rational ego receives. In contrast, postmodernity examines the construction of identity itself. For modernity, violence is based on learned behavior. In postmodernity, violence is foremost a *social representation*.[23]

A social representation is a symbolic system held by a group of people. A common example of a social representation is *money*. While coins and bills hold negligible intrinsic worth, we all agree to use these symbols to represent units of value. Social representations define social reality and create social order. In addition they provide a common code of meaning that enables communication.[24] The social representations that my society holds become influencers of my identity and behavior.

In the postmodern view, both masculinity and femininity are understood as social representations. These genders are symbolic systems that we use to define identity and establish social order. As a cis-gendered man, I have been acculturated with male and masculine identities that describe my roles in society. I have equally been acculturated with a set of expectations and roles for how I relate with female and feminine identities. In the tables below, fill out the man and woman social representations that you hold today.

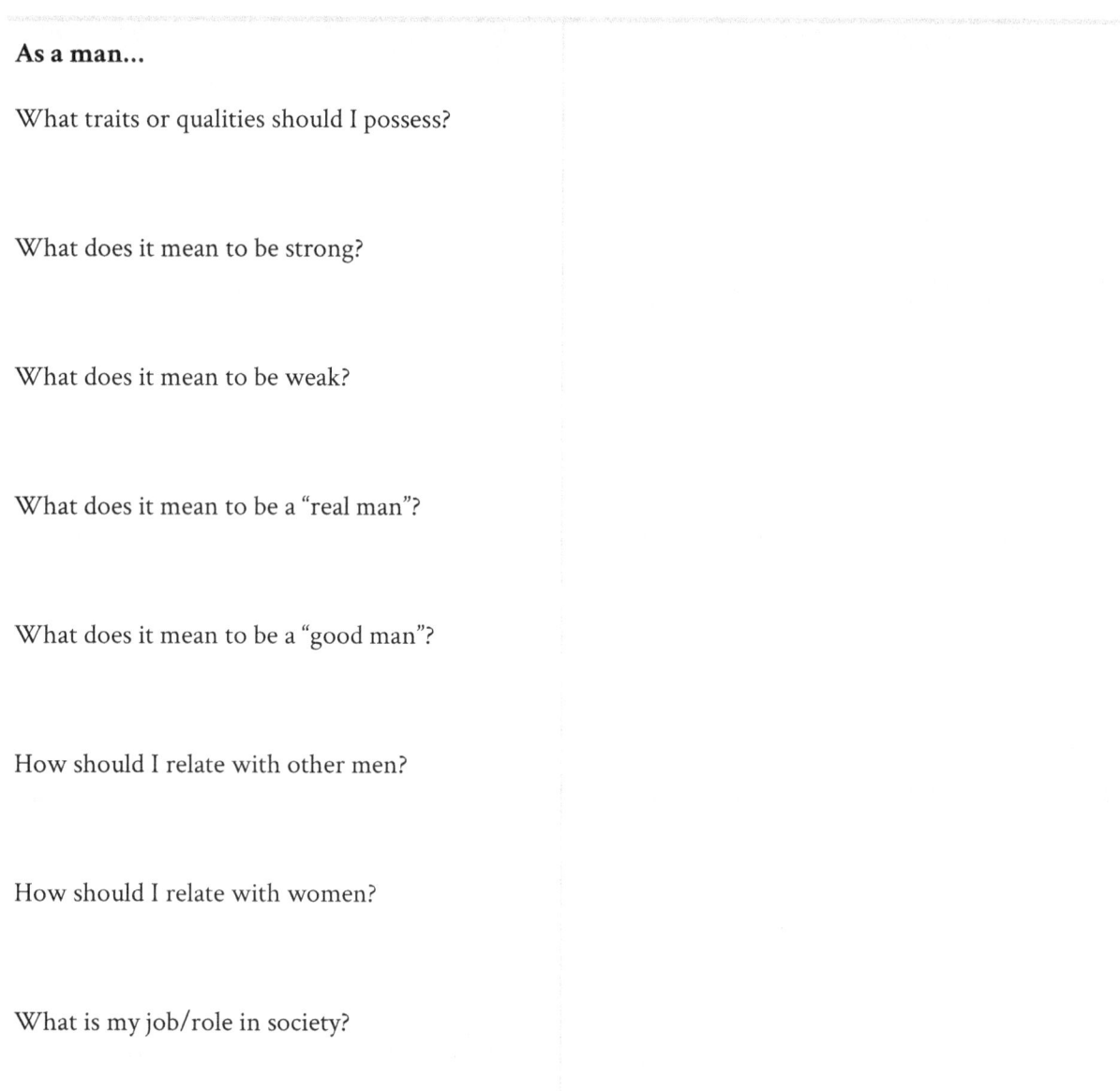

As a man...

What traits or qualities should I possess?

What does it mean to be strong?

What does it mean to be weak?

What does it mean to be a "real man"?

What does it mean to be a "good man"?

How should I relate with other men?

How should I relate with women?

What is my job/role in society?

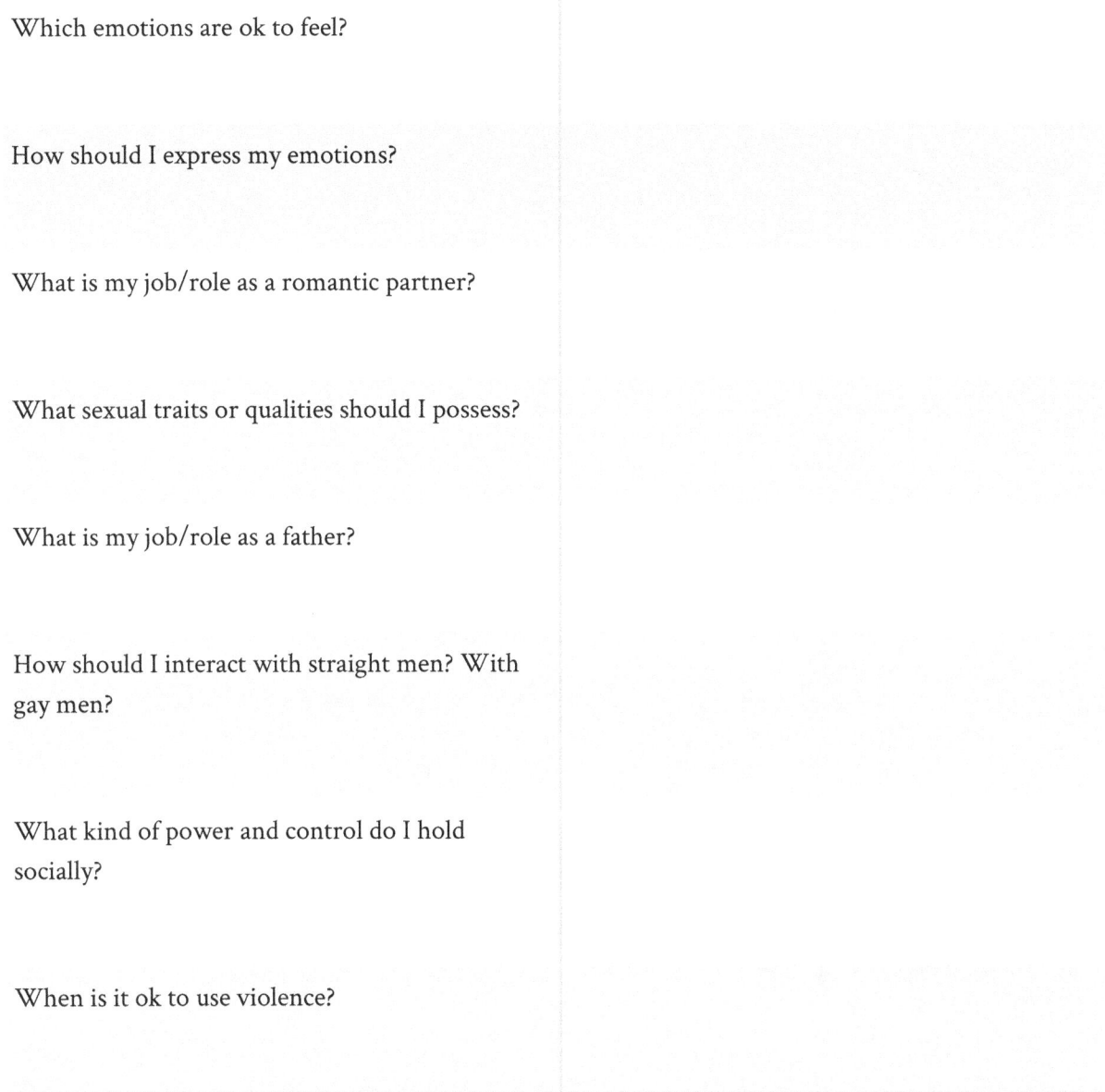

Which emotions are ok to feel?

How should I express my emotions?

What is my job/role as a romantic partner?

What sexual traits or qualities should I possess?

What is my job/role as a father?

How should I interact with straight men? With gay men?

What kind of power and control do I hold socially?

When is it ok to use violence?

Figure 6.5 Social representation of being a man

As a man interacting with a woman...

What traits or qualities do I feel she should possess?

Who should be in control?

What is her job/role in society?

What is her job/role as a romantic partner?

What sexual traits or qualities do I expect from her?

Who is responsible for birth control?

How much attention do I give to her body and sexuality?

Is it ok for me to pressure her into sex?

What is her job/role as a mother?

Which emotions do I expect her to feel?

How should she express her emotions?

What kind of power should she hold socially?

When is it ok for her to use violence?

How do I respond when she doesn't meet my expectations?

Is it ok for me to interrupt her?

When is it ok for me to yell, hit, or leave her?

When is it ok for her to yell, hit, or leave me?

Figure 6.6 Social representation men hold toward women

Having taken your inventory, let's now compare your social representations with some existing models of the social construction of hegemonic masculinity. In 1976, Robert Brannon and Samuel Juni developed the Brannon Masculinity Scale which defines the male role using four traits:

No "Sissy Stuff"	The stigma of anything vaguely feminine
The Big Wheel	Success, status, and the need to be looked up to
The Sturdy Oak	A manly air of toughness, confidence, and self-reliance
Give 'Em Hell	The aura of aggression, violence, and daring

Figure 6.7 Brannon Masculinity Scale criteria for the male sex role[25]

In 1992, based on his work with the Oakland Men's Project, Paul Kivel published the "Act Like a Man Box," which is a set of behaviors and qualities that men are supposed to possess:

Men...	Men are...
Yell at people	Aggressive
Have no emotions	Responsible
Get good grades	Mean
Stand up for themselves	Bullies
Don't cry	Tough
Don't make mistakes	Angry
Know about sex	Successful
Take care of people	Strong
Don't back down	In control
Push people around	Active
Can take it	Dominant over women

Figure 6.8 The Man Box[26]

As of 2020, Ronald Levant's revised Male Role Norms Inventory includes the following seven traits:

Avoidance of femininity
Negativity toward sexual minorities
Self-reliance through mechanical skills
Toughness
Dominance
Importance of sex
Restrictive emotionality

Figure 6.9 Male Role Norms Inventory[27]

There are commonalities between these three assessments of the socialization of masculinity. In the social script for hegemonic masculinity, men are strong, tough, self-reliant, unemotional except for anger, dominant, and aggressive. It is important to note however, that postmodernity recognizes a plurality of masculinities. White Anglo-Saxon Protestant masculinity, latino *machismo* masculinity, and metro-sexual masculinity are just a few examples from American culture, each with its own unique feel. Furthermore, within the postmodern paradigm, all of these masculine scripts are seen as conditioned identity layers impressed upon us by society that separate us from our true selves.

> Until we are willing to question many of the specifics of the male sex role, we are going to deny men their full humanity. Indeed, until we are willing to question the very idea of a male sex role, one that draws lines between appropriately male and appropriately female behaviors, we will be denying both men and women their full humanity.
>
> —Olga Silverstein[28]

Even though both men and women may behave aggressively, aggression is considered to be a masculine trait. More importantly, these two genders carry different social representations of violence.[29] Violence for men means something different than violence for women.

For men, there are two distinct representations of interpersonal violence: peer violence and domestic violence. Peer violence is most commonly enacted between "high risk" teenage and young adult men. Domestic violence is most commonly enacted upon women and children. Women also commit domestic violence, but for different reasons. In each of these three cases, the meaning (i.e., the *social representation*) is unique and embedded within the cultural and institutional influences on the individual.

Peer violence amongst males is a social symbol that confers respect and recognition. Unlike the mythic/traditional paradigm, which interprets peer violence in terms of access to resources, the plural/postmodern paradigm understands these acts in terms of the social meanings that they confer. Securing recognition and respect through peer violence is essentially an enactment of *power relations*.

> The male role demands that no matter what our inner state, we must act and appear to be confident, strong, and in control. This contradiction can make us want to control and abuse others to prove that our appearance of power is no facade. The resulting anxiety pushes us toward violence.
>
> —Paul Kivel[30]

Domestic violence is also an assertion of power. However, while peer violence is about *recognition*, domestic violence committed by men is about *control*.

The literature, then, is very largely in agreement that male violence in the home is an instrumental act aimed at asserting or maintaining control and that men who beat their wives are most likely to be those who in terms of marital power structure, personality, sex-role adherence or peer-group affiliation have a particular sensitivity to issues of masculine control.

—Campbell and Muncer[31]

Often violence happens in situations where the man is in an inferior social position to his partner, or is experiencing low self-esteem, depression, or jealousy. The recipients and meanings differ between peer and domestic violence for males, but the core motivation of social power is the same. This is our first instance of making explicit the connection between violence and power.

While each act of domestic violence is specific to the individuals involved, it is also inextricably linked with the power dynamics and social representations of the culture within which it takes place. Generally, male domestic violence is a specific expression of *hegemonic masculinity*. Kivel is worth quoting at length on this topic.

Since the links between sexuality and violence run so deep in our male training, issues of power and control can easily get acted out in sexual ways. The primary message we receive is that having sexual access to women, having someone who is sexually vulnerable to us, is the epitome of male power...

The act of incest epitomizes the male dilemma in our society. The men in this [incest] support group were able to control others, thereby proving they were successful. At the same time, they proved their failure as men because they had to hurt someone they loved in order to assert their control. Hurting those we love destroys our sense of moral integrity and achieves only a momentary and ultimately empty sense of respect and control, thus increasing our sense of failure and pain. The men in this group were caught in a cycle of sexual abuse that they knew was wrong and that they even abhorred, but they couldn't stop without admitting they were utter failures as men.

—Paul Kivel[32]

In contrast, it is estimated that about half of domestic violence acts committed by women are in self-defense.[33] The social representation of violence for women is the *loss of control*.[34] As stress builds up and other options become more and more limited, women increasingly turn to violence.

Men who kill can be characterized as demanding that the wife 'Do what I tell you to do.' Women who kill seem to be saying, 'I can't take this any more.' Though the result in both cases is equally tragic, these two messages are quite distinct and a predictable result of men and women's differing understanding of aggression.

—Campbell and Muncer[35]

All three of these social representations of violence trace to the core theme of *power relations*. Violence is one means to communicate power within a relationship. As a more complex world-view, postmodernity is able to see violence within larger social systems of power relations.

Power is a complex topic, particularly within the various schools of postmodernism. At the simplest level, power means agency: the capacity to direct one's will successfully toward a goal. In this context, power includes access to resources and opportunity. Thus defined, power is a neutral capacity, neither inherently good nor bad.

However, most postmodern theories focus on how individuals hold power over each other in society. The standard sociological definition for power is the capacity to motivate or coerce the actions of others.[36] Michel Foucault, the paradigm's most notable thinker on the topic of power, defines power relations as actions that influence the actions of others.[37] He contends that power relations are a core feature of society, inherent in the nature of a *governed* collective.[38] Power relations are an inescapable part of all social interactions. In addition, the social construction of power is inextricably linked with the social construction of knowledge. Power legitimates what is true. Knowledge defines what power is and how it acts.[39]

Violence, then, is a broad category which includes numerous social representations, depending on my identity-based socialization and the context of the culture in which I live. Violence is just one means of the exercise of power. Postmodernism sees power relations as the root of violence. Power influences every interaction in society across individuals, identity groups, and institutions.

The bad news is that power is everywhere and the abuse of power causes not only inter-personal violence, but collective oppression, deep-seated conflict, and war. The good news is that all of these social structures—including individual identities, group identities, social institutions, violence, power, and knowledge—are socially constructed representations, and thus are subject to change. How we go about making these changes is one of the main themes of this workbook and a primary goal of today's Warrior.

The problem is not changing people's consciousness—or what's in their heads—but the political, economic, institutional regime of the production of truth. It's not a matter of emancipating truth from every system of power (which would be chimera, for truth is already power) but of detaching the power of truth from the forms of hegemony, social, economic, and cultural, within which it operates at the present time.

—Foucault[40]

This is the *great work* of postmodernity: to deconstruct the systems of oppression, suffering, and violence in society; to redefine knowledge, history, and social norms in sensitive, just, and inclusive terms; and to rebalance the power structures of hegemonic masculinity, racism, extractive capitalism, and religious bigotry. The plural/postmodern paradigm is the first paradigm that is able to bring systems of violence into awareness because it holds a systems view. It is the first paradigm that offers any seemingly credible solutions to deal with violence. Solutions in this paradigm range across trauma healing, social and restorative justice, and political activism.

Looking systemically, every act of violence includes a variety of actors: the two parties involved, the family members and people closest to those parties, the community in which the event took place, and the larger society which holds the social representations that are being enacted.

Men commit acts of violence partly because (1) there is little critical judgment of our actions, (2) there is denial that we make decisions about what we do, and (3) there is no strong and articulate community holding us accountable for our intentions and our actions. Relying on personal resolve not to hit, abuse or violate people cannot work in a social environment where assault and interpersonal violence is accepted, extolled, and modeled…If we intend to stop being violent, we must decide to step out of male roles that encourage violence.

—Paul Kivel[41]

If we want to change male violence, we have to change the social representations of masculinity which condone and legitimate violence, as well as the cultural systems in which violence is enacted.

Summary of First-Tier Perspectives on Violence

The mythic/traditional paradigm holds that violence is an inherent quality of male-ness. It is a natural effect of hormones, social challenge, and male instincts. The mental/modern paradigm views violence as learned behavior that is passed down through generations of children. The plural/postmodern paradigm sees violence as a social representation within interlocking systems of power relations. Each of these perspectives holds some truth. Instead of arguing for a singular correct model, the integral paradigm's approach is to look across all theories to synthesize a more holistic meta-theory.

I can use these perspectives to work toward a more peaceful world. Young men under pressure with few social prospects are at greatest risk for violence.[42] With an understanding of the situations that activate male violence, we can work together to create social stability for young men at the peak of their testosterone. For the men who are not in the high-risk category (myself included), part of our responsibility is to provide mentorship, guidance, and opportunities for men who are high-risk:

> The old peoples of the earth, the tribal peoples, all knew that you'd better initiate the Warrior in a young man. If you don't initiate the Warrior, that aggression energy in a young man is going to damage his community and probably himself. So they came up with software, tribal initiations, from the Masai to the Zulu to the Zuni, helping the young male learn what his aggression is for because he's got it so early in his life, he hasn't got any life experience to tell him how to use it wisely.
>
> —Robert Moore[43]

Moreover, I need to come to terms with these aggressive influences within myself. I have a capacity for violence that no amount of wishful thinking, sensitivity training, or spiritual nicety can erase. This is in me and all men. Once I admit this to myself, I can begin the process of integrating my violence in a meaningful and useful way.

Looking across these theories, I can reflect on times I engaged in violence in my life. Personally, I got into my share of fights with other boys as a middle-schooler; I participated in cycles of emotional and verbal abuse with romantic partners in early adulthood; and I can now recognize being influenced by the arguments I witnessed by my parents and other adults as a young child. With these perspectives, I can explore how the hormonal/instinctual, cognitive/behavioral, and social conditioning layers have each contributed to my experiences of violence.

Examining Experience of Violence

	What happened?	Contribution of testosterone and social challenge?	Contribution of learned behavior from childhood?	What was the social meaning? How was power exercised?
A time I witnessed violence:				
A time I caused violence:				
A time I received violence:				

Figure 6.10 Inventory of violent experiences

Prompts for Journaling and Discussion

Compare your social representation for being a man in Figure 6.5 with the hegemonic masculinity traits in Figures 6.7, 6.8, and 6.9. How is your socialization of masculinity similar? How is it different?

When you were growing up as a child, what were you taught about being a boy and being a man?

How does violence define masculinity? In what ways is masculinity a response to it?

Integral and High Integral Approaches to Violence

But those of us who are seriously intentioned can investigate our own lives; we can see how we are violent in daily life, in our speech, in our thoughts, in our actions, in our feelings, and we can be free of that violence, not because of an ideal, not by trying to transform it into non-violence, but by actually facing it, by merely being aware of it; then, when war comes, we shall be able to act truly.

—J. Krishnamurti[44]

One way to understand the giant leap into the integral paradigm is the discovery of the whole self. This is not an intellectual shift and it does not happen by *trying* to be whole. Rather, I have a direct, internal experience where *I find myself*. The center of my being is sacred, capable, adult-aged, and loving. Psychological wholeness means *I'm good with me*. I'm not avoiding myself, and I'm not trying to fill some wound or trauma from external sources. Wholeness does not mean perfection, it does not mean I'm fully healed, and it does not mean I never become triggered. Wholeness means I recognize the foundation of my being is goodness. When I get shaken off my foundation, I am able to find my way back again. I step into greater sovereignty by recognizing that my state of being is my choice. I am choosing to stay, to feel, and to love. I am choosing to inhabit my whole human self.

First I find wholeness within, and from that experience, I begin to synthesize wholeness all around me. I experience myself as a locus of consciousness in relational exchange with systems (and systems of systems) all around me: food/waste systems, familial systems, ecosystems, cultural networks, etc. Paradoxically, by centering more fully in myself, I become available to experience an interweaving of myself within holonic networks and holarchies. Experiencing my wholeness enables the discovery of my whole/partness, my holonic nature.

The first-tier paradigms discussed above respond to violence in the world through solutions that attempt to fix it or accommodate it. At integral, I begin by exploring the causes of violence within myself. By experiencing my own violence, by becoming intimate with it, I am able to integrate my violence into my wholeness.

In order to do this, I need to have a strong enough *center* in my adult self to be able to hold the intense emotions and instability that come with confronting my capacities for violence. I need to embody enough *integrity*—energetically, emotionally, and psychically—to not become overwhelmed or consumed by the force of my violence.

> Men cannot confront the naked truth of their own violence without the risk of abandoning themselves to it entirely.
>
> —Rene Girard[45]

By choosing to be intimate with my violence, I discover my own safety in the face of both internal and external violence. Safety in this case means: I am able to stay open and available in myself in the presence of violence. Remarkably, this has the effect of de-escalating violence (the harmful effect) back into aggression (the act).

The World Health Organization's definition of violence from the opening of this chapter is useful for tracking statistics but gives me only a superficial and limited view of violence. Without understanding—and indeed without becoming intimate with the roots of violence—I will never be able to transform the violence within myself or in the world around me. It is to this deeper inquiry that I now turn.

Types of Violence

> Suicide, sexual assault, battery, murder—these are clearly violent acts. But alcohol and other drug use, emotional psychological intimidation and abuse, and dangerous sports and hobbies are also violent. Workaholic patterns that lead to heart attacks; chronic neglect of our bodies that can lead to early death; failure to get help or medical care that leads to preventable deaths; and cutting off wives, partners, children, and friends so that intimacy is destroyed—this is also violence. These are common ways for men to respond to their own pain and abuse.
>
> —Paul Kivel[46]

Violence is not merely a physical act. On any level where I find a need, I will also encounter the capacity for violence. Following the work of Abraham Maslow, I can understand my needs as a hierarchy: *physiological, safety, belonging, esteem,* and *cognitive* needs, which then transition from needs to capacities for *aesthetics, self-actualization,* and *transcendence.* I have core needs which take priority. As those needs become met, I expand to meet more complex needs.

At every level of the hierarchy, I can be an agent or recipient of violence. Violence looks and feels different depending on the developmental need that it is operating upon (Figure 6.11). There are many types of violence beyond physical force: *emotional, cognitive, aesthetic, actualization,* and *spiritual.* Because the integral lens prioritizes developmental and evolutionary pathways toward self-actualization, the integral approach examines violence within the context of needs and growth.

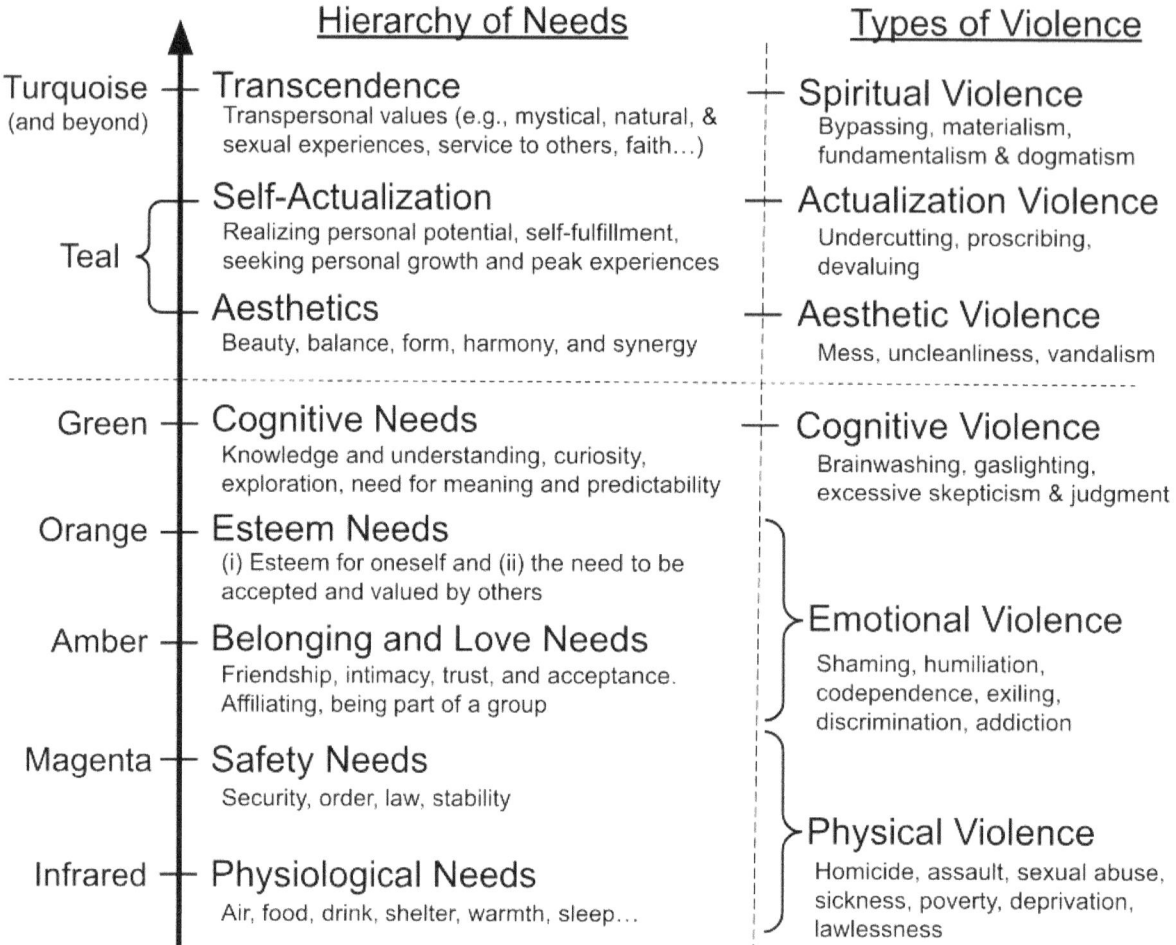

Figure 6.11 Maslow's hierarchy of needs and corresponding types of violence

My most primal needs are physiological. I need food, water, and air to sustain my body. I also need warmth, shelter, and sleep in order to remain alive and nominally functional. Once I have my physiological needs satisfied, I become available to work on my safety needs. These include the need for stability, order, and law. I need to be able to rely on my environment for security. This allows me to down-regulate my nervous system, relax, and be productive.

Violence at these two levels largely expresses itself on the physical level. Homicide, assault, and sexual abuse are examples of interpersonal violence, and endemic sickness, poverty, deprivation, and lawlessness are examples of systemic or collective violence. These acts prevent basic safety and physiological needs from being met.

After my safety needs are met, I begin to focus on belonging and love needs. I need to know that I am part of a social group. I need to have a secure place within my family, workplace, and community groups. I need to be able to trust others and be accepted by them. Above the belonging needs are my esteem needs. At this level, I need to feel positively about myself and my ability to succeed at my tasks. In addition, I need to be recognized and valued for my contributions by others.

Violence at these two levels acts on the emotional level (and also *affects* which are precursors to emotions).[47] Shaming, humiliation, and codependence are examples of interpersonal emotional violence. Exiling and discrimination are examples at the collective level. When I am the recipient of these types of violence, they tend to block my access to the esteem and belonging levels of the hierarchy. There is a particularly strong link between violence and humiliation, which I will devote a section to below.

The next layer holds my cognitive needs. I have needs to understand, to be curious, to explore, and to find meaning in my life. Examples of cognitive violence include brainwashing, gaslighting, and excessive judgment or skepticism. These types of violence impair my capacity to think rationally, prioritize, manage, and execute tasks in my life.

Above cognitive needs, I pass the threshold into the second tier of development where instead of meeting *needs*, I am now focusing on *capacities*. My capacity for aesthetics shows up in my perception of beauty and harmony. This includes how I arrange and decorate my living spaces. This extends beyond physical cleanliness and order to include the sound, felt-sense, "vibration" and "energy" of a space. It may include gardening, landscaping, or tending to natural landscapes. It includes my artistic projects. Violence at the aesthetic level includes mess, uncleanliness, and vandalism.

In the next layer, I am focusing on my capacity for self-actualization. This is the core of the integral paradigm of consciousness. Here, I am discovering how to give myself peak experiences; how to evolve, learn, and grow; and how to cultivate purpose-driven work. Violence at this level is any act that inhibits my capacity for self-actualization. Examples here are undercutting my vision or confidence, proscribing a method that inhibits my creativity, and devaluing my self-worth or work.

The top layer of Maslow's hierarchy is the transcendent layer, which focuses on trans-personal capacities like compassion, love, and service. Here, I am focused on spiritual development and mystical experiences. Examples of violence at this level include spiritual bypassing (the spiritual is more real than the mundane), spiritual materialism (aggrandizing spiritual identity), and any types of religious, spiritual, or metaphysical fundamentalism and dogmatism.

Unmet needs cause strong emotions like fear, anger, pain, and grief,[48] which lead to conflict and violence.[49]

Needs are universal. We call them *basic human needs* because all people are subject to them. The ways I satisfy my needs are individual and cultural. I may satisfy my need for shelter in a thatched hut, a skyrise apartment, or a suburban house. Individuals and groups create identities based on their unique ways of satisfying needs. Threatening a need therefore threatens the identity of a party. So in addition to the missing need and the strong emotion that accompanies that missing need, I perceive a threat to *who I am*. All of these work together to motivate violent behavior.

> Deep-rooted conflict occurs when the most significant human needs satisfiers of a group are taken away or threatened... Needs, then, are inextricably bound to identity and identity formation; a threat to satisfying needs leads to frustration and, potentially, to violence. There is a relationship between human needs and cultural values: "While needs are universal, values form the culturally specific array of needs satisfiers for particular individuals, groups and communities. In other words, they help to give specific definition to identity." [Montville, 1990] Deep rooted conflict occurs when values linked to the specific identity of a group are violated.
>
> —Vern Redekop[50]

I will feel the impulse to act violently in response to having a need threatened or removed. My family group, peer groups, and affiliation groups (ethnicity, nationality, subculture, etc.) will similarly respond forcefully to threats to their needs. When a group I hold membership in resorts to violence, I will likely feel the urge to participate. This will generally come in the form of protecting my loved ones or standing up for "my people." Self-defense, protection, and securing my/our needs are unequivocally the most common rationalizations I will use when I commit an act of violence.

A complementary perspective is the recognition that conflict can be reconciled by satisfying the needs of all parties involved. If I have my needs met, then my strong emotions subside and my identity is no longer threatened. Violence is actually a highly volatile and risky act with dire potential consequences physically, emotionally, and socially. When I am free of the perceived threat to who I am and what I need, I can return to harmonious relations.

Taking an even wider view, we can address violence in our society by supporting all individuals and groups to address their needs (and emotions and identities). As people advance upward along the hierarchy of needs, they gain more resilience and become agents of support for others to advance. As Ramashray Roy eloquently puts it:

Needs theories insist that only by satisfying or creating opportunities for individuals to satisfy their basic needs can there exist the possibility of a fully developed human person, a whole [human], and a harmonious, progressive society. If needs are satisfied and individuals grow into "healthy," multilaterally developed, mature persons, the pursuit of individual good will become the vehicle of social or public good. The claim of needs theories is not simply that the satisfaction of basic human needs ensures the healthy and proper development of the individual. It is also that need satisfaction is, in fact, the only way for the individual to become moral.[51]

To put it another way, my needs trump my morality. I can only be as peaceful as I am safe. When I am not safe, all bets are off.

Humiliation

Missing needs do not universally lead to violence. I've had plenty of experiences where my needs were threatened and I responded peacefully. Yet at other times, seemingly more trivial threats elicited violence in me. Why is this? For starters, *fighting* is one of three primary survival responses. The other two are *flight* and *freeze*. These mechanisms are hard-wired into our nervous systems. When I become triggered, sometimes I'm violent, sometimes I run away, and sometimes I freeze. But there is yet another mechanism that triggers violence, which is the experience of humiliation.

In order to understand humiliation, I first need to understand shame. Shame is the internalized judgment that my identity-picture for myself is *bad* or *wrong*. I am the problem. Shame is accompanied by the impulse to hide or collapse. The internalization can happen because someone tells me I'm wrong and I believe it. Or, as is often the case with small children, we internalize shame in order to protect a relationship which is causing us harm, for example, "It's because I'm bad that this happened to me."

Humiliation is a close relative to shame. Whereas shame is a self-distortion of my validity (*bad, wrong*), humiliation is a self-distortion of my dignity (*unworthy, untouchable*). In the moment of experiencing humiliation, I go into helplessness, fawning, or subservience.

To be humiliated is to internalize external perceptions of oneself as subhuman and treatment of oneself as if one were nonhuman. Internalization entails being exposed and displayed before oneself as radically individuated: stigmatized, and therefore unworthy of freedom and inclusion in the human community.

—Taylor[52]

Humiliation is relational—meaning I see myself as unworthy in comparison to another person or group of people. I can shame myself alone based solely on my self-image, but humiliation always happens through power relations with another. One party is in control, powerful, dignified, and worthy; the other party is being controlled, powerless, disgusting, and worthless. This, by the way, makes humiliation the universal feature of *dominator hierarchies* and *hegemonic masculinity*. Humiliation is both an outcome of these systems of power and a tool that the system uses to perpetuate itself.

As I mentioned above, in the moment when I am internalizing humiliation, I become subservient. This experience is so odious that most of us will do *anything* to avoid it. After a humiliating experience, I become vengeful. I experience the violation of being humiliated as an affront to my basic human rights to such an extent that I vow to return this harm *in-kind* or *with interest* to the other party or a convenient surrogate. Humiliation is the reason violence begets more violence. It also explains why sometimes, when I am the recipient of harm but I retain my dignity, I feel no need to retaliate. Without humiliation, harm is far less likely to incite further violence.

A key insight of Gandhi's was that not only does dignity in the face of harm break the cycle of violence for the recipient, but it also opens the heart of the agent of violence. By willingly subjecting himself to violence in his dignity, Gandhi awakened the dignity of his oppressors. When I am connected to my sense of dignity, I have no need to be violent.

A Deeper Understanding of Violence

> Since men do not know that the conflict occurs inside themselves, they go mad, and one lays the blame on the other. If one-half of mankind is at fault, then every man is half at fault. But he does not see the conflict in his own soul, which is however the source of the outer disaster. If you are aggravated against your brother, think that you are aggravated against the brother in you, that is, against what in you is similar to your brother.
>
> —Carl Jung[53]

We can now appreciate that there are many different types of violence that operate across the ladder of human development. Violence either prevents growth to the next higher need-level or eliminates access to the current level. Because each need-level is a necessary foundation for the levels above it, when an act of violence takes out any given layer, then all higher layers also collapse.

Here is my first deeper truth about the nature of violence:

    1. Violence keeps myself or another small.

The effect of violence is arrested development. This is true for all types of violence, whether it is self-inflicted, interpersonal, or collective. Violence is destructive.

In addition, violence always happens in relationship. Violence between two parties can only happen to the extent that they share resources, communicate, or are in some form of connection with each other. The relationship may be anonymous or fleeting, as in a crime of opportunity, but there will always be a larger relational system that holds the two (or more) parties involved in the act of violence.[54] Self-violence occurs in the presence of fragmentation and discord between parts of myself. The integral perspective recognizes "me" as an inter-relational self-world system. Because the act of violence keeps at least one actor in the relational system small, the integral view can see that violence limits the capacities of the relational system holding the actors.[55] This is my second deeper truth:

2. Violence keeps relational systems small.

> To truly address male pain and male crisis we must as a nation be willing to expose the harsh reality that patriarchy has damaged men in the past and continues to damage them in the present. If patriarchy were truly rewarding to men, the violence and addiction in family life that is so all-pervasive would not exist.
>
> —bell hooks[56]

Another reality that immediately becomes apparent after examining Figure 6.11 is that all of us are both agents and recipients of acts of violence on a regular basis. On the collective level, I both collude with and am kept small by the systems of violence in our society. This is one way to understand oppression, which I'll explore in Chapter Eight. On the interpersonal level, when I sit with a client in my role as a therapist and I subtly push my interpretation of their situation, that's a form of violence. When I rush my four-year-old nephew into his car-seat because I have an appointment to make, that's a form of violence. We are doing this to each other *all the time.*

The most horrifying recognition of all is the amount of violence that I perpetrate against myself. Every belittling thought, the ways I shame myself, how I habitually force myself to overeat, the pressure I put on myself to perform, the stress I cause myself by constantly worrying, and on and on... The self-violence that I engage in is utterly staggering. Just speaking for myself, the amount of self-violence that I regularly commit is orders of magnitude beyond all violence that I am either agent or recipient of with external sources.

This brings me to my third deeper truth about violence:

3. Every external act of violence is a consequence of self-inflicted violence.

Here is what I mean by this statement: I will only enact violence upon others to the extent that I am already experiencing violence within my psyche. When I push my agenda on a client, I do that because I habitually push my agendas upon myself. When I rush my nephew into the car, I do this because I habitually rush myself. My actions toward every other person in my life are simply an externalization of the way I am treating myself.[57] External acts of violence are always symptoms of internal self-cruelty.

> The first act of violence that patriarchy demands of males is not violence toward women. Instead patriarchy demands of all males that they engage in acts of psychic self-mutilation, that they kill off the emotional parts of themselves. If an individual is not successful in emotionally crippling himself, he can count on patriarchal men to enact rituals of power that will assault his self-esteem.
>
> —bell hooks[58]

I cannot hope to change the violence I see in the world without first coming to terms with the violence I hold within myself. Finding peace within myself is necessarily the first step to living in a peaceful world.

> Although attempting to bring about world peace through internal transformation of individuals is difficult, it is the only way.
>
> —The 14th Dalai Lama[59]

Use the table below to bring awareness to the ways that you enact violence upon yourself. The intention is to be honest about what is already happening. I want to understand what I do to me or what I don't do for me. The intention is not to use this material to make myself wrong, shame myself, or beat myself up—those are yet more types of self-violence. Instead, I want to come into ownership of the fact that these are choices I am making in my internal landscape.

Need	Self-Violence Examples	What I do to myself
Transcendence	Spiritual bypassing, spiritual materialism, dogmatism	
Self-actualization	Unworthiness, perfectionism, workaholism	
Aesthetic	Messiness, uncleanliness, image-obsession	
Cognitive	Self-doubt, pressuring, performing, distraction, confusion	
Esteem	Self-shame, inner criticism, narcissism, overwhelm	
Belonging & Love	Self-abandonment, self-isolation, group-think	
Safety	Unemployment, crime, addiction, self-abuse	
Physiological	Self-harm. Over/under eating, sleeping, or exercising	

Figure 6.12 Inventory of types of self-violence

By filling out the table above, I am taking the first step in transformation: being honest. I am choosing to expose my cruelty. It's an act of admitting that "I do these things to myself." It is only by bringing my habitual patterns and hidden agendas into the light of awareness that I can address them.

Now, my natural response to a list like this is to want to fix it. I immediately label these habitual actions as a problem. I want to set a goal for myself to eat healthier. I write down some affirmations like "I am worthy of love" and tape them to my desk. Whatever it is that my conceptual mind wants to "do" about my habitual cruelty very quickly becomes yet another agenda. The question arises, "Why have I hidden my cruelty patterns from myself in the first place?". Most likely it's in response to the judgments and condemnations of my conceptual mind. I don't accept myself and so I hide me from me.

I want to propose a different approach. Instead of trying to fix my habitual self-cruelty, I choose to love myself in my pattern. I choose to accept that *I do this*. From the wholeness of my adult self, *I welcome my cruelty*. I am not talking about a rote platitude along the lines of "I love and accept myself." What I am proposing is to choose to accept that my patterns of woundedness, addiction, codependence—whatever—may never change. And without needing to analyze why I do what I do, I can simply allow my pattern of self-cruelty to be. I can abide with myself, hurting myself.

This brings me out of my head and into feeling. My head is never in control of what I feel. Sometimes when I drop in, I feel the hurt of my violence to myself. Sometimes I feel the anger of how I've suppressed myself—how I keep myself small. Other times I feel the grief of welcoming this exiled part to come home. I may even feel my dark pleasure and determined commitment to my habit of cruelty—after all, on some level, I do this to myself because I want to be doing it. None of these descriptions of feeling will make much sense from the abode of the conceptual mind. But if you've had the opportunity to come into feeling in this way, you'll understand what I'm talking about. The point is to feel how it is to be in this cruelty pattern—to become intimate with it.

Feeling erases the illusion of separation upon which violence is predicated. In feeling there is communion. Without feeling, isolation. When I am in communion with myself, self-harm is not only impossible, it is utterly meaningless. When I am in communion with another person or group, the divide between self and other has dissolved into a transcendent *us*. Coming into my heart and feeling re-members me into connection beyond the possibility of violence.

Recall the mental/modern observation that all violence is learned behavior. Because such-and-such events happened in my childhood, I learned to be violent to myself. Consequently, I learned to be violent to others. While this may be true, holding this position is also a trap that keeps me beholden to my history of violence. Am I merely a victim to my past, doomed to endlessly re-enact violence upon myself and others? Here is what works for me to find my agency: Whatever action I am taking now—whether it is habitual, whether it sources in my history, whatever horrific story is attached to it—this action is always my choice in the present moment. It may not be a conscious choice. But at some level of my being, I am doing this act of self-cruelty because it is the best option I've learned I have. Owning that I choose my actions liberates me from my history of wounding and victimhood. Owning that I choose my actions centers me into the present moment and opens the possibility to choose something new. This brings me to my final deeper truth about violence:

4. My self-violence is always a choice I make.

Why do I choose violence? On the surface level, I would say: hormones, instincts, learned behavior, and social conditioning. On the inner level, the answer is to secure a need, emotion, and identity. But on the deepest level, my answer is much more profound. Hurting myself is an innate aspect of the human condition. It is a mechanism of the soul's journey to know itself. I hurt myself to know myself. I am not speaking about martyrdom or fatalism here. From the center of my being, I can own that my patterns of self-harm are my love unfolding. It is the nature of my soul to experience itself through pain. At this level, it is not my ego's choice, but my soul-self—my heart—which has chosen this path. And every step along the path, wounded or whole, pure or distorted, violent or peaceful, is a step of love. At the soul level, every choice I have ever made and will possibly make is an act of love. Paradoxically, my self-violence is the unfolding of my self-love.

This is just as true for me as an individual human as it is for society and as it is for the whole of the kosmos on its evolutionary journey. At the most primal level, the separation into *self* and *other* hurts. And this separation allows *self* to witness *other*. In that relationship, love is born. Through the reconciliation of the hurt, a more transcendent unity is known.

I will continue my habit of hurting myself until I completely love myself in that place. At which point, I will be free to find novel ways to enact the pain of separation on myself in my ever-unfolding journey of becoming. Through this lens, the word violence loses its meaning. The inherent judgment that I carry about the harm, the blame, and the wrongness of the act is replaced by an acceptance of the nature of life moving through me and as me. More than acceptance, it's an embrace of the excruciating wisdom of this process. This embrace, of course, is called *compassion*. And this deeper understanding of the nature of the soul's journey is the experience of violence from the high integral paradigm.

Summary

Physical violence is overwhelmingly perpetrated by men. Why is this so? My best explanation is that a combination of testosterone, male instincts, and social challenges have evolved the propensity for aggression in males. Specific acts of violence are witnessed and experienced by male children which are then normalized and become patterns of behavior that carry forward into adulthood. In addition, social representations (or *memes)* are conditioned into masculine identities which promote and reward violence. Violence is then used to legitimate male power and authority across individuals, identity groups, and social institutions.

In order to address physical violence, our most effective tools include healing the underlying trauma held by men from childhood. Somatic (meaning *body-based*) healing techniques include Somatic Experiencing[60], NARM[61], the Hakomi Method[62] (in which I'm trained), and MDMA-assisted psychotherapy[63] (in which I'm also trained), just to name a few. Since the turn of the millennium, somatic therapies have taken monumental leaps in our understanding of trauma and our ability to heal it. Cognitive behaviors and narratives are secondary responses to what is happening in our bodies. Our emotions, limbic resonance, and nervous-system states are the core places that require healing. Trauma is stored in the body. Because somatic approaches address the core of trauma, I consider them to be the most direct pathway to healing.

Archetypal maturation through the life-cycle works hand-in-hand with trauma healing. Traumatized children remain psychologically frozen as they grow older. By unfreezing trauma, healing empowers boys to become adolescent heroes and then adult men. This maturation process requires rites of passage and the community support of other initiated men. This is the masculine path of the Warrior in today's world.

Beyond physical violence, *conflict needs theory* identifies the potential for violence wherever a need is threatened or taken away. Needs are universal human traits. When needs are unmet they trigger intense emotions that act as motivators for extreme behavior. In addition, the satisfiers of needs are building blocks of culture and identity. When needs are threatened, identity is threatened. Situations of unmet needs lead to violence.

Conversely, satisfying needs leads to health, growth, and cooperation.

> For a person to experience well-being means that person has appropriate satisfiers for the human identity needs of meaning, connectedness, action, security, recognition, and the like, and that these are all well-integrated around a high level of Selfness.
>
> —Vern Redekop[64]

In order to address violence, we must empower individuals and groups in our society to meet their needs.

Finally, by turning within, I can become intimate with the mechanism of violence itself. This is where true transformation happens. Here are my four deeper truths about violence:

1. Violence keeps myself or another small.
2. Violence keeps relational systems small.
3. Every external act of violence is a consequence of self-inflicted violence.
4. My self-violence is always a choice I make.

These four truths act like stepping stones that form a contemplative pathway into the core experience of violence. The result of immersing oneself in these four steps is an ownership of violence and then an opening to feel what it's like to experience violence. As men and as Warriors, perhaps the single most important action we can take today for the advancement of humanity is to *own* and *feel* the violence we experience within ourselves.

Prompts for Journaling and Discussion

As a child, what did you learn about violence? Aggression?

What is your relationship with violence today?

In your community, how are boys, teenagers, and young men either supported or neglected?

As a man, how do you experience power relations with individuals, with groups, and with institutions? Be as specific as possible.

Notes

[1] Athanadoros, CC0

[2] "Male Violence, Towards an Integration," in *Male Violence*, Archer.

[3] "Global Status Report on Violence Prevention 2014," World Health Organization.

[4] "This added emphasis on the damage caused is, in my opinion, the crucial distinction between physical aggression and violence. The first concentrates on the act and the second on the consequences." *Male Violence*, Archer.

[5] "Global Study on Homicide," United Nations Office on Drugs and Crime.

[6] "Women, children and elderly people bear the burden of the non-fatal consequences of physical, sexual and psychological abuse." "Global Status Report on Violence Prevention 2014," World Health Organization.

[7] "Physical injuries themselves are outweighed by the wide spectrum of negative behavioural, cognitive, mental health, sexual and reproductive health problems, chronic diseases and social effects that arise from exposure to violence. All types of violence have been strongly linked to negative health consequences across the lifespan, but violence against women and children contributes disproportionately to the health burden." "Global Status Report on Violence Prevention 2014," World Health Organization.

[8] "National Intimate Partner and Sexual Violence Survey," CDC.

[9] "It has long been known that testosterone (T) increases aggressive behavior in male vertebrates... In general, it appears that T is most immediately involved in aggression associated with reproduction, such as the establishment and maintenance of a breeding territory and mate-guarding behavior, rather than with other forms of aggression (e.g., anti-predator aggression, irritable aggression). An increase in the frequency or intensity of reproductive aggression as an effect of T is strongest in situations of social instability, such as during the formation of dominance relationships, the establishment of territorial boundaries, or challenges by a conspecific male for a territory or access to mates (e.g., in birds, in reptiles, in fish). Conversely, the level of aggression declines during socially stable periods and when territories have been established, with status or boundaries maintained by social inertia. Thus, circulating levels of T increase during periods of heightened aggression, possibly stimulated by male-male interactions, and decline during less aggressive periods, possibly as a result of decreased male-male interactions." "The Challenge Hypothesis," Wingfield et al.

[10] "We hypothesize that an ancestral history of frequent and violent intergroup conflict has shaped the social psychology and behavior of men in particular. Compared with women, men

are more likely to engage in intergroup rivalry because for them the (reproductive) benefits, for example, in access to mates and prestige gains, sometimes outweigh the costs. Indeed, research on traditional societies shows that tribal warfare is almost exclusively the domain of men, and that male warriors have more sexual partners and greater status within their community than other men do… Thus, there is some theoretical and empirical support for the idea that men's behaviors and cognitions are more intergroup oriented than women's. We refer to this idea as the *male-warrior hypothesis.*" "Gender Differences in Cooperation and Competition: the Male-Warrior Hypothesis," Van Vugt et al.

[11] "The Male Warrior Hypothesis: Testosterone-related Cooperation and Aggression in the Context of Intergroup Conflict," Muñoz-Reyes et al.

[12] "Evolutionary Psychology of Male Violence," in *Male Violence*, Archer.

[13] "Wherever it is widely practised, polygamy (specifically polygyny, the taking of multiple wives) destabilises society, largely because it is a form of inequality which creates an urgent distress in the hearts, and loins, of young men… The taking of multiple wives is a feature of life in all of the 20 most unstable countries on the Fragile States Index compiled by the Fund for Peace, an NGO." "The link between polygamy and war," *The Economist.*

[14] "The relationship-specificity of human violence bespeaks its functionality: circumstances eliciting it are threats to fitness, and the targets of violence are generally not merely those available but those with whom assailants have substantive conflict, and hence have something to gain by subduing them." "Evolutionary Psychology of Male Violence," Daly and Wilson in *Male Violence*, Archer.

[15] "Traditional Socialization Theories of Violence," in *Male Violence*, Archer.

[16] "One may therefore learn violent behaviour through modelling or reinforcement of behaviour in the family, in peer groups, and from television and movies." "Traditional Socialization Theories of Violence," Hoffman et al in *Male Violence*, Archer.

[17] Ibid.

[18] "Dodge's research indicates that aggressive children attribute more hostile intentions to others than non-aggressive children, and also interpret aggression as positive. These research findings suggest that aggressive children tend to have deficient social processing capabilities and a lack of behavioural strategies to settle interpersonal disputes. Interestingly, research on adult violent offenders also indicates that they tend to overattribute hostile intentions to others, and see aggression in a favourable light." Ibid.

[19] "For abused children, the whole world is filled with triggers. As long as they can imagine only disastrous outcomes to relatively benign situations, anybody walking into a room, any stranger, any image, on a screen or on a billboard might be perceived as a harbinger of catastrophe…When something reminds traumatized people of the past, their right brain reacts as if the traumatic event were happening in the present. But because their left brain is not working very well, they may not be aware that they are reexperiencing and reenacting the past—they are just furious, terrified, enraged, ashamed, or frozen. After the emotional storm passes, they may look for something or somebody to blame for it." *The Body Keeps the Score*, van der Kolk.

[20] "Because childhood abuse occurs during the critical formative time when the brain is being physically sculpted by experience, the impact of severe stress can leave an indelible imprint on its structure and function. Such abuse, it seems, induces a cascade of molecular and neurobiological effects that irreversibly alter neural development. The aftermath of childhood abuse can manifest itself at any age in a variety of ways. Internally it can appear as depression, anxiety, suicidal thoughts or posttraumatic stress; it can also be expressed outwardly as aggression, impulsiveness, delinquency, hyperactivity or substance abuse." "Scars That Won't Heal: The Neurobiology of Child Abuse," Teicher.

[21] "Evolutionary Psychology of Male Violence," in *Male Violence*, Archer.

[22] "One central proposition offered to explain the gender gap in delinquency and crime is that males are socialized from an early age to be more physical and to engage in more rough-and-tumble play than females. In at least one study, males were found to be punished physically more harshly. Aggression amongst boys is reinforced to a greater extent by peers and by those in authority." "Traditional Socialization Theories of Violence," Hoffman et al in *Male Violence*, Archer

[23] "Violence, and what is meant by violence, is historically, socially and culturally constructed. Talk and (men's) talk about violence is not just representation (of norms): it is (creation of) reality in its own right."[sic] "Men, masculinities and the material(-)discursive," Hearn.

[24] "Social representations are systems of communication and social influence that constitute the social realities of different groups in society." *Encyclopedia of Critical Psychology*, Sammut and Howarth.

[25] *The Forty-Nine Percent Majority: The Male Sex Role*, David and Brannon.

[26] *Men's Work: How to Stop the Violence that Tears Our Lives Apart*, Kivel.

[27] *The Tough Standard: The Hard Truths About Masculinity and Violence*, Levant and Pryor.

[28] *The Courage to Raise Good Men.*

[29] "Part of gender socialization entails the acquisition of appropriate social representations of specific phenomena, including aggression...It is likely that gendered differences in social representations of aggression may be traced to contemporary structural factors and to the socialization experience of boys and girls." "Men and the Meaning of Violence," Campbell and Muncer in *Male Violence*, Archer.

[30] *Men's Work: How to Stop the Violence that Tears Our Lives Apart.*

[31] "Men and the Meaning of Violence," Campbell and Muncer in *Male Violence*, Archer.

[32] *Men's Work: How to Stop the Violence that Tears Our Lives Apart.*

[33] "Of the 14 studies that ranked or compared motivations based on frequency of endorsement, four found that self-defense was women's primary motivation (46–79%) for using intimate partner violence, with one additional study reporting self-defense as the second most common motivation (39%)." "Why Do Women Use Intimate Partner Violence? A Systematic Review of Women's Motivations," Bair-Merritt et al.

[34] "From an expressive aggression perspective, the salient dimension of the women's experience is the traumatic build-up of stress. The husband's ability to restrain her movement and to isolate her from social and legal assistance, combined with the constant threat and use of violence, leads to the build-up of an intolerable level of stress in which self-control snaps and lethal violence ensues." "Men and the Meaning of Violence," Campbell and Muncer in Archer, *Male Violence*.

[35] "Men and the Meaning of Violence," Campbell and Muncer in *Male Violence*, Archer.

[36] Max Weber defines power as the probability that an individual will be able to realize their own objectives against opposition from others with whom they are in a social relationship.

[37] "The exercise of power is not simply a relationship between 'partners,' individual or collective; it is a way in which some act on others...[Power] operates on the field of possibilities in which the behavior of active subjects is able to inscribe itself. It is a set of action on possible actions; it incites, it induces, it seduces, it makes easier or more difficult; it releases or contrives, makes more probably or less; in the extreme it constrains or forbids absolutely, but it is always a way of acting upon one or more acting subjects by virtue of their acting or being capable of action. A set of actions upon other actions." "The Subject and Power," in *Power, Essential Works 1954-84*, Foucault.

[38] "Power relations are rooted deep in the social nexus, not a supplementary structure over and above 'society' whose radical effacement one could perhaps dream of. To live in society is, in any event, to live in such a way that some can act on the actions of others. A society without power relations can only be an abstraction." "The Subject and Power," in *Power, Essential Works 1954-84*, Foucault.

[39] "In a society such as ours, but basically in any society, there are manifold relations of power which permeate, characterise, and constitute the social body, and these relations of power cannot themselves be established, consolidated nor implemented without the production, accumulation, circulation and functioning of a discourse. There can be no possible exercise of power without a certain economy of discourses of truth which operates through and on the basis of this association. We are subjected to the production of truth through power and we cannot exercise power except through the production of truth." "Power/Knowledge," *Selected Interviews and Other Writings 1972-1977*, Foucault.

[40] "Truth and Power," in *Power, Essential Works 1954-84.*

[41] *Men's Work: How to Stop the Violence that Tears Our Lives Apart.*

[42] "Men in young adulthood are the principal perpetrators of potentially lethal violence and its principal victims, too...Young men are both especially formidable and especially risk-prone because they constitute the demographic class upon which there was the most intense selection for confrontational competitive capabilities amongst our ancestors." "Evolutionary Psychology of Male Violence," Daly and Wilson in *Male Violence*, Archer.

[43] *The Archetype of Initiation.*

[44] *On Conflict.*

[45] *Violence and the Sacred.*

[46] *Men's Work: How to Stop the Violence that Tears Our Lives Apart.*

[47] "Affect is the innate, biological response to the increasing, decreasing or persistent intensity of neural firing. This results in a particular feeling, facial and body display, and skin changes. Affects feel rewarding, punishing, or neutral in their own ways. Affect makes things urgent." "Nine affects, present at birth, combine with life experience to form emotion and personality," The Tomkins Institute.

[48] "Human needs are ontologically grounded in emotions and negative emotions are triggered in humans when there is a threat to the survival of either the physical organism or the developing self." "Needs as Analogues of Emotions," Sites in *Conflict, Human Needs Theory*, Burton.

[49] "At every social level, [a party's] natural and universal needs are the fundamental, first causes of conflict and disputes, from the simple to the complex...Successful and final *resolution* of any conflict must involve satisfying those needs of the parties involved that are being frustrated by existing conditions and relationships." "Necessitous Man and Conflict Resolution: More Basic Questions about Basic Human Needs Theory," Mitchell in *Conflict: Human Needs Theory*, Burton.

[50] *From Violence to Blessing.*

[51] "Social Conflicts and Needs Theories: Some Observations," in Burton, *Conflict: Human Needs Theory.*

[52] *Sexual Violence and Humiliation.*

[53] *The Red Book*, Jung.

[54] "'Relational system' is a phrase I coined in response to the question: Where do deep-rooted conflicts take place? To answer this in a general sense, I developed the concept as follows: 're-lational' speaks of having interaction or mutual impact through time and 'system' comes from the Greek words meaning, literally, to stand together. A relational system creates a context - such as a family, a workplace, or a region - in which parties have to deal with one another." *From Violence to Blessing*, Redekop.

[55] "When people in mimetic structures of violence interact with one another they are worse off for the encounter. Sometimes if they 'won' in a competitive exchange they might have a fleet-ing feeling of vindication, pride of smugness but this is inevitably short-lived. This leads to the question of the meaning of violence." *From Violence to Blessing*, Redekop.

[56] *The Will to Change: Men, Masculinity, and Love.*

[57] "Humans punish themselves endlessly for not being what they believe they should be. They become very self-abusive, and they use other people to abuse themselves as well. But nobody abuses us more than we abuse ourselves, and it is the Judge, the Victim, and the belief system that make us do this. True, we find people who say their husband or wife, or mother or father, abused them, but you know that we abuse ourselves much more than that. The way we judge ourselves is the worst judge that ever existed." *The Four Agreements*, Ruiz.

[58] *The Will to Change.*

[59] From the introduction to *Peace Is Every Step*, Hanh.

[60] Somatic Experiencing (SE™) aims to resolve symptoms of stress, shock, and trauma that accumulate in our bodies. When we are stuck in patterns of fight, flight, or freeze, SE helps us release, recover, and become more resilient.

[61] The NeuroAffective Relational Model, NARM, is a mindfulness-based clinical treatment, as its method is grounded in a phenomenological approach to addressing identity and consciousness of self—who we truly are beneath these patterned ways of relating to ourselves and the world.

[62] Hakomi Mindful Somatic Psychology is a mindfulness, somatic, and experience-based approach to change.

[63] "In our first Phase 3 study, 88% of participants with severe PTSD experienced a clinically significant reduction in PTSD diagnostic scores two months after their third session of MDMA-assisted therapy, compared to 60% of placebo participants." maps.org

[64] *From Violence to Blessing.*

| 7 |

Power and Justice

Figure 7.1 Justice, Rider-Waite-Smith Tarot

For whatever the source of masculine abuse of power, it is our responsibility as contemporary men to understand it and to develop the emotional and spiritual resources to end it. The issue should never be how to get rid of the urge for power, masculine or feminine. The real issue is how to steward it, and how to channel our other instincts along with it into life-giving and world-building activities.

—Moore and Gillette[1]

In the prior chapter I covered violence on the individual level. In this chapter, I will explore collective level dynamics for power and justice through the lenses of the paradigms. This material will lay the foundation for our discussion of collective violence in the next chapter. To begin, let's use integral's four-quadrant model to define and understand the collective entities called socio-cultural holons. You may wish to take a few moments to read the *Sociocultural Holons* section in Appendix I, where I examine these topics in more depth.

Integral's four quadrants can be used to distinguish between individuals, culture, and society. As an individual in the upper left quadrant, I hold my own personal agency as an entity: I'm a holon. In addition, I participate in the cultural we-spaces of humanity. I'm a member of a culture. Culture confers belonging in a group and occupies the collective *interior* of experience (lower left quadrant: LL). When I am in a cultural group, I hold membership within the "we" or "us" through acquaintance and shared understanding (sometimes called a hermeneutic circle). Cultures are the cohesive feelings of groups of humans, including language, values, and morality. Culture occupies a different quadrant from society, which holds the material, behavioral its-spaces of humanity. Society occupies the collective *exterior* of experience (lower right quadrant: LR). Society confers membership in the system through interactions like communications and transactions. I participate within the system by behavior and exchange. Societies are the cohesive networks of human groups, including institutions and techno-economic modes of production. So: our three important groups are individuals, cultures (shared identity), and societies (shared material system).

A culture is a cohesive group that functions like a holon, but because it lacks a singular will (aka dominant monad or individual agency), we call it a collective holon. The same is true of a society. Both cultures and societies instead have an emergent agency which arises through the networking interactions of its members. We call this *nexus agency*.[2]

With these distinctions in mind, I want to examine how individuals, culture, and society interact to produce systems of violence. I cannot attribute war, oppression, or ecological violence solely to the actions of individuals. Our systems of culture and society have emergent properties with chaotic behaviors and levels of complexity that make reductive analysis impossible. Our global behaviors are not arbitrary however. Patterns are discernable. When contextualized as the interplay between individuals (UL), cultural identity groups (LL), and social institutions (LR), we can begin to understand why we do what we do and gain insights to change our patterns.

The primary actors at the collective level are political identity groups, which I call *power-wielding sociocultural holons*. Political collectives utilize their nexus-agency to communicate, pursue their interests, compete, and struggle for self-preservation. Power-wielding sociocultural holons define what constitutes justice in society and then use power to enforce it. These three social constructs are therefore intertwined: sociocultural holons, justice, and power.

How Sociocultural Holons Define Social Power and Justice

The paradigms of consciousness provide a framework to understand the evolution of power-wielding sociocultural holons. Each worldview enacts and inhabits a distinct cultural world with its own definition for justice. What constitutes justice is not one fixed ideal, but has been evolving along with humanity. As culture becomes more complex, the enforcement of power also grows, and so do the types of power that are wielded. So by looking through each successive lens, I see a unique interpretation of the social system that creates and maintains power. How we define the primary *power-wielding sociocultural holons*, how we define *justice*, and the *types of power* these social holons exercise—all are dependent on the paradigm of consciousness that the society holds. Let's explore how collectives within distinct paradigms define social holons, justice, and power-relations.

	Sociocultural Holons	Justice	Power
Integral	Paradigms	Well-being (Agape, liberation) & evolution (Eros, transformation)	Organicity, kaizen, semiotics
Plural/ postmodern	Ethnonational identity groups	Equal liberty principle, restorative	Socialization, informational
Mental/ modern	Nation-states, corporations	Utilitarianism, Libertarianism, retributive	Techno-economic, individualizing
Mythic/ traditional	Monarchies & colonies, religious institutions	Might makes right, religious moralism, primitive	Political, military, & pastoral

Figure 7.2 Political definitions through the paradigms

1. Mythic/Traditional Sociocultural Organization

Back at the beginning of recorded history, humanity moved from tribal groups of about 150 people into larger settlements and towns. In a tribal group, everyone is able to recognize the face and name of everyone else in the group. Kinship bonds keep the group together and allow members to recognize threats from outsiders. When humans shifted into larger settlements, beyond this capacity to be familiar with every member of the group (known as Dunbar's number), humans invented a new way to organize themselves into coherent groups: myths and traditions. As the name suggests, the mythic/traditional paradigm unifies large groups of people under a common belief system with a shared moral code using myths and traditions. The collective need at this level is for *authority*. The central authority instills a shared cultural story in members of the group so it can function harmoniously. A single strong leader, whether political or religious, unifies the group vision and determines the collective will.

Viewed in this light, I can appreciate the incredible adaptation of mythology to organize people. From Dunbar's number of 150 people in a tribal unit, the use of myths and traditions has scaled up to 2.4 billion members of Christianity today, for example. When we share a mythology and the morality that comes with it, I can easily determine who is *in my group* and who poses a threat by being *outside my group*.

For the mythic/traditional paradigm, the power-wielding social holons are monarchies and their colonies together with religious institutions. This reflects the political landscape during the Middle Ages in Europe when the mythic/traditional paradigm was the most advanced world-view in Western civilization. People in this paradigm are focused on the core need of belonging. Whether the collective is a church, sports team, political party, or national identity, the collective provides a membership into "our people."[3]

Justice at mythic/traditional is determined by the person at the top. Within political empires, the leader makes the rules. It is "might makes right," where strength confers the capacity to define what is just. In religious institutions, the *transcendent divine authority* has a "revealed morality," which is accessed through religious leaders and sacred texts. Justice is determined by adherence to the rules. Those who disobey the rules are subject to punishment, exile from the group, or death. Outsiders do not hold an equal inherent value as in-group members. Outsiders are "other" and as such should either be saved by conversion into the group, colonized or enslaved to benefit the group, or killed to remove the threat to the group.[4] Violence in any of these pursuits is justified. The goal of religious institutions is salvation after this life, and for political monarchies, it is the glory of the ruler.

At the low end of the mythic/traditional paradigm, the social system of justice is known as *primitive justice*.[5] In this system, justice is conceptualized as a balance. If someone does something "bad" or "wrong," then they deserve an equal amount of punishment. This is epitomized in the phrase, "An eye for an eye, a tooth for a tooth." Justice means any act of violence is met with an equal act in return. Vern Redekop notes that this type of justice is prone to creating runaway cycles of vengeance. He calls these *mimetic systems of violence* because violence creates a mirroring or mime-like repetitive cycle.

A mimetic structure of violence is a relationship that builds up in such a way that the parties in the relationship say and do things to harm one another... Violent actions are returned mimetically through escalating cycles of revenge.

–Vern Redekop[6]

Examples of these types of cycles include feuds like the Hatfields and McCoys and the Cold War arms escalations between the U.S. and U.S.S.R. In primitive justice, individuals take responsibility into their own hands for determining and enforcing justice.

The next step, at the high end of the mythic/traditional paradigm, is *retributive justice*. In this system, a neutral third party determines whether injustice has been done and administers the punitive, justice-restoring action. This system interrupts the vengeful passion involved in primitive justice. In addition, the form of the punishment becomes standardized and is usually different from the offensive action.

When we identify something as a crime, a number of basic assumptions shape our responses. We assume that:

1. Guilt must be assigned.
2. The guilty must get their "just deserts."
3. Just deserts require the infliction of pain.
4. Justice is measured by the process.
5. The breaking of the law defines the offense.

–Howard Zehr[7]

The three types of power that this paradigm utilizes are *political power, military power*, and *pastoral power*. Political power is the capacity of the state to define and enforce its will amongst its subjects. Political power influences through authority and law. Military power is the capacity for the state to engage in conflicts with other states. Military power influences through force.[8] Pastoral power is behavioral influence used by religious institutions to moralize individuals.[9]

Power in this paradigm was famously articulated by Thomas Hobbes in *The Leviathan* in 1651. He conceives of the natural state of humans to be anarchy and war. The monarchy is a Leviathan-like creature which is our best hope to ensure peace.[10] In this paradigm, I need a strong state to protect me from a dangerous world and other evil humans. The exercise of violence by my political or religious institutions is validated by their necessity to prevent the far greater chaos that would ensue without them.

In summary, the mythic/traditional paradigm organizes around authority, whether political or religious. Monarchies, dictatorships, and organized religions are the power-wielding sociocultural holons in this paradigm. These institutions use military, political, and pastoral power to instill order, morality, and collective identity among large groups of people. This central authority defines what is just and enforces justice.

Prompts for Journaling and Discussion

Describe how colonization (historical or present) has shaped your world and your life.

Describe how organized religion has shaped your world and your life.

What is your relationship with authority?

When have you experienced primitive justice and when have you experienced retributive justice?

2. Mental/Modern Social Organization

Now let's consider the mental/modern paradigm. Here, representative democracy and capitalism form the core organizing principles of society. Modernity *includes* the groups, justices, and power-relations of the mythic/traditional paradigm, but *transcends* that view into a more complex (i.e., modern) world. So political power and military power are still recognized and utilized, but the actors and rules of engagement have evolved. This developmental process will be true for each successive paradigm. The worldview is transcended while the valuable social constructs are included.

The power-wielding sociocultural holons for modernity are political nation-states and economic corporations. Modern nation-states have evolved from monarchies into democracies which hold greater complexity in executive, legal, and judicial systems. In modern states, individuals are united by a social contract rather than a singular authority.

The view in international relations that the world is governed by the interactions of nation-states is known as *classical realism*. Because trans-national authority is limited and ineffective, nation-states are free to pursue power with minimal moral restrictions.

> In a world whose moving force is the aspiration for power of sovereign nations, peace can be maintained only by two devices. One is the self-regulatory mechanism of the social forces which manifests itself in the struggle for power on the international scene, that is, the balance of power. The other consists of normative limitations upon that struggle in the form of international law, international morality, and world public opinion. Neither of these devices, as they operate today, is capable of keeping the struggle for power within peaceful bounds.
>
> —Hans Morgenthau[11]

Marxists, in contrast, view the actions of nation-states as a consequence of capitalism. Corporations, therefore, are the primary social actors who strive to maximize profit by subjugating workforces, extracting resources, and monopolizing markets. This pursuit of power and profit is checked by similarly limited and ineffective government regulations and public opinions.

Justice in this paradigm is discernible by the rational mind foremost, rather than being externally defined by authorities. Justice is now seen to be a universal right for all humans. Citizens in modern society recognize equal treatment under civil law, moral freedom to pursue their individual interests, and political representation through democratic institutions.

Right is defined by the decision of conscience in accord with self-chosen ethical principles appealing to logical comprehensiveness, universality, and consistency. These principles are abstract and ethical (the Golden Rule, the categorical imperative); they are not concrete moral rules like the Ten Commandments. At heart, these are universal principles of justice, of the reciprocity and equality of human rights, and of respect for the dignity of human beings as individual persons.

—Jurgen Habermas[12]

I'd like to highlight two systems of justice at the modern level. Utilitarianism defines justice as the highest good for the most people. Happiness and pleasure are the measures of what is good and should therefore be maximized.[13] In contrast, Libertarianism seeks to maximize the autonomy and freedom of individuals. In this perspective on justice, the power of nation-states, corporations, and social institutions is best limited to minimum necessities in order for individuals to hold more power.[14] Both the utilitarian and libertarian conceptions of justice recognize that nation-states and corporations will pursue power amorally (i.e., without regard for morality) if not checked in some way. In addition, all of the individual actors within either a corporation or nation-state are essentially vying for power to their fullest extent within the confines of external limitations.

Competitive contests between business enterprises as well as labor disputes between employers and employees are frequently fought not only, and sometimes not even primarily, for economic advantages, but for influence over each other and over others, that is, for power. Finally, the whole political life of a nation, particularly of a democratic nation, from the local to the national level, is a continuous struggle for power. In periodical elections, in voting in legislative assemblies, in law suits before courts, in administrative decisions and executive measures - in all these activities men try to establish their power over other men.

—Hans Morgenthau[15]

Justice at the modern level moves beyond retributive justice to *procedural justice,* which adds the following two principles. First, the rights of all parties must be defined and honored through the process. This ensures the justice process does not create injustice along the way. The institutions of justice must therefore be transparent. Second, the same rules and principles are applied to every case. The procedure should be uniform and therefore fair. Procedural justice in some form is utilized by every democratic society today.

In the mythic/traditional paradigm in Western civilization, punishment for crimes often took the form of physical torture or execution in a public spectacle. With the onset of modernity, the infliction of physical pain as punishment is replaced by the removal of the offender's liberties and disciplining their actions.[16] In addition, punishment became hidden within institutions from the view of the public.[17] Further, modernity's systems of justice for criminal behavior expanded to include circumstantial evidence and the sanity or insanity of the offender, far beyond the simple ascertainment of whether the illegal act was or was not committed. This paradigm shifts from judges being the sole arbiters of justice to experts and psychiatrists supporting the process and verdicts being rendered by a jury of one's peers. All of this has the effect of systematizing, standardizing, and de-personalizing the judicial process.

It is worth noting that in modernity's system of justice, little is done to support the victims, and criminals are punished but are not actually rehabilitated, even if this notion is given lip-service. Instead, the prison system creates a social stigma for offenders and serves as a hub where criminals learn from each other. This form of justice does not take into account the structural or systemic factors that created violence, and therefore does little to change the violence-inducing conditions in society.

In modernity, political power and military power are preserved from the traditional social structures and embedded in a more complex social fabric. However, the refutation of religion and religious institutions by the mental/modern paradigm de-legitimates pastoral power. Foucault notes that even though modernity did not preserve pastoral power within religious institutions, this type of power evolved into use by the institutions of the modern family, medicine, psychiatry, education, and employers. This power is *individualizing* in that it seeks to influence the actions of people as individuals. The egoic self, as the central actor at the mental/modern paradigm, seeks its individual empowerment now that it has evolved beyond the *group-think* and *role membership* of the mythic/traditional paradigm. Modernity's social institutions evolved to wield power over this new egoic individual through *individualizing power*.[18] Foucault further analyzes individualizing power in terms of *bio-power*, referring to influences over sexuality, and *disciplinary power*, referring to influences over behavior to produce obedience to a norm.

In addition, modernity overtly recognizes that power is conferred by technological innovation (ex: guns, germs, and steel) and by economic influence. Corporate actors within the capitalist system utilize their own forms of techno-economic power. Even before modernity, productive capacity was a tool for the empire-building power of the traditional paradigm. But with the emergence of modernity, techno-economic capacities explicitly assume both the means and goals of power-relations for nation-states and corporations.

Prompts for Journaling and Discussion

Describe how your nation-state has shaped your life.

How do you experience the power wielded by corporations?

Write your own list of *universal human rights.*

How have behavioral or sexual norms exercised power over you?

3. Plural/Postmodern Social Organization

The plural/postmodern paradigm sees the world through an even more complex lens than modernity. Postmodernity recognizes the harm caused by the power-wielding sociocultural holons of the prior two paradigms and is actively engaged in deconstructing, delegitimizing, and disempowering them. This view condemns the colonization and dominator hierarchies, both political and religious, from the mythic/traditional paradigm. In equal measure, it condemns profit-hungry corporations and war-mongering nation-states for their oppression of people and exploitation of the planet. Instead, postmodernity is working on empowering a different class of sociocultural holons, called *ethnonational identity groups.*

An ethnonational identity group is a sociocultural holon which represents a nexus of several group identity categories. These include ancestry, religion, ethnicity, land/territory, and political affiliation. In addition, these groups must hold a unified collective will (nexus-agency) toward sovereignty. There is no strong, clear definition for this type of group, except that the members believe themselves to be a group.

> Objective criteria, in and by themselves, are therefore insufficient to determine whether or not a group constitutes a nation. The essence of the nation is a psychological bond that joins a people and differentiates it, in the subconscious conviction of its members, from all nonmembers in a most vital way. With but very few exceptions, authorities have shied from describing the nation as a kinship group and have usually explicitly denied any kinship basis to it. These denials are customarily supported by data showing that most nations do in fact contain several genetic strains. But this line of reasoning ignores the dictum that it is not what is but what people perceive as is which influences attitudes and behavior. And a subconscious belief in the group's separate origin and evolution is an important ingredient of national psychology.
>
> —Walker Connor[19]

This sociocultural holon carries a cultural cohesion (*ethno-*) with a desire for self-determination (*-nationalism*). Ethnonational groups rarely comprise one and only one nation-state. It is much more common for a nation-state to span several ethnonational groups which coexist within its power dynamics. It is also common for one ethnonational group to be represented across multiple nation-states.[20] The plural/postmodern paradigm is sensitive to the rights of these sociocultural holons and recognizes them as the primary political actors above and frequently in opposition to nation-states.[21] Whereas there are around 200 nation-states in the world today, there are thousands of ethnonational groups.

For conflict theorist, Vern Redekop, ethno-identities are complexly woven together through five strands of culture: land, religion, ethnicity, ancestry, and politics. These factors become the basis not only of a group's identity, but also of that group's claim to sovereignty, self-determination, and nationalism.

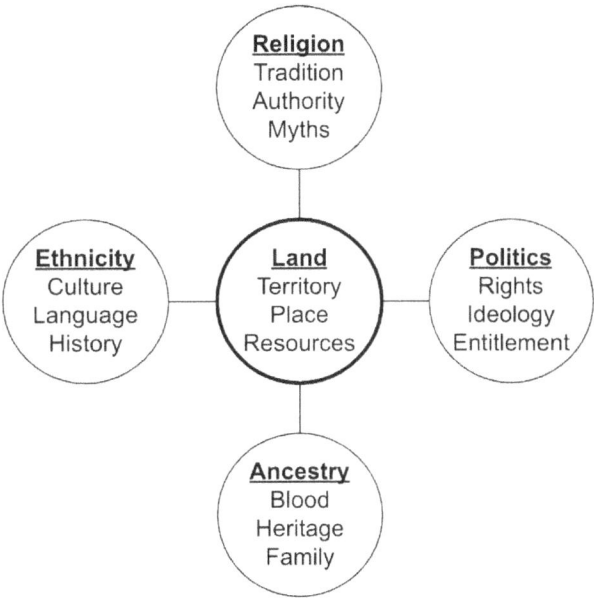

Figure 7.3 Interrelated strands of ethnonationalism[22]

Land is the central component of ethnonationalism. On the most basic level, every nation controls a territory, so land and nationhood are inextricably connected. Groups form connection to land as a *place*—a meaningful aspect of *who we are*. The connection to land as *place* makes it special and ties into religion, ethnicity, ancestry, and politics. In addition, land provides resources that groups benefit from and identify with.

As we already explored in the mythic/traditional paradigm, religion creates group identity, organizes people around a central authority, and instills a collective moral code. Religion can be used to legitimate violence and inter-group conflict. Paradoxically, religion can also be used as a vehicle for peace. A group's religion confers rights and entitlement to resources, and homogenizes the ideology of the members.

Ethnicity includes culture, race, language, and history. When I'm in a group of people of my ethnicity, I have the sense that these are *my people*. We share the same customs and mannerisms. We *get* each other, and that brings both belonging and comfort. Our ethnicity will have a history or an oral tradition with our people's chosen stories. These are both chosen traumas and chosen glories. Retelling these stories, marking these historical events or holidays, and remembering the historical figures unifies the ethnic group in the same way religious traditions unify a religious group.

Ancestry includes the family ties, genes, and DNA of a group. Often the metaphor of having the blood of a people is used—for example, Italian blood or Hawaiian blood. Shared ancestry creates bonds and is used to legitimate participation in a group.

The politics of a group determines the norms for the other four categories. Legal structures determine who accesses which land and how that land is used. Politics defines the allowable religious practices, ethnic practices, and ancestry qualifications for the ethnic group. In addition, the political ideology of the group may become woven into the identity of the group itself. The political power of this ethnonational group in relation to other groups determines its legitimacy, sovereignty, and entitlement to resources.

Use the table below to describe your ethnonational group along these categories. Redekop considers these categories through the two lenses of enframing, meaning *who we are*, and emplotting, meaning *where and when we began*.

	Enframing: who we are	Emplotting: when & where we began
Ethnonational group		
Land		
Religion		
Ethnicity		
Ancestry		
Politics		

Figure 7.4 Ethnonational group characteristics

The most frequently cited plural/postmodern formulation of justice was put forward by John Rawles in his *Theory of Justice*. This distributive theory of justice centers on the *equal liberty principle,* which states, "Each person is to have an equal right to the most extensive total system of equal basic liberties compatible with a similar system of liberty for all."[23] This is a formulation of justice through a systemic lens. The ideal social system is one in which each individual is granted maximum liberty. This is in contrast to utilitarianism which seeks to maximize happiness. Libertarianism seeks liberty *from* social institutions, whereas the equal liberty principle seeks liberty *through* social institutions. In the postmodern conception, social and economic inequalities are only permitted if they offer the greatest benefit to the least advantaged and if they offer equal opportunities to all.

John Rawls poses the *veil of ignorance* thought experiment.[24] Here, I want to imagine designing the society that I would most want to inhabit from an original position where I do not know what roles I will eventually hold. If I could end up anywhere in this society, my self-interest would lead me to design the social system to maximize the liberty of all members, and in particular for those with the fewest advantages.

Rawls' theory of justice represents the specific theory most commonly referenced by the postmodern paradigm in Western culture. More broadly, this formulation of justice belongs to *social welfare* politics, where the obligation of society is to care for all its members. The plural/postmodern paradigm recognizes each individual and group as a moral actor capable of determining right action as they interpret it through their unique cultural lens.[25] Morality is *relative* to the actors involved. Interestingly, the moral relativism of postmodernity holds an absolute stance *against* the moralities of the traditional and modern paradigms.

Justice in the plural/postmodern paradigm is known as *restorative justice* and utilizes both the wider systems view of an act of violence together with the core value of sensitivity. Restorative justice recognizes that the needs of both offenders and victims are not met by punitive systems. Recall from the prior chapter the special relationship between violence and needs. Missing or threatened needs instigate violence, and violence inherently limits or removes the needs of the victim. Restorative justice focuses on needs. In addition, it looks at the community and societal situations that may have contributed to the act.

> Restorative justice: crime is a violation of people and relationships. It creates obligations to make things right. Justice involves the victim, the offender, and the community in a search for solutions which promote repair, reconciliation, and reassurance.
> —Howard Zehr[26]

In restorative justice, acts of crime and violence are understood to harm all parties involved: the victim, the relationships, the offender, and the community. The focus therefore is on the actions required to address the damages caused. "Unlike retributive justice, which finds a punishment to fit the crime, restorative justice emphasizes finding consequences to fit the context."[27]

Imagine a sliding scale measurement of a relationship with hostility at one end and strong connection at the other end. Every act of violence or crime moves the relationship more toward the hostility end. Without active engagement, relationships will tend to stay where they are or slide even farther downward. The restorative justice system aims to promote relationships upward along this scale while meeting the needs of all parties involved. In some cases, only partial restoration may be possible. The goal of this approach is to provide the opportunities for repair to occur.

In addition to supporting the needs of the victim and offender, this model attempts to change the systemic factors that contributed to the violent act. It does this by engaging stakeholders, community members, and institutions. Communities have needs that may be unmet or may have been harmed by the crime. Restorative justice recognizes community needs and provides a framework to address them.

New forms of power are recognized using the systems lens of the plural/postmodern paradigm. Systemic power is emergent and instead of being *possessed* by a group or individual it is *expressed* through the networked interactions of the system. While it is true that individuals, groups, or institutions may benefit from the privileges of systemic power, the source of systemic power cannot be localized. Rather, systemic power is multiform and constantly evolving as social actors engage in the ongoing creation of culture and techno-economic production.[28]

Modernity's individualizing power is included and transcended by postmodernity into *socializing power*. Whereas individualizing power works on the *behaviors* of individuals, socializing power also works on the *identities* of individuals and groups.[29] All social identity groups are understood by this paradigm to be social constructs, including race, ethnicity, gender, sexual preference, etc. These collective identities are labels that are *learned* and *conditioned* into me. Social identity is not intrinsically true, it is only true relative to my culture. An important point for the plural/postmodern paradigm is that because these social identities have been created by humans, they are subject to change. Therefore, I can put social identities into service of the *equal liberty principle*. From this perspective, I now understand colonization not simply as a political system of empire-building, but also a cultural process of interrupting the identity of the subjected group and imposing a new identity and worldview. Thus colonization is viewed through the systems lens as a form of socializing power.

The shared ideologies, values, feelings, attitudes and behaviors of the dominant identity groups, together with the structures and dynamics leading to their institution-alization - collectively and historically - are what have given rise to that which can be called the culture of imposition. Within this culture of imposition: the ideas and beliefs of the dominant groups coalesce into imposed ideologies on members of all groups in a society regardless of other perspectives and ways of thinking; values traditionally held, even by dominant groups' original cultures, become distorted and corrupted, yet are upheld as the cultural norms to be abided by all.

—Raúl Rosado[30]

In addition, the plural/postmodern paradigm recognizes the power of language, information, and knowledge, i.e., *informational power*. The words and grammar of my language(s) define the space of thinkable thoughts. Without the language to describe a phenomena, that experience effectively does not exist in a shared symbolic system. This is known as the Sapir-Whorf hypoth-esis.[31] Language wields power over my thoughts. In addition, the information that I have access to influences my thoughts, beliefs, identity, and experience of reality. Biased news sources are the prime example of the power of information. The use of propaganda to influence behavior has existed for hundreds of years, but postmodernism is the first to recognize the power of information to create and reinforce *social identities*.

In the postmodern era, new systems and networks have emerged including the internet and social networks, which utilize power in new ways. *Connectedness* is its own form of power within a social network. Those with the most connections hold the most influence over the network.[32] *Information* as power evolves into a new expression within networks. The traditional paradigm's singular authoritative media, gives way to the democratic mass media of modernity, which is then surpassed by a plurality of user-generated content in social networks. *Memes* now have the potential to *go viral*, within a landscape where the authority of news and information sources has been fragmented and dispersed. Those who manage the network now hold a tremendous amount of power and responsibility for the ways information flows through it:

Facebook has a population of 2.5 billion people – larger than any country in the world. It has the capability to wage information warfare to change the national narrative (formerly a role of national governments and before that of kings, emperors, and church) and trigger regime change without firing a single bullet.

—Seba & Arbib[33]

Finally, as I described in the previous chapter, knowledge and power are so closely inter-twined that several thinkers have claimed *knowledge is power*. Knowledge defines the relationships and structures through which power acts. Power enforces the dissemination and authority of knowledge.[34] Language, information, and knowledge are all socially constructed forms of power that the plural/postmodern paradigm is utilizing to reshape society according to its ideal picture of justice.

Now that I've explored how these three first-tier paradigms view the social world differently, let's consider the United States of America as an example. Each paradigm views this entity through its unique lens and sees vastly different *meanings, goals,* and *methods.* The mythic/traditional paradigm sees "the best country in the world," which is essentially a contemporary empire exerting its power and influence to "make America great" and defend its constituents from a fundamentally hostile world of outsiders. Meanwhile, the mental/modern paradigm views America as a techno-economic actor within a globalized competition of states pursuing profit and political influence. Modernity views America as advancing the values of democracy, human rights, and increased standards of living through economic development (at least theoretically, if not in practice). Third, the plural/postmodern paradigm sees the US as a system of oppression where the white, male, Christian, euro-centric ethnonationals wield power over other ethnonational groups, both within the US and across the globe. The *plurality* of ethnonational groups are struggling for sovereignty and equal treatment in a globalized world. Three paradigms: three internally-valid and mutually-exclusive interpretations of the US. It is from within these disparate worldviews that collective violence is defined or invisible, justified or condemned, and reconciled or tolerated.

Prompts for Journaling and Discussion

For your ethnonational group, what makes this group special, and how has this group shaped your life?

How does your ethnonational group either a) define the norms for justice; or b) hold different needs than the norms for justice?

What other ethnic groups does your group define itself in relation or opposition to?

4. Integral Social Organization

Each paradigm manifests through both individual consciousness and collective consciousness. As the cutting edge of our evolution, the integral paradigm has not yet formalized a sociocultural structure. A growing number of individuals in the world today operate from integral, but the identity groups which transmit culture and institutions of social production have not yet assimilated the integral paradigm. So the big caveat here is that any claims I make about integral social organization are provisional at best. The exciting news is that by engaging in discourse about integral culture, like we're doing here, we are creating the foundations to bring these collective structures into the noosphere and into 3D reality.

Integral is the first paradigm that is able to see paradigms, and it recognizes the necessary and natural developmental holarchy of paradigms. Individuals and collectives evolve through these universal self-worldviews. Each paradigm is a necessary step on the ladder and contains its developmentally appropriate values, ethics, capacities, and identities. Integral recognizes *paradigms* as the social and *worldviews* as the cultural power-wielding collective holons of society. It doesn't matter which tradition, religion, or mythic-membership organization one belongs to, all people and groups at this level are going to follow the same deep features of the mythic/traditional value-system. Similarly, it doesn't matter which corporation or nation-state (mental/modern) or which ethnonational group (plural/postmodern) that an individual or group holds, they are all going to act according to the capacities and values of the paradigm they inhabit. Integral views the world as a series of organizing principles of consciousness whose members compete (i.e., the culture wars) but whose evolution is interwoven and mutually reinforcing.[35] From integral, it is not specific religions, or nation-states, or ethnonationals who are shaping the world. Rather, it is the interplay of the traditional, modern, and postmodern paradigms that are shaping the world today.[36] By reading and contemplating everything in this chapter, you have been joining me in an integral-level exploration of social holons.

Justice at the integral level works toward two goals: well-being and evolution. Social action aims to *liberate* society and individuals from oppressive systems that hamper well-being, and to *transform* both society and individuals toward greater self-actualization.[37] Justice is any process that promotes increasing levels of sociocultural well-being (Agape, liberation) and evolution (Eros, transformation).

At the plural/postmodern level, I am focused on the system of society. Now at integral, justice becomes a function of the change process that society is engaged in. The same structure/system/process layers of complexity that I covered in Chapter 4 apply here as well. The modern paradigm holds free individuals as its ideal. The postmodern paradigm holds a maximally free system as its ideal. The integral paradigm holds a *liberative process* as the mark of justice. Movement toward more well-being and evolution is just. Any movement toward death and fear is injustice.

Both well-being and evolution are viewed through an even more comprehensive frame. In order to fully understand the effects of collective action, Raúl Rosado argues that simultaneously holding five perceptual positions is required. These are (1) my own perspective; (2) the perspective of the other individual; (3) the perspective of a detached observer; (4) the system in which we are embedded; and (5) "increasingly more expansive points of view, ranging from an entire society, a hemisphere, humanity as a whole, the planet's ecosystem, higher spiritual realms, to The Great Nest of Being itself."[38] Integral's amazingly comprehensive lens for the world is able to hold all these perspectives and understand the meta-systemic effects of an action. This is a holistic approach to justice.

Similarly, Isaac and Ora Prilleltensky view well-being as a web that spans across individuals, cultures, and institutions (the big three):

> Well-being is situated in individuals, organizations, and communities. To promote one, you need to promote the others. To understand one, you need to understand all of them. Our basic premise is that individual well-being cannot be fostered in isolation from the organizations that affect our lives and the community ties where we live. Promoting personal well-being in isolation is inefficient. Personal, organizational, and community well-being exist in a tight web of reciprocal influences.[39]

Integral recognizes that the capacity of individuals to move toward wellness and self-actualization are inextricably linked with our cultures, social systems, and ecosystems. Isaac and Ora Prilleltensky go on to outline a web of interrelated values that work together to create a just society (Figure 7.5).

Figure 7.5 Interdependent web of values[40]

Individuals, identity groups, and institutions each hold their own types of values. These values are balanced within each group between growth (Eros) and well-being (Agape). In the graphic above, the top half of each circle represents growth values, while the bottom halves list the well-being values. The main point is that all of these values work together (or against each other). Society is an interrelated web that is formed by the values held by each type of social actor. Justice emerges naturally as the social system engages virtuous processes of Eros and Agape. Injustice arises through imbalance or suppression of these values, or in other words, through the processes of Thanatos and Phobos.

Justice at integral is no longer about right versus wrong or adherence to an external morality. Punitive systems are seen as active contributors to suffering. Rather, integral processes are focused on understanding the roots of violent and destructive behavior, so that individuals and systems can address those core causes and move into virtuous cycles (which has been our focus throughout Part II of this workbook). Here is Gabor Maté on the topic of drug addiction:

> Not only do we avert our eyes from the hardcore drug addict to avoid seeing ourselves; we do so to avoid facing our share of responsibility. As we have seen, injection drug use more often than not arises in people who were abused and neglected as young children. The addict, in other words, is not born but made. His addiction is the result of a situation that he had no influence in creating.
>
> His life expresses the history of the multigenerational family system of which he is a part, and his family exists as part of the broader culture and society. In society, as in Nature, each microcosmic unit reflects something of the whole. In the case of drug addiction, the sins of entire societies are visited unevenly on minority populations.[41]

It is the responsibility of integral individuals (and eventually of integral cultures as they come online) to understand the unique developmental needs of each paradigm, to support individuals and collectives within that paradigm to become healthy, and to provide access to the appropriate resources so folks in those paradigms can transition upward along the developmental ladder. Integral advocates for well-being and evolution for each paradigm. At integral, I understand that the paradigms are not going away, and the goal is not to get everyone into the integral paradigm. Every human begins life at the archaic level and must grow through each successive stage. Therefore, justice means honing effective processes to support this development. Here is Ken Wilber:

> Culture needs to resume its primary function as a pacer of transformation, with the bar set beyond hyperindividuality to transindividuality (Integral and Super-Integral Awareness), and religious systems recalibrated as conveyor belts, picking people up at prepersonal levels, helping them move into personal levels, and then delivering and releasing them into transpersonal and superconscious levels altogether—a wholeness upon wholeness upon wholeness, everlastingly.[42]

The integral paradigm recognizes all of the prior forms of power and includes them, but also incorporates wholly new forms of power. The Hakomi Method has coined the term *organicity* to describe the innate capacity of individuals to move toward their own wholeness. We each have an organic drive toward growth, health, and well-being. As an aside, *the organic masculine* is this inborn life-affirming aspect of masculinity. Here is the Hakomi principle of organicity:

The second Hakomi principle, organicity, is respectful and trusting of a living system's inner wisdom and integrity as it participates in and interacts with its environment... The organicity principle acknowledges that, as opposed to a machine that can be fixed from without, a living organism can only be healed from within, through enrolling its own creative intelligence when dealing with issues of worldview and meaning. The implication for psychotherapy is that it looks for and follows natural processes, inner movements, inner rhythms, and spontaneous, nonverbal signs of the collaboration of the unconscious orienting toward increased wholeness; this, as opposed to artificially prescribing structures or agendas from without.

—Weiss, et al[43]

Organicity is the innate wisdom of life to become. It is the nature of every individual and of human society as a whole. This is a new form of power which has also been termed self-authorship, the internal locus of control, and self-actualization. Power at integral acknowledges and celebrates the unique paths that each individual and collective will traverse. To put it another way, integral trusts in virtuous processes.

Integral community development is premised on an understanding that community well-being in a cultural, behavioral, and systemic sense tetra-arises with the health of human consciousness as it moves through developmental stages. "Development," therefore, means much more than accumulated wealth, built infrastructure, or economic growth, although it can include these, in one form or another. It is about aligning and attuning to the evolutionary unfolding of self, community, and environment, and recognizing where people are at and where their deepest vision can carry them, creating spaces to explore self-in-relation, and consciously enabling self-growth and new discourse to flow through the collective into more compassionate action.

—Gail Hochachka[44]

In equal measure, integral has the ability to see where and how processes become stuck and then to provide resources to unstick them and make them more effective. This is another use of power, called *kaizen*, which is a Japanese term referring to the continuous improvements of processes.[45] Kaizen was introduced to Western culture in the 1980s as an approach for business supply chains, production, and management. But the tools for process improvements are applicable to any system. One example of a Kaizen tool for process improvement is illustrated below:

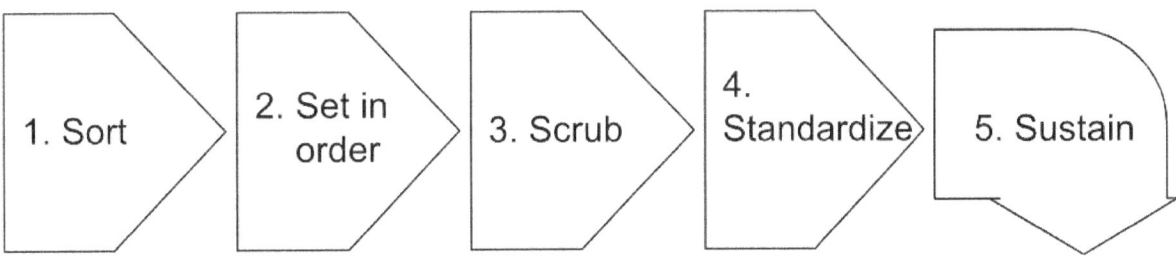

Figure 7.6 The Five S's of Kaizen[46]

The third type of integral power that I'd like to highlight is semiotics. Inclusive of language, but even more comprehensive, semiotics is the study of symbols and meaning. As we saw in the post-modern paradigm, the Sapir-Whorf hypothesis claims that my language reflects and affects how I view the world. Because of this, language holds power. Integral applies this concept within a more nuanced and holistic framework for reality.

Each paradigm inhabits its own valid and coherent self-world system. Within this world, each paradigm creates its developmentally appropriate interpretations, meanings, and identities. Each paradigm holds its own semiotics. Whatever phenomena are symbolized and named enter into the intersubjective thought-space for a culture, and thus become collectively *real*, or more accurately, *valid within the worldview.*

For example, the mental/modern paradigm sees a world that is scientifically, objectively measurable. When presented with phenomena of the subtle realm like a kundalini awakening, individuals in this paradigm will interpret it with the tools available. In this case it is often labeled as a psychotic episode. The modern paradigm uses its own diagnosis and tools to address this experience. The integral paradigm, with a world-space that includes subtle energy and spiritual awakening, will label the same phenomenon differently and apply its level-appropriate tools to work with it.

Each paradigm sees and interprets its own true version of reality. However, there is no single interpretation of reality that is *completely real* or *finally true.* In the first place, language and symbols can never fully represent reality. Every experience is ungraspable and beyond words. In addition, because worldviews are constantly evolving, our experiences and interpretations of reality are constantly evolving. More advanced worldviews are more inclusive than junior ones, but every worldview is valid and every paradigm uses its own semiotic system.

> Every language form carries a kind of dominant or prevailing world view, which tends to function in our thinking and in our perception whenever it is used, so that to give a clear expression of a world view contrary to the one implied in the primary structure of a language is usually very difficult. It is therefore necessary in the study of any general language form to give serious and sustained attention to its world view, both in content and in function.
>
> —David Bohm[47]

The integral paradigm requires not simply a step to the next paradigm, but represents a shift to a whole new tier of consciousness. This *giant leap* brings new recognition to the human experiences of consciousness, spirituality and the sacred, wholeness of the self, the interconnected web of life, and the evolutionary journey of the kosmos. All of this new territory requires an *integral semiotics*. The mythic/traditional conception of God as an old man on a throne in heaven will be reinterpreted as Spirit from integral's *vision logic* lens on reality. Mental/modern's understanding of science will be woven into a world of radical empiricism that includes the four quadrants of being-in-the-world, not solely the material world. The plural/postmodern conception of nature as the victim of capitalist greed will be released from the drama triangle and recontextualized within developmental ecosystems theories or *integral ecology*.[48] There is a massive amount of new terrain that the integral paradigm accesses, and therefore needs to symbolize. By creating new language and new meanings for this terrain, integral semiotics opens the shared mindspace for humanity to experience this terrain, to know that it is real, and to share these experiences with each other. The effect of this new semiotics, and the power that it represents, is the power to evolve and liberate humans.

> *Semiotics is a matter of emancipation.* It is driven, in its highest reaches, by an emancipatory interest. By naming and signifying the higher structures and states, it opens the doorway to our own growth and development into those states; it gives the mind permission to begin thinking in those directions; it reassures us that those realities are indeed really there.
>
> —Ken Wilber[49]

Moreover, at integral, I view symbolism and meaning as inherent features of the kosmos, indelibly woven throughout all of reality. I live in a symbolic kosmos. This position is known as pansemiotics.[50] Semiosis is coextensive with the kosmos. All matter is encoded light. Each organism is encoded life. Every human communication is encoded reflexive consciousness. The symbolic is the unifying link between form and consciousness, mind and matter. Thus semiotics is the power of creation itself. Experiencing new meaning, naming those experiences, and sharing them with others constitutes the semiotic advance into novelty of the kosmos.

In each instance of integral power, the focus has moved to *empowerment*. Organicity, kaizen, and semiotics each actualize individuals and collectives through their skillful use. The adage that *power corrupts and absolute power corrupts absolutely* is only true for first-tier types of power. Integral power is about harnessing and participating with the power of life. At integral, I'm more interested in becoming a conduit for power than holding power over someone else. Integral's primary focus is on harnessing our self-arising natural power toward well-being and growth. External, proscriptive, and authoritative forms of power may still serve a developmentally appropriate purpose, but these are no longer the primary tools of the integral paradigm.

> Power at its best is love implementing the demands of justice, and justice at its best is love correcting everything that stands against love.
>
> —Dr. Martin Luther King, Jr.

Summary

Each paradigm centers its own power-wielding sociocultural holons using distinct forms of power and definitions of justice. Members of a paradigm may recognize other paradigms' sociocultural holons, for example the mental modern view recognizes the existence of both monarchies and ethnonational groups. But what first-tier paradigms don't do is grant validation or authority to the sociocultural holons of other paradigms. The mental/modern nation-states do not recognize or support the sovereignty of ethnonational groups, by and large.

The types of power in each paradigm negate the worldview of the junior paradigms, but preserve the uses of those powers. Often these forms of power are adapted into even more complex self-world systems. Thus each step diversifies and expands how it utilizes social power.

The evolution of justice moves from an authoritative set of rules and punishments, to universal rights for humans, to a culturally contextual system of equal opportunities, to virtuous processes of empowerment.

Integral advances each of these social dynamics to a wholly new level, a second tier. In the integral world that is coming our way, I expect to see humanity investing in well-being and self-actualization across the big three of individuals, culture, and institutions. This represents the cutting edge of social evolution for humanity.

Prompts for Journaling and Discussion

Which paradigm of consciousness holds your center of gravity?

How is your paradigm influencing the ways you relate to colonization, organized religion, national citizenship, and ethnonational identity in your life?

Describe a time you experienced *organicity* unfolding in your process of growth or healing.

Return to *Figure 7.5, The interdependent web of values*, above. How does the well-being of each social actor contribute to the well-being of the other two actors? Why does each circle need to balance between the top values of Eros and the bottom values of Agape?

Notes

[1] *The King Within.*

[2] "The governing 'nexus'—or 'nexus-agency'—of the group provides certain rules, values, guidelines, ethics, and semantics that influence, to one degree or another, its members. But there is no 'super-I' that fully controls every member of the group." *The Religion of Tomorrow,* Wilber.

[3] "At this level, maintaining the expectations of the individual's family, group, or nation is perceived as valuable in its own right, regardless of immediate and obvious consequences. The attitude is not only one of *conformity* to personal expectations and social order, but of loyalty to it, of actively *maintaining*, supporting, and justifying the order, and of identifying with the persons or group involved in it." *Communication and Evolution of Society,* Habermas.

[4] "In addition there were barbarians, whom one attempted either to conquer or to convert - aliens who were potential members but who, so long as they had not the status of citizen, did not count as fully human." *Communication and Evolution of Society,* Habermas.

[5] "Humankind is generally attuned to primitive justice, which is often framed as 'good guys versus bad guys.' Someone is hurt in what we interpret as a gratuitous or oppressive action, and we want the perpetrator to suffer." *Introduction to Conflict Studies,* Rioux and Redekop.

[6] *From Violence to Blessing.*

[7] *Changing Lenses.*

[8] "Political power must be distinguished from force in the sense of the exercise of actual physical violence. The threat of physical violence in the form of police action, imprisonment, capital punishment, or war is an intrinsic element of politics. When violence becomes an actuality, it signifies the abdication of political power in favor of military or pseudo-military power...The actual exercise of physical violence substitutes for the psychological relation between two minds, which is of the essence of political power, the physical relation between two bodies, one of which is strong enough to dominate the other's movements. It is for this reason that in the exercise of physical violence the psychological element of the political relationship is lost, and that we must distinguish between military and political power." *Politics Among Nations,* Morgenthau.

[9] "1. It is a form of power whose ultimate aim is to assure individual salvation in the next world. 2. Pastoral power is not merely a form of power that commands; it must also be prepared to sacrifice itself for the life and salvation of the flock. Therefore it is different from royal power, which demands a sacrifice from its subjects to save the throne. 3. It is a form of power that looks after not just the whole community but each individual in particular, during [their] entire life. 4. Finally, this form of power cannot be exercised without knowing the inside of people's minds,

without exploring their souls, without making them reveal their innermost secrets. It implies a knowledge of the conscience and an ability to direct it." "The Subject and Power," in *Power, Essential Works 1954-84*, Foucault.

[10] "And in him consisteth the Essence of the Common-wealth; which (to define it,) is *One Person of whose acts a great Multitude, by mutuall Covenants one with another, have made themselves every one the Author, to the end he may use the strength and means of them all, as he shalt think expedient, for their Peace and Common Defence.* And he that carryeth this Person, is called SOVERAIGNE, and said to have *Soveraigne Power*; and every one besides, his SUBJECT. The attaining to this Soveraigne Power, is by two wayes. One, by Naturall force; as when a man maketh his children, to submit themselves, and their children to his government, as being able to destroy them if they refuse ; or by Warre subdueth his enemies to his will, giving them their lives on that condition. The other, is when men agree amongst themselves, to submit to some Man, or Assembly of men, voluntarily, on confidence to be protected by him against all others. This later, may be called a Politicall Common-wealth, or Common-wealth by *Institution*; and the former, a Common-wealth by *Acquisition.*..It belongeth therefore to him that hath the Soveraign Power, to be Judge, or constitute all Judges of Opinions and Doctrines, as a thing necessary to Peace ; therby to prevent Discord and Civill Warre." *The Leviathan*, Hobbes.

[11] *Politics Among Nations.*

[12] *Communication and Evolution of Society.*

[13] "The creed which accepts as the foundation of morals, Utility, or the Greatest Happiness Principle, holds that actions are right in proportion as they tend to promote happiness, wrong as they tend to produce the reverse of happiness. By happiness is intended pleasure, and the absence of pain; by unhappiness, pain, and the privation of pleasure." *Utilitarianism*, Mill.

[14] "Society in every state is a blessing, but government, even in its best state, is but a necessary evil; in its worst state an intolerable one: for when we suffer, or are exposed to the same miseries by a government, which we might expect in a country without government, our calamity is heightened by reflecting that we furnish the means by which we suffer." *Common Sense*, Paine.

[15] *Politics Among Nations.*

[16] "From being an art of unbearable sensations punishment has become an economy of suspended rights… The guillotine takes life almost without touching the body, just as prison deprives of liberty or a fine reduces wealth. It is intended to apply the law not so much to a real body capable of feeling pain as to a juridical subject, the possessor, among other rights, of the right to exist." *Discipline and Punish: The Birth of the Prison*, Foucault.

[17] "Punishment, then, will tend to become the most hidden part of the penal process." Ibid.

[18] "1. We may observe a change in [pastoral power's] objective. It was no longer a question of leading people to their salvation in the next world, but, rather, ensuring it in this world. And in this context, the word 'salvation' takes on different meanings: health, well-being (that is, sufficient wealth, standard of living), security, protection against accidents. A series of 'worldly' aims took the place of the religious aims of the traditional pastorate, all the more easily because the latter, for various reasons, had followed in an accessory way a certain number of these aims; we only have to think of the role of medicine and its welfare function assured for a long time by the Catholic and Protestant churches. 2. Concurrently, the officials of pastoral power increased. Sometimes this form of power was exerted by state apparatus or, in any case, by a public institution such as the police...Sometimes the power was exercised by private venture, welfare societies, benefactors, and generally by philanthropists. But ancient institutions, for example the family, were also mobilized at this time to take on pastoral functions. It was also exercised by complex structures such as medicine, which included private initiatives with the sale of services on market economic principles but also included public institutions such as hospitals. 3. Finally, the multiplication of the aims and agents of pastoral power focused the development of knowledge of man around two roles: one, globalizing and quantitative, concerning the population; the other, analytical, concerning the individual." "The Subject and Power," in *Power, Essential Works 1954-84*, Foucault.

[19] *Ethnonationalism: The Quest for Understanding.*

[20] "If we exclude both the multinational states and those states which, although themselves homogeneous, are characterized by that so-called irredentist situation in which the dominant group extends beyond the state's borders, our only illustrations would be Denmark, Iceland, Japan, Luxembourg, the Netherlands, Norway, and Portugal. These states would account for less than 4 percent of the world population and, if we exclude Japan, for less than 1 percent. With so few nation-states, analyzing ethnonationalism in terms of total economies (G.N.P.s, labor forces, etc.) is not apt to prove very edifying." *Ethnonationalism: The Quest for Understanding*, Connor.

[21] "But in a world containing thousands of ethnonational groups and less than two hundred states, it is evident that for most people the sense of loyalty to one's nation and to one's state do not coincide. And they often compete for the allegiance of the individual." *Ethnonationalism: The Quest for Understanding*, Connor.

[22] Adapted from *From Violence to Blessing*, Redekop.

[23] *Theory of Justice, Revised Edition*, Rawls.

[24] "The idea of the original position is to set up a fair procedure so that any principles agreed to will be just. The aim is to use the notion of pure procedural justice as a basis of theory. Somehow we must nullify the effects of specific contingencies which put men at odds and tempt them

to exploit social and natural circumstances to their own advantage. Now in order to do this I assume that the parties are situated behind a veil of ignorance. They do not know how the various alternatives will affect their own particular case and they are obliged to evaluate principles solely on the basis of general considerations." *Theory of Justice, Revised Edition*, Rawls.

[25] "If needs are understood as culturally interpreted but ascribed to individuals as natural properties, the admissible universalistic norms of action have the character of general moral norms. Each individual is supposed to test monologically the generalizability of the norm in question. This corresponds to Kohlber's stage 6 (conscience orientation)." *Communication and Evolution of Society*, Habermas.

[26] *Changing Lenses*.

[27] *Introduction to Conflict Studies*, Rioux and Redekop.

[28] "[Postmodernity's political technology of power] is diffuse, rarely formulated in continuous, systematic discourse; it is often made up of bits and pieces; it implements a disparate set of tools or methods. In spite of the coherence of its results, it is generally no more than a multiform instrumentation. Moreover, it cannot be localized in a particular type of institution or state apparatus... The overthrow of these 'micro-powers' does not, then, obey the law of all or nothing; it is not acquired once and for all by a new control of the apparatuses nor by a new functioning or a destruction of the institutions; on the other hand, none of its localized episodes may be inscribed in history except by the effects that it induces on the entire network in which it is caught up." *Discipline and Punish: The Birth of the Prison*, Foucault.

[29] "No one can construct an identity independently of the identifications that others make of [them]. These are, naturally, identifications that others make not in the propositional attitude of observers, but in the performative attitude of participants in interaction. Indeed the ego does not accomplish its self-identifications in a propositional attitude. It presents itself to itself as a practical ego in the performance of communicative actions; and in communicative action the participants must reciprocally suppose that the distinguishing-oneself-from-others is recognized by those others. Thus the basis for the assertion of one's own identity is not really self-identification, but intersubjectively recognized self-identification." *Communication and Evolution of Society*, Habermas.

[30] *Consciousness-in-Action, Toward an Integral Psychology of Liberation and Transformation*.

[31] "We are thus introduced to a new principle of relativity, which holds that all observers are not led by the same physical evidence to the same picture of the universe, unless their linguistic backgrounds are similar, or can in some way be calibrated...It will be found that an 'event' to us means 'what our language classes as a verb' or something analogized therefrom. And it will be found that it is not possible to define 'event, thing, object, relationship,' and so on, from nature,

but that to define them always involves a circuitous return to the grammatical categories of the definer's language." *Language Thought and Reality*, Whorf.

[32] "In a social network, people are empowered by being connected to the network. Power as empowerment means facilitating this connectedness. The network hubs with the richest connections become centers of power." *The Systems View of Life: A Unifying Vision*, Capra and Luisi.

[33] *Rethinking Humanity: Five Foundational Sector Disruptions, the Lifecycle of Civilizations, and the Coming Age of Freedom.*

[34] "We should admit rather that power produces knowledge (and not simply by encouraging it because it serves power or by applying it because it is useful); that power and knowledge directly imply one another; that there is no power relation without the correlative constitution of a field of knowledge, nor any knowledge that does not presuppose and constitute at the same time power relations." *Discipline and Punish: The Birth of the Prison*, Foucault.

[35] "Take the famous 'Culture Wars,' for example, which is a zealously overheated argument as to which system of values is the one true system. There are generally agreed to be three major contestants in these Culture Wars: the traditional, often fundamentalist, mythic-literal, religious believers, advocates of God's truth as literally revealed in the Bible; the modern, rational, scientific believers, advocates of progress and achievement; and the postmodern, multicultural, sensitivity believers, advocates of nonmarginalizing attitudes and ecological sustainability. ...Integral stages go one step further and ask, 'What partial truths do each of those 1st-tier truths have to contribute to a fuller view of humankind?' and then work on creating integrating frameworks, such as AQAL, to pull all of these fragments together to more accurately reflect the Whole of reality and all of its various interpretations." *The Religion of Tomorrow*, Wilber.

[36] "Worldviews are the foundational structures of cultural evolution and are therefore the most basic units of cultural analysis." *Developmental Politics*, McIntosh.

[37] "While liberation could be characterized as the *struggle against* oppression, transformation could be characterized as the *movement toward* a future vision. Yet, from the perspective of this integral framework, liberation and transformation are not approaches in opposition to each other. Instead they are complementary forces for change." *Consciousness-in-Action*, Rosado.

[38] *Consciousness-in-Action.*

[39] *Promoting Well-Being.*

[40] Adapted from *Promoting Well-Being*, Prilleltensky and Prilleltensky.

[41] *In the Realm of Hungry Ghosts.*

[42] *The Religion of Tomorrow.*

[43] *Hakomi Mindfulness-Centered Somatic Psychotherapy.*

[44] From "Integrating Interiority in Sustainable Community Development: A Case Study with San Juan del Gozo Community, El Salvador," quoted in *Integral Ecology,* Esbjorn-Hargens and Zimmerman.

[45] "Kaizen fosters process-oriented thinking because processes must be improved for results to improve. Failure to achieve planned results indicates a failure in the process. Management must identify and correct such process-based errors. Kaizen focuses on human efforts—an orientation that contrasts sharply with the results-based thinking in the West." *Gemba Kaizen,* Imai.

[46] Adapted from the Kaizen Institute.

[47] *Wholeness and the Implicate Order.*

[48] "Thus the classical definition of ecology (the study of the interrelationship between organisms and their environment) becomes the study of the interrelationship between organisms' experiences and behaviors, and their cultural and systems environments. In other words, *Integral Ecology is the study of the subjective and objective aspects of organisms in relationship to their intersubjective and interobjective environments at all levels of depth and complexity.*" *Integral Ecology,* Esbjorn-Hargens and Zimmerman.

[49] *The Religion of Tomorrow.*

[50] "The universe is perfused with signs, semiosis is not only a process found in all living nature among beings which are organic, functional wholes (organisms as interpreters, or interpretants). The sign, its object and its interpretant are universal categories, which existed (eventually in degenerate form) even before the origin of life…The pansemiotic thesis may be read as a version of panpsychism: the idea that matter is effete mind, or that qualities of experience, sensation, pain or feeling come in degrees, and that even inorganic systems may have, eventually to very small degrees, such qualities." "The Biosemiotics of Emergent Properties," Emmeche, quoted in *Integral Ecology,* Esbjorn-Hargens and Zimmerman.

| 8 |

Collective Violence

Figure 8.1 Riot in Vancouver, 2011[1]

There is recognition that none of us is immune to the same dynamics and structures that lie behind the worst violence we can imagine. But there is also an invitation to victims and perpetrators to join in the quest for a healing path, and an unfailing passion to search out the human worth of everyone.

–Desmond Tutu[2]

The dynamics that create and sustain collective systems of violence are different from those for interpersonal violence. Social forms of violence are emergent and self-organizing. They do not necessarily arise from any singular cause; nor can I predict any definitive outcomes. However, the underlying group dynamics can be understood. Patterns are discernable.

Collective violence arises through the nexus-agency of the group. These systems of violence hook into the unintegrated Warriors within each of us. Collective forms of violence sweep us into them so that we become active agents of violence, often to the point where it seems like the only choice we have. In Jungian terms, unintegrated archetypal energy builds like pressure in the collective. At a certain point, these repressed energies become stronger than the individual wills of the members of the group. When this happens, a mob forms. Mobs have their own mentality, acting out the shadows of the collective unconscious:

As soon as people get together in masses and submerge the individual, the shadow is mobilized, and, as history shows, may even be personified and incarnated.

–Carl Jung[3]

The first step in meaningful action toward collective violence is understanding. It is only by understanding how these social forces incite violent behavior that I become free to make a new choice.

To me, the biggest problem is that by not being able to see the broader picture and how all struggles are interrelated, people in social movements do not seem to be able to come together to effectively organize against oppression and for fundamental social change.

–Raúl Rosado[4]

In this chapter I'll begin by examining how sociocultural holons and power enact collective forms of violence. I'll discuss how *group identity needs* motivate violence. Then, I'll cover specific types of collective violence: mimetic systems, scapegoating and hazing, oppression, and ecological violence.

One challenge with this topic is that these systems involve identities, cultures, and politics which I identify with (or against), making this discussion both personal and potentially triggering. Because I'm looking at patterns of relationships, these power structures may be either invisible where I identify with a privileged group or internalized where I identify with a marginalized group. In general, my participation in the system makes it difficult for me to see the system without bias.

How Sociocultural Holons Enact Violence

Sociocultural holons are complex. Each paradigm's social holons discussed in the prior chapter include individuals, one or more social identity groups, and one or more institutions. For example, the British colonial empire included British citizens and individuals acting on Britain's behalf throughout the colonies, all the various social groups within British culture, and countless institutions spanning commerce, military, religion, and governance.

Collective violence can happen at any scale, from bullying dynamics in a middle-school playground up to world wars. However, the most sweeping forms of violence are enacted by the social holons with the most power. These social holons pursue their own interests utilizing the forms of social power that are available to them. When the interests of two power-wielding sociocultural holons conflict, violence often ensues. As I mentioned in the prior chapter, a key insight of Hans Morgenthau was that the nexus-agency of nation-states (and more generally, sociocultural holons) pursues its own interests amorally. These entities will utilize overt and systemic forms of violence to win power. They will also pursue power for its own sake. And by holding power, they legitimate the use of violence on their behalf.

Each type of social power in the first-tier paradigms has the potential to be used for violence. Military power can be used for war and genocide. Political power can be used for oppression. Informational power can be used for propaganda, and so on. Sometimes the definitions become blurry or crossed, for example in a *junta*, the military institution assumes political power. For each type of power in the table below, I list the paradigms and social holons that utilize it and the types of violence that result.

Type of Power	Paradigm	Sociocultural Holon	Types of Violence
Military	Mythic, modern, and postmodern	Monarchies and colonies, nation-states, and ethnonational groups	War, civil-war, genocide, terrorism, insurrection
Political	Mythic, modern, and postmodern	Monarchies, religions, nation-states, and ethnonational groups	Oppression, corruption, insurrection, colonization
Pastoral	Mythic	Organized religions	Religious war, oppression, persecution, and discrimination
Individualizing	Modern	Nation-states, corporations, and social institutions	Discipline, repression, conditioning, withholding rights and services
Techno-Economic	Modern and postmodern	Nation-states, corporations, and social institutions	Economic inequality, workforce subjugation, sanctions, monopolies
Socializing	Postmodern	All social holons	Conditioning, oppression
Informational	Postmodern	Media institutions and particularly social networks	Propaganda, character assassination, canceling, oppression
Organicity	Integral	Potentially all social holons, all paradigms	Not applicable
Kaizen	Integral	Potentially all social holons, all paradigms	Not applicable
Semiotics	Integral	Integral & post-integral social holons	Not applicable

Figure 8.2 Social powers, paradigms, holons, and types of violence

First-tier forms of social power are frequently used to create collective forms of violence. The myriad types of power correspond with a diversity of violence that spans increasing levels of complexity.

Some violence is overt and physical. Other forms of violence are systemic and therefore more difficult to discern. For example, societies with high levels of economic inequality have measurable differences in health, happiness, and life expectancy along the wealth gradient between the poor, middle class, upper class, and the very rich.[5] This is true even in developed countries where most of the population have all basic needs met. As Michael Marmot argues in the quote below, people with more wealth are healthier and live longer. This is not due to basic needs, but rather to social opportunity. Because poorer people die younger and are less healthy, wealth disparity is considered a systemic form of violence.

The higher the status in the pecking order, the healthier [people] are likely to be. In other words, health follows a social gradient. I call this the status syndrome... For people above a threshold of material well-being, another kind of well-being is central. Autonomy—how much control you have over your life—and the opportunities you have for full social engagement and participation are crucial for health, well-being, and longevity. It is inequality in these that plays a big part in producing the social gradient in health. Degrees of control and participation underlie the status syndrome.

—Michael Marmot[6]

Beyond the status syndrome within developed countries, economic inequality also operates between developed and developing countries, between transnational corporations and laborers, and between men and women.

The most pervasive form of violence in capitalism, however, is the structural violence exercised by economic coercion. On the one hand, debt and Structural Adjustment Programs are excellent examples of such coercion exercised over entire peoples and nations. On a more general level, capitalism uses the unequal division of labor as a structure for appropriating wealth. Wage laborers are paid less than the value they create, thus allowing for capital accumulation. The exploitation of both women and ecosystems is greater still because their contribution to the economy is simply not recognized (it is kept invisible, for instance, by indicators such as GDP).

—Hathaway and Boff[7]

Economic inequality and the status of wealth produce their own forms of Thanatos. The concept that the wealth gap is a form of violence requires a systems level perspective to fully understand. There is no man with a gun shooting people in overt aggression. It is the invisible, accumulated interactions of people, group identities, and institutions in which these harmful patterns emerge. This is true of all *systemic* forms of violence. One of the big gifts of the plural/postmodern paradigm is systems thinking which illuminates these forms of collective violence.

Repression and discipline are two other forms of systemic violence. These utilize individualizing power. A common example is sexuality. Sexual repression is imposed through a complex web of silence, taboo, rules (moral, legal, psychiatric, medical, etc.), and proscribed actions (again: moral, legal, psychiatric, medical, etc.). The effect is to shape and coerce the behaviors of members of a society. By way of analogy, imagine a plant attempting to grow in a volume of space that is too small. The environment restricts the realization of the fullness of the plant. Likewise, repression and discipline are forms of growth-limiting constrictions on human behavior and represent systemic forms of violence.[8]

In contrast, integral's new forms of power are inherently nonviolent. While it is true that the plural/postmodern paradigm recognizes the principle of nonviolence, becoming truly nonviolent requires an experience of the wholeness of the self and the sacredness of life. These qualities begin to come on board at integral, and become ever stronger and more thorough as we continue into high integral and beyond.

Because integral sociocultural holons do not yet fully exist in society, much of the social dynamics at integral remains speculative. But I would expect integral's virtuous processes of organicity, kaizen, and semiotics to reach downward into military, political, pastoral, and other forms of power. Integral's downward embrace would theoretically transform these systems of violence. This is the optimistic promise I am holding for the benefits of the integral paradigm.

In today's pre-integral society, sociocultural holons pursue the accumulation of many types of power. The competition to win or hold power results in the array of collective forms of violence. Simultaneously, the maintenance of power results in ongoing patterns of violence.

Now take a moment and consider the relationship between masculinities and collective forms of violence. In Western culture, men have held most leadership roles in institutions that wield social power (see Figure i in the Introduction). Men in power are the ones who are defining and shaping social systems of violence, who are committing acts of violence, and who are benefitting as a result of these power structures. Collective violence is primarily carried out by men on behalf of the narrow interests of men as a power-wielding cultural group.

> War has historically almost exclusively been undertaken by men, and still is. Because of this, both military violence and the principles of military organisation and discipline are strongly linked to masculinity. In many historical and contemporary contexts militarised masculinities have achieved or strongly contributed to political dominance.
>
> —Christensen and Rasmussen[9]

The exchange happens in both directions. Men as a cultural identity group (LL) shape institutions and social systems (LR). Simultaneously, military, political, economic, and educational institutions shape individual men (UL) and normalize these hegemonic cultural models of masculinity (LL). All of the individual factors which contribute to male violence that we explored in Chapter 6 (i.e., testosterone and challenge, the male-warrior psyche, learned violent behavior, and the social representation of masculinity) are inextricably woven together with these collective forms of violence. Later in this chapter, we'll dive deeper into the relationships between individuals, collective identities, and institutions.

Prompts for Journaling and Discussion

What types of violence are occurring in your society today? What are the corresponding types of power? Who are the sociocultural holons enacting this violence and wielding this power?

Describe how overt violence like war differs from systemic violence like economic inequality.

Group Identity Needs

Recall that in Chapter 6, I identified individual needs as drivers for violence. When my needs are not met, I feel strong emotions and become motivated to take drastic action. The reciprocal is also true: when I commit an act of violence, it either removes a current need or blocks access to higher-order needs from being satisfied for the target of the act. Unmet needs motivate violence, and violence keeps relational systems small.

Groups of humans have needs in a similar way that individuals have needs. However, group needs are about *identity*, so I'll call these *group identity needs*. When a group identity need is threatened or destroyed, it motivates groups of people into collective acts of violence.

> Deep-rooted conflict is about identity: the beliefs, values, culture, spirituality, meaning systems, relationships, history, imagination and capacity to act that form the core of an individual or group. Identity can be defined by needs, which are variously described in the literature as human identity needs, ontological needs (need relating to the nature of being), or simply human needs. The unique and particular satisfiers of human needs make up the unique and particular identity of a given individual or group. Deep-rooted conflict occurs when the most significant human needs satisfiers of a group are taken away or threatened.
>
> —Vern Redekop[10]

The types of needs for groups are universal. However, the specifics of how these needs become satisfied are unique. Groups satisfy their identity needs through *culture*. So when a group need is attacked or denied, the nexus-agency of the group registers violence toward its culture. The patterns of exchange (language, communication, shared values, etc.) constitute the sociocultural holon itself. Individual members of the group hold a merged identity with the identity of the group. So when a group need is attacked, the members register a threat to their identity. When this happens, members *will* respond on a survival level, even if this means violence.

In my model, which is adapted from Vern Redekop, there are six primary group identity needs: self-worldview, security, connectedness, recognition, deconstruction, and agency (Figure 8.3).[11] Like Maslow's hierarchy of needs for individuals, group identity needs form a ladder where lower-order needs take precedence over higher-order needs.

Agency Needs
Action, autonomy, capacity, and control over environment.

Deconstruction Needs
De-conditioning, social liberation, and anti-oppression.

Recognition Needs
Dignity, acknowledgement, appreciation, and significance.

Connectedness Needs
Community, language, customs, and relationships in society.

Security Needs
Physical and emotional safety. Housing, rights, and welfare.

Self-Worldview Needs
Basic group identity. Core sense of self and world.

Figure 8.3 Hierarchy of group identity needs

The most fundamental group identity need is a shared self-worldview.[12] Without a shared interpretation of identity and reality, there is no unifying cohesion for the group. This represents an integral interpretation of social dynamics: Worldviews define cultural holons. In the same way that physiological needs ensure the survival of an organism, the shared self-worldview is the most basic aspect of survival for a group's identity.

The next group need is for security. This includes physical and emotional security for individual members, as well as housing, rights, and welfare for the population. In addition, whatever institutions are controlled by the group are also subject to securing their ongoing existence and capacity to function.

Connectedness needs include the relational aspects of culture within the group and between other groups in society. Spaces to gather, forums to communicate, and resources for cultural expressions like art or dance are all part of this need.

Recognition needs for groups parallel esteem needs for individuals. Both are about being witnessed by others in society for the accomplishments, value creation, and contributions being made. For groups this includes a sense of dignity (both internally felt and externally validated), acknowledgement, and appreciation. Groups not only need to be connected to the larger society, they also need to be recognized for their worth by society.

Deconstruction needs fit within the plural/postmodern paradigm and represent a group's need to strip away the identities, values, and stereotypes that have accrued through history, have been imposed by other groups, or apply solely to prior levels of development. Deconstruction is the need to de-condition, and includes both social liberation and anti-oppression work.

At the top of the ladder of group needs is agency. A group needs to be able to act, to carry out its collective will, and follow its desires for self-manifestation in the world. Group agency is usually enacted through social institutions. A group's action, capacity, and self-determination are largely a function of its ability to form and manage institutions across the PESTEL spectrum.[13]

As an individual, I source aspects of my identity through my social groups. This has a number of implications. As already noted, when a group identity need is threatened or removed, each individual in the group may register that their own identity is threatened too. In addition, wherever the group exists on the developmental ladder of needs will strongly influence the position of each individual. So if a group is collectively realized in society (generally the dominant group), that opens the doorway for individuals to move up their respective developmental ladders. Conversely, if a group is at the bottom of the ladder (for example, during a genocide the group identity faces existential threat), this will strongly inhibit individuals in the group from advancing upward.

In Chapter 4, as part of my integrity work on the subject of culture, I listed my cultural affiliations across a number of group identity categories. Take a moment to flip back and revisit Figure 4.18. In the table below, for each of your identity categories, position yourself along the group needs hierarchy.

Identity Category	My Affiliation	Which group needs are fulfilled: Paradigm, Security, Connectedness, Recognition, Deconstruction & Agency?
Race		
Nationality		
Ethnicity / Ancestry		
Political Party		
Generation / Age		
Sex		
Gender		
Sexual Orientation		
Body Ability		
Mental Ability		
Class		
Education Level		
Education Focus / Major		
Professional Role		
Professional Industry		
Community		
Hobby		

Figure 8.4 Inventory of group identity needs

Filling out the chart above makes this work more than theoretical; instead, it becomes personal and immediate. Each of us carries an *intersection* of identities that have varying levels of group needs being met.

Violence impacts needs and also can be used to secure needs. This means violence often shapes identity. Take a few moments to compare the types of social violence from Figure 8.2 with the history and current situation of your social groups. For your identities where the group needs are not all met, how has violence shaped this group's position? For your identities where all the group's needs are met, how has violence contributed to that position? How have your social groups enacted violence? How have they been the targets of violence? In what ways have collective forms of violence influenced your identity and your position on the hierarchy of group identity needs in Figure 8.3?

Here is a personal example. Non-heterosexual people are eleven times more likely to be targets of violent hate crime than heterosexual people in the United States.[14] When I was in high school, a gay college student named Matthew Shepard was beaten, tortured, and left to die a hundred miles north of my home. This incident particularly impacted my sense of safety as a queer teen. I learned that if I shared my identity with the wrong people in the wrong situation, my life was on the line. From that event, I internalized that in order to be safe, I needed to hide this identity, which, in turn, impacted my recognition, connection, and agency group identity needs in this category. Even though this incident was a form of interpersonal violence, the media attention it received placed it into the collective dialogue. Matthew Shepard tragically lost his life. Countless LGBTQIAA folks, including myself, experienced an interruption to their identity as a result. Violence interrupts identity.

Here is another example. I am a psychotherapist as both a professional role and industry affiliation. This role carries a high degree of power in our society. At the extreme end, therapists hold the power to prescribe personality-altering drugs, to call police or social services to have someone institutionalized, and to testify in the court of law to influence sentencing. Beyond that, clients disclose their deepest secrets to therapists. Therapists hold the capacity to shape the inner lives and biggest decisions of their clients with their guidance. Because of this socially granted power, therapists are afforded all of their group identity needs: paradigm, safety, connectedness, recognition, and agency. By holding this group identity, I receive the benefits our society bestows to this group. People view me as an authority in certain contexts. And most importantly, none of my personal development is being hampered by my culture's relationship with this professional identity. In sharp contrast, I also identify as a sex-worker. This identity carries a significant amount of social taboo and has detracted from my personal needs being met at times.

Violence not only interrupts identity, it can be used to define identity and to continually maintain it. When an identity group is embedded in a system of violence, individuals learn that violence is a necessary part of life. Identity needs become satisfied through violence. For example, for someone in an inner-city gang, violence defines the paradigm of the group. Safety is derived from the capacity to be violent. Connection to comrades in the group happens through committing acts of violence together. Recognition is bestowed based on violence and personal agency is defined by one's capacity for violence. When violence defines identity, peace becomes impossible.

Consider the national and religious holidays that celebrate occasions of violence. These occasions honor an historical act of violence that defined the identity of a group. By celebrating the holiday each year, the violence, power-structure, and group identity are renewed within society.

In addition, people who are victims of violence may have their identity defined by the role of victimhood. My self-worldview is that of being harmed or wronged by hostile forces. Security may be met through obsessive measures for protection. I connect primarily with other victims and my need for recognition is to be seen as a victim of harm. Action is directed toward retribution for violence. When victimhood defines identity, violence is never over.

In this sense there are two identity-layers of social conditioning. I hold the group identities that society acculturates into me, and violence adds the role-based identities of victim, perpetrator, and savior from the drama triangle.

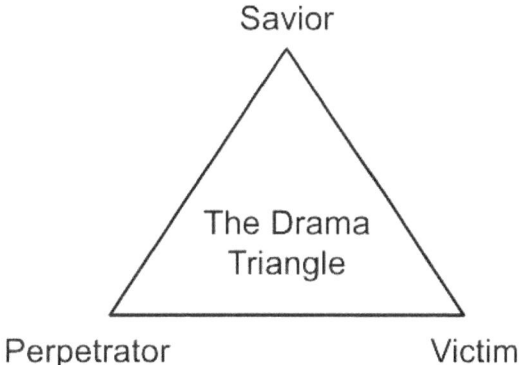

Figure 8.5 The drama triangle

In the first-tier paradigms, conditioned identity, power, and violence are mutually constituting forces. Social power is frequently established through violence by an identity group or sociocultural holon. Put another way, collective violence creates social power structures and hegemony. In addition, social power confers the *capacity* to use violence to the social groups that wield it. Group identity, power, and collective violence are mutually constituting and sustaining aspects of human society. They enroll individuals and institutions in their propagation and advancement.

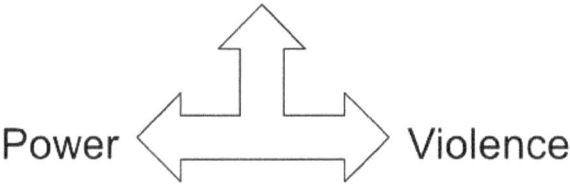

Figure 8.6 Mutual constitution of conditioned identity, power, and violence

The relationship between violence, power, and identity is perhaps the most important concept in this chapter. It provides the organizing principle to understand each type of collective violence in the sections that follow. In addition, this understanding allows me, as an individual, to redefine my relationships with social identities in order to exit these cycles of violence and become an empowered agent for peace.

Prompts for Journaling and Discussion

How has violence interrupted your identity?

How has violence defined your identity?

Make a list of holidays in your country or religion. Which of these maintain a group identity? Which of these honor an occasion of violence?

How has the experience of violence enrolled you into the drama triangle?

Mimetic Systems of Violence

Humans have the natural inclination to imitate one another. This is how culture is learned and how innovations are propagated. Our imitation also extends to desires. I see what someone else has and I want the same thing. I see someone who is successful and I want to be like them. René Girard calls this *mimetic desire*. We copy each other's desires in a mime-like way.

The value I place on an object of desire is based on my perception of how others value it. The more fully I identify with someone else, the more intensely I will imitate their desires. This imitation of desires can, and often does, lead to conflicts. When I perceive that another party desires an object, I will compete for that object. The other party may also imitate my desires mimetically. This creates a rivalry.

Instead of desiring an object, I may desire to *be* the other party—meaning the object of desire is identity. If the other party also takes on this desire, we become doubles for each other, each trying to best the other through a narcissistic fascination. Girard calls this process *mimetic doubling*. In this case the identity needs of each party are perceived to be fulfilled at the expense of the other party. The distinction between the identities of the two parties blurs and they become doubles of each other.

These types of rivalries may enter escalating feedback loops. Competition, one-upmanship, obsession, and even the destruction of the other become part of the system of mimetic desire. Although I see myself in the other party, the competition stirs an increasing level of hatred for them.

The process of imitation and escalation with desires also applies to violence, which Vern Redekop calls *mimetic systems of violence*. Any act of violence to hinder a rival in a competition will naturally be returned. When this punishment is returned *with interest*, the cycle of violence escalates. Left to our own devices, two humans or groups of humans will perpetuate rival violence, or vengeance, in a never-ending cycle. Each party believes that they must have the final word, and so the retribution passes back and forth.

The imitative character of violence is in fact most manifest in explicit violence, where it acquires a formal perfection it had not previously possessed. At the level of the blood feud, in fact, there is always only one act, murder, which is performed in the same way for the same reasons, in vengeful imitation of the preceding murder. And this imitation propagates itself by degrees. It becomes a duty for distant relatives who had nothing to do with the original act, if in fact an original act can be identified; it surpasses limits in space and time and leaves destruction everywhere in its wake; it moves from generation to generation. In such cases, in its perfection and paroxysm mimesis becomes a chain reaction of vengeance, in which human beings are constrained to the monotonous repetition of homicide.

—René Girard[15]

There are a number of factors that intensify the process of mimetic violence. When the two parties are in a closed relational system, the violence only focuses on one object or relationship. When there are no external mediators, the two parties will be more likely to escalate. This may be the case within a family system. The arms race between the U.S.A. and U.S.S.R. during the Cold War is another example, as these were the only two world superpowers.

When the two parties strongly identify with one another, the mimetic doubling becomes more intense—for example, in a sibling rivalry or in neighboring sports teams. This is also the case when the object of desire has great value, like the attention of a parent. Finally, if the other party carries social prestige, that spurs the rivalry, as with star athletes and celebrities.

Countries and ethnonational groups are just as prone to mimetic structures of violence as individuals. Groups mirror each other's desires and compete for those objects. For example, Turkey and Greece compete for control of Cyprus. Group mirroring includes desires, identity needs (and needs satisfiers), and each other's violent behaviors and attitudes. Historical violent events are reenacted, keeping the cycle alive and present. Vengeance is a cyclical pattern that plays out between rival groups. Violence not only keeps groups stuck in past victimizations and glories, it also co-opts the future: Fantasies of violence and wishing for more violence dominate the possibilities of future events.

Mimetic systems of violence lead to *entrenchment*. Violent attitudes and behaviors enter into institutional structures and become part of a society's hegemony. The production of arms and security measures become part of the economy. Individuals within systems of violence define their identities through violence, meet their group needs through violence, and become obsessed with retribution. This all leads to a curtailment of creativity, tolerance, learning, and growth. These systems become increasingly limited and stuck.

Deep-rooted conflict pulls people into mimetic structures of violence, within which they feel that they have no choice but to be violent. Violence shapes identity and tends to escalate. Objects of violence, the ones to whom violence is done, become non-persons. In the process, perpetrators of violence lose their own humanity. The violent Self becomes narcissistic, caught up in a personal woundedness and unable to see things from another perspective. Emotions drive the violence, but they are sometimes camouflaged by cool logic. People's roles are framed as adversaries. Sometimes the urge is to win, sometimes to get even, and sometimes to destroy.

—Vern Redekop[16]

Violence is limiting for everyone involved. Because violence disrupts identity, it affects the core aspects of group needs and powerfully compels individuals to act on behalf of the group. When two groups exchange violence, the identity needs of individuals in those two groups become threatened and are sometimes perceived to be mutually exclusive. The only way our people will survive is to remove these other people. The needs and identities of all parties suffer as a result.

Prompts for Journaling and Discussion

When in your life have you responded to violence with violence?

Choose one ongoing conflict that you are intimate with. How has mimetic violence contributed to this conflict?

What factors might prevent mimetic violence from escalating into mutual destruction?

Hazing and Scapegoating

Hazing and scapegoating are two collective forms of violence that are used by groups to maintain identity. In the case of hazing, identity is defined through violence, while in scapegoating, identity is preserved through violence.

Hazing uses violence to initiate new members into a group. It often involves intense trials, physical or emotional abuse, humiliation, and alcohol or other inebriants. Hazing most frequently occurs in universities, fraternities, sports teams, military units, and gangs. Hazing is most common in groups where a strong sense of identity is required, where a high degree of trust between members is necessary, or where there is strong competition to enter the group.

For new individuals, hazing bestows membership in the group. This functions similarly to a rite of passage, except instead of entering sacred space—what Victor Turner calls *liminal space*[17]—the initiate enters a warped version called *liminoid space*. Liminal spaces are transformational containers which are stewarded by ritual elders. This is where initiation happens. In sacred space, the raw power of life moves the initiate through the stages of death and rebirth, and the ritual elders understand that they cannot control the process. By contrast, hazing's liminoid space bestows identity through violence. The leaders of the group utilize power dynamics, humiliation, and aggression to shape the rite of passage.

At the level of the group, hazing reinforces the collective identity. New members of the group earn the right to wield this violence against outsiders and to re-enact the hazing ritual for the next round of recruits. The re-enactment of the violent act itself is what perpetuates the identity of the group.

Scapegoating operates differently from hazing, but is driven by similar deep features of group identity. When a group chooses to sacrifice or exile a scapegoat, the purpose is to reestablish cohesion amidst group turbulence.

> Any community that has fallen prey to violence or has been stricken by some overwhelming catastrophe hurls itself blindly into the search for a scapegoat. Its members instinctively seek an immediate and violent cure for the onslaught of unbearable violence and strive desperately to convince themselves that all their ills are the fault of a lone individual who can be easily disposed of.
>
> —René Girard[18]

Here is how a scapegoat event works. When a crisis breaks out within a group, the power structures, identities, and culture of the group become threatened. This crisis can take many forms:

a terrorist attack, an escalation of cycles of violence between members of the group, high unemployment, a pandemic, or a natural disaster. The crisis leads to chaos and to mimetic violence, escalating through cycles of vengeance and retribution without end.[19] In this sense, it is also contagious. Violence sweeps people into it and ripples throughout the whole group, threatening the existence of the group itself. Both riots and civil wars escalate through these mimetic systems of violence.

In order to break a mimetic system of violence, groups select and sacrifice a scapegoat. Paradoxically, scapegoating is a type of violence that ends violence. René Girard calls sacrificial violence *purifying*—it removes violence from a group. This is in contrast to the impure, contagious violence of vengeance.

The scapegoat must have two characteristics. First, they must be an outsider to the violence and threat facing the group. Whether the scapegoat is an animal, a person, or a group of people, they must be innocent of the present cycle of violence. Second, the scapegoat must come from a social niche which is incapable of taking revenge for the sacrificial act. This is why throughout history slaves, children, and marginal members of society were used in ritual sacrifice. Because the scapegoat is both innocent and free of the possibility of retribution, they are safe targets to receive the violence of the group and thereby end the cycle.

Figure 8.7 Azazel and the scapegoat[20]

The final crucial element is that the members of the group must fully believe in the guilt of the scapegoat and the necessity of the sacrifice.[21] There is always a mysterious element to the sacrifice, which is often attributed to religion or divine will. But on a purely social level, the belief in the guilt of the scapegoat is absolutely required in order for the act to be successful. When the mob does not fully believe the guilt of the scapegoat, then more chaos and intergroup struggle will follow.

After the scapegoat is successfully banished or sacrificed, the impure contagious violence is expelled and the group reunites in a shared identity. This restores normal power relations and peace. The sacrificial act is then mythologized by the group and potentially reenacted through rituals or holidays.

> [Sacrificing the scapegoat] is a deliberate act of collective substitution performed at the expense of the victim and absorbing all the internal tensions, feuds, and rivalries pent up within the community… [The victim] is a substitute for all the members of the community, offered up by the members themselves. The sacrifice serves to protect the entire community from its own violence; it prompts the entire community to choose victims outside itself… There is a common denominator that determines the efficacy of all sacrifices and that becomes increasingly apparent as the institution grows in vigor. This common denominator is internal violence—all the dissensions, rivalries, jealousies, and quarrels within the community that the sacrifices are designed to suppress. The purpose of the sacrifice is to restore harmony to the community, to reinforce the social fabric.
> —René Girard[22]

The use of a scapegoat is prevalent in tribes and villages in the magic/tribal paradigm. This is because primitive justice is arbitrated by individuals and is therefore prone to the runaway vengeance effect. One of the major cultural advancements of the mythic/traditional paradigm is the presence of a central authority that dispenses retributive justice. Today's criminal justice system interrupts cycles of violence by dispensing retribution in a systematic and impersonal way. Because justice and the necessary punishment has been declared by the central authority, individuals have no legitimate basis to pursue violence in the name of vengeance. The criminal justice institution replaces the scapegoat function and ensures group cohesion for post-tribal social paradigms. However, for power-wielding sociocultural holons (i.e., political groups), there is no effective criminal justice system, so runaway vengeance, like the Israel-Palestine conflict, and scapegoating, like the U.S.'s war on terror, are still prevalent collectively.

Prompts for Journaling and Discussion

Have you ever experienced hazing as either the initiate or the elder? What was it like?

In groups that use hazing, what is the relationship between identity, power, and violence?

Have you ever experienced scapegoating as either the victim or as part of the mob? What was it like?

Where in mythology or popular history do you recognize the scapegoat? How did the sacrifice bring cohesion to the group?

Oppression

We need to take that energy, that Warrior energy, that's very likely the most noble thing in the male soul and bring it into the service of an inclusive nonracist, non-sectarian, non-cultic vision about a world of justice and peace.

—Robert Moore[23]

Oppression is a systemic form of violence that operates at the societal level. Oppression permeates individuals, group identities, and institutions in complex, emergent, and interconnected patterns. As a systemic phenomenon, oppression is not held by any specific part of society and cannot be traced to any singular cause. Oppression is an ongoing process that limits the well-being and development of individuals and society as a whole. The vicious processes of oppression utilize conditioned identities, first-tier forms of power, and both systemic and overt forms of violence.

From an integral perspective, oppression is described as a complex system of systems involving and impacting all aspects, all levels, and all dimensions within the sphere of human activity. Moreover, oppression is simultaneously a process and structure that supports, aggravates, and/or gives rise to virtually all major problems in society.

—Raúl Rosado[24]

All societies create social conditioning that influences the identities of its members. Oppressive societies encode the attitudes, beliefs, norms, power dynamics, and identities of the dysfunctional system into the conditioning of its members.

In order to understand oppression, let's position it within the integral framework we've been using. In my model of self-identity, the psyche has four parts with the self situated at the center. The four quadrants correspond to the capacities for thinking, acting, feeling, and being. This mandala of the psyche is itself situated within the four-quadrant model of Integral Theory: individual interior, individual exterior, collective interior, and collective exterior (Figure 8.8). My individual exterior is my body, inclusive of my sex, skin color, and physical features. My collective interior includes the memberships and identities I share with groups of humans. And finally, my collective exterior includes all the structures and institutions of society. Institutions impart customs and norms of behavior. The two collective quadrants (LL and LR) contribute to my identity through acculturation and socialization.

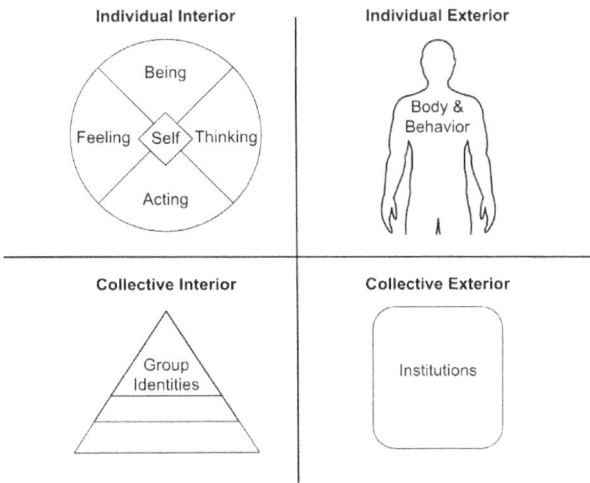

Figure 8.8 Four-quadrant model of humanity

In addition, I form my identity in relationship with other people that I'm close with. Family members, peers, and authority figures all assign identity to me through our interactions. People in my life perceive me, name me, value me, and interact with me based on their concepts of my identity. Therefore, I form my identity in partnership with all the other people in my life.

The group identities of the collective interior include race, nationality, ethnicity/ancestry, political affiliation, generation/age, sex, gender, sexual orientation, body ability, mental ability, and class. Each of these identities influences my sense of self. Importantly, these identities are not value-neutral in an oppressive society. Each identity category exists in a power dynamic with other identities: some dominant, others subordinated. In Chapter 4, I also distinguished *border identities* that don't fit neatly into either of the other power positions. In addition, each of these identity categories exists in dynamic interrelationship with each other. My personal identity across all these categories inhabits a particular social *intersection*.

The institutions of the collective exterior include political, economic, social, technological, environmental, and legal organizations and structures. Institutions define and enforce the norms of a society. They codify the way we create culture, preserve it, and carry it forward. Institutions legitimate the power dynamics that are held between identity groups. In a self-reinforcing cycle, institutions are generally led by individuals who hold dominant identities across multiple categories. Dominant groups control institutions, which normalize and enforce the dominant power position. This creates a systemic ideology of oppression (Figure 8.9).

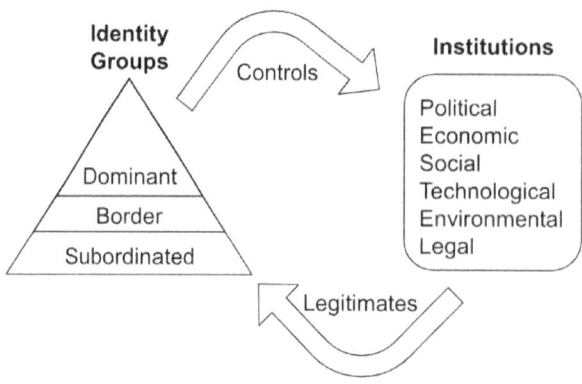

Figure 8.9 Systemic ideology of oppression

The ideology of oppression includes all the -*isms* that are generated by identity groups (racism, classism, ableism, sexism, etc.) together with all of the structural powers wielded by institutions (laws, norms, repression, discipline, political discourse, access to economic and educational opportunities, etc.). This is the systemic nexus of knowledge and power.

The effect is that individuals in the dominant groups are systemically privileged while individuals in the subordinated groups face discrimination. The ideology of oppression influences not only how individuals are able to act within society, it influences each person's identity. Individuals internalize the limiting norms, beliefs, behaviors, and identities from oppressive societies. This is known as the *internalization of oppression* within a *culture of imposition*. Internalization acts upon the four quadrants of the psyche: Beingness is supplanted by conditioned identities; the intellect takes on limiting beliefs about self and others; actions become strategies to fulfill unmet needs (known as character strategies); and the capacity to feel is impaired by trauma and attachment wounding, which in turn produce strong emotions. All of these effects limit the natural self in its capacities for well-being and growth.

Isabel Wilkerson uses the term *caste* to refer to the ideology of oppression.

> The social pyramid known as a caste system is not identical to the cast in a play, though the similarity in the two words hints at a tantalizing intersection. When we are cast into roles, we are not ourselves. We are not supposed to be ourselves. We are performing based on our place in the production, not necessarily on who we are inside.
> —Isabel Wilkerson[25]

Wilkerson outlines eight cultural pillars which create and sustain the social hierarchy of caste: (1) Dominant groups hold their position due to divine will, mythology, tradition, the natural order, or an external authority which has decreed the power hierarchy; (2) members of each group are born into it (race, class, gender, ethnicity, etc.) and hold that social group for life; (3)

endogamy, which means restricting marriage to people within the same social identity group, keeps people, resources, and identity separate; (4) the culture holds a belief that the dominant groups are pure while subordinated groups are polluted; (5) each group holds defined occupations; (6) subordinated groups are dehumanized, degraded, and humiliated to justify their place at the bottom of the hierarchy; (7) violence, terror, and cruelty are used for enforcement and control of the social order; and (8) the culture propagates beliefs in the inherent superiority of the dominant group and inherent inferiority of the subordinated groups. These eight pillars work together in an interlocking mesh between group identities and social institutions to maintain the caste system, or ideology of oppression.

Divine Will and the Laws of Nature	Caste is decreed by myth, tradition, and natural order
Heritability	People are assigned their position at birth and cannot change it
Endogamy and the Control of Mating	People can only marry and mate with those of the same group
Purity versus Pollution	The dominant group is clean and the subordinated groups are dirty
Occupational Hierarchy	Each group holds defined professional roles
Dehumanization and Stigma	Subordinated groups are less-than-human
Terror and Cruelty	Violence is used for enforcement and control
Inherent Superiority versus Inferiority	Culture propagates the ideal images of beauty and worth

Figure 8.10 The eight pillars of caste[26]

In the table below, fill out the cultural narratives you have received about men's dominant position and women and trans-folks' subordinated positions in our society. The focus is not on what you believe, but what stories our culture holds—for example, "Men are supposed to . . . and women are supposed to . . ."

Pillar of Caste	Narratives for men, women, and trans-folks
Divine Will and the Laws of Nature	
Heritability	
Endogamy and the Control of Mating	
Purity versus Pollution	
Occupational Hierarchy	
Dehumanization and Stigma	
Terror and Cruelty	
Inherent Superiority versus Inferiority	

Figure 8.11 Inventory of gender hierarchy narratives

In addition, systems of oppression interact with group identity needs. Satisfiers of group needs for subordinated identities are limited by oppressive systems. Subordinated groups generally have less agency, are recognized through negative stereotypes that they are unable to deconstruct, are disconnected from land, heritage, and organic sources of empowerment, face threats to security, and have their cultural self-worldview imposed upon by the dominant group. Dominant groups are also impacted by distorted, exaggerated, and inflated satisfiers of group needs. Members of dominant groups learn to source their needs through the existing power structure. For example, the upper class meets its material needs by subjugating a low-wage working class. Although sometimes less obvious, dominant group members are also negatively affected by the culture of imposition. And because just about every member of society carries both dominant and subordinated identity categories, this system negatively impacts everyone.

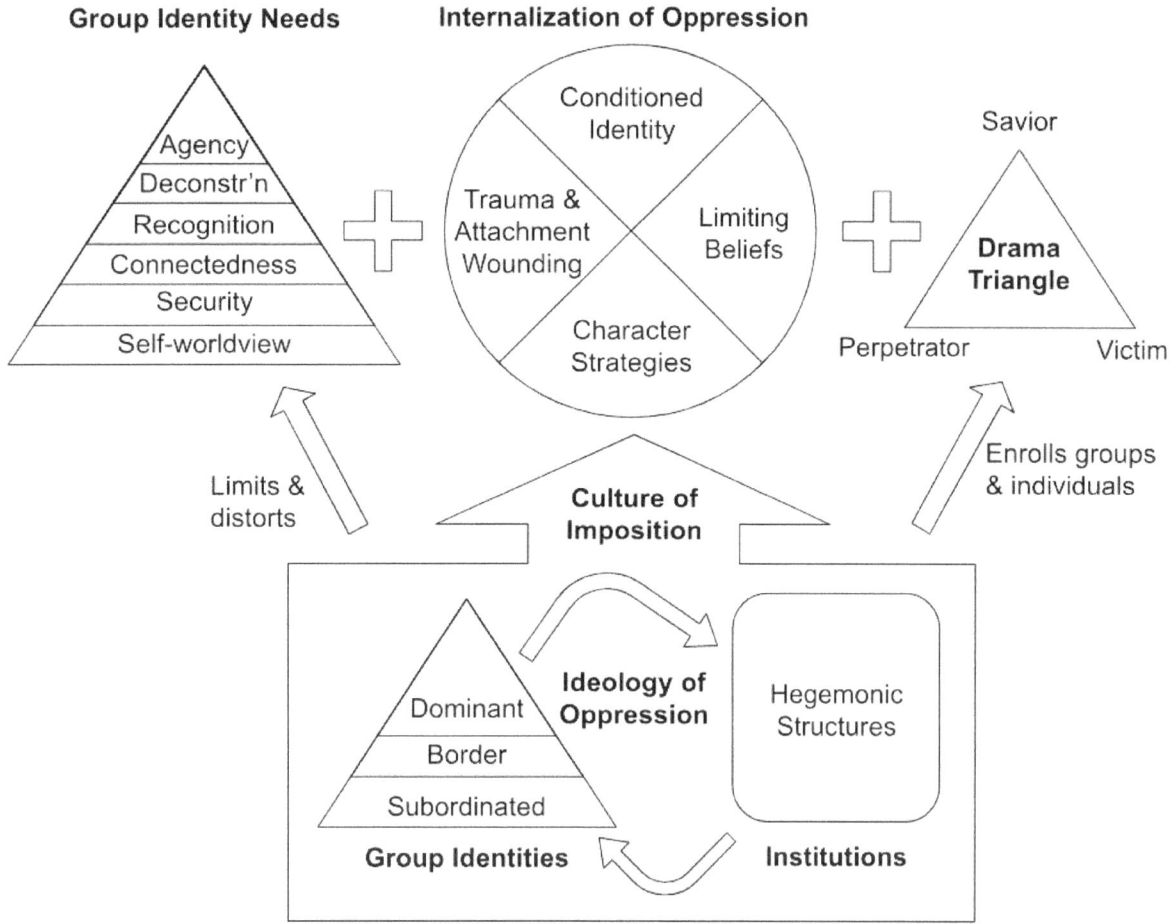

Figure 8.12 Culture of Imposition and the Internalization of Oppression

The oppressive culture imposes conditioned identities onto individuals. Because these identities are limited, warped, and ultimately disempowered in both dominant and subordinated positions, this conditioning also naturally enrolls individuals and groups into the role-based identities of the drama triangle: victim, perpetrator, and savior. It is interesting to note that an individual may internally identify with one role, while other individuals simultaneously hold that individual in a different role. For example, through the lens of white fragility, I may experience myself as a victim of cancel culture.[27] Another individual may view me as a hegemonic oppressor—a perpetrator. Yet another individual may view me as a white savior. Whenever I am viewing myself or another through one of the roles of the drama triangle, true empowerment as well as genuine forgiveness and healing remain impossible to reach. These role-based identities feed back into the collective power dynamics of dominant and subordinated groups and become institutionalized in social systems.

Members of both dominant and subordinated groups internalize oppression, which maintains the system.[28] However, the ways the two groups internalize oppression is different.

Subordinated members who are in acceptance of systems of oppression will internalize a sense of inferiority. These individuals assimilate the oppressive ideology and then collude with the system. Rosado describes a psychological downward spiral from internalized inferiority that moves "from a sense of invisibility to confusion to doubt to pain to shame to anger to despair to powerlessness to passiveness to helplessness to apathy to cynicism to hopelessness to emotional numbness to self-hate to self-destructiveness."[29] These traits may not be experienced linearly and may loop back around on each other. But the point is that oppressive systems debilitate individuals. They warp and collapse the healthy psyche, prevent access to the satisfiers of group identity needs, and enroll individuals into the drama triangle.

In contrast, members of dominant groups internalize a false sense of *superiority*. The systemic patterns that develop together with internalized superiority are social privileges that maintain a dominant position of power, i.e., *hegemony*. It is important to recognize that superiority and privilege are still internalizations of systems of oppression. Conditioned superiority exists hand-in-hand with conditioned inferiority. So even though members of dominant groups may be more capable or resourced, they have still been indoctrinated by the limiting culture of imposition.

The integral lens takes even wider views: of the entire society, of humanity as a species, and of the living planetary system. Within these contexts, oppression can be understood as a self-perpetuating social process which hinders not just specific groups of humans, but the well-being and development of these larger systems as a whole. Oppression is a collective form of violence that all members of society are enacting upon themselves and each other.

Prompts for Journaling and Discussion

Select one subordinated group that you feel connected to or identify with. How does oppression limit this group?

Select one dominant group that you feel connected to or identify with. How does oppression benefit this group? How does it limit this group?

Choose one dominant identity group. What is the cultural ideology of oppression for this category, including values, myths, and beliefs? What attributes mark this group as dominant? How do institutions reinforce that power dynamic?

Ecological Violence

Over the last 150 years, humanity as a species and Western civilization in particular has destroyed a significant portion of life on this planet. This sixth planetary extinction is now being called the *anthropocene extinction event*.[30] Humanity's destruction of ecosystems, biodiversity, and habitat is its own form of collective violence.

Let's examine the scope of ecological violence. When scientists consider the planet as a homeostatic ecological system, they identify nine distinct self-regulating processes that humans are impacting. These processes each have a tolerance boundary that our planet is able to absorb. Beyond these boundaries, humanity is causing harm—ecological violence—to the living systems that sustain us. The planetary boundaries model considers human impacts on ecosystem integrity through a system's lens. Each individual driver interacts with all the others in emergent, nonlinear ways. We need to consider the biosphere as a dynamic whole in order to accurately understand our impacts.[31]

The Planetary Boundaries framework measures nine drivers, illustrated in Figure 8.13. *Biosphere integrity* is measured across genetic diversity, which includes extinction rates, and the human appropriation of the biosphere's net primary production. This driver measures the capacity of ecosystems and human systems to maintain themselves, reproduce, differentiate, network, and grow. Both in terms of biodiversity and production, humanity has strongly breached the earth's safe operating space.

Climate change is measured in the concentration of atmospheric carbon dioxide, which was 417 ppm in 2022, well beyond the scientifically established minimum of 350 ppm to keep warming under 1.5 degrees celsius. It is also measured by radiative forcing, which is the balance of thermal energy that the earth's atmosphere retains: 2.91 w/m^2 in 2022 versus the ideal target of 1 w/m^2.

Novel entities refers to any synthetic or man-made materials that are being introduced into the environment. These include plastics, styrofoam, pharmaceutical chemicals, nuclear waste, and myriad other materials that are foreign to natural habitats.

Stratospheric ozone depletion measures the concentrations of substances that deplete the ozone layer. Thanks to the 1987 Montreal Protocol, these emissions are within planetary boundaries.

Atmospheric aerosol loading refers to particulate matter like dust from deserts and soot from wildfires. These emissions are also within the safe operating space today.

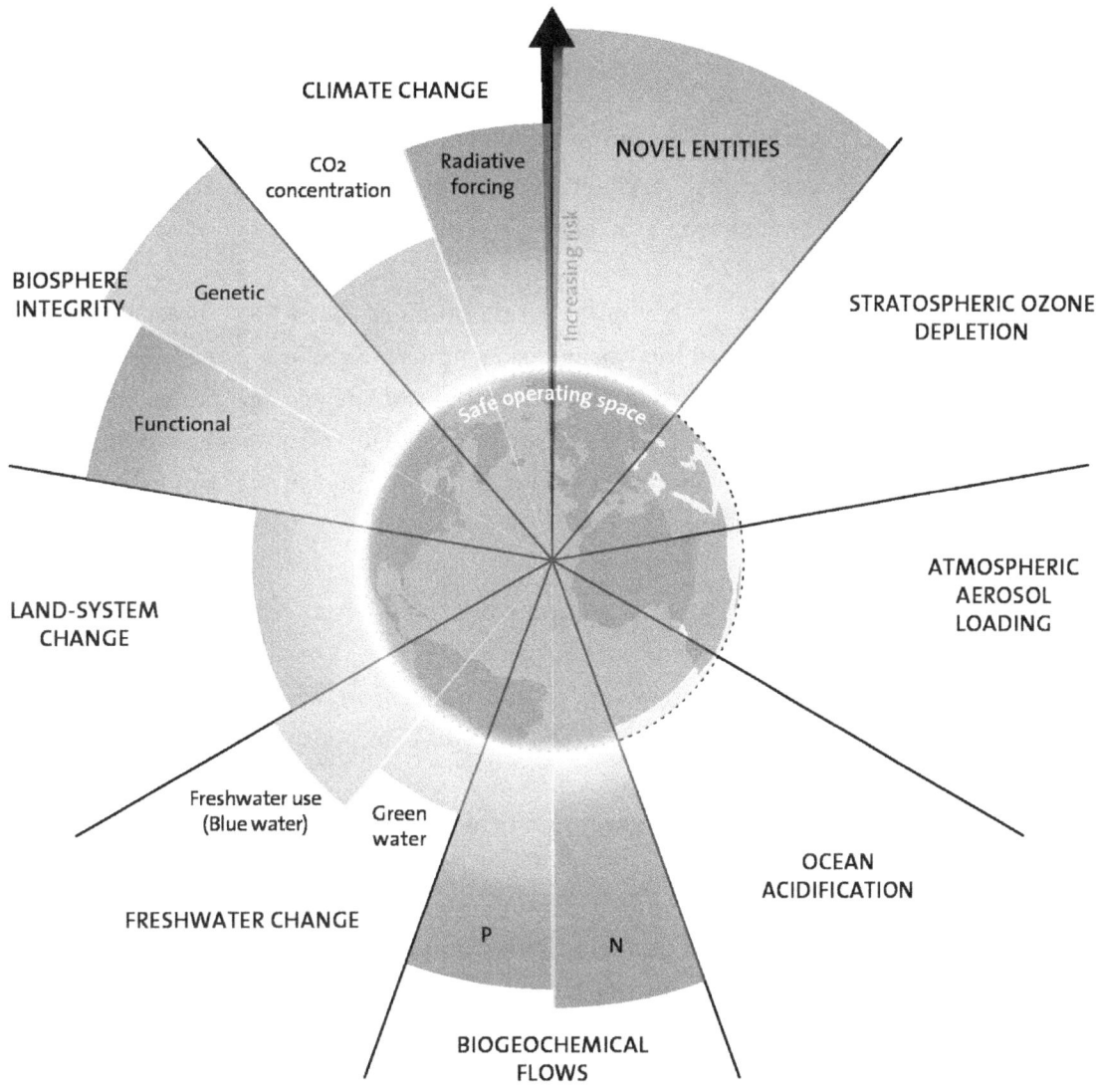

Figure 8.13 2023 Planetary Boundaries[32]

Ocean acidification occurs as carbon dioxide emissions rise and oceans dissolve the gas into carbonic acid. This effect deteriorates the shells of marine life like corals and mollusks. At present, acidification is near the boundary of the ocean's capacity, but increasing atmospheric carbon dioxide is threatening to breach it.

Biogeochemical flows measure the disruption of phosphorus and nitrogen through agricultural and industrial processes. In particular, this refers to the use of chemical fertilizers which run off into wetlands and oceans. At present, both of these flows are well beyond the planetary boundary.

Freshwater change measures human impacts on water systems. Blue water use includes stream flows, surface freshwater, and groundwater. Green water refers to "root-zone soil moisture," or the fresh water that is available to plants. All of our impacts on freshwater flows are outside the safe operating space.

Finally, *land-system change* refers to the amount of land that is wild forest versus habitat that has been converted to human development, agriculture, or lost to wildfires or desertification. Globally, we are destroying forests at a rate beyond the planetary boundary.

Today, six of the nine drivers are beyond our safe boundaries. In these breached categories, the drivers continue to move toward increasing risk. Importantly, these categories interact with each other in systemic ways. So, for example, increasing climate change causes more extreme heat events which increases wildfires. This increases aerosol loading and negatively impacts land-system changes, which in turn degrades biosphere integrity. No single driver can be understood or addressed in isolation from the others.

The planetary boundaries model gives us a framework to understand the large-scale, collective-level, physical impacts that humanity is having on the planet. On the surface, the causes of this violence are straightforward: A growing human population with rising levels of material consumption has led to increasing resource extraction and a commensurate increase in waste.

The four quadrants of the integral framework provide a structure to understand ecological violence on an even more comprehensive level. The first quadrant is individual interior, which corresponds to the ecopsychology, or more accurately ecopathology, of how individuals participate in and are affected by ecological violence. The second quadrant is the individual exterior, which includes behaviors of individuals and how we physically interact with ecosystems. The third quadrant is the collective interior, which describes how culture organizes around ecological violence. And the fourth quadrant holds the impacts of the planetary boundaries together with all of humanity's institutional systems that are driving these impacts.

> We feel that the AQAL framework provides a powerful analysis of the many currents involved in creating, perpetuating, and responding to our historical and contemporaneous environmental crises. Integral Ecology highlights that any anthropogenic ecological crisis is the result of a complex tetra-mesh of the 4 terrains and their various levels of complexities. Thus, any crisis is the result of a complex and unique mixture of fractured consciousness, unsustainable behaviors, dysfunctional cultures, and broken systems. To identify only one or a couple of these contributing factors and hold them up as the main culprit will not help anyone to effectively address these crises.
> —Esbjorn-Hargens and Zimmerman[33]

Having outlined the outward systemic violence of the lower right quadrant through the Planetary Boundaries Model, now let's explore ecological violence through the other three quadrants.

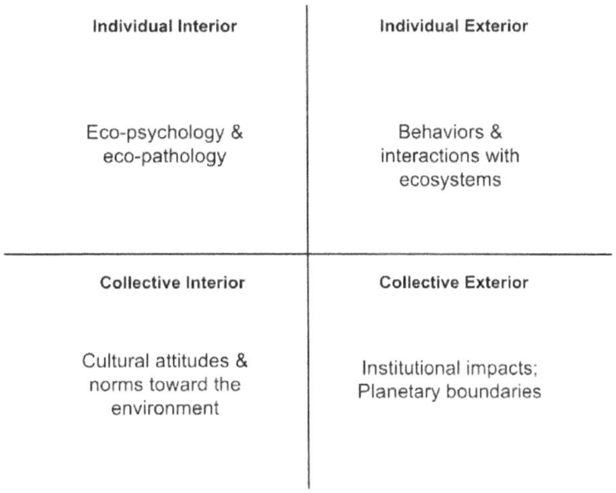

Individual Interior	Individual Exterior
Eco-psychology & eco-pathology	Behaviors & interactions with ecosystems
Collective Interior	**Collective Exterior**
Cultural attitudes & norms toward the environment	Institutional impacts; Planetary boundaries

Figure 8.14 Four-quadrant model of ecological violence

At the individual interior level, I am both an agent of ecological violence and suffer harm as a result. The core internal experience is disconnection. My modern lifestyle has insulated me from the rhythms of nature. This process of disconnection has been developing through successive generations over the last ten thousand years. I am disconnected from the beauty and abundance of nature. At the same time, I'm disconnected from the places where harm is being caused: I'm not exposed to the strip mines or deforestation or pacific trash gyres. In addition, the impacts on nature are happening slow enough that it's challenging to recognize. Each year, the fish are a little smaller and fewer, and the forests are a little drier. On a geological timescale, this change is happening incredibly quickly, but on a human timescale it's almost invisible. All of these factors contribute to my disconnection from the natural world. For most of our history, humans were not only immersed in nature, we *were* nature. Today, "nature" is a place I go to visit for recreation.

My psychological disconnection from nature then causes a whole host of other distortions and coping mechanisms, illustrated below.

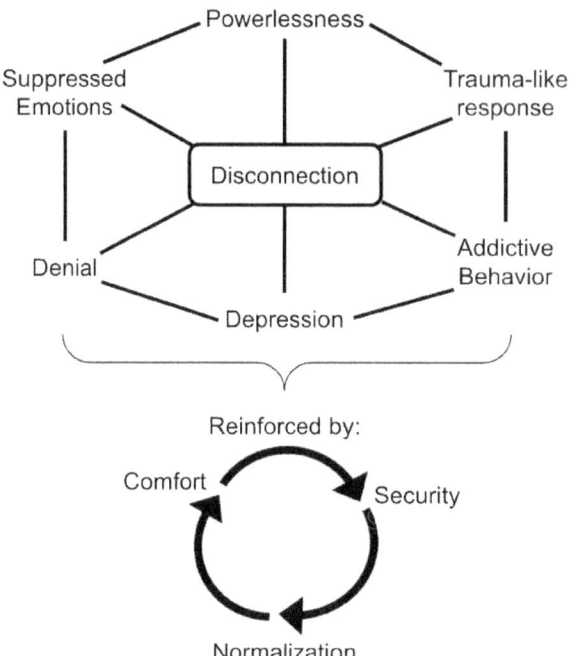

Figure 8.15 Web of disconnection and cycle of continuation

My psychological disconnection from both the gifts of nature and the harm that I am participating in contributes to powerlessness, suppressed emotions, trauma-like responses, addictive behavior, denial, and acceptance of the status quo. This forms a web of maladaptive pathology that I get stuck in. The web of disconnection is reinforced by my comfort, perceived security, and the normalization that this is *the way things are*. My ego's first priority in selecting between options will be to choose what is familiar. These three factors, comfort, security, and normalization, keep me participating in the process of ecological violence, even when I'm able to recognize it's not in my best interest. Let's consider each aspect in the web of disconnection.

Powerlessness occurs as I internalize the system of ecological violence. I view the problems as so large and pervasive that there is literally nothing I can do to make a positive impact. In addition, I give precedence to securing my individual needs before working toward the collective good: "I would do more for the environment, but I need to work just to make ends meet." This powerlessness creates a belief that large-scale transformation is impossible, which becomes a self-fulfilling prophecy. I then collude with the broken system.

> Powerlessness could be defined as that which prevents us from realizing the fullness of both our power-from-within (the creative potential that serves as the basic foundation for our renewed vision) and our power-with (our ability to act in concert with others).
> —Hathaway and Boff[34]

The next node on the web is *suppressed emotions*. In the face of ecological violence, I will suppress both my challenging emotions like pain, grief, fear, and anger, as well as the more pleasurable ones like joy and awe. I see the state of what's happening to the planet and my natural response would be to *feel*. The natural world is undergoing a mass death event. The pain that I feel is a sign of my connection with the suffering of the world. However, I habitually suppress these emotions, manage my state, and distract myself. The more I cut myself off from feeling, the more of my lifeforce I *disconnect* from. By suppressing the challenging emotions, I also limit my capacity to feel the positive emotions. It is natural to grieve for the earth, to be angry about what's happening, to fear for future generations, and to feel the pain of ecological collapse. But it is equally important to enjoy the earth, to love her passionately, and to celebrate nature. Moreover, making space for these feelings is necessary in order to heal and to step out of the web of disconnection.

> What we are dealing with here is akin to the original meaning of compassion: "suffering with." It is the distress we feel on behalf of the larger whole of which we are a part… That pain is the price of consciousness in a threatened and suffering world. It is not only natural; it is an absolutely necessary component of our collective healing.
>
> —Macy and Brown[35]

The next node covers *trauma-like responses*. As a somatic therapist, I recognize a few different types of trauma. An acute trauma is a single shocking event where a person's nervous system moves outside the window of tolerance and the excess emotional energy becomes stuck in the body. Chronic trauma, on the other hand, develops through repeated exposure to a harmful stimulus or environment. Over time, chronic trauma negatively impacts a whole host of developmental processes including "emotion regulation, impulse control, attention and cognition, dissociation, interpersonal relationships, and self and relational schemas."[36] My disconnection from the natural world functions like chronic trauma. Connection with nature, plants, animals, rivers, oceans, forests, and ecosystems are regulating and relational. Without these stimuli and relationships, I become increasingly prone to the same numbing out and immobilization that is characteristic of chronic trauma.

Understanding my disconnection from nature as a trauma-like response also illuminates why I feel a draw toward the next node, addictive behavior. Addiction is a coping mechanism to avoid pain.[37] In addition to the more commonly understood forms of addiction like drug use or pornography, the ecopathology of addiction includes consumption, workaholism, and social media. These are all forms of distraction which keep me from feeling the pain of ecological violence and simultaneously further disconnect me from the natural world.[38]

Technological society's dislocation from the only home we have ever known is a traumatic event that has occurred over generations, and that occurs again in each of our childhoods and in our daily lives. In the face of such a breach, symptoms of traumatic stress are no longer the rare event caused by a freak accident or battering weather, but the stuff of every man and woman's daily life. As human life comes to be structured increasingly by mechanistic means, the psyche restructures itself to survive. The technological construct erodes primary sources of satisfaction once found routinely in life in the wilds, such as physical nourishment, vital community, fresh food, continuity between work and meaning, unhindered participation in life experiences, personal choices, community decisions, and spiritual connection with the natural world. These are the needs we were born to have satisfied. In the absence of these we will not be healthy. In their absence, bereft and in shock, the psyche finds some temporary satisfaction in pursuing secondary sources like drugs, violence, sex, material possessions, and machines. While these stimulants may satisfy in the moment, they can never truly fulfill primary needs. And so the addictive process is born.

—Chellis Glendinning[39]

The next aspect of the web of disconnection is *denial.* At the extreme end, this manifests as outright negation of the scientific community's consensus about humanity's harmful impacts. On a more subtle level, I find myself holding a cognitive dissonance about this crisis. It's too much to be present to. So I focus on other things and push my awareness of ecological violence into the background. Again, this has two effects: It allows me to continue to participate in, and benefit from, our exploitation of ecosystems, and it further isolates me from the natural world, which embeds me deeper into the web of disconnection.

The same psychological defenses, distortions, and inauthenticies that contribute *to* global crises may also result *from* them. For as stresses mount, so also does the temptation to resort to defensiveness and inauthenticity. Yet denial, repression, or other defenses are always purchased at the cost of our full potential and humanity. When we distort our image of the world we distort our image of ourselves. When we fear to look out at the world we fear to look into ourselves. Therefore we remain unaware of the powers of potential that lie within us and are us; the powers of potential that are the major resources we have to offer to the world.

—Roger Walsh[40]

Although this model is by no means exhaustive, the final node on my web of disconnection is *depression.* Today, the World Health Organization ranks depression as the single largest contributor to disability.[41] Depression is a complex mental health process that frequently interconnects with powerlessness, suppressed emotions, trauma, addictive behaviors, and denial—every other node in the web of disconnection. Depression often goes hand in hand with anxiety, and for me, the core experience is one of despair. It is a case, not just of powerlessness, but of *hopelessness* to address the pain of the natural world and my role in it.

Use the table below to examine how each aspect of the web of disconnection and cycle of continuation may contribute to ecological violence and how they may be reinforced by your psychological experience of ecological violence.

Aspect	How it contributes to eco-logical violence	How it is caused by ecological violence
Disconnection		
Powerlessness		
Suppressed emotions		
Trauma-like response		
Denial		
Addictive behavior		
Depression (& anxiety)		
Comfort		
Safety		
Normalization		

Figure 8.16 Inventory of eco-pathology

Each of the traits in the web of disconnection is linked with all the others. In addition, they all feed into the cycle of continuation (comfort, security, and normalization), which keeps the dysfunctional process entrenched in my psyche. These psychological forms of suffering are then complexly linked with the other three quadrants in the integral matrix: my individual behaviors, our cultural adaptations, and our collective physical impacts.

Let's now turn to the upper right quadrant, which holds my individual physical experience of ecological violence. This comes in two flavors. The first are my behaviors that directly harm ecosystems—for example, littering or driving a gas-powered vehicle. These are physical interactions between myself as an individual and the environment.

The second aspect of the individual exterior quadrant is the time I spend isolated from ecosystems. The more time I spend indoors, or in suburban or urban built environments, the less physical visceral connection I make with the green spaces. A quick note here: Because humans are inherently part of nature and everything that we create is therefore also natural, it's not strictly accurate to hold the dichotomy of built environments versus nature—it's all nature, and we are all nature. But the underlying point is that living ecosystems with a diversity of species impart richer connections for me as an organism than urban concrete-scapes. The physical aspect of disconnection from ecosystems mirrors the psychological experience of disconnection.

> How can we revere the living world if we can no longer hear the bird song through the noise of traffic, or smell the sweetness of fresh air? How can we wonder about God and the Universe if we never see the stars because of the city lights? If you think this is an exaggeration, think back to when you last lay in a meadow in the sunshine and smelt the fragrant thyme and heard and saw the larks soaring and singing. Think back to the last night you looked up into the deep blue black of a sky clear enough to see the Milky Way, the congregation of stars, our Galaxy.
>
> —James Lovelock[42]

But the impacts of physical isolation flow in two directions. Yes, I cut myself off from the life-giving wisdom of the natural world—but I also deprive nature from my presence. The natural world benefits from human engagement when we show up in reciprocity. Robin Wall Kimmerer poses the question, "Do you think the earth loves you back?" This is what creating a relationship means. I love the plants, animals, stars, and earth; and they love me in return. I steward them, and they provide for me. When I isolate myself, I disconnect from this cycle of mutual support and care.

Knowing that you love the earth changes you, activates you to defend and protect and celebrate. But when you feel that the earth loves you in return, that feeling transforms the relationship from a one-way street into a sacred bond.

—Robin Wall Kimmerer[43]

The final quadrant in this inventory is the lower left, collective interior. This quadrant holds the cultural beliefs, attitudes, and identities toward ecological violence, as well as cultural responses to the ongoing harm. In the West, we hold a worldview that contributes to ecological violence. Joanna Macy and Molly Brown call it the Industrial Growth Society.[44] David Korten calls it Empire.[45] Mark Hathaway and Leonardo Boff call it a Cosmology of Domination:

The vacuum of meaning inherent in the mechanistic worldview, together with the quest of science to control nature, led to the formulation of what we might call the first "surrogate cosmology." Living in a dead and hostile universe, humanity would find its purpose in improving its own living conditions by accumulating wealth and working for social and economic "progress." In time, these goals were largely combined into the pursuit of economic "growth."

—Hathaway and Boff[46]

I could say the techno-economic activity of the mental/modern paradigm is propagating most of the ecological violence throughout the world today. But this paradigm does not act alone. It is supported by the mythic/traditional paradigm, which is where the largest number of humans reside today, and in turn it supports the plural/postmodern and integral paradigms. All paradigms of globalized society are engaging in ecological violence.

Similar to the eco-pathologies of individual interiors, our culture suffers through disconnection. It can be called a collective-level forgetting.[47] I think my lifestyle is normal. I don't recognize that how I'm living today is vastly different from how humans lived in the past.

We as a species are suffering from a kind of *collective amnesia*. We have forgotten something our ancestors once knew and practiced - certain attitudes and kinds of perception, an ability to empathize and identify with nonhuman life, respect for the mysterious, and humility in relationship to the infinite complexities of the natural world.

—Ralph Metzner[48]

This amnesia is actually a double forgetting. My culture forgot how to connect with nature, and then we forgot that we forgot. Today's patterns seem so normal that I don't even understand that I'm missing these vital connections.[49]

I trace this back to two splits. The first is the domestication of humans that began with the mythic/traditional paradigm. This is where we separated ourselves from the wildness of the natural world and began to create civilization. We tamed plants and animals and in the process became tame ourselves.

The second split began with the mental/modern paradigm, articulated by Descartes' separation of mind and matter. My ego believes itself to be separate from my body and the material world. Both of these *disconnections* require a remembering in order to heal. *Re-member* means to re-embody the wholeness that I am. My conceptual mind is coextensive with my body and my body is coextensive with the earth. But instead, I live in a society that acculturates this double-separation: mind is separate from body, and body is separate from nature. Our culture has forgotten that anything could be different and normalizes this disconnected lifestyle.

Another way to understand our collective violence toward the biosphere stems from the perspective that Western civilization is an archetypal adolescent. Collectively, we are behaving as heroic egos in competition with each other to accrue wealth and glory. The men in our culture aggressively position themselves to secure resources and mating opportunities. This pathological adolescence is then magnified through our power-wielding sociocultural holons.

> The notion of a species-wide fixation at the stage of early adolescence fits with the kind of boisterous, arrogant pursuit of individual self-assertion that characterizes the consumerist, exploitative model of economic growth, where the short-term profit of entrepreneurs and corporate shareholders seems to be not only the dominant value, but the only value under consideration. It also fits with the aggressive and predatory militarism and emphasis on the values and ideals of male warrior cults that have characterized Western civilization since the Bronze Age.
>
> —Paul Devereux[50]

The individuals in our culture are lacking initiatory rites of passage to mature through the archetypal life-cycle. Traditionally, these rites of passage are gendered, for example: Boys become men. Initiation into adulthood doesn't happen through the other group identities like race or class. Because of this, gender holds a unique position which points to the significant role that men must play in the transformation and maturation of our culture. Rites of passage need to be a primary focus of men's work.

As individuals undergo the transformational processes of initiation into adulthood and elderhood, this will create a ripple effect for our culture and institutions. Indigenous cultures largely had (and still have) these rites of passage. Western culture has lost access to them. This again is a double-edged sword where our disconnection from the natural cycles of life has cut off our culture from maturation through the archetypal lifecycle, which in equal measure leads to our wanton destruction of the cycles of complex life. This is another example of the nexus of identity (i.e., pathological adolescence), power, and violence working in a vicious process.

In summary, ecological violence can be best understood as a process of flux across the four-quadrant field of our planetary physiosphere, biosphere, and noosphere. The dynamics in each quadrant are complex, emergent, and feed into themselves. I like to view these quadrants through the structure/pattern/process levels of complexity. Acts of violence make up the structure or content. This act is contextualized within the social and environmental patterns that produced it (the systemic level). And the present-moment interactions between structures and patterns produce a process that moves either virtuously or viciously. The processes of violence drive toward both Thanatos and Phobos. In addition, the processes of ecological violence interact with the processes of oppression and other mimetic systems of violence within human collectives.

Because these processes are self-constituting, self-sustaining, and self-reinforcing, Vern Redekop refers to them as processes of *entrenchment*. It is only by understanding these processes at the level of complexity at which they operate that I can hope to find meaningful actions toward change. It is to these opportunities that I will turn next.

Prompts for Journaling and Discussion

What is the most prominent way that you experience disconnection from and through ecological violence?

Who would you be and how would you act if you did not experience any of the aspects of the web of disconnection (Figure 8.15)?

How has culture influenced your relationship with nature—both positive and negative?

How do you love the earth? How does the earth love you?

Notes

[1] Elopede, CC SA 3.0

[2] From the introduction to *From Violence to Blessing*, Redekop.

[3] From "On the Psychology of the Trickster Figure," Carl Jung in *The Trickster: A Study In American Indian Mythology*, Radin.

[4] *Consciousness-in-Action, Toward an Integral Psychology of Liberation and Transformation.*

[5] "The gap in life expectancy between the richest 1% and poorest 1% of individuals was 14.6 years (95% CI, 14.4 to 14.8 years) for men and 10.1 years (95% CI, 9.9 to 10.3 years) for women." "The Association Between Income and Life Expectancy in the United States, 2001-2014." Chetty et al.

[6] *The Status Syndrome: How Social Standing Affects Our Health and Longevity.*

[7] *Tao of Liberation: Exploring the Ecology of Transformation.*

[8] "The disciplines of the body and the regulations of the population constituted the two poles around which the organization of power over life was deployed. The setting up, in the course of the classical age, of this great bipolar technology—anatomic and biological, individualizing and specifying, directed toward the performances of the body, with attention to the processes of life—characterized a power whose highest function was perhaps no longer to kill, but to invest life through and through. The old power of death that symbolized sovereign power was now carefully supplanted by the administration of bodies and the calculated management of life." *The History of Sexuality: An Introduction*, Foucault.

[9] *Masculinity, War and Violence.*

[10] *From Violence to Blessing.*

[11] In *From Violence to Blessing*, Redekop's five needs are: meaning, security, connectedness, recognition, and action. One notable difference is that Redekop arranges his needs in a matrix, not a hierarchy.

[12] "Worldviews are arguably the basic units of cultural analysis and interpretation—the most fundamental structures of cultural evolution." *Developmental Politics: How America Can Grow Into a Better Version of Itself*, McIntosh.

[13] PESTEL: Political, Economic, Social, Technological, Environmental, and Legal.

[14] "LGBT people experienced 6.6 violent hate crime victimizations per 1,000 persons compared with non-LGBT people's 0.6 per 1,000 persons." "Hate crimes against LGBT people: National Crime Victimization Survey, 2017-2019," Flores, et al.

[15] *Things Hidden Since the Foundation of the World.*

[16] *From Violence to Blessing.*

[17] "Liminality, marginality, and structural inferiority are conditions in which are frequently generated myths, symbols, rituals, philosophical systems, and works of art. These cultural forms provide men with a set of templates or models which are, at one level, periodical reclassifications of reality and man's relationship to society, nature, and culture." *The Ritual Process, Structure and Anti-Structure*, Turner.

[18] *Violence and the Sacred.*

[19] "Vengeance, then, is an interminable, infinitely repetitive process. Every time it turns up in some part of the community, it threatens to involve the whole social body. There is the risk that the act of vengeance will initiate a chain reaction whose consequences will quickly prove fatal to any society of modest size. The multiplication of reprisals instantaneously puts the very existence of a society in jeopardy, and that is why it is universally proscribed." *Violence and the Sacred*, Girard.

[20] Image from Collin de Plancy's Dictionnaire Infernal (Paris, 1825). "And Aaron shall lay both his hands upon the head of the live goat, and confess over him all the iniquities of the children of Israel, and all their transgressions in all their sins, putting them upon the head of the goat, and shall send him away by the hand of a fit man into the wilderness: and the goat shall bear upon him all their iniquities unto a land not inhabited: and he shall let go the goat in the wilderness." Leviticus 16:21-22

[21] "For the surrogate victim to effectively distract individuals and groups from their internal violence, they have to believe fully that the suffrage victim is guilty. This belief is confirmed when peace is restored after the scapegoat event." *From Violence to Blessing*, Redekop.

[22] *Violence and the Sacred.*

[23] 1995 address to the New Warrior Network, quoted in *The Archetype of Initiation.*

[24] *Consciousness-in-Action.*

[25] *Caste: The Origins of Our Discontents.*

[26] Derived from *Caste: The Origins of Our Discontents*, Wilkerson.

[27] "We consider a challenge to our racial worldviews as a challenge to our very identities as good, moral people. Thus, we perceive any attempt to connect us to the system of racism as an unsettling and unfair moral offense. The smallest amount of racial stress is intolerable—the mere suggestion that being white has meaning often triggers a range of defensive responses. These include emotions such as anger, fear, and guilt and behaviors such as argumentation, silence, and withdrawal from the stress-inducing situation. These responses work to reinstate white equilibrium as they repel the challenge, return our racial comfort, and maintain our dominance within the racial hierarchy. I conceptualize this process as *white fragility*. Though white fragility is triggered by discomfort and anxiety, it is born of superiority and entitlement. White fragility is not weakness per se. In fact, it is a powerful means of white racial control and the protection of white advantage." *White Fragility*, DiAngelo.

[28] "The maintenance of dominance systems also depends on the self-debilitating behaviors of subordinates. More to the point, except for extreme cases of coercion, the persistence of group-based dominance rests on the coordinated and choreographed actions of both dominants and subordinates alike." *Social Dominance: An Intergroup Theory of Social Hierarchy and Oppression*, Sidanius and Pratto.

[29] *Consciousness-in-Action.*

[30] "Around 1 million species already face extinction, many within decades, unless action is taken to reduce the intensity of drivers of biodiversity loss. Without such action, there will be a further acceleration in the global rate of species extinction, which is already at least tens to hundreds of times higher than it has averaged over the past 10 million years." "The Global Assessment Report on Biodiversity and Ecosystem Services," Intergovernmental Science-Policy Platform on Biodiversity and Ecosystem Services.

[31] "Currently, anthropogenic perturbations of the global environment are primarily addressed as if they were separate issues, e.g., climate change, biodiversity loss, or pollution. This approach, however, ignores these perturbations' nonlinear interactions and resulting aggregate effects on the overall state of Earth system. Planetary boundaries bring a scientific understanding of anthropogenic global environmental impacts into a framework that calls for considering the state of Earth system as a whole." "Earth beyond six of nine planetary boundaries," Richardson, et al.

[32] Azote for Stockholm Resilience Centre, based on analysis in Richardson et al 2023. CC BY-NC-ND 3.0

[33] *Integral Ecology.*

[34] *Tao of Liberation: Exploring the Ecology of Transformation.*

[35] *Coming Back to Life.*

[36] See *The Body Keeps the Score: Brain, Mind, and Body in the Healing of Trauma*, van der Kolk.

[37] "Not all addictions are rooted in abuse or trauma, but I do believe they can all be traced to painful experience. A hurt is at the centre of all addictive behaviours. It is present in the gambler, the Internet addict, the compulsive shopper and the workaholic. The wound may not be as deep and the ache not as excruciating, and it may even be entirely hidden—but it's there. As we'll see, the effects of early stress or adverse experiences directly shape both the psychology and the neurobiology of addiction in the brain." *In the Realm of Hungry Ghosts: Close Encounters with Addiction*, Mate.

[38] "Our inability to stop our suicidal and ecocidal behavior fits the clinical definition of addiction or compulsion: behavior that continues in spite of the individual knowing that it is destructive to self, family, work, and social relationships." "The Psychopathology of the Human-Nature Relationship," Metzner in: *Ecopsychology: restoring the earth, healing the mind*, Kanner.

[39] "Technology, Trauma, and the Wild," in *Ecopsychology : restoring the earth, healing the mind*, Kanner.

[40] *Staying alive: the psychology of human survival.*

[41] "Depression and Other Common Mental Disorders: Global Health Estimates," World Health Organization.

[42] *The ages of Gaia: a biography of our living earth.*

[43] *Braiding Sweetgrass.*

[44] "To the Industrial Growth Society, the Earth is supply house and sewer. The planet's body is not only dug up and turned into goods to sell, it is also a *sink* for the often toxic products of our industries. If we sense that the temp is accelerating, we are right - for the logic of the Industrial Growth Society is exponential, demanding not only *growth*, but rising rates of growth and market share. The logic of ever-expanding need for resources and markets is generating what is increasingly recognized as a global corporate empire, secured by military threats, interventions and occupations." *Coming Back to Life*, Macy and Brown.

[45] "Empire is a label for the hierarchical ordering of human relationships based on the principle of domination. The mentality of Empire embraces material excess for the ruling classes, honors the dominator power of death and violence, denies the feminine principle, and suppresses realization of the potentials of human maturity." *The Great Turning: From Empire to Earth Community*, Korten.

[46] *The Tao of Liberation: Exploring the Ecology of Transformation.*

[47] "The problem, then, is how to bring about a striving for harmony with land among a people many of whom have forgotten there is any such thing as land, among whom education and culture have become synonymous with landlessness." *A Sand County Almanac*, Leopold.

[48] "The Psychopathology of the Human-Nature Relationship," *Ecopsychology: restoring the earth, healing the mind.*

[49] "For a long time now we have been unable to remember our former closeness with the Earth. Due to this amnesia, the ecological problems now thrust upon us have come as a shock, unforeseen because of our condition… We notice the gradual emergence of an amnesia that is really a double forgetting, wherein a culture forgets, and then forgets that it has forgotten how to live in harmony with the planet." *Earthmind: a modern adventure in ancient wisdom*, Devereux.

[50] *Ibid.*

| 9 |

Developing Toward Sustainability

Figure 9.1 Depiction of Gaia by DALL*E

It is not a question of who has the greatest military might, but rather it is man against man, man who has put together ideologies, and these ideologies, which man has made, are against each other. Until these ideas, ideologies, end and man becomes responsible for other human beings, there cannot possibly be peace in the world.

–J. Krishnamurti[1]

At this point it is fair to ask, "Is my fate as an individual determined by the position of my social identities in my society?" Prior to undertaking any social deconditioning work, the answer is that individuals are strongly, but by no means completely, influenced by their social groups. One benefit of social deconditioning is that it liberates individuals from the worst influences of group dynamics. This work has begun in the plural/postmodern paradigm and promises to become even more emancipatory in the integral paradigm.

As I develop my Warrior more fully, he shifts from being a liability for violence to a staunch advocate for peace. For me, my Warrior battles first and foremost against my own complacency. This archetype calls me to see the truth about my situation and the world that I live in. The Warrior's dedication will not allow me to settle or to hide into my little comfortable retreat when there is injustice in the world. As Desmond Tutu famously said, regarding his fight to end apartheid in South Africa, "If you are neutral in situations of injustice, you have chosen the side of the oppressor." There can be no doubt that our world today contains an incredible amount of injustice. When the immensity of suffering in our world overwhelms me, the Warrior inspires me to show up anyway.

Having laid out the mechanisms for collective forms of violence in the prior two chapters, I will now offer a path toward peace. In order to shift my participation in mimetic and systemic forms of violence, I must form a new relationship with power and redefine my conditioned identities. Both of these undertakings are natural results of developing through the paradigms and emerging in the integral worldview. In this chapter, I'll lay out my map for how individuals develop group identities for ecology and culture through the paradigms. We'll build on this new identity framework to understand how to create virtuous processes across individuals, cultures, and institutions. Finally, I'll take a fresh look at the topic of sustainability—what it means for humanity to live sustainably on planet earth—within the context of the integral approach.

Eco-Cultural Identity

My first exploration is into *identity*. As an individual in the upper left quadrant, I hold a psychological identity: my self-sense. This self-sense develops through the paradigms of consciousness (archaic, magic, mythic, etc.). Upon closer examination, my self-sense includes multiple distinct *lines* of intelligence, each of which develops through the *levels* of the paradigms. Here are the lines that Ken Wilber has articulated:

> These different developmental lines include morals, affects, self-identity, psycho-sexuality, cognition, ideas of the good, role taking, socio-emotional capacity, creativity, altruism, several lines that can be called "spiritual" (care, openness, concern, religious faith, meditative stages), joy, communicative competence, modes of space and time, death-seizure, needs, worldviews, logico-mathematical competence, kinesthetic skills, gender identity, and empathy—to name a few of the more prominent developmental lines for which we have some empirical evidence.[2]

Some of these lines clearly occupy the upper left quadrant of individual interior experience, including cognition, meditative stages, and logico-mathematical competence. Some of these lines extend across both individual subjective experience (UL) and collective inter-subjective experience (LL), including psychosexuality, needs, communicative competence, and worldviews. These are relational intelligences that develop through cultural interactions.

My identity, my self-sense, is one such line that extends across both individual and collective domains. Clearly, part of my identity is a solo endeavor. I have an experience of myself, I know who I am, and that internal psychological "me" holds an egoic (or pre-egoic or trans-egoic) agency. But in addition, other people reflect my identity back to me, which I also use to form my self-sense. *Who I am to you* informs *who I believe myself to be*. In addition, because I think in language, and language is culturally defined, my self-sense must arise culturally within the context of my language(s).

> These ideas, values, feelings and behaviors are culturally bound to language: that through which we name and give meaning to particular images of self, or to assign value or worth, albeit always relative to other people and things; that through which, within the collective context, particular emotional charges are stimulated, neuro-linguistically associated, and triggered again and again, in relation to the aspects of our perceived "self" or "I." Therefore, the personal dimension of identity can only arise within the overall social and cultural context of the collective, if not for anything else, because language, so central to how we internally represent our self to ourselves and to others around us, is both a product and an instrument of culture.
> —Raúl Rosado[3]

My identity is therefore both a subjective individual experience and an inter-subjective collective experience.

In addition, the nexus-agency of a cultural group holds a collective identity. The Rotary Club, the United States of America, and the Roman Catholic Church are all group identities. As an individual, I hold membership within the group and share in the group identity. My group identities are either assigned or chosen through cultural affiliations. We are already familiar with these group identities in this workbook from the *cultural integrity* and *environmental integrity* sections of Chapter 4. Here they are again:

Race	Nationality	Ethnicity/Ancestry	Political Party
Generation/Age	Sex	Gender	Sexual Orientation
Body Ability	Mental Ability	Class	Education Level
Education Focus/Major	Professional Role	Professional Industry	Community
	Hobby	Environmental Identity	

Figure 9.2 Group identity categories

This list should not be taken to be exhaustive either. I assume each of these group identities to be part of "me," i.e., aspects of my self-sense. In addition, other people see me through these filters; they associate these group identities with me and project them onto me.

A key insight of Raúl Rosado is that each of the social identity categories listed above constitutes a line of development.[4] Growth through the paradigms applies to social identity. So I can now add to the purview of integral's evolutionary model: racial development, class development, gender development, and so on. My development across each line happens independently. So, for example, I could simultaneously be at plural/postmodern racially and mythic/traditional sexually.

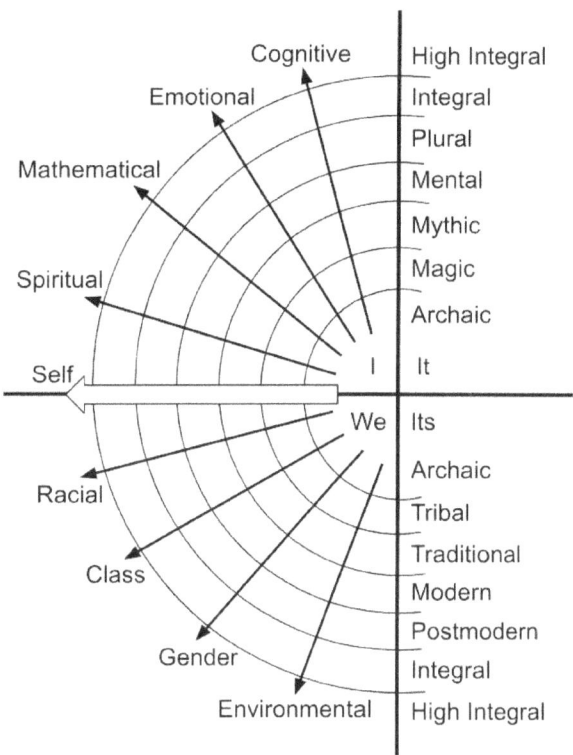

Figure 9.3 Examples of individual and group developmental lines

The figure above illustrates a handful of individual developmental lines in the upper left quadrant and a handful of group identity developmental lines in the lower left quadrant. I have psycho-spiritual intelligences in my I-space which evolve through the archaic, magic, mythic, mental, plural, integral, and high integral levels, and I have cultural intelligences in my we-space which evolve through the archaic, tribal, traditional, modern, postmodern, integral, and high integral levels. Several of these lines, including my self-sense, straddle both individual and collective dimensions. It is worth noting that although I am labeling my self-sense as a distinct developmental line, every line of intelligence contributes to my identity. Some aspects of my identity are in-born through the traits that are individual to me, and other aspects of my identity are culturally constructed, assigned, or assumed.

Now let's examine how these group identity lines progress through the paradigms of consciousness. To do so, I turn to the work of Sean Esbjorn-Hargens and Michael Zimmerman, who created a progression of ecological selves using the integral paradigms.[5] These eco-selves describe how an individual within a paradigm will hold an identity in relationship with the environment. Their map, which is presented below, draws on Susan Cook-Greuter's Ego Development Theory. Esbjorn-Hargens and Zimmerman confine their progression of selves to ecological-based identities, but in my view, this model applies equally to all group identities: race, class, nationality, ethnicity, gender, and so on. Accordingly, I have broadened the label from *eco-selves* to *eco-cultural identities* (Figure 9.4).

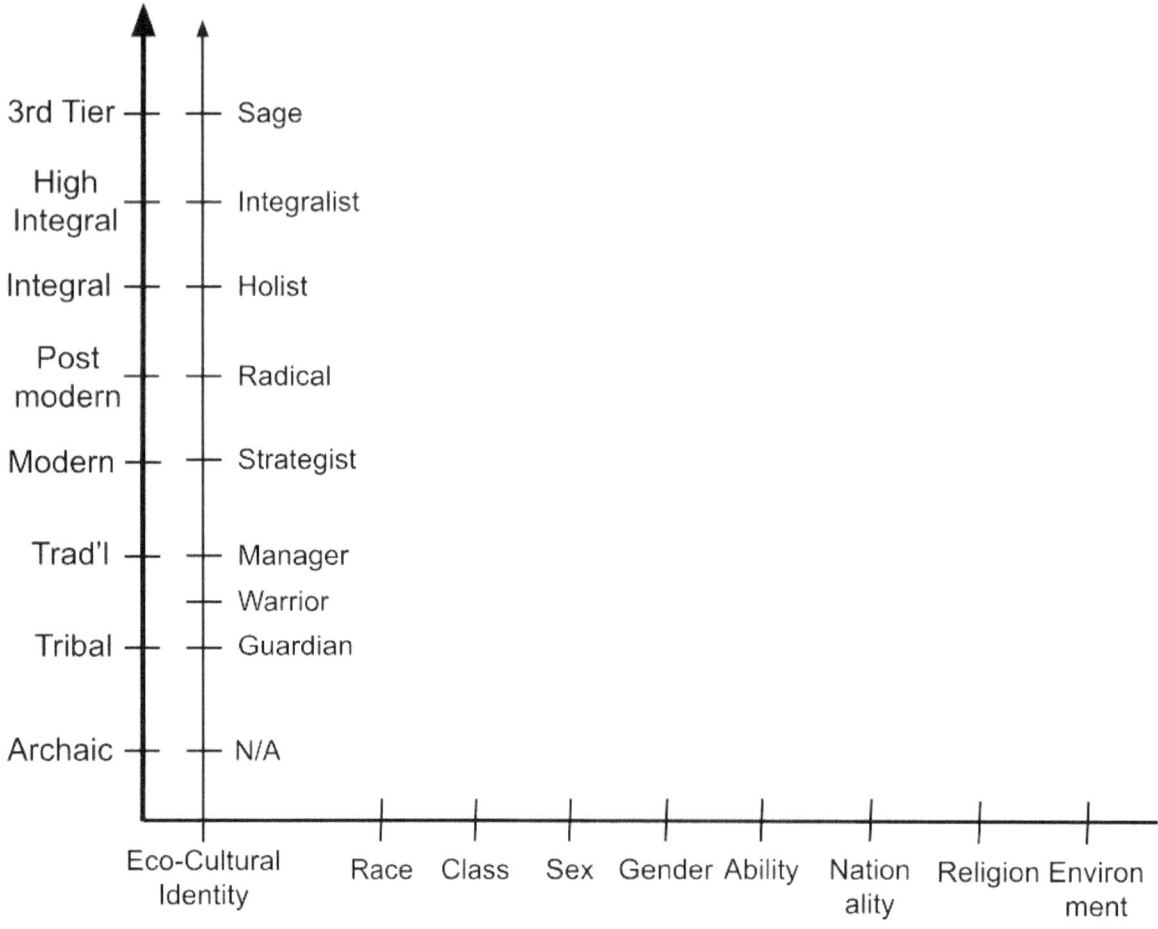

Figure 9.4 Developmental spectrum of eco-cultural identities

Here is a short description of the eight eco-selves from Esbjorn-Hargens and Zimmerman:

> Each eco-self has a unique way of relating to itself, others, and the natural world. In brief, the Eco-Guardian respects and fears nature; the Eco-Warrior wants to conquer nature (or in some cases culture); the Eco-Manager is dedicated to managing nature from a religious or secular position; the Eco-Strategist not only wants to manage nature but wants to use nature, and in many cases exploit it for some kind of profit (usually capital); the Eco-Radical wants to save nature for all of humanity and often for its ground value; the Eco-Holist wants to unite nature's multiple flows so the complex system can flourish; the Eco-Integralist celebrates nature as holonic and honors all ecological perspectives; the Eco-Sage is "one with" nature (and Nature and NATURE).[6]

Each of these eco-cultural identities represents how I create my self-sense from a given world-view with regards to each of the group identity categories. The Guardian corresponds to the tribal worldview. The Warrior occupies the space between tribal and traditional worldviews (more on this below). The Manager is the eco-cultural self in traditional culture. The Strategist represents the self at modern. The Radical is the postmodern eco-cultural self. The Holist is integral, the Integralist is high integral, and the Sage covers all third-tier structure states.

These eight eco-cultural identities represent universal patterns of how the culturally embedded self develops and expresses. In addition to applying to my ecological self, these identities apply to my racial self, my class self, my sex self, my gender self, and so on. This means for my racial identity, I am somewhere on the ladder of racial Guardian, racial Warrior, racial Manager . . . all the way up to racial Sage. The same is true for my gender identity—I could be a gender Guardian, gender Warrior, gender Manager, and so on.

Let's take a look at each of these eight eco-cultural selves in more detail. For the purposes of this workbook series, sex, gender, and sexual orientation are the most immediately relevant cultural identities, so I'll spend more time examining the selves through these three aspects, keeping in mind that these eight selves apply equally to all cultural group identities from Figure 9.2.

The Guardian

The Guardian is the eco-cultural self in the magic/tribal worldview. The ethos of the Guardian is Romantic. The Guardian is impulsive. They are focused on safety and immediate gratification. The world is filled with magical powers of good and evil. Culture is tribal with strong connections to elders, ancestors, and the spirit world.

Very few adults exclusively hold this identity, though the content of this identity is often accessed or idealized by Romantic and New Age perspectives. Approaches to sex and gender that look back in time to a better period, a paradise or golden age, in which the true versions of sex and gender proliferated are appealing to the Guardian self. As I mentioned in Chapter 1, this includes both Gimbutas' pre-agricultural Goddess hypothesis and the mythopoetic conception of the pre-industrial deep masculine. The Guardian works to re-establish a lost cultural ideal as well as protect or *guard* the remaining pristine cultures that still preserve the idealized pre-globalization, pre-industrial, or pre-agricultural periods. This is equally true of racial/ethnic Guardians, religious Guardians, political Guardians, and so on.

Eco-cultural Guardians may be found in *elements* of tribal cultures and cultural appropriations there-of—including neo-shamanism, neo-Luddism, paganism, wicca, tribalism, animism, totemism, and nature worship. By no means are these cultures fully defined by Eco-cultural Guardians.

The Warrior

The Warrior occupies the space between the magic/tribal worldview and the mythic/traditional worldview. I haven't included the Warrior as a paradigm of consciousness, though other authors do specify this as a distinct stage:

> The warrior stage of consciousness and culture arises as a result of the inevitable transition from the long and stable stage of tribal culture to a more complex form of human social organization. In human history, as tribes become successful, as they develop wealth and new technologies, their expanding populations bring them into conflict with their neighbors. And as life conditions become increasingly warlike, a new worldview emerges. This worldview can be aggressive and egocentric, but it can also be splendid and noble.
>
> —Steve McIntosh[7]

The Warrior eco-cultural self is self-protective and self-serving with a heroic ethos. The Warrior acts to empower the idea of the self instead of gratifying immediate needs and desires, like the Guardian. As the name suggests, the Warrior is willing to fight, seeks power, and protects the self.

McIntosh gives examples of the historical Hawaiian and Lakota cultures that incorporated the Warrior into beautiful cultural expressions. At the other end of the spectrum, street gangs, war zones, and child-slave rings offer examples of the brutality and hostility of this eco-cultural identity.

Gender portrayals of Tarzan, Conan, and Rambo exemplify the Warrior with bulging muscles, wearing little clothing, and fighting within the natural environment. The archetypal image of gender relations is the large strong man standing powerfully, with a slender woman being protected or carried by him. Often, the appeal of the *male warrior* in men's work harkens to this eco-cultural identity. Racial Warriors, political Warriors, ethnic Warriors, religious Warriors, eco-Warriors, and so on, are all willing to fight for personal power in their identity of choice.

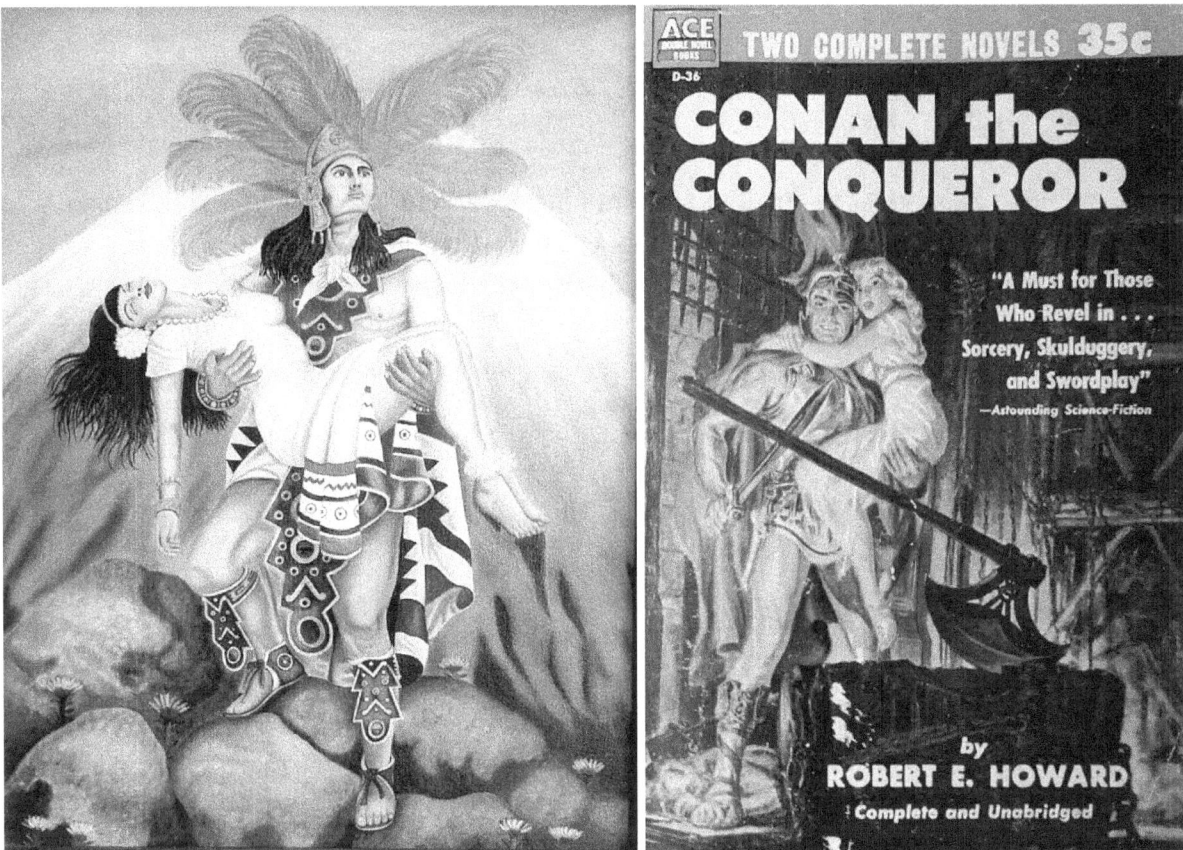

Figure 9.5 Popocatépetl & Iztaccihuatl;[8] Figure 9.6 Conan the Barbarian

Eco-cultural Warriors may be found in *elements* of primitive skills and wilderness survival culture, trophy and sports hunting, off-grid homesteading, gangster and mafia cultures, martial arts, and social Darwinism.

The Manager

The Manager is the eco-cultural self in the mythic/traditional worldview. The ethos of the Manager is social and ecological conservation. Managers in traditional cultures receive their identity from the group and adhere strongly to group norms. My role within the group or the identity of the group itself are blended with my individual self-sense. I hold strong dichotomies of right/wrong, us/them, and good/bad. I follow concrete rules, moral absolutes, and the authority of hegemonic power structures.

Because my group's traditions, rules, and laws maintain the social order, and because my identity is tied to the identity of the group, I am invested in maintaining these structures. I am socially conservative. I hold the norms of my religion, political party, ethnic group, or nationality as the singular truth.

I may view nature as the providence to my in-group from the transcendent divine. For example:

> And God blessed them, and God said unto them, Be fruitful, and multiply, and replenish the earth, and subdue it: and have dominion over the fish of the sea, and over the fowl of the air, and over every living thing that moveth upon the earth.
>
> —Genesis 1:28

Conservation-based approaches to the environment are typical of this paradigm. I want to *manage* nature for the sake of future generations or to maintain the natural order.

How I relate to sex, gender, and sexual orientation is inherited from tradition, scripture, and family values. Male Managers include patriarchs, pastors, cowboys, farmers, and soldiers. Female Managers include housewives, secretaries, nurses, and the like.

Eco-cultural Managers include *elements* of socially, politically, and environmentally conservative groups, patriotism, Puritanism, religious missionaries and monotheistic religions, the Boy Scouts and Girl Scouts, Focus on the Family, the Promise-Keepers men's organizations, and Support Our Troops.

The Strategist

The Strategist is the eco-cultural self in the mental/modern worldview. The ethos of the Strategist is rationality. This self has individuated from the natural world, the tribal unit, and the social group and therefore strongly values independence and individual freedom. It's interesting to observe that even though the Strategist's self-sense has become an individuated ego, the eco-cultural self nevertheless creates a culture of individualism that it belongs within.

The Strategist utilizes logic, the scientific method, and rational thought to become as efficient and successful as possible. I am focused on achievement, self-esteem, and creating value. I view culture and nature as problems to be solved, challenges to be overcome, and games to be won. I employ strategy and technology to maximize my value creation, wealth, and standard of living. I recognize that the natural world is governed by laws. I view nature as an asset of resources to be utilized for building and consumption. I recognize the personhood of every human which leads me to value universal human rights.

I value competition and work to create level playing fields across economics, politics, and sports. I believe in meritocracy and the *invisible hand* of economics. I fight for equal rights, higher education, and liberal values. Strategists support the equality of legal coverage and political representation across all group identity categories: race, gender, class, etc. Employee rights, affirmative action (positive action, quota systems), and equal opportunity are all movements within the Strategist worldview.

Eco-cultural Strategists include *elements* of socially and politically liberal groups, Newtonian scientific materialism and the Lockean worldview, scientists, businesspeople, behavioralists, Utilitarians, and liberal feminists.

The Radical

The Radical is the eco-cultural self in the plural/postmodern worldview. The ethos of the Radical is equality. Radicals value social responsibility, emotional sensitivity, tolerance, and political correctness. Here, I value marginalized viewpoints and work for a more communal, equitable world. The affirmative action of the Strategist is succeeded by the more pluralistic *diversity, equity, and inclusion* approach. Radicals are activists who are socially and environmentally engaged to overcome oppression, injustice, and restrictive social conditioning.

> Critical understanding of oneself, therefore, comes through the struggle of political "hegemonies," of opposing directions, first in the field of ethics, then of politics, culminating in a higher elaboration of one's own conception of reality. The awareness of being part of a determined hegemonic force (i.e. political consciousness) is the first step towards a further and progressive self-consciousness in which theory and practice finally unite. So the unity of theory and practice is also not a given mechanical fact but an historical process of becoming, which has its elementary and primitive phases in the sense of "distinctiveness," of "separation," of barely instinctive independence, and progresses up to the real and complete possession of a coherent and unitary conception of the world. That is why we should emphasize that the political development of the concept of hegemony represents a great step forward in philosophy as well as in practical politics, because it involves and presupposes an intellectual unity and an ethic conforming to a conception of reality which has surpassed common sense and, even though still within restricted limits, has become critical.
>
> —Antonio Gramsci[9]

As Gramsci notes in the passage above, written in 1934, political consciousness is its own form of personal development. This ladder spans from *barely instinctive independence* up through a *unitary conception of the world*. The recognition of hegemony is an important step in this evolutionary process whereby I move from *common sense* (i.e., acceptance of the way things are) into critical, progressive consciousness where theory and practice unite (i.e., the Radical).

Second-wave feminism, which moves beyond equal rights into the social construction of gender itself is the domain of the Radical. Queer theory, post-structuralism, and intersectionality are all schools of thought available to the Radical. My sensitivity as a Radical extends to the ethnonational group of which I am a member—giving voice to the marginalized groups and dismantling the hegemonic groups. Radicals find a cause and advocate. My approach at this level is to dismantle the roles and identities that are no longer serving me. Race Radicals, class Radicals, and eco-Radicals all work to update society within the sensitivity and systems views of postmodernity.

> From the perspective of postmodernism, those who have been wronged by modernity include: victims of racism and ethnic discrimination at home, victims of colonialism and imperialism abroad, female victims of sexism and an oppressive patriarchy, gay victims of homophobia, working class victims of capitalism, animal victims of an unethical food industry, as well as modernity's overall victimization of the world's natural environment.
> —Steve McIntosh[10]

Eco-cultural Radicals include *elements* of critical academia, New Age spirituality and many of the "neo" movements like neo-tantra and neo-shamanism, psychotherapy, the United Nations, the woke movement, #metoo and #blacklivesmatter, and social, political, and environmental progressive activism.

The Holist

The Holist is the eco-cultural self in the integral worldview. I approach environmental and social justice using a holistic ethos. I am able to hold multiple perspectives, have tolerance for ambiguity and paradox, and synthesize holonic unities. The self-sense is centered in wholeness. I am able to distinguish my social conditioning from my authentic self. I am ready to move beyond the blame and hurt of the Radical, and I develop increasing capacities for resilience, humor, and curiosity. As such, the Holist is the first cultural identity that is not *given* by society but which is *self-defined*. This marks a shift into active participation in the creation of cultural identities. It is not the case that the cultural deconditioning of postmodernism removes all cultural identity from the self. Cultural identity is unavoidable. The Holist embraces cultural identity from a place of choice and agency, engaging in cultural self-authorship.

Because I am less merged with my eco-cultural identities (race, class, gender…)—meaning I take these roles less personally—I become free to play and explore with these categories. Gender fluidity, sexual orientation fluidity, and identifying with multiple religions (e.g., Jew-Bu or Christian-yogi) are ways that the Holist explores a greater range of identity.

This may seem redundant, but Holists embrace holism and view each aspect of ecosystem and culture through a holistic framework.

> The '"key-log"' which must be moved to release the evolutionary process for [a land] ethic is simply this: quit thinking about decent land-use as solely an economic problem. Examine each question in terms of what is ethically and esthetically right, as well as what is economically expedient. A thing is right when it tends to preserve the integrity, stability, and beauty of the biotic community. It is wrong when it tends otherwise.
>
> —Aldo Leopold[11]

The masculine Holist has digested and embodied the postmodern feminist critique of hegemonic masculinity. Instead of supporting or silently abiding the masculine abuse of power, the holist is an advocate for change. This means doing the inner work that we've been undertaking in these workbooks, speaking up in the face of injustice, and standing in allyship of feminine empowerment. Masculine Holists have transcended the over-sensitivity of postmodernism into a resilient ownership of their masculinity. This expression of masculinity reveres the sacredness in all genders and all life. Through this recognition, the masculine Holist steps into ever stronger embodiments of nonviolence.

> The core of feminist masculinity is a commitment to gender equality and mutuality as crucial to interbeing and partnership in the creating and sustaining of life. Such a commitment always privileges nonviolent action over violence, peace over war, life over death.
>
> —bell hooks[12]

Eco-cultural Holists include *elements* of integral organizations and schools (integral medicine, integral spirituality, integral philosophy, integral business, and so on), and holistic organizations and schools (holistic medicine, the Gaia hypothesis and sustainable development, holistic education, and so on).

The Integralist

The Integralist is the eco-cultural self in the high integral worldview. For starters, the cultural worldview at high integral has not yet been established in our society. Because the culture is still in formation, the identity must be too. In this sense, Integralist individuals are like trailblazers who are defining the frontiers of identity and culture.

Simultaneously though, the high integral paradigm brings an increasing disenchantment with the egoic self. The ego becomes transparent to itself and so the vestiges of eco-cultural identity are increasingly falling away. The Integralist is able to adopt and play with identity when useful, but is also able to move beyond identity, social constructions, and language into a more direct experience of the ineffable mystery of reality.

Integralists are characterized by compassion, Agape, and an embrace of all aspects of life, both internally and in the world.

> For the Eco-Integralist the heart opens and increases the individual's capacity to feel the widespread suffering around the planet. This capacity for remaining open to such suffering without being consumed by it is an important quality of the compassion that emerges with this Eco-Self. Wilber has captured this paradox with the phrase "hurts more, bothers you less." The Eco-Integralist is deeply committed to the integration of transcendence and innocence. This is a marriage of wisdom and compassion, which recognizes that nothing needs to be done, because everything is always already perfect.
> —Esbjorn-Hargens and Zimmerman[13]

Race, class, sex, gender, and the other group identity categories become opportunities for the Integralist to explore shadow work and embrace the ugly, wounded, or exiled places within themselves. In this light, these categories are like fertile manure for the Integralist's garden. The roles where we as humans are most divided become the catalysts for the eleutheropoetic unfolding of the Integralist. Whereas the Radical seeks liberation *from* proscribed race, gender, and so on, the Integralists finds liberation *through* race, gender, and so on.

Eco-cultural Integralists include *elements* of all of the same organizations and schools of thought mentioned above in the Holist section. What separates Integralists from Holists, is greater capacity for *vision logic*, or the capacity to see cross-paradigmatically or even trans-paradigmatically, more comfort with paradox, and a deeper trust in the process itself. Integralists recognize that every paradigm's solutions for culture and ecosystem create new problems, often in unforeseen ways, including the high integral approach itself. This comfort with messiness is embraced by the Integralist identity.

The Sage

At the level of the Sage, we are now discussing a sampling of highly developed people rather than a culture which imprints identity. This move requires another monumental step into the third tier of development, which entails passing through the *dark night of the ego* into a stable trans-egoic experience of reality. In this sense, the Sage is primarily a soul-self instead of an egoic self. In addition, the Sage is basically a catch-all for the higher structure-states of development. Therefore, I would also include those who've made it through the even more daunting *dark night of the soul* into a stable experience of the transpersonal Self in this category.

With that in mind, the identity of the eco-cultural Sage is most prominently marked by on-going intimacy with Spirit. Saints and mystics are other names for the Sage. The identity is fluid, expansive, open, and available. At the level of the Sage, I see myself in others, not in a conceptual way, but directly and immediately. I feel myself interwoven and interconnected with the natural world and all of life. I experience my "self" as part of the Great Web of Life.

The focus of the Sage is to integrate the individual consciousness back into the kosmic tapestry of consciousness. At each step along the developmental ladder of eco-social identities, the self-sense has been both individuating and integrating—its unique version of *transcend and include.*

These eight selves form a holonic ladder where the self at each stage includes the selves below and becomes a part in the next more inclusive, more expansive version of self. The eco-cultural selves occupy the cultural experiences of an individual in the lower left quadrant. They form a system of roles and identities that I wear in relationships and cultural groups.

Prompts for Journaling and Discussion

Return to Figure 9.4, *Developmental spectrum of eco-cultural identities*, and plot your eco-cultural selves across each group identity category.

Development of Eco-Cultural Selves and Culture

I began life as an infant fully enmeshed in the phenomenal world. This does not mean I was enlightened. It means my self-reflexive consciousness was at the very beginning of its emergence. We all began at the Archaic level and progressed from there. As a Guardian, I am embedded in the animistic natural world and my self-sense has distinguished its own desires and needs. As a Warrior, I now know I am a "self" instead of a collection of impulses. By the level of the Manager, I have individuated from my environment and the natural world, but my self-sense is still fused with my social group. Strategists free the ego from groups and truly become individuals. I recognize the individuality of all humans at this level and become a self amongst other selves. At the level of the Radical, two things are happening. First, I am now individuating from acculturated identities, or *deconstructing* this conditioning. Second, I am integrating back into my social group from a position of individual sovereignty. I become an ethno-centric individual. I am able to re-assume my bond with the group without losing myself into it. As a Holist, the self that I identify with becomes my adult self or soul-self. I increasingly center in this experience of wholeness. The deeper I go into my center, the more I discover the wholeness of society and the environment. I move beyond ethno-centrism to human-centrism and see myself as an integral member of this one race. Another label for this is species-identification. Somewhere between the Holist and the Integralist, my scope expands even wider to include all life and the entire planet—yet another aspect of self integrating into wider contexts. I begin to think and act from a planet-centric orientation with life-identification. Finally, in the developmental levels that the Sage traverses, I am seeing, feeling, and intuiting my "self" back into the kosmos. The entire universe increasingly begins to feel like my very own body. I become kosmo-centric and kosmo-identified.

The movement of self-identity is from egocentric (me) to enthnocentric (me + *my group*) to sociocentric (me + my group + *my nation*) to worldcentric (me + my group + my nation + *all peoples*) to planetcentric (me + my group + my nation + all peoples + *all beings*).

—Esbjorn-Hargens and Zimmerman[14]

Figure 9.7 Self individuation and integration

Each of the group identity categories (race, class, gender, etc.) will hold a center of gravity somewhere on this developmental ladder of eco-cultural selves. Each category progresses somewhat independently of the other categories, so I may simultaneously be a race Radical and a gender Warrior. As the center of gravity of my *psychological self* in the upper left quadrant advances through the paradigms, it will exert a pull on my various eco-cultural selves in the lower left quadrant to develop. Additionally, the paradigm and worldview of the sociocultural holon that I participate in will strongly influence the developmental altitudes of my eco-cultural selves. In a traditional culture, the most natural and common eco-cultural level would be the Manager. Advancing to the Radical, Holist, or Integralist within a traditional culture is possible, but much more challenging because cultural selves and culture co-enact each other. In an integral culture, advancing to the Holist will be much more common and easy. When the cultural water is already at the integral temperature, I am spared the effort of heating it myself.[15]

As we have seen, it is highly desirable for both sociocultural holons and individuals to advance upward into integral. Doing so transforms the nexus of *conditioned identity, power, and violence* into the *redefined identity, empowerment, and blessing* nexus. I've illustrated this transition in the figure below and, for me, this is amongst the most important concepts in this entire workbook.

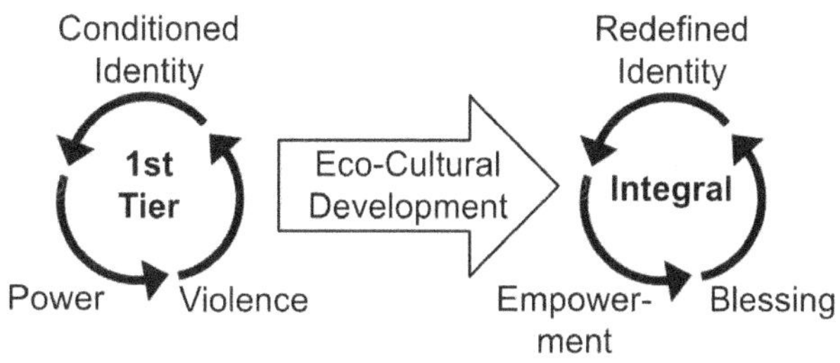

Fig 9.8 Moving from the nexus of violence to the nexus of blessing

As an individual, when I transition my eco-cultural identities from first tier levels into integral and beyond, I undergo a redefinition process that is massively transformational. The Holist is not simply one step up from the Radical. The Holist is the first eco-cultural identity that I define and choose for myself. Guardians, Warriors, Managers, and Strategists are identities that are acculturated givens. I receive them from the culture I inhabit. As its name suggests, the Radical rebels against those prior conditioned identities. Because the Radical is primarily a reaction *against* what came before, it is still partial. The Holist is whole. This identity arises from the centered truth of my adult self and co-enacts with culture. I become an equal partner with my culture in the expression and evolution of these identity categories. We call this level of the process *redefinition.*

As identities become redefined in wholeness, both individuals and sociocultural holons transform their relationships with power. Power-over, dominance, and hegemony from the first tier levels transform into power-with, empowerment, and self-actualization.

When each holonic entity is held in dignity and supported to grow in its unique way, this leads to the true and trustable experience of nonviolence. Mimetic systems of violence transform into mimetic systems of blessing. Instead of acting to keep relational systems small through violence, individuals and culture begin to enact the virtuous cycles of uplifting each other. Blessing is a deep topic that I will explore in depth in the Monarch's Lore Book. In this context, *blessing* means supporting another to meet their personal and group identity needs. When our needs are met, we are free to grow and violence becomes both irrelevant and undesirable. The motto of the integral Warrior archetype is: *blessing conquers violence.*

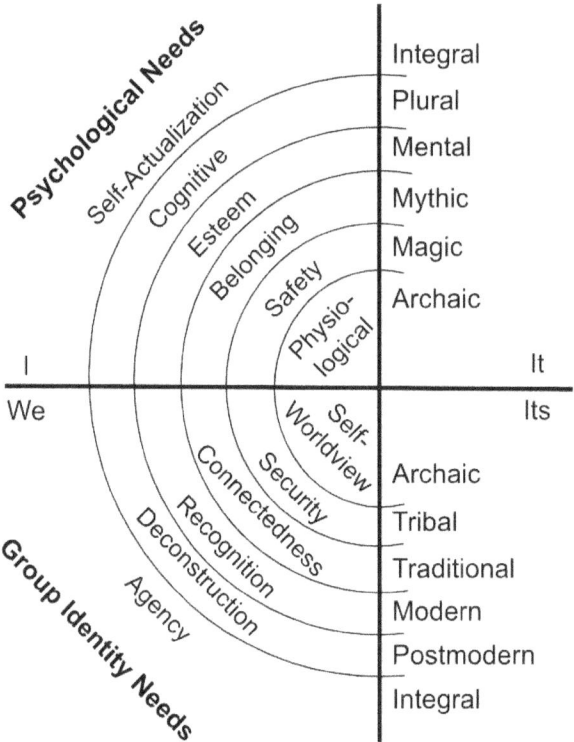

Figure 9.9 Psychological needs and group identity needs

Like curses, mimetic structures of violence constrict the movement of people, limit life options, and are directed toward death. In contrast, blessings are empowering, lead to creative and ever-expanding options, and are oriented toward life… Within mimetic structures of blessing, a dynamic of mutual desire for the well-being of the Other develops, in which both model and imitator become more fully functioning Subjects in the process…Blessing is oriented toward the development of the Self as a fully functioning, fulfilled Subject, that is, a person with the dignity and inner resources to act directly in the world.

–Vern Redekop[16]

Mimetic systems of blessing support more holistically re-defined identities (like the organic masculine, as a prime example), which in turn, leads to greater self-empowerment, and feeds back into a greater capacity to offer blessings to others. This is the virtuous cultural nexus of blessing. This virtuous cycle becomes mirrored by other individuals and groups *mimetically*. The more trust and support I extend to you, the more likely you are to do the same in return for me.

Eco-cultural identities use distinct processes to advance through the selves. In Chapter 4, I introduced three models for anti-oppression processes: *social identity development theory*, *consciousness-in-action*, and *the cycle of liberation*. Take a moment to turn back to Figure 4.21. Each group identity line (race, class, gender, and so on) uses the cultural development processes to advance through the same universal levels (Guardian, Warrior, Manager, and so on). While each group identity category advances in its unique way (race focusing on racial material, gender focusing on gender material), the process of advancement itself is universal. I can now plot the *social identity development theory* of Hardiman and Jackson together with integral's developmental worldviews to map the individual's advancement through the collective interior of eco-cultural selves (Figure 9.10).

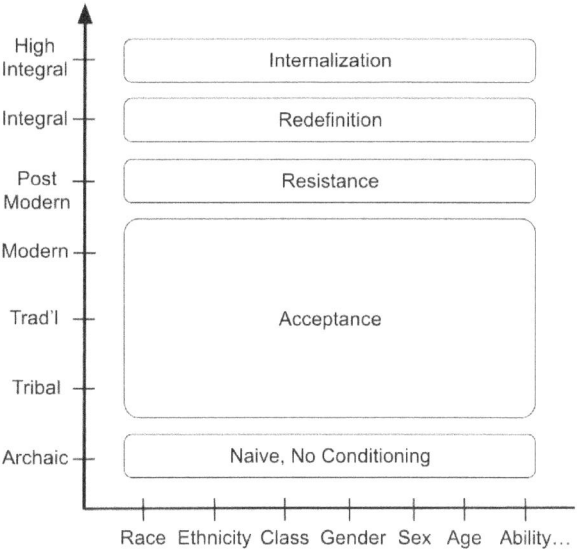

Figure 9.10 Integral mapping of Hardiman & Jackson's social identity development process

Let's explore what this means. Humanity as a species (and each individual) begins at the archaic worldview. Here, there are no groups, no conditioning, and no awareness or participation in power structures. Then, as humans developed civilization, cultural grouping began. This corresponds to the magic/tribal worldview. For me as an individual, this represented the first few years of my life when I was learning the basics of language and culture. In this paradigm, as well as the next two, I am in *acceptance* of my social conditioning as *the way things are*. The mythic/traditional worldview stresses belonging. This is where I learn in-group and out-group affiliations, together with stereotypes and social hierarchy. In the mental/modern worldview, I move beyond role adherence to egoic achievement. Even though my sense of self has individuated from my social group, I am still operating within the rules of the system which carries all the inequalities and biases of my society.

As I move into the plural/postmodern worldview, I begin to recognize that the rules don't work. By following the rules, I am limiting myself, and I see that the system is subject to change. I enter the *resistance* phase. Hardiman and Jackson note that this may be passive resistance or active resistance. What I am resisting is identification with the social groups that have been assigned to me, and the rules that these groups operate under. This phase is often accompanied by feelings of alienation, shame, pain, hurt, anger, or frustration. I may distance myself from my former identity category and community members. I may challenge instances of injustice and find a sense of power as I reject oppressive behaviors and identities.

> First of all, resistance means opposition to being invaded, occupied, assaulted, and destroyed by the system. The purpose of resistance, here, is to seek the healing of yourself in order to be able to see clearly. This may sound as though it falls short of a positive act of resistance. Nevertheless, it's very basic.
>
> —Thích Nhât Hạ nh[17]

Bridging between the plural/postmodern and integral worldviews, I begin to *redefine* my eco-cultural identity in relation to society. I search for new definitions, names, and framing. This requires me to critically examine how these systems of conditioning operate and are perpetuated. Here is where Rosado's consciousness-in-action process engages. I move through the phases of perceiving, recognizing, understanding, and responding. Ultimately, this leads me to find a new, authentic definition of this aspect of my cultural identity. Through this process, I am able to reclaim some positive aspects of the heritage or culture of my group.

At integral and beyond, my redefined sense of self then begins to integrate across all aspects of my life. My new identity becomes increasingly *internalized*. This liberates me to work more broadly on systemic issues or apply the same process to other developmental lines of my eco-cultural identities.

At integral, the wholeness of my self is able to hold my conditioned identities without becoming fused with them. These identities live *within me*, but I don't hold them *as me*. This is the crucial point. I individuate my identity needs from the identity needs of my groups. With this step, I am vastly less susceptible to social dynamics of violence that stem from missing group needs. Because I am not as invested in *our story*, I become liberated to see a bigger picture in the social system. This opens me more fully to universal compassion instead of the paradigm-specific favoritism I held in the first tier levels. In addition, I become more resilient to hold my strong emotions so that I can become responsive to injustice instead of reactive against it.

This social identity development process outlines how individuals grow through the eco-cultural selves. Let's plot it together with the individuation and integration journey of the self and the eco-cultural selves (Figure 9.11).

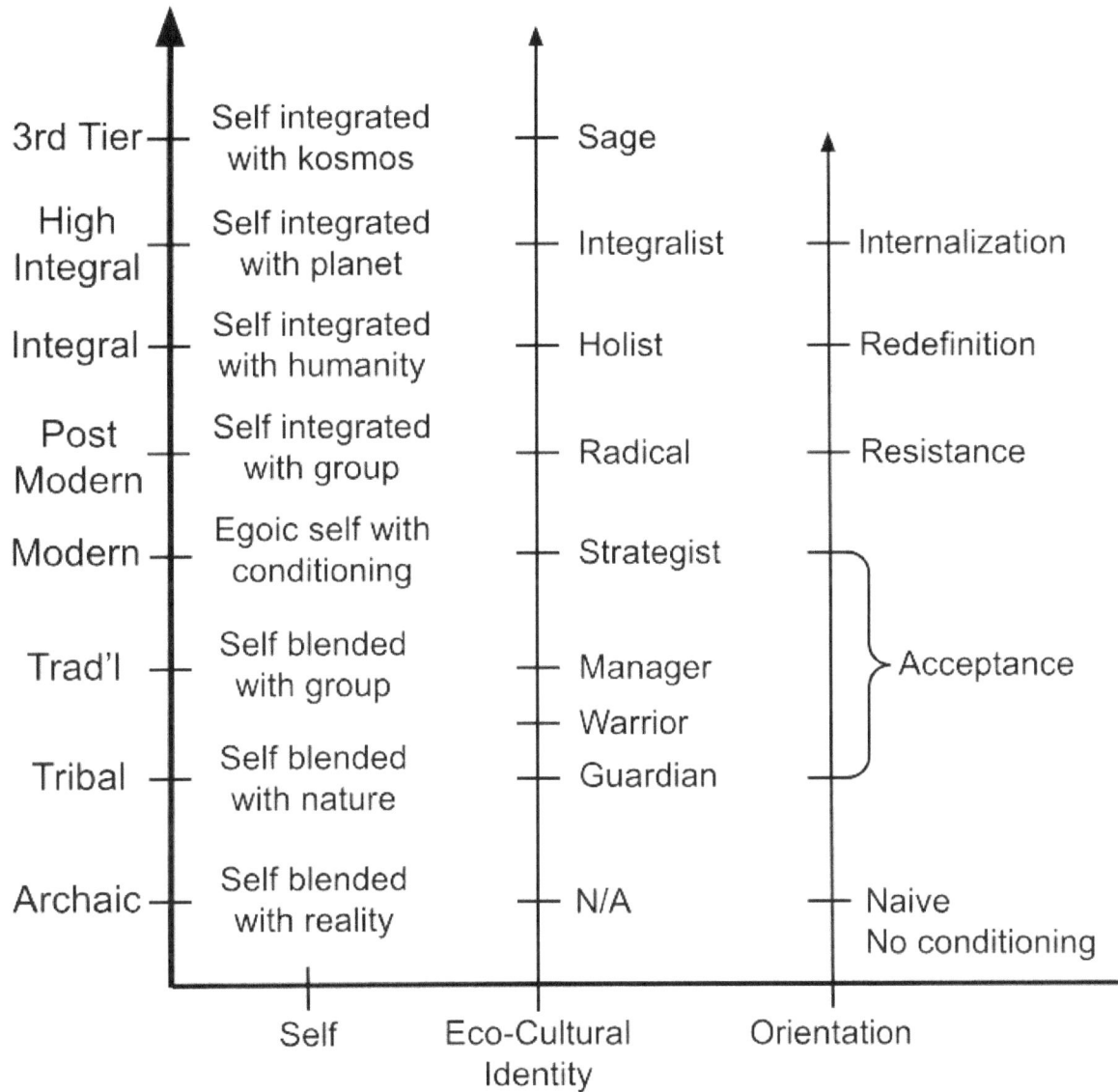

Figure 9.11 Developmental journey of the selves

Now let's make this more immediate and visceral. I'm assuming you've been filling out the tables and prompts as we've progressed through this workbook. You should already have a considerable amount of information about your cultural positioning. In Figure 4.18, you took inventory of which group identities you hold, and in Figure 7.4, you went deeper into your ethnonational group identity. In Figure 4.20, you identified whether these categories are dominant, border, or subordinated and listed concrete examples for how this arises in your sociocultural experience. In Figures 4.22 and 4.26, you made self-assessments of where in the eco-cultural development processes you are today. Then in Figure 8.4, you examined how your group identity needs are being met. Take a few moments to review these inventories.

Your next bold and exciting step is to re-imagine each of these identity categories in wholeness. This next piece of work is what is required to become an archetypal Warrior at integral. For each group identity category, imagine an authentic, empowered, blessed and blessing version that lives within you. Redefine this identity for yourself. Imagine that both your psychological needs and group identity needs are fully met for each category (Figure 9.9). In particular, imagine how both personal self-actualization and collective agency would express through the nexus of empowerment and blessing. Who would you become? What would need to shift in yourself and in your relationships in order for you to step into this new identity?

Fill out the table below with your Holistic selves in redefinition. Take your time with this exercise. If you run into resistance or other strong emotions, tend to them. It's part of the de-conditioning process. You may find that for some categories you don't know what a re-imagined self would look like. That's ok. Do some research. Talk to your friends and community. Listen and learn. This complex process often requires time to formulate and digest.

Identity Category	Redefined Identity	Who would I become? What does self-actualization, agency, empowerment, and blessing look like?
Race		
Nationality		
Ethnicity / Ancestry		
Political Party		
Generation / Age		
Sex		
Gender		
Sexual Orientation		
Body Ability		
Mental Ability		
Class		
Education Level		
Education Focus / Major		
Professional Role		
Professional Industry		
Community		
Hobby		
Ecological self		

Figure 9.12 Redefinition of group identities

I'll give just one personal example here. In our cultural lexicon, I hold a "Master's" degree as my level of education. Having undertaken the exploration we've been through, I can see that there is nothing subtle about the hegemonic privilege baked into this title. Most people never give these social implications a moment's thought. But this educational title gives me the social legitimation to call myself a *master* as I move through my career. If I'm a "master," then how will I view the people who work for me? Even if I don't hold myself with the inflated power from the word master, do I want to use this title knowing that others will likely project that power structure onto me? Master is the label that has been given to me by our culture and that I have unconsciously accepted.

In redefinition, I would say that my education level is "postgraduate". This is both accurate and culturally neutral. I am not subtly elevating myself into a position of power over others through my title. Instead, I am acknowledging my achievement in self-empowerment.

Once I move into the stage of redefinition for a group identity, I begin to act in the world from that new place. Rosado stresses that understanding is not enough. Action is required for real cultural change to happen. And although the Radical is good at taking action, this is frequently in reaction from a place of emotional trigger and blame. As a Holist in redefinition, I begin to *respond* instead of react. Thus, the final and most important step in *consciousness-in-action* is *responding*. Hence, we are doing Warrior's work.

> Critical consciousness is not, in and of itself, liberating; consciousness without action only leads to cynicism. It is consciousness-in-action–*conciencia-en-acción*–nurtured by a vision and a sense of hope, that can lead to liberation and transformation.
>
> —Raúl Rosado[18]

At this juncture, I begin to move into the third cultural-transformation process, Bobbie Harro's *cycle of liberation*. Here, I am focusing on changing the social and cultural systems of my community and society. This is collective work that acts upon sociocultural holons. New collective holons are formed as redefined social, environmental, and political groups coalesce. Existing collective holons are transformed as institutions and social systems (LR), and group identity, language, and values (LL) become engaged in the cycle of liberation.

Figure 9.13 Cycle of liberation[19]

This is the integral vision for the transformation of collective processes of violence into collective processes of blessing. It begins with the individual's journey of *waking up* out of passive acceptance with the status quo into the possibility of cultural change. Waking up corresponds with the Radical eco-cultural self and the phases of resistance and understanding. I then begin *getting ready* when I enter the Holist and redefinition of limiting, conditioned identities and oppressive social systems. I am now ready to act, to respond. I *reach out* to others, I speak up, I make new connections, and I seek experiences of changing culture. Once I find my niche, the next step is to grow. I begin *building community* by connecting with other Holists doing activism work in redefinition. This will include people in my identity category and people outside of my identity category, from both dominant and subordinated groups. The next step is *coalescing*, where the community organizes, gathers resources, educates, and plans for collective action. We then enter *creating change* to transform culture and institutions. These changes must be continually *maintained*, and part of this process is to shepherd new individuals into the community.

Looking broadly across our three processes of cultural transformation, I recognize two aspects of the evolutionary journey. I evolve as an individual through my social and cultural interactions. In addition, the socio-cultural holons with their own nexus-agencies are transformed. This requires both inner work and outer work.

> Therefore, we need people who commit themselves to two types of service. The first is to the symptomatic relief of suffering in the world. The second is to psychological awareness, both their own and that of others, to relieve the mental causes of this suffering and to make themselves more effective.
>
> —Roger Walsh[20]

Even though I view collective action as a natural outcome of the eco-cultural evolution process, it is by no means easy or straightforward. Changing culture is challenging work. For me personally, I am able to engage in collective action insofar as it is directly connected to my personal growth. Working from a place of goal-oriented agendas, from my guilt, or from caretaking have led me to burnout. But using this model, I can see how my personal development is innately interwoven with the evolution of the collective. Aligning with my own self-actualization provides the trustable place from which I can engage in collective action.

Prompts for Journaling and Discussion

When you consider redefining your eco-cultural identities, what emotions arise?

When you consider engaging in the cycle of liberation, what emotions arise?

How are personal growth and public advocacy related for you, and how are they different?

The Empowerment Dynamic

In concert with redefining my eco-social identity categories, I want to disenroll myself from the drama triangle. Each of the three roles in the drama triangle (victim, perpetrator, and savior) fundamentally carries relational disempowerment. The victim feels disempowered, the perpetrator wields power over another, and the savior holds the power to fix the situation. As long as I'm holding myself and others in these roles, I will maintain a system of disempowerment.

David Emerald Womeldorff has introduced *The Empowerment Dynamic*, or TED, as the antidote to the roles of the drama triangle. The new roles he presents are the creator, the challenger, and the coach.

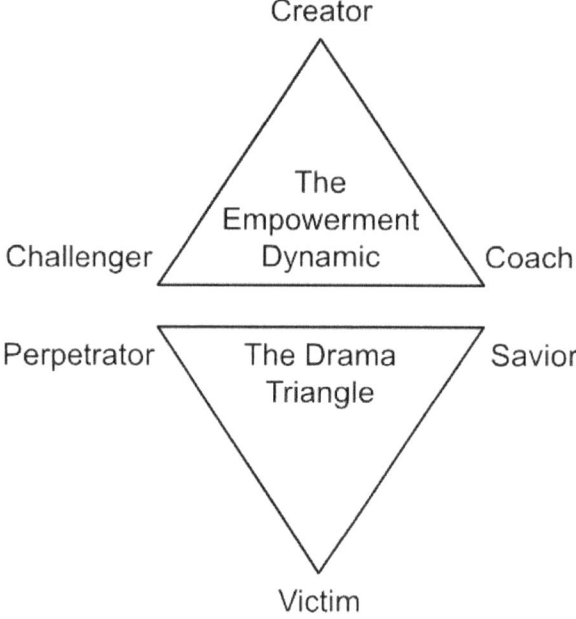

Figure 9.14 The Empowerment Dynamic[21]

The most important orientation change is from victim to creator. As the victim, I am powerless to life circumstances and the manipulations of others. As the creator, I am connected to my own power to respond and manifest the outcomes that I want for myself. Aligning myself to the role of a creator in my life opens the door for serendipity, synchronicity, play, and fun to emerge.

As a perpetrator, persecutor, or villain, I blame others and cut them down. As the challenger, I provide the encouragement and skepticism to align to deeper truths and achieve greater successes. The confrontation of the challenger is like a purifying fire that strips away distortions and energizes the system. In the Buddhist context, this can be called *wrathful compassion*.

As the savior or rescuer, I reinforce the powerlessness of the victim and the blameworthiness of the perpetrator. When I shift to the coach, I foremost recognize the dignity and capability of others, and then work to offer support and guidance for them to grow and learn. Coaching enables empowerment.

The three empowerment roles—creator, challenger, and coach—work together to spur virtuous relational dynamics. This reorientation is typical of individuals as they step into the holism of the integral paradigm. It works together with the Holist eco-cultural self to counteract systems of violence and oppression.

In Figure 8.12, I sketched out a comprehensive framework to describe how systemic violence operates across the individual, cultural, and social Big Three dimensions. I am now able to outline a comprehensive framework for a system of well-being and empowerment:

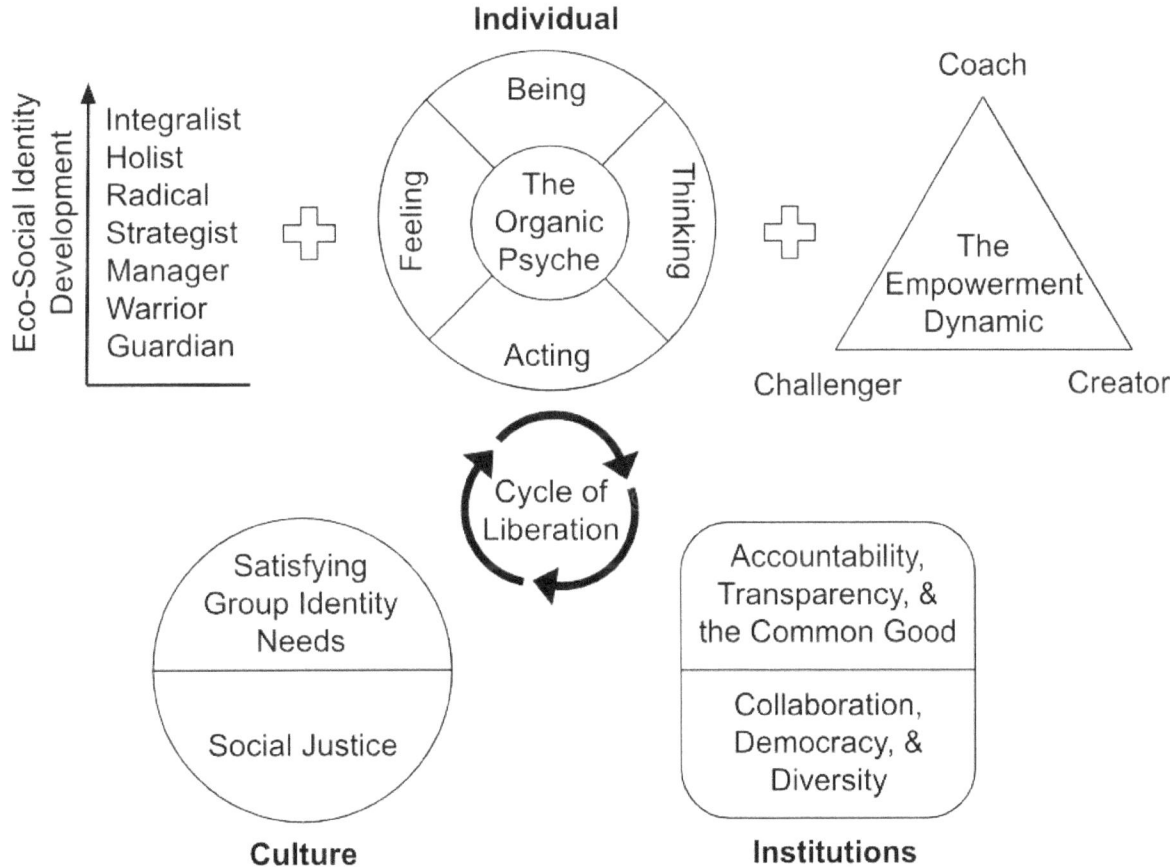

Figure 9.15 Meta-process for AQAL wellbeing

This framework draws on the incredible work of many social pioneers, and in integral fashion synthesizes them into a coherent whole across the AQAL matrix. I'll acknowledge each source as I pull it all together: The mutually reinforcing virtuous process has been described by Vern Redekop as a mimetic system of blessing. The values held by each domain are based on Prilleltensky and Prilleltensky's interdependent web of values (Figure 7.5). As individuals engage in identity development (Hardiman & Jackson) through the eco-cultural selves (Esbjorn-Hargens & Zimmerman) and step into the empowerment dynamic (Emerald), they will naturally center in the organic psyche. These collective and relational aspects of individual work go hand-in-hand with the three individual developmental pathways I outlined in the introduction, namely: growth through the paradigms of consciousness, awakening through states of consciousness, and archetypal maturation via initiation. As more and more individuals come online through their healing and growth, we will increasingly engage in the collective process of the cycle of liberation (Harro).

This is not a single process, but an interlocking system of processes (i.e., meta-process) where the virtuous results of each aspect feed into the overall well-being of humanity and ultimately, the entire planet. This model is not a destination—it says nothing about what the world we create will come to resemble. Rather, it describes the journey. If we get individuals, institutions, and culture working together in this way, then we will naturally engage in a creative advance into well-being.

Sustainability

Sustainability is defined as meeting the needs of the present without compromising the ability of future generations to meet their own needs.
–United Nations Brundtland Commission, 1987

The most widespread definition of sustainability is about meeting needs. There are two requirements here: The first is meeting our needs today, and the second is empowering future generations to meet their needs. We have a myth in environmental circles that humanity was at one point sustainable. We lived in balance with our ecosystems and did not compromise future generations. While it may have been true that ancient humans were so small in number and consumed so few resources that the planetary biosphere was not impacted, it is also true that humans throughout our history have moved through cycles of build-up and collapse, have hunted species to extinction, and have profoundly shaped the natural environment for our purposes.[22] All of these activities were natural, and are still natural today. So, at best, the second half of the sustainability equation was provisionally true in some historical cases.

But at no point in human history, have we ever met the needs of the present. On just a basic physiological level, the child mortality rate was about 50% for all of human history up until modernity.[23] Child mortality is a useful statistic to track how well a society is meeting their most basic needs.

Until the last few centuries, there was almost no way for us to stop children from dying. It wasn't until the rise of clean water, proper sanitary conditions, vaccines, better nutrition and other advances in health care that rates of child mortality started to plummet. As recently as 1800, about 43% of the world's children died before reaching their fifth birthday. Today that figure is 4% – still woefully high, but more than 10-fold lower.

—Hannah Ritchie[24]

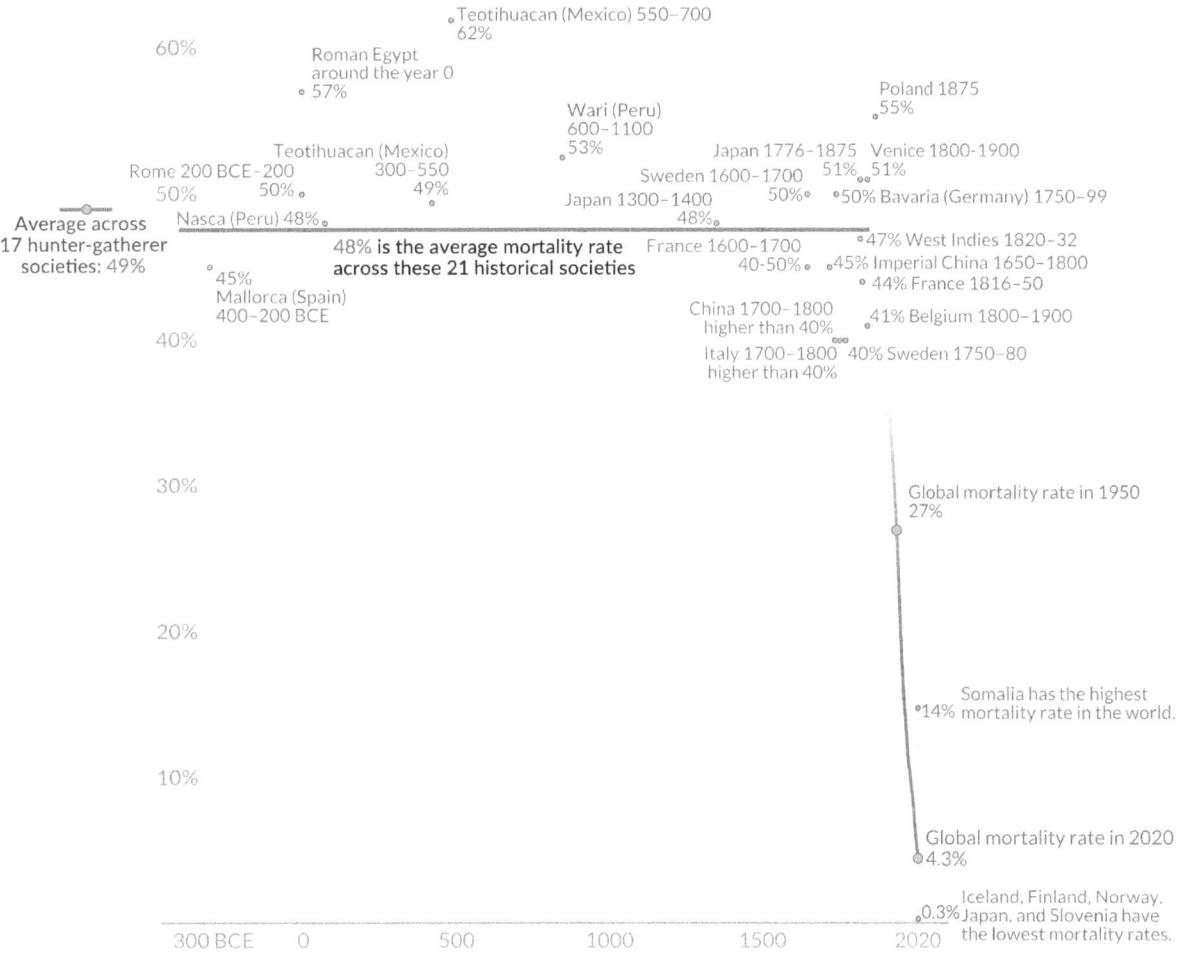

Figure 9.16 Historical rates of child mortality[25]

From this metric, I can see that every human society across our history prior to modernity failed to meet the sustainability definition of satisfying the most basic needs of its present members. As we have been discussing, humans have many needs, with physiological being the most fundamental level for individuals. We also have safety, belonging, esteem, and cognitive needs. In addition, groups of humans and our eco-cultural selves have self-worldview, security, connectedness, recognition, and deconstruction as group identity needs (Figure 9.9). These needs operate in a hierarchy where the basic needs are prerequisites for more sophisticated needs. The first half of sustainability means every human as well as every ethnic group, animal, and ecosystem is able to meet their needs across these hierarchies. The second half requires us to meet these needs without negatively impacting the future. Sustainability is a very tall order indeed.

Some societies may have been environmentally balanced in the past, but that was only because child mortality (among other factors) kept populations low. The needs of tomorrow were safeguarded, but the present needs were never met. Today, we are rapidly advancing toward a world where the vast majority of humans have every physiological need met (see Figure 9.16 on child mortality). Our advancement in meeting today's needs has come at the cost of creating a dangerous imbalance with our ecosystems (see Figure 8.13 for the Planetary Boundaries model). The needs of today are being better met, but at the expense of the needs of tomorrow. At no point have humans as a species ever met the definition for sustainability.

Here is my task as an integral Warrior: to meet all of my own needs, to create a civilization that meets the needs of every member, and to ensure the opportunity for future generations to meet their needs as well. At integral, we become Warriors for sustainability. With the maps and tools we've explored in this workbook, we can now take a sober look at what is required from us and for our world to become sustainable.

We stand in a very special place today. Never before in the history of our species have we been able to understand the complex, systemic, multi-systemic challenges posed by the interlocking needs of biosphere and noosphere. Never before have we had a realistic roadmap for sustainability, or even a basic understanding of what was truly required. Today, you are joining me in stepping into this bold new understanding of what is possible for our planet. It is a precious experience to behold.

> We need to make sure that everyone in the world can live a good life *and* we need to reduce our environmental impacts so that future generations can flourish too. That puts us in uncharted territory. No previous generation had the knowledge, technology, political systems, or international cooperation to do both at the same time. We have the opportunity to be the first generation that achieves sustainability. Let's take it.
>
> —Hannah Ritchie[26]

This task may seem impossible. But consider this: When Gandhi took up the cause of Indian independence, the majority of colonial rebellions had been unsuccessful, bloody affairs; India not only didn't have an army, it didn't have a shared identity or even speak a unified language; the British empire was the most powerful social-holon on the planet; and nonviolent protest had never been attempted at large scale. Common sense would have stopped this movement before it ever began. And yet . . . India achieved independence through nonviolent means.

When we look today at the prospect of becoming nonviolent as a species, meeting the needs of every being on the planet, and living in true sustainability, the task may seem equally impossible. But listen:

> When I despair, I remember that all through history the way of truth and love have always won. There have been tyrants and murderers, and for a time, they can seem invincible, but in the end, they always fall. Think of it - always.
>
> —Gandhi

What does it mean to have all my needs met? It does not mean I am perfectly satisfied all the time. Nor does it mean I never face challenges. As I move into the integral paradigm, my primary focus shifts from needs to capabilities. I still have needs and sometimes they go unmet. But most of the time, most of my needs are met. When a need is challenged or missing, I am able to respond by mobilizing my capable adult (or Holistic eco-cultural self) to satisfy my missing need. I have cultivated a greater capacity for resilience to ride the inevitable waves of expansion and contraction. The wholeness of my self-system becomes its own resource that can satisfy some of my connection, self-esteem, or cognitive needs. I am self-resourcing. In addition, in self-actualization I create networks of support and social safety nets. I weave myself into more resilient social systems. Finally, I completely change my orientation to the experience of missing needs. Instead of holding myself as a victim of life or circumstance where missing needs are happening *to me*, I hold each experience as an opportunity for learning and growth that is happening *for me*. Thus I am no longer bound as a victim to my missing needs in the same way I was in tier one. In fact, at integral, I actively seek out challenges and explore experiences where my triggers become activated in order to become more whole. Moving into self-actualization is a profound step on the developmental ladder.

We can apply this same perspective to humanity's collective crises:

> From this perspective our current crisis can be seen not as an unmitigated disaster but as an evolutionary challenge, not just as a pull to regression and extinction but as a push to new evolutionary heights. It can be seen as a call to each and every one of us, both individually and collectively, to become and contribute as much as we can. This perspective gives us both a vision of the future and a motive for working toward it.
>
> —Roger Walsh[27]

As we have seen, violence of all forms is closely linked with missing needs. As I step into the integral paradigm, non-violence becomes a way of life. This is not the conceptual or aspirational approach of my ego. I am not thinking my way into peace. I am *being* nonviolent. This means I'm choosing to suffer. As more and more Peacemakers are forged in the world, we will engage *the cycle of liberation* (Figure 9.13) to enact sweeping changes collectively.

> There are laws, regulations, and institutions to protect the environment from harmful behaviors, but if people act in accordance with worldcentric morality, they would not knowingly harm other people or the environment. We must create circumstances for interior development. Were a critical mass of people to operate from worldcentric morality, they would most likely demand that social and political institutions conform to worldcentric values.
>
> —Esbjorn-Hargens and Zimmerman[28]

It is important for me to stress, however, that the goal is not to get everyone to integral. Because each human begins life at archaic, and because each paradigm includes the prior ones as essential parts in its own wholeness, human society will always incorporate the magic/tribal, mythic/traditional, mental/modern, and plural/postmodern paradigms. Our goal is to foster healthy versions of each paradigm and to support the members of each paradigm to develop in their own way. Further, my task is to love each individual exactly where they stand and to honor each person's capacity for development—including recognizing that some people's present worldview may be their station for life.

Here is a profound implication: the social nexus of *conditioned identity, power, and violence* is a feature of the human developmental journey. We can and should aim to move our individuals and power-wielding sociocultural holons out of that nexus and into the *redefined identity, empowerment, and blessing* social nexus. But the wound, the struggle, and the victimization carry a larger wisdom for the soul's journey. They are part of the great perfection of this human experience.

Within this context, I can see that "sustainability" is not a fixed destination that we will someday definitively reach. Rather, it is the virtuous process that matters. When we focus on the process, the results will take care of themselves.

Moreover, there will always be a crisis. It turns out, the contents of the crisis depend on the paradigm through which I'm making meaning of the world.[29] The mythic crisis is different from the modern crisis, is different from the postmodern crisis, etc. Our reactions to "the crisis" are a form of suffering, and our solutions to "the crisis" inevitably create new problems. Each successive paradigm arises to address the crisis of the previous paradigm, and unavoidably causes a more complex crisis (or polycrisis) in the process. To put it in Buddhist terms, our relative human world of samsara will always contain suffering. Our task is not to fix samsara. Our task is to embrace our suffering and the suffering of the world.

The great paradox that reveals itself in the integral paradigm is, *things are getting better and things are getting worse.* Both are simultaneously true. Now we can add yet another layer of paradox from the high integral perspective: *Things are getting better, things are getting worse, and everything is already perfect.*

Let's conclude this chapter and Part II of the workbook with a dedication:

> I take a breath in gratitude for the merit that has brought me to this place, now.
> I recognize the preciousness of my position.
> I celebrate the fruits of my work and my practice.
> Whatever goodness my practice has brought,
> I dedicate to the well-being and wholeness of all beings everywhere.
> We are the living blessing of love.
> I offer a breath of gratitude back to life.

Prompts for Journaling and Discussion

What does sustainability mean to you?

How do you see the crisis that is facing humanity and the world today? How does this differ from other interpretations of the crisis?

Imagine humanity living in nonviolence, creating generative processes of blessing. What does this look like? Articulate your optimistic vision for humanity and the planet.

How would you like to offer your blessings today?

Notes

[1] *On Conflict.*

[2] *Integral Psychology,* Wilber.

[3] *Consciousness-in-Action.*

[4] "My own critique of Wilber's work relates to its failure to include social group identity development as one of the multiple developmental lines identified as crucial for the overall development of consciousness, both at individual and collective levels." *Consciousness-in-Action,* Rosado.

[5] See *Integral Ecology.*

[6] *Integral Ecology.*

[7] *Integral Consciousness and the Future of Evolution.*

[8] Image by AntoFran Creative Commons 3.0

[9] "The Study of Philosophy and of Historical Materialism," in *The Modern Prince and Other Writings.*

[10] *Developmental Politics.*

[11] *A Sand County Almanac.*

[12] *The Will to Change: Men, Masculinity, and Love.*

[13] *Integral Ecology.*

[14] *Ibid.*

[15] "Thus, what we find in the real world—and in real groups, collectives, and 'We's'—is a 'layer cake' of different structures (and states) of development, with each layer containing a nexus-agency that exerts a significant influence on the members at that layer, and then a central cultural layer, or nexus-agency, which defines the group's overall characteristics and how the group officially defines itself (amber, orange, green, and so forth). This nexus-agency exerts a particularly strong influence on those members whose center of gravity is at the same basic level as the group's central level. *The Religion of Tomorrow,* Wilber.

[16] *From Violence to Blessing.*

[17] *The Raft is Not the Shore,* Berrigan.

[18] *Consciousness-in-Action.*

[19] Adapted from *Teaching for Diversity and Social Justice,* Harro.

[20] *Staying Alive: the Psychology of Human Survival.*

[21] Adapted from *The Power of TED,* Emerald.

[22] "Earth's most recent major extinction episode, the Quaternary Megafauna Extinction, claimed two-thirds of mammal genera and one-half of species that weighed >44 kg between ≈50,000 and 3,000 years ago. Estimates of megafauna biomass (including humans as a megafauna species) for before, during, and after the extinction episode suggest that growth of human biomass largely matched the loss of non-human megafauna biomass until ≈12,000 years ago. Then, total megafauna biomass crashed, because many non-human megafauna species suddenly disappeared, whereas human biomass continued to rise. After the crash, the global ecosystem gradually recovered into a new state where megafauna biomass was concentrated around one species, humans, instead of being distributed across many species." "Megafauna biomass tradeoff as a driver of Quaternary and future extinctions," Barnosky.

[23] "What is striking about the historical research is how similar child mortality rates were across a wide range of very different historical cultures: No matter where in the world a child was born, about half of them died." "Mortality in the past: every second child died," Roser.

[24] *Not the End of the World: How We Can Be the First Generation to Build a Sustainable Planet.*

[25] Source: Max Roser, CC-BY. Data sources: Volk and Atkinson (2013), Human Mortality Database, and UN IGME. From OurWorldinData.org

[26] *Not the End of the World.*

[27] *Staying Alive: the Psychology of Human Survival.*

[28] *Integral Ecology.*

[29] "An ecological crisis is too complex for any single individual to comprehend, so people select the information to include in their construction of that crisis. The construction of a crisis enables a society (or a group of individuals) to cope with the uncertainty that the crisis represents. It allows individuals to communicate about the crisis and to simplify the problem by selecting what is possible." *Integral Ecology,* Esbjorn-Hargens and Zimmerman.

PART III - SEX

| 10 |

The Gift of the Warrior: Sexual Self-Mastery

Figure 10.1 Shiva Ekamukhalinga[1]

The attainment of wholeness requires one to stake one's whole being. Nothing less will do; there can be no easier conditions, no substitutes, no compromises.

—Carl Jung

In the world today, men face an apparent dilemma of how to be both sexual beings and respectful humans. This dilemma has variously been framed as *the bad boy versus the nice guy*, as *the cock versus the heart*, and as *dominance versus sensitivity*. These frames shine light on the symptoms: We carry unintegrated sexual impulses that either over- or under-express. The answer is not to cultivate more of this side or more of that side. We need both turned on—sexuality and respect, cock and heart, penetration and presence—and they need to be activated in service to our sovereign center. The process to integrate our erotic impulses is what we've been lacking as men.

My focus here in Part III is to intentionally engage with my body and arousal in order to learn full-body non-ejaculatory orgasm. Cultivating this skill brings my arousal into conscious choice and it amplifies the flow of erotic energy. Through this approach, I become *more sexual, consciously*. This is Warrior's gift of sexual self-mastery.

The chapters that follow lay out a complete pathway to intentionally engage and master your sexual energy. These are my field notes. They are the guidance that I wish I had been given as I was traversing this rite of passage. The practices in these chapters are meant to be used. Use them. Conceptual understanding is not the point—the point is to practice.

I have structured the practices in a progression to ensure your safety in the transmission of the teachings. In yogic tradition, there is a powerful sexual energy that lies dormant at the base of the spine called *kundalini*. By cultivating large amounts of sexual energy, there is a real risk that kundalini can uncoil suddenly and intensely—known as a *premature kundalini awakening*. These events can and do land students in the hospital or psychiatric ward. If you jump straight to the advanced practices, you increase your risk of premature kundalini awakening.

Everything that I'm sharing in these pages, I have tested in my own body and with a myriad of students over the last decade. Following this progression and listening to my body has kept me safe. When used skillfully, accessing kundalini is like slowly turning up a dimmer switch on a light bulb. This gives my body and mind space to integrate the power of my full erotic life-force as the light becomes brighter and stronger.

Sexual self-mastery is among the most daunting initiations I'm aware of for a man and is the Warrior's gift being offered here. This entails an active engagement of sexual energy to develop increasing levels of awareness and control. In contrast, Gandhi undertook a vow of sexual celibacy. For him, celibacy was incredibly powerful—it laid the foundation for his life's work of Satyagraha and nonviolence. The initiation I am sharing here is not celibacy—sexual self-mastery is an embrace, not a denial. In my view, the intentional cultivation of sexual potency is both more challenging and more empowering than the monk's sexual celibacy.

Through this sexual self-mastery initiation, you will learn how to access *full-body non-ejaculatory orgasms*. As you read and engage with these chapters, you will understand why sexual self-mastery is the gift of the Warrior more so than the Lover. The path requires focus, boundaries, committed action, and resolve. While the Lover delights in erotic pleasure, it is the Warrior who teaches me how to purify and channel my sexual vitality.

For the majority of my sexually-active life, I believed that orgasm and ejaculation were one inseparable event for men. Everything I experienced and every porn video I watched confirmed this. I had no reason to question that anything could be different. I couldn't possibly imagine the vast realms of pleasure, intimacy, and consciousness that would be unlocked by intentionally exploring my capacity for orgasms.

Ejaculation is a physiological process. It's a physical thing my body does. Certain muscles rhythmically contract to pump fluid. Orgasm, on the other hand, is a pleasurable energetic expansion. It's an experience in my subtle-energy system. It turns out that orgasm and ejaculation are two distinct phenomena that often trigger together. With practice, it is possible to separate the physical process of ejaculation from orgasmic energy.

Orgasm cannot be defined in terms of physical function because it is an energetic phenomenon. The worldview pervading our medical, biological, and academic institutions does not include subtle energy, so the best scientists can do is point to the physiological responses that accompany orgasm.[2] This sheds some light on why there are not more resources in our culture around orgasm—we cannot manage what we are not able to measure. Once I shifted paradigms to one that is inclusive of subtle energy, the exploration of orgasm became readily available.

To understand orgasm, imagine that the body is a pot full of water. The water represents my subtle-energy. It is the aliveness permeating each cell. Orgasming is like bringing this pot of water to a boil. I heat the pot and the temperature rises in the liquid water until it gets close to boiling. At a certain point, the entire pot begins to boil as liquid water changes states into steam.

By analogy, *pleasure* is the heat that I apply to my body's subtle energy through sexual stimulation. I intensify the pleasure until my energy reaches a peak of intensity. Past a certain point, I experience a state-change into orgasm. This is the *orgasm threshold*.

I can feel pleasure and subtle energy anywhere in my body. Every cell is infused with this vital energy. Accordingly, it's possible for me to have an orgasm centered in any location in my body. In my exploration, I've tested my pinky toe, elbow, ear, and eyelids, and they are each every bit as capable of orgasming as my cock. I can feel orgasmic waves ripple throughout my whole body or I can learn to concentrate this energy in any specific part of my body. In the coming chapters, I'll share how I learned to do this.

When my orgasm is centered in my cock, my body has an automatic program to rapidly pump the muscles in my groin while my testes and various glands release semen and fluid. By default, the physiological process of ejaculation occurs together with the energetic phenomenon of orgasm. The really exciting discovery is: Orgasm does not depend on ejaculation. I can orgasm anywhere in my body independently from ejaculation. I can even learn to orgasm in my cock without triggering ejaculation. This is a total game-changer.

In the past, I held a story that sex has one culminating event: ejaculation. Without that event, sex is not a success. And after that event happens, sex is over. I have since learned that this is only one way to approach sex and self-pleasure, and a rather narrow one at that. By separating orgasm from ejaculation, I have learned how to have orgasm after orgasm after orgasm while withholding ejaculation. Although I can only ejaculate once or twice a day, there is no upper limit to the number and duration of orgasms I can experience. Learning this has resulted in nothing less than a total revolution in my experience of sex.

Not only has this brought vastly more pleasure into my life, but it has exploded the cultural narrative about what sex could be. Sex and self-pleasure no longer have a singular goal or a definitive ending point. This, I learned, is a massive relief of performance pressure for both me and my partners.

On the other side of this initiation, sex has become an open-ended playground of discovery and a place of profound intimacy. My sexuality is now one of my most direct doorways for shadow work. It has become a practice that supports both my purpose in the world and my pathway of spiritual realization. In short, my sexuality has become perhaps the richest area of exploration in my life.

> Understanding who you are and how you operate sexually is fundamental to personal growth, self-integration and achieving your full potential.
>
> —Sheri Winston[3]

Let's take a look at the progression into orgasmic mastery:

5 Phases to Orgasmic Mastery

1. Arousal control. I learn to control my arousal so that I can last as long as I want during sex and I can choose when I ejaculate.

2. Edging. I learn to experience and sustain higher and higher states of pleasure.

3. Body orgasms. I start igniting mini-orgasms in my body. They're not as strong as when I ejaculate, but I can have them again and again and again.

4. Full non-ejaculatory orgasm. I am able to hold my body steady while I have an energetic orgasm in my cock—this is a *full non-ejaculatory orgasm.* The strength and duration of my energetic orgasms now regularly surpass the ejaculatory orgasms I was having prior to Phase 1.

5. Orgasmic articulation. I learn how to include my entire body in orgasmic states. My orgasms come in peaks, ripples, waves, colors, and textures. I can extend my orgasms for multiple minutes. I can orgasm in different locations in my body. I have the ability to access orgasms readily, on demand. I learn to ride orgasms into expanded states of consciousness. Orgasmic energy becomes a tool for spiritual awakening and potentiates my mission in life.

Next, it's important to understand what this undertaking will require:

- Stop watching porn.
- Stop ejaculating for anywhere from six months to two years.
- Self-pleasure or have sex *daily* for this duration.
- Practice yoga *daily* to support the sexual practice.
- Confront and heal an epic amount of sexual shadow: performance, shame, insecurity, judgment, attachment to outcome, etc.
- Completely re-learn how to have sex, rewire your nervous system, bring articulation to muscles you never knew existed, and overcome millions of years of evolutionary instincts to *spread the seed.*

This is no small feat. It requires a Warrior's dedication to practice. It works across physical, emotional, energetic, and relational levels of my being simultaneously. It disrupted my sleep, increased my horniness, and pushed me outside of my comfort zone in the exact places I would really rather not have opened up.

Here is why *stop watching porn* is number one on this list. As men, we have a natural capacity to stimulate arousal visually. Porn vastly amplifies this circuit. I am seeing sexually arousing images via porn and I am turning myself on through that stimulation. In order to move through the *5 Phases* I needed to learn somatic arousal. I had to unlearn my habit of turning myself on visually, and discover how to access arousal through feeling sensations in my body. Somatic arousal is not subject to the addictive response cycles that porn induces. Instead of the *craving - consumption - relief* pattern of porn, I am using sexual stimulation to become more alive, energetic, and vital. Instead of artificially ramping my arousal with images of many novel sexual mates, I am cultivating my authentic erotic drive. I need to become so finely tuned to the instrument of my body that I can feel the subtlest pitch-shifts in my pleasure. So I am not advocating any moral judgment against porn. Rather, I am simply delineating the practical reasons why porn is not compatible with this path.

Benefits

As I progressed on this path, I began having better sex and I became a better sexual partner. Vastly more pleasure became available to me. Pleasure is rightly understood as an aspect of the path—not as the goal. What really blew my mind is everything beyond sex that shifted in my life as a result. How I treat my cock is a mirror for how I relate to everything and everyone. When I stopped using my cock as a tool for instant gratification and began working together with it as a sacred teacher, my entire life changed.

My first realization was how much I was stuck in my head during sex and how focused I was on pleasing my partner. Practicing arousal-control required me to feel my body during sex. I know it sounds obvious, but learning to feel my body during sex was a huge shift for me—one that opened many additional layers of depth to my sexual experience. As my practice deepened, my capacity for focused feeling became a meditative experience. In addition, being so attuned to myself made space for many repressed emotions and memories to surface. Sex became an avenue for my healing.

I used to be very quick to come. When I picked up these practices, I started having intercourse for 30 minutes… 45 minutes… an hour… two hours. I had never lasted more than 15 minutes before and I had no idea how much more my entire body could open into sex.

In order to avoid spilling over, I needed to slow way down. The sexual script that I learned from porn was vigorous pumping at high velocity. This simply wasn't an option as I was learning to withhold ejaculation. Not only did I access more control by slowing down, I also opened up a whole world of feeling and sensation that I had been numb to. Higher speed actually dampens sensitivity. Instead of just following maximum pleasure into climax, I began to pace myself. I cultivated presence. I began to enjoy the experience of slow sex. It's the difference between savoring a five-course meal over a number of hours and scarfing down some fast-food.

My goal in sex changed from "getting off" to "do everything to avoid getting off." I had no idea how deep and how pervasive the agenda to ejaculate ran in me. Through my practice, I came to feel and understand how the build-up and release of semen was controlling my sex drive, and thus my behavior. I began to see how I was unconsciously using sex to feel relief. Even more broadly, I came to see how my desire to go to parties, my desire to meet and flirt with people, even which humans I was attracted to, were all subtly in service to getting myself off. Taking ejaculation off the table literally freed me from a whole host of seduction strategies and drama in my life.

It's obvious in retrospect, but once I stopped harboring this unconscious agenda to get off, I was able to connect with people I was attracted to more openly. I started relating to *what is* instead of to *where this will go.*

As my internal relationship with sex transformed, the responses I received—particularly from women—shifted dramatically: I became safe, and because of that, I became way more attractive than I had ever been before.

Learning to withhold ejaculation took all the pressure off during sex—there was nowhere to get to and nothing that needed to happen. No more pressuring my partner or myself. No bar for whether I succeeded or not.

When I talk to women who have partnered with non-ejaculating men, the primary benefit they list is: no pressure. Not, "He can last a long time." Not, "He's in his heart more" or "He can give me better orgasms." Instead, simply: "He's not pressuring me to get him off."

Throughout my entire adolescence and into adulthood, I was ejaculating once or twice a day. So I had no baseline for what that output was costing me. Semen carries an incredible amount of life-force. When I was regularly releasing it, that meant my body was constantly investing in making more. When I stopped ejaculating, I tapped into more creativity, more drive, and more focus than I had ever experienced in my life. It was like an extra motor kicked into gear. I found that my need to vegetate virtually disappeared, while each morning I awoke with clarity and excitement for my day. A fog lifted. This clarity and focus has only strengthened for me through the subsequent years of my practice.

I had a client once who was beginning to retain ejaculation. He is an avid runner and would track his run times. He was noticing that his times would get better and better, then suddenly drop back, then start improving again. He couldn't find a reason for why his times were improving, or especially why they would drop back and erase all previous progress. Finally, he put it together that when he started practicing semen-retention, his run-times began to improve. And the night after a hot date where he spilled his seed was where his times dropped. This boost of energy and focus is the most immediate, direct, and in many cases profound benefit that men will access through semen retention.

As I have learned how ejaculation has affected me across all these levels, my relationship with my semen has changed. Instead of viewing it as a pregnancy liability or a mess to be contained and cleaned up, I now view my semen as the most sacred gift my body has to offer. Sharing it is precious. I know that I'll feel an energetic dip for a few days afterward. Today, when I do choose to ejaculate, I do so with intention and I honor the sharing of my creative essence through the act.

On the other side of ejaculation control is orgasmic mastery. There are entire realms of pleasure, bliss, and consciousness that become available for exploration through orgasm. Used in this way, sex has become an avenue for my spiritual evolution.

Beyond orgasms, this path has led me to become vastly more available for connection during sex. Investing so deeply in orgasms has freed me from needing to worry about them. Whether orgasms happen or not is no longer my real focus. What really turns me on is intimacy. Today in my life, sex has become a playground where I open as fully as I can to my honest truth, where I share nakedly with my partner and get to witness them in return. Sex is an ever-evolving dance that expresses itself through me and as me. It is the raw creativity of the kosmos channeled through my body as a prayer and given as an offering back to life.

Challenges

Advancing through the *5 Phases to Orgasmic Mastery* is a major undertaking. For most men, it requires the Warrior's committed action on a daily basis for a year or two. Initiation into full-body orgasm offers profound freedom, personal growth, healing, and maturing as a man—and it's worth it. But it will ask everything of you. In the yogic texts, this is considered a *siddhi*: a miraculous super-power attained through depth of practice.

Learning full-body orgasms has been one of the most challenging and rewarding experiences of my life. It has pushed me more than anything I've known. It has worked me across all layers of my being: physically, emotionally, relationally, energetically, and karmically. When I first received these teachings, I was in a committed relationship. It took me nine months of sexual practice to make it to full non-ejaculatory orgasm (Phase Four). During those nine months, my partner and I committed to be in intercourse together for 45 minutes a day, every day. In addition, my commitment to myself during this time was to practice a minimum of 20 minutes of yoga before sex. If I hadn't done my yoga practice, I wasn't ready for sex, no exceptions. Looking back, I can say that without that level of dedicated consistency, I wouldn't have made it.

Talking to other men who have undertaken this initiation, the common thread is a fanatical level of devotion to their practice. It is the Warrior archetype that carries us through. Some men get it within six months. Some men take two years. It depends on where you're starting from, the amount of time and energy you put in, and your natural affinity for this practice. Like playing a musical instrument, this is something that every man has the potential to achieve, regardless of trauma, physical capability, age, etc. Orgasm is an innate capacity of life-force and it is our birthright as humans to experience. With practice and dedication, every man can step into this level of sexual self-mastery.

Now let's look at the challenges on this path:

1. The post-porn libido purge

For men coming off a porn addiction there is a *libido purge* where we can lose our arousal for a period of six to twelve months. Porn addiction causes a desensitization to non-porn sexual stimuli.

When I stopped using porn, I lost my libido for six months. I had to resensitize myself to pleasure. This is a physiological process that takes time. During this time, it's common for men to lose their erections. The good news is that this is normal, and our libido does eventually return.

Often men will attempt to stop porn at the same time they start non-ejaculation practice. While the aspiration is commendable, my recommendation is to tackle one major sexual achievement at a time. For most men, breaking the porn habit is a major undertaking on its own. First, stop using porn and find your new solid ground. Then, come back to the Five Phases to Orgasmic Mastery.

2. The sensitivity and intensity convergence

Here is how this process often unfolds: As I begin to withhold ejaculation, the semen and energy that I am accustomed to releasing now builds up in my system. I feel more powerful urges to get off. I get blue-balls: a painful pressure in my testes. My ejaculation goes onto a hare trigger. I start having wet dreams. I become unbelievably sensitive to erotic stimulation. Semen retention skyrockets my sensitivity.

At the same time, these practices are designed to intentionally bring more and more pleasure into my body. I am slowly building my capacity to hold sexual energy through daily sex or self-pleasure. I am training myself to increase my energetic tone to hold more intensity.

In this phase, my sensitivity is going through the roof at the same time I am intentionally bringing myself to greater levels of intensity. This is by design: sexual abstinence does not lead to orgasmic mastery. It is the combination of semen retention and consistent sexual stimulation that opens the initiation.

These two forces—greater sensitivity and greater intensity—create a double-whammy, like two waves crashing into each other. It can feel overwhelming at times. It disrupts my sleep. I experience waves of desire and lust beyond anything I've felt before. I feel like I am high on cocaine all day long. The convergence of intensity and sensitivity can be massively disruptive.

In order to make it through, the yoga practices that I'm offering here are essential. They taught me to move and channel all this new-found energy into useful places in my life.

It is normal in this practice to spill your seed. It happened for me again and again and again. Here is the bad news: Every time I ejaculate, I start over from scratch, day one, fully resensitized and rebuilding my capacity from the beginning again. One slip and I can lose weeks of progress. It can be frustrating, demoralizing, and embarrassing. It often feels like I am moving backwards or regressing in sexual performance. "I'm supposed to be getting better at sex and this practice has only made me more horny and unbearably sensitive—I'm getting worse, not better." This is where many men call it quits. Hopefully this is also where the resources in the pages that follow will support you to stay with your practice and make it through.

The good news is that as I hold off from ejaculation for longer stretches, I develop more capacity to hold, and my body adjusts. There seems to be a recalibration that my body undergoes at about seven weeks without ejaculation. I normalize and adapt to all the new erotic energy that I now have access to. Seven weeks is a long time to make it. But from this point, it gets easier. I still need to practice withholding, but the immediacy of my urge to ejaculate has now abated considerably.

3. Shame, judgment, and cruelty

Very few places are as tender for me as my sexual performance. When I'm not having sex well, it cuts straight to my insecurity and my fear of being weak. Rather than admit to my insecurity, I have a whole host of strategies at my disposal: I shame myself, I blame my partner, I isolate myself, I judge myself, and generally just act cruelly towards myself. All of this can and will surface. Shame spirals have completely hijacked my practice. In these times of challenge, I definitely felt tempted to just go back to what worked in the past.

When I undertook this initiation, it meant I completely sucked at sex for an extended period of time. I intentionally disassembled all the skills and techniques I had working for me. This humbled me, yes, but whether I humiliated myself was my choice.

If you are harboring sexual agendas, insecurities, and shame, this practice will expose them. My advancement through this process happened *to the extent that* I was able to meet and transform these wounds. So when my self-judgment kicks in, I hold it as *part of the initiation*—something arising to be healed.

4. Buried pain and trauma

I spent years using masturbation for trivial reasons. I was bored, I wanted a distraction, or I wanted to fall asleep. When I gave up ejaculation, no more sleepy hormone cocktail for my brain at the end of a long day! Instead, I was now energized and more connected to my feelings after self-pleasure and sex. This was incredibly confronting. I was no longer able to use sex or self-pleasure to avoid myself. Instead, it began bringing me directly into all of my emotions, including the ones I would rather not feel.

I have had many challenging sexual experiences in my life. Some were painful, emotional, and even overwhelming. My natural response was to push these experiences away. The thing is, for better or worse, there is no *away*. "Away" means I push the challenging energy and emotion into my body where I lock it down with tension so that I don't have to feel it. Subconsciously, I invest my energy in this pushing, tensing, and locking—and then I do my best to forget about it. This is one way to understand trauma.

Using these sexual practices, I began bringing more and more energy into my body. At some point, that energy was enough to unlock the tension holding down my old pain. Back it came, rising to the surface to be felt again.

I told myself, "Of course I want to be more connected to myself through sex." But I can't count the number of times that an old wound has come up and my response has been, "Anything but this. Take it back. I don't want to go here."

Fortunately, my body has its own intelligence. As long as I'm staying attuned to my body—not overriding it or pushing past it—I will not open anything that I'm not 100% resourced to handle. So I can trust that I am ready for whatever is arising.

Of course, I get to choose whether I go into my trauma or painful history. But understand that there are no shortcuts on this path to sexual self-mastery. All the exciting sexual awakening happens *to the extent that* I face my shadows and heal my wounds.

5. Plateauing

Plateauing means hitting a lull or pause in my advancement. Everything seems to be moving nicely forward and then, for no apparent reason, I stop making progress. A few weeks go by and it's just the same old thing. I lose momentum. I start skipping my practice days. Next thing I know, I'm off the wagon.

This phenomenon is not unique to sexual practice. Athletes and musicians call it a *training plateau*. Our bodies adapt to a given regimen and we stop progressing.

On my sexual journey, I've hit many plateaus. I've fallen out of practice and come back again plenty of times. Here is what has worked for me to address a plateau:

> A) Return to my inspiration and passion for this path—remember why I'm doing this;
> B) Talk to other men to get advice on where I'm stuck and have them help me stay accountable;
> C) Change how I'm practicing—time of day, duration, technique—mix it up; and
> D) Change my mindset during my practice—am I here "to do the program," or am I here to enjoy these gifts of life, body, and pleasure?

I deeply trust the wisdom of my body and the timing for what's happening. After going through a relationship break-up, I have commonly taken a break from sexual practice. Trying to force myself into practice is usually counter-productive. There's a larger arc to my journey beyond sex that I've learned to have faith in. Every time I've set down my sexual practice, it has come back in its own time, from a new place.

I am sharing these pitfalls here in the introduction to offer a realistic picture of what this path entails. This practice is not simply an exercise in expanding one's capacity for pleasure. For me, it required layer upon layer of healing and personal growth. Along the way, my relationship to my sexuality massively transformed.

Commitment

Now that you're informed about the benefits and requirements of this path, it's time to open the practice container. The first step on this path is commitment. My commitment is not to achieve some future state. True commitment only happens in the present. Every minute I spend in practice is simply an extension of the power of my commitment. My actions are the truest expression of my commitment. Every day that I reaffirm my commitment through my actions makes it stronger—makes *me* stronger.

The most trustable commitment I can make is to my own life, and the way that works is by aligning with my purpose. Take a moment now and turn back to Figure 5.2 where you listed your purpose statements for your child parts and copy your mission into this section:

Who I'm here to be: I am _____, living a life of _____.

What I'm here to learn: I am _____, using _____ to meet my needs.

How I'm here to love: I am _____ in a world that is _____.

Take three deep breaths

At the deepest level of my being, I am honoring my missions for this life.
By following my purpose, I am loving myself.
I am aligning my will in service to love. Will in service to love: this is commitment.

Now, I am including my sexuality.
I am considering my sexual history solo and with partners,
and how this has aligned with my three purposes above.
Looking forward, I am imagining how my sexuality could align more fully with my missions.

In this moment, I am feeling my erotic life-force energy in my body.
I am saying "Yes" to my aliveness.
With these words, I align my eroticism in service to my missions.
With these words, I connect my missions with the Eros of life that flows through me and all around me.

Blessed be and thus it is!

In the meditation above, you were guided to connect your life's missions with your sexual energy. If you don't feel connected to your purpose yet, take your time here. Go back through the material in Chapter 5. Talk to other men. Do some journaling. And allow your purpose to come to you. Even if you begin with "My mission is to discover my true purpose," that's an honest place to start and will orient you into deeper levels of self-knowledge.

Once you feel confident in your life's purposes, connecting your erotic energy to these missions will accomplish two things: first, it fully aligns your life-force with your path; and second, it gives you a trustable experience of your sexuality. As long as your eroticism is supporting one of your missions, you can trust it. Meaning: You can trust yourself to be sexual.

In order to walk this path, it is imperative to commit to self-pleasuring or intercourse as a daily practice. A very strong devotion to the practices is required, which is why we are connecting it with our core missions in life. I can think of plenty of examples of friends who have become fanatics about a workout routine or a particular diet. They are so deeply committed to their *thing* that they live it, they breathe it—everything they read is about it, and all they talk about is *the thing*. This is the level of total commitment that one can have towards sexual practice; indeed, it is generally what is required in order to move through all the trials along the path. Men like us who self-initiate into sexual mastery do it through dedicated daily practice. Here is the commitment:

**Every day, I will self-pleasure or have sex while withholding ejaculation
and abstaining from porn—starting at 20 minutes per day
and working up to 45 minutes or longer.**

In addition to self-pleasuring daily, the meditations, energy-work, and yoga practices outlined in these chapters should become part of regular practice. My larger commitment is to *knowing myself through sexual and spiritual practice.*

Personally, in the time since I started intentional sexual practice, I've had three long-term partners, interspersed with periods of solitude and dating. Just over half of my time has been in dedicated partnership where regular sexual practice was feasible, and just under half of my time has been devoted to solitary self-pleasure practice. Both sexual partnership and solo self-pleasure are rich experiences that offer different challenges and benefits. Neither is better or preferable to the other, and the full path is attainable regardless of relationship status.

Solo Practice

Loving yourself well takes courage, practice and perseverance. You can choose to be a great self-lover by accessing every bit of pleasure that you're capable of—it's a radical act.

—Sheri Winston[4]

For everyone entering onto this path, solo self-pleasure is the foundation. Whether I am in partnership or not, I am making regular space to connect with my body and my arousal. With consistent practice, self-pleasure gives me a clear reflection of my state of being: physically, emotionally, mentally, and spiritually. Through this practice, I can see where I'm blocked or resistant. I have space to receive my fantasies and work with my shadows. And because it's just me, I can intentionally hone in on exactly what is happening in my body and with my energy. I have total control over the speed and intensity of stimulation.

The self-pleasure practices and techniques discussed below lay out a developmental path-way—a progression. I am not pressuring myself to advance on the path and I am not judging my performance. My focus is on the process rather than the outcome. How am I feeling now and where does this feeling want to take me? I measure success not by the strength of my orgasm, or whether I orgasm or not, or even whether I get hard or not. Success looks like authentically connecting through my body and through pleasure with what is actually present for me. This is worth repeating:

I measure success in self-pleasure to the extent that I connect to my authentic experience through my body and through pleasure.

The main challenge with solo practice is activation energy. With a partner, there is an *other* to polarize with and build attraction. Self-pleasuring, in comparison, may feel flat or empty. Under-standing this, I learn to use my energetic tools to generate extra energy to get my arousal flowing.

In order to advance through the 5 Phases, self-pleasure needs to be a dedicated daily practice. Self-pleasuring only when it feels good does not stimulate enough energy for most men. The length of time spent self-pleasuring should be slowly lengthened to 45 minutes. Extended periods of time spent in high arousal is where I will most effectively learn these new skills. Without agenda or attachment to my sexual performance, I am investing my time and energy to cultivate the conditions for my sexual development.

Partnered Practice

Regular sexual practice with a partner is another animal entirely. Intercourse calls me to fully participate and bring all of myself. In solo-self pleasure, it's possible to avoid certain places and mellow out my intensity. When I'm using these practices with a partner, I am consistently called to give everything, hide nothing, and feel completely. Other benefits of partnered practice include more energy and a more dynamic play of experience.

Most partners have sex when they feel in the mood or follow a routine for sex. In contrast, this is an intentional sexual practice. It is therefore a radically different approach to sex. My partner and I make an agreement to make time for sex, ideally daily. Then we show up for it and we help support each other to stay in it. This mutual commitment deepens a relationship beyond anything I've ever experienced. In various Tantric traditions, this practice forms the foundation for the consort relationship—the path of spiritual awakening through partnership. The commitment is to show up. I am committing to taking care of any emotional, physical, or logistical needs so I can be available for sex. From here, the intention is to be in penetrative intercourse together for 45 minutes or longer. During that 45 minutes, as a man learning the 5 Phases, I am training my body to be aroused without spilling over into ejaculation.

It's incredible how having sex daily with another human asks everything of me. It triggers my wounds, my traumas, my resistance, my strategies for getting my needs met, AND it does the same for my partner. The nature of deep sexual practice is that it raises my karma to the surface directly. Stepping into a committed sexual practice with a consort is rightfully terrifying—it is the path of the Love Warrior.

Giving or receiving orgasm is not the point. Just be in the experience together for whatever arises. I stay aroused enough that I can continue to have sex, but avoid spilling over. If I need to stop sex, practice a few *uddiyana bandas*[5] in order to pull the energy up from my cock, and then continue with sex—so be it. The physical and energetic practice of stabilizing at increasingly higher levels of arousal is what matters for the man's initiation into non-ejaculatory orgasm. And it's also important to play, improvise, and explore during lovemaking with my partner. It's worth mentioning that intercourse is the preferred mode of practice but not the only way to stimulate pleasure together.

Every excuse imaginable to not have sex will come up: *we'll get in a fight, I'm not in the mood, she's not in the mood, I'm too busy...* I can't count the number of times I "haven't been in the mood" or wasn't getting hard only to discover that by sharing a resentment I was withholding towards my partner, my arousal sprang right up. Daily sex is the most honest and direct form of couple's therapy I've encountered. If I'm not getting an erection, we trade massage or we talk through what emotions are here or I simply insert my soft cock. If my partner has a yeast infection, we use that opportunity to explore giving and receiving anal, for example. We make a full conscious commitment together to daily sexual practice. Then we make the time and hold each other to it. We do whatever it takes, and we do it with total love and kindness.

Both partners will need to learn patience and slowness during sex to advance along the *5 Phases to Orgasmic Mastery*. Learning Phase One: Arousal Control is like picking up a violin for the first time and trying to find different notes. It's screeching, halting, inconsistent, and frustrating. Meanwhile, my partner is on the receiving end of this. All of my performance habits together with all of my partner's agendas are going to come up to be worked through. In solo-practice, I'm only attuning to my energy. In intercourse, my partner may suddenly start orgasming or my partner may lose arousal and I am called to ride those waves of energy as well as my own.

Just as I am choosing to let go of my attachment to ejaculation and orgasm, my partner is being called to a commensurate type of surrender. My partner must be willing to let go of being taken by me (for now), receiving my full orgasm without me holding anything back (for now), and any attachment to receiving my ejaculation. This is a major undertaking for both partners. When I was learning this, my partner was willing to patiently show up for sex while I was haltingly relearning arousal and rewiring my nervous system. During this time, it was important for the balance of our relationship for me to spend time lavishing her and celebrating her highest sexual expression.

This practice is for committed partnership. I strongly recommend *against* trying this path with casual partners. For one thing, having daily sex for 45 minutes will accelerate any connection straight into partnership or explode it. I don't believe it's possible to remain casual in this practice. The daily consistency IS the strong container for the practice to grow within. Inconsistent practice simply isn't strong enough for this initiation. In addition, most men find that changing between partners is confusing for the body and energetics. Consistency is key.

It is also absolutely crucial for me to have an open conversation with my partner about what I'm practicing during sex and to have my partner's full enthusiastic buy-in for the process. Even with consent, feeling me hold back from ejaculation during sex can be confusing or trigger feelings of rejection.

The good news for people who are partnering with men learning these practices is that even if the sex is not initially as powerful or masterful, relaxing into 45 minutes of non-goal-oriented intercourse is generally immensely pleasurable. When my former partner started this practice with me, she quickly learned how to enter extended states of orgasm by relaxing and letting go more and more deeply.

With consistency, sex becomes the core of the relationship. It is the place where both partners open their bodies, emotions, and energy together. It provides a safe space to be honest, which in turn leads to more profound experiences of intimacy. As both partners learn to ride the waves of higher and higher levels of arousal, expanded states of consciousness begin to open. The *hieros gamos*, the divine union of opposites, naturally begins to awaken as a consciousness that transcends and includes both individual partners. This is among the most precious experiences available in this human life.

Summary

Start with your core desire. What do you want through sex? Who do you want to be sexually? And how is your sexuality empowering your life's mission? This connection to your true purpose will motivate you in your process of discovery. Keep coming back to it.

We all start this journey from our own position. There's a humility that is required to simply make the time every day and show up for the practice. When I started on this path, I was in a relationship that was in crises around sex. I had no sexual confidence and I was totally stuck. In addition, I had minimal awareness of my body, zero awareness of subtle energy, and very little control over my libido. But I was willing to put in the time to learn.

Wherever you are right now is your starting point. It is no better or worse than anyone else's. It's yours. Your life purpose is your fuel—it will move you along this path. All of the practices outlined in the coming chapters are here to support you on your path. They are by no means definitive, dogmatic, or prescriptive. You are in the driver's seat, and these are maps drawn by someone who's traveled this countryside already.

While each practice has a skillful fruition to it, I hold them as non-goal-oriented explorations. Every day I am making the space to breathe deeply and touch myself to cultivate pleasure. Then I get curious to see what unfolds. It's important to feel good and enjoy self-pleasuring. Ultimately each session is an end in itself: today I made space to drop into my body and feel pleasure. This is one of the most direct and profound forms of self-love I've encountered.

Initially, it was my individual purpose that drove me on the path of sexual exploration. Over time, I have come to understand that cultivating my sexuality goes far beyond my personal benefit. As I release my shame, heal my wounds, and step into sexual sovereignty, that profoundly affects every human I'm in a sexual encounter with for the rest of my life. This is a gift that I pass forward simply through embodiment. Moreover, by saying Yes to my sexuality and welcoming aliveness into my body every day, I am becoming the fullest, brightest version of myself. I can choose to take that energy and offer it back to life, back to the earth, and outward for the benefit of all beings everywhere.

Feeling fully alive is the highest place to be in service from. For Gandhi, it was only after committing to his version of sexual self-mastery that he became available to truly pursue his life's work, and I believe it is the same for every man. Our erotic nature is perhaps the strongest aspect of our human lives. Harnessing that energy with intention opens us fully to the Warrior's path of service.

Ejaculation, Men, and the "Male Sex"

In the most specific terms, the practices I'm outlining here in Part III are for people who ejaculate semen. This workbook series is geared for *men*, in which I include biological males, masculine-gendered folks, and people who initiate through the masculine archetypal roles and parts. A person can hold any combination of these categories and still identify as a man. In addition, the category *biological male* exists on a spectrum across anatomy, hormones, and genes. There is no singular definition. The same goes for masculinities and the masculine archetypes. I bring this up because my intention is for these teachings to benefit people without my language and framing getting in the way.

The non-ejaculation practices that I'm presenting here are geared toward anyone whose body produces sperm. They will also be useful for anyone who is in sexual connection with a person whose body produces sperm. With this in mind, I'm going to use the terms *men* and *male* throughout these chapters—but mostly, I'm going to focus on sharing my own experience as a person who produces sperm and trust you to adapt these teachings as needed.

I will also note that these sections are primarily focused on how to operate a male ejaculatory system: a cock and testes. My focus here does not include *conscious sex* or *sacred sex* practices. I'll cover those topics in *Lore Book III: The Lover*. I have not included any information on how female or non-binary arousal operates. My intention is not to exclude the feminine or the androgyne, but simply to focus on the material from my lived experience that is mine to share. I highly recommend Sheri Winston's *Women's Anatomy of Arousal* as a feminine compliment to the man-focused material presented here. Her book is immensely educational for anyone having or in relationship with a pussy.

Prompts for Journaling and Discussion

What is the longest stretch you've ever gone without ejaculating? Did you notice any differences in your body or arousal?

Have you ever had an orgasm without ejaculating? What was it like?

If you were to begin a practice regimen for full-body non-ejaculating orgasm, what obstacles might get in your way?

What would be meaningful about intercourse if you took orgasm and ejaculation out of the equation?

If you imagine yourself at Phase Five: Orgasmic Mastery, how would your life change?

Notes

[1] Photo by redtigerxyz CC SA 3.0

[2] "We recognize there is no universally accepted definition of orgasm. For example, orgasm has been defined as the apex and culmination of sexual excitement (Miller and Keane, 1987); a sexual climax, marked by a peak in myotonia, vasocongestion, psychological tension, and erotic pleasure (Francoeur, 1982); and a reflex (Kaplan, 1974). Graber (1982) attributed orgasm to the perception of activity in specific genital muscles and organs. Komisaruk (1978, 1982) speculated that orgasm is generated by afferent activity that increases in intensity and synchrony (in response to somatic and visceral afferent and reafferent stimulation), which generates a peak of sensory and motor excitation. After conducting extensive interviews with researchers studying the physiological components of orgasm, Gallager (1982) concluded that an orgasm is an involuntary response to a stimulus. The stimulus is usually thought to be physical, although as cited above, there are indications that imagery is an adequate eliciting stimulus." "Physiological correlates of imagery-induced orgasm in women," Whipple, et al.

[3] *Women's Anatomy of Arousal.*

[4] *Ibid.*

[5] see Yoga Sequence II.

| 11 |

Arousal Control

Figure 11.1 Saraha[1]

Holy places, shrines, and lesser shrines: all are right here—I've been there in my travels, but I've seen no place of pilgrimage more blissful than the body.

—Saraha, *Couplet 48*[2]

To begin, I am simply spending time every day touching my body for pleasure. I want to listen to how my body likes to be touched. I want to learn how to turn myself on, and how to keep myself turned on. This first practice is called *arousal control*.

I can conceptualize my sexual arousal on a scale from zero to ten, where zero means no arousal and ten means orgasm. The *arousal curve* is a graph of how my sexual arousal changes over time. In conventional sex or self-pleasure, I move directly towards increasing arousal until I get to orgasm and ejaculation, after which, there is a steep drop in my arousal back to baseline (Figure 11.2). Studies report that most men last between five and seven minutes during intercourse.[3] This is what our bodies are instinctually wired for, and it is this habit that we will be working to retrain.

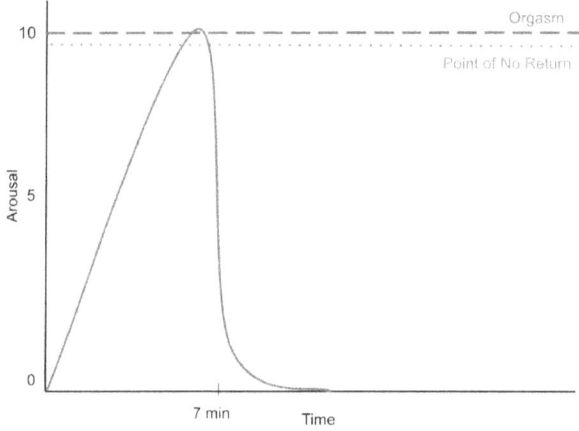

Figure 11.2 - Conventional Sex

On the chart, ten is an orgasm, demarcated with a dashed line. In conventional sex this is the goal. Notice that there is also a dotted line just below orgasm, labeled, the *Point of No Return*. Moments before my body begins the rhythmic contractions of ejaculation, there is a switch where ejaculation is definitely going to happen—this is the *point of no return.*[4] My basic orientation is: As long as I don't reach the point of no return, I'm not going to ejaculate.

My first step is to bring awareness to the level of arousal I'm feeling during self-pleasure and intercourse. Frequently, I skip right over 4, 5, 6, 7, and 8 in my goal to maximize my pleasure. I sometimes refer to four through eight as *flyover country*. But it is a mistake to think there's nothing worth exploring in these middle ranges of arousal. There is an incredible richness and depth that opens when I meet this space with curiosity instead of agenda.

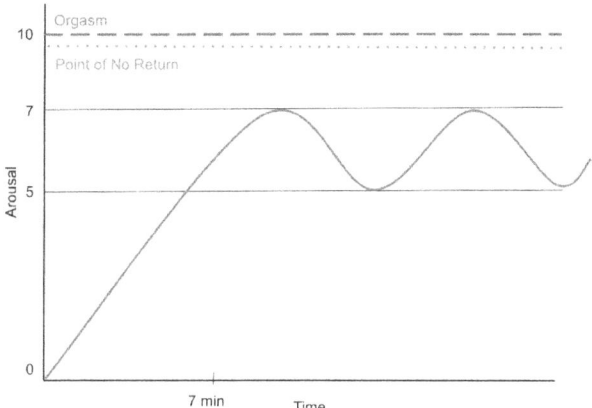

Figure 11.3 - Arousal Control

In the *arousal control* practice, I am finding the zone between about five and seven in my arousal and stabilizing there (Figure 11.3). Remember to breathe deeply. The more I breathe, the more I feel. At first, my arousal levels may be spiky and irregular. I can have a big swing either up or down suddenly. Seven provides a safe buffer beneath the point of no return. Five keeps me aroused enough to not lose my erection. The practice is to identify intuitively where these numbers are, and to learn to stay in this zone and enjoy. Notice that Figure 11.3 has a slower ramp of arousal than the first graph—I am taking my time to slowly build pleasure in my body. There is no destination and no need to rush. My arousal will naturally rise and fall in waves. By going more slowly, my arousal becomes less erratic and more steady. I can use my awareness, breath, sound, touch, and movement to modulate my arousal and stay in the zone. I want to focus on the physical sensations and the energy of arousal and not get lost in thinking or fantasizing. The point is to feel pleasure in my body. This practice provides a safe space to try different techniques and learn how my erotic energy flows.

Now is the moment to commit to doing your very best to withhold ejaculating. No ejaculation from this point forward, no exceptions. Notice what happens with your arousal and general energy levels as you begin to contain your sexual energy. For me, it built up strongly and quickly. It was a major adjustment. Understand that you will slip up, especially if your body is accustomed to ejaculating daily. I cannot count the number of times I spilled. Notice what happens to your energy after you spill. Each time you spill, you will begin building your sexual container again from ground zero. This is normal. It is part of the process. Treat yourself with kindness and recommit to your practice. The beginning few weeks are usually the most challenging.

Embodiment

Embodiment is the process of dis-identifying from my conceptual mind and bringing my presence into the raw experience arising in my body. This is the foundation that supports arousal control. Put another way, in order to control my arousal, I must inhabit my body. And in order to do that, I need to get out of my head.

Embodiment is also termed, *somatic awareness*. By coming into my body, I contact my unfiltered sensations, emotions, and desires. The world becomes more immediate, more visceral, and more alive. Embodiment catalyzes curiosity, creativity, and growth—all natural qualities of being human. In contrast, my conceptual mind will pre-consciously filter raw sensory data to affirm the biases and beliefs that I already hold.[5] Because of this, my conceptual mind naturally selects for what is familiar, comfortable, and safe. Embodiment therefore requires me to risk my comfort and safety to step into the wild and primal terrain of my *soma*.

My body remembers. My "baggage" is what keeps me small, keeps me repeating wounded patterns, and keeps me stuck. It lives in my body and can be resolved through embodiment. Unresolved emotions are held in my body. Traumatic experiences get locked into my body. Shame is stored in my body. Processing my baggage on a cognitive level has been useful for me to understand my issues, but has done little to actually help me change. On the other hand, embodiment and somatic forms of therapy bring me into the places where my unresolved or fragmented parts are held, which enables real transformation. The word *remember*, literally *re + member*, connotes a returning and integrating into my body more fully.

My body feels. The path to more aliveness takes me out of my head and into feeling. This is true of the emotions I resist like grief, anger, and raw fear, as well as the yummier ones like joy, pleasure, and love. Feeling is my unfiltered response to reality. In this way, feeling shows me my truth. Feeling connects me to me. Human connection and intimacy happen through my limbic system and my body. In contrast, my conceptual mind makes meaning of my feelings, often judging them and insulating me from their intensity.

My body is wise. There is a natural intelligence in my body. Consider: Every cell in my body is a tiny point of awareness. Each of these trillions of cells is connected to its environment and carrying out its functions. Each cell is acting in coordination with the surrounding cells, tissue, and in concert with its organ, which in turn is working in harmony with every other organ and the functions of my body as a whole. My conceptual mind is largely unaware of the symphony being played continuously by these trillions of points of awareness, magnificently interconnected with each other and my environment. Embodiment closes the gap so that my conceptual mind can *hear the music* and begin to *sing along* with the wisdom of my body.

In Buddhist philosophy, the body holds Buddha-nature. My body is already awake and already enlightened. My journey is to integrate my conceptual mind into the awakened state that I already abide in somatically. The body is the path. The body is the teacher. The body is the Way.

Relaxed Arousal

Relaxed arousal is the practice of feeling sexual pleasure while maintaining a down-regulated nervous system. In my experience, it has been a foundational tool for learning to orgasm without ejaculation. By keeping my body relaxed, I am able to gently open into orgasmic states without threatening to spill into ejaculation.

Let's take a brief tour of the science behind this. The autonomic nervous system (ANS) is responsible for many of the tasks that my body accomplishes without conscious guidance. Examples include digestion and breathing. The three modes of the ANS are the **parasympathetic** system, the **sympathetic** system, and the **dorsal-vagal** system. The parasympathetic mode governs digestion and relaxation. Sympathetic switches on for fight-or-flight activation. Finally the dorsal-vagal system governs freeze and fold responses to extreme threats.

In the parasympathetic mode, I have slower breath, lower heart-rate, lower blood-pressure, and am able to relax my attention and musculature. In this mode, I am available to feel. The sympathetic mode, in contrast, is high-energy, quick responding, vigilant, and tense. In the sympathetic mode, I am bypassing feelings in order to act. Here's the crucial point: Pleasure and arousal build within the parasympathetic mode, and I switch into sympathetic mode to ejaculate.[6] Therefore, I want to learn how to stay in the parasympathetic mode, which means relaxed arousal.

Learning about relaxed arousal instigated a total lifestyle change for me. Prior to undertaking this path, I would amp up my nervous system to be productive and then numb myself out to relax. I would use stimulants like coffee,[7] nicotine,[8] and media[9] to upregulate my system into sympathetic mode. At the end of the day, I'd use depressants like alcohol and sugar to shut my nervous system back down. The combined effect of stimulant and depressant use is that I was hijacking my nervous system and disrupting my body's natural capacity to self-regulate. Here's the kicker: In this cycle, I became increasingly desensitized to sexual arousal. This is in addition to the litany of health issues baked into this pattern.[10] Again, arousal happens in the resting state of the parasympathetic mode. Recognizing this, my task is to recondition my nervous system from the cultural norm of amp and numb into parasympathetic living.

The body automatically (i.e., autonomically) swaps between parasympathetic and sympathetic modes as needed. With awareness and practice, I can work with my ANS to spend more and more time in a down-regulated state. I want to practice shifting into parasympathetic mode and staying there. All of the practices that follow are directly relevant for re-training the nervous system in this way.

Porn and media nearly universally portray sex in sympathetic mode: fast-pumping, high-intensity, clenched-bodies. This maximizes stimulation and quickly moves towards climax. The natural effect of intense stimulation is desensitization and numbing. The sympathetic mode actually constricts blood flow and suppresses erections. The truth is, I feel more pleasure the slower I go. Relaxing during sex opens up vast new landscapes of pleasure, emotion, healing, and intimacy.

To tie it all together: If I learn to keep my body in the parasympathetic mode during sex, then I won't go into ejaculation. Staying relaxed, I can learn to cross the *orgasm threshold* without triggering ejaculation.

Prompts for Journaling and Discussion

When and where do you feel most connected with your body?

How can you tell that you are connected to, or disconnected from your body?

What prevents you from prioritizing your relationship with your body?

How do you judge your body?

Draw a graph of your pleasure curve during sex.

Self-Pleasure Practice I: Self-Touch

Growing up, I learned to activate my arousal through visual stimuli. Porn and other media were the primary imprints for how I learned this, and in turn, I began to view women's bodies this way. In contrast, the path to full-body non-ejaculatory orgasm requires that I access pleasure and arousal through touch and through feeling. If I want to have an orgasm in my "full-body," that means I'm feeling pleasure in my *full body*.

Therefore, I need to rewire my turn-on from visual arousal to *somatic arousal*. In addition to feeling more pleasure through this practice, I've uncovered many additional benefits: I started objectifying women less and I became more sovereign in my erotic experience. Every nerve-ending (and indeed every individual cell) became increasingly included in my pleasure—I was awakening into my body. Finally, I began to align with the innate wisdom of my body's turn-on instead of artificially manipulating it with visual stimuli.

Learning somatic arousal is an initiation in its own right embedded within the larger full-body orgasm initiation. Touching my body for pleasure confronts me with the places that I am shut down. I meet my resistance, numbness, frustration, boredom, and distraction immediately and directly. Pleasure brings me out of my head and into more aliveness. Strangely enough, it is my aliveness itself that I resist. I want comfort, control, and familiarity. Awakening more pleasure in my body disrupts all of these.

I access somatic arousal through awareness, breath, and sensation. I place my awareness inside my body, focusing on the places where touch and sensation are arising. If I'm thinking about my to-do list, then I'm not feeling pleasure in my body. Pleasure arises to the extent my awareness is immersed in my body.

The more I breathe, the more I am going to feel. My breath should be *deep and free*. I can expand into each inhale with my full torso and then simply relax on the exhale. Breathing out requires zero effort. I want to create the habit of sustaining these full, relaxed breaths.

Finally, I activate sensation through touch. In the self-touching exercise below, I am both giving and receiving touch simultaneously. First, I focus on feeling pleasure in my body as I touch. Second, I shift my focus to feeling pleasure through my hands as they give touch to my body. Third, I broaden my awareness to feel pleasure both as my hands give and my body receives.

When I'm touching myself or a partner, I want to feel for *the resilient edge of resistance*. This is a term that was coined by Chester Mainard and it means finding the level of engagement where my touch is met by the body.

But in Tantra, we want to go a step further. We want to *become* the touch. To do that, we need to find the narrow realm of touch that lies between too much pressure and too little. When you touch the body, you want to touch deeply enough that the body pushes back just a little. If a muscle becomes rigid under your touch, you've gone too far. If the muscle feels flaccid, you haven't gone far enough.

—Barbara Carrellas[11]

The resilient edge of resistance is not one fixed place or type of touch. It means attuning with the body being touched and finding the place of meeting. Sometimes this edge is delicate. Other times this edge is deep and powerful. The edge is the place where aliveness springs up through touching.

There are many types of touch I can explore. For this exercise, I am experimenting with A) gentle caressing, tickling, and light touch; B) grabbing, squeezing, and holding firmly with pressure; C) scratching, pinching, and pulling and; D) deep-tissue massage, kneading, and rolling.

Elements of Arousal	Steps to Immersive Touch	Modalities of Touch
Awareness	1. Receive pleasure in body	Caressing
Deep, free breathing	2. Feel pleasure in hands giving	Squeezing
Touch	3. Feel pleasure in body & hands	Scratching
		Deep massaging

Figure 11.4 Tools to access pleasure through touch

Duration: 20+ minutes

Instructions:

Set a timer and create a space where you won't be interrupted. If you're like me and you naturally ejaculate quickly during sex, it's important to practice staying aroused for longer periods of time. However long you would like to last during sex, you should practice staying aroused during your daily self-pleasure.

Breathe deeply and fully. Slowly caress your entire body: feet, legs, belly, chest, back, arms, neck and head. As you self-touch, imagine that you are breathing directly into the part of your body that is feeling sensation. It's as if the air is being inhaled into fingertips and skin instead of lungs.

Practice the three steps of immersive touch. First, as you touch, focus on receiving pleasure in your body. Second, focus on feeling pleasure in your fingers giving touch. Third, combine both so you are feeling pleasure in your hands and body simultaneously.

Explore the four modalities of touch: caressing, squeezing, scratching, and deep massage. As you touch your body, focus on feeling pleasure. The only goal of this practice is to generate pleasure. Breathe pleasure. Touch pleasure. Immerse in pleasure. As you do this, welcome whatever emotions or sensations are arising.

Bring yourself into arousal. Locate five out of ten—this is purely a subjective feeling of half-way to the top. Locate seven out of ten—again a subjective felt sense of two notches higher yet still safely below the point of no return. Stay in the five to seven zone on your pleasure curve. Play with breathing your arousal higher. Practice breathing your arousal lower. Touch the intensity higher and lower. Follow your intuition and experiment. Most importantly, let go of any attachment to outcome and simply enjoy feeling pleasure.

Repeat this practice daily and notice how your awareness and control develop. Try the Yoga Sequence I, described below, directly beforehand and see how that changes this practice. Try Yoga Sequence I directly afterward and notice how that feels. Practice first thing in the morning and last thing before sleep. It is this type of curiosity and exploration which will lead you to progress most effectively on your path.

Meditation I: Interoception

Tension includes any restriction, holding, knot, or contraction in my body. In addition to physical tension, I also hold tension energetically, mentally, and emotionally. I put tension into my body, largely unconsciously, as a coping mechanism for the intensity of my raw experience. When an experience is *too much* and I don't have space or capacity to feel it, I use tension to lock that experience into my *soma*, into my body. Tension stops movement and restricts feeling. I use tension for safety.

If I feel cut off from my feelings, disconnected from my aliveness, or numb to my passion, a very likely reason is that I'm holding tension in my body. Although I use tension to lock away experiences I don't want or don't like, the effect is frequently that this process distances me from *all* emotions and vitality. I so frequently find that my passion for life is right here, underneath all the grief I've been avoiding. Releasing tension is a way for me to expand my consciousness.

In this Interoception Meditation, I bring my breath and awareness into my body. I spend time breathing into each particular body part, beginning with my toes and working my way up. As I breathe into each part of my body, I feel for tension.

At first, I experience tension as an *other* in my body. It's a foreign object. It's numb and solid. I allow my in-breath to gently meet the surface of the tension. With each out-breath, I relax completely. Slowly, I feel my in-breath reach all the way around the tense area, encapsulating it. As I spend more time breathing and feeling, my tension begins to melt. The solid surface of the tension becomes more porous and my breath begins to flow into it. Movement returns. Often, the unlocking of tension is accompanied by pain or intense emotion as whatever I had been avoiding is now welcomed to be felt.

Eventually, more of my awareness is able to enter the tension. Instead of the tension being an object, I come to recognize that I am the one doing the tensing. I experience the tension as my willful resistance to life. By owning that *I am tensing*, I become free to choose whether to continue to hold or to loosen up.

Through this practice, I am relaxing and opening up more flow in my body. This meditation greatly enhances my capacity to feel pleasure and arousal. I am also building my capacity to be present with intensity. Further along, this becomes important for reaching higher states of arousal without spilling into ejaculation. The most rewarding aspect, however, is that each block of tension I melt reunites me with more of me.

Duration: 15 minutes to start, working up to 45 minutes.

Instructions:

As in corpse pose, lie down on your back with your legs stretched out straight. Allow your toes to fall open. Rest your hands at your sides, palms facing up. Make any adjustments you need to be comfortable. Without changing your breathing, follow your breath with your awareness. Notice the rise and fall of each breath in your body. Feel each breath.

Follow the breath into the space of the big toes. Feel the tension. Relax on the outbreath.

> Beginning with the big toe of each foot, imagine that the in-breath is entering directly into both toes. Feel the breath enter each toe. As the breath enters, sense for tension. Tension might feel painful, tight, stuck, dull, numb, or solid. You may encounter resistance. Emotions or memories may arise. Whatever shows up, breathe with it. On each out-breath, relax the toes. Melt the tension. Let go completely.

> Your awareness follows the in-breath into the space of the big toes. Release everything on the out-breath.

Follow the breath into the space of the second toes. Feel. Relax.

When your body feels complete with the big toes, move onto the second toes and repeat the process. Then the third toes, fourth toes, and pinky toes. Each time follow your breath into the space of the given toes, feel for tension, and then relax on the exhale.

If you get lost in thinking, come back to the last body part you remember working with. If something starts to release somewhere else in your body, make space for the release to happen, and then come back to the given body part. Follow your breath into the body. Feel for tension. Relax on the outbreath.

Follow the breath into the space of each part of the body. Feel. Relax.

After you work with all five toes on both feet, the sequence is:

Bottoms of feet, tops of feet, ankles, calves, shins, knees, quads, inner thighs, groin and genitals, belly, low-back, ribs, chest, mid-back, upper-back, thumbs, each finger, palms, back of hands, wrists, forearms, upper arms, shoulders, neck, jaw, tongue, cheeks, eyes, temples, forehead, and scalp.

Follow the breath into the space of the whole body. Feel. Relax.

Finally, follow the in-breath into your whole body. Inhaling, feel your whole body and notice for tension. Exhaling, melt your whole body.

Yoga Sequence I: Opening the Body

If one has control of the reproductive fluid, one has control of nature, the body and the mind. Of course, it is not easy to develop this control, but hatha yoga provides the methods.

—Swami Muktibodhananda[12]

When I first began to study sacred sexuality, I learned it within the framework of yoga's spirituality and philosophy. The sexual practices that we are learning here are a type of yoga. The word *yoga* literally means *to yoke* - like an ox is yoked to a cart. In this analogy, the body is the ox and our mind is the driver in the cart. Yoga brings the mind and body together. More broadly, yoga means *union* and it represents a richly developed pathway of realization. Yoga leads to union with all that is. At first, I had no idea that yoga was anything more than a trendy fad for stretching.

There are certain branches of yoga that focus on purification and renunciation in order to ascend to unity consciousness. I would call this an upward path, and it is most famously represented by the yoga sutras of Patanjali. Personally, I find these paths beautiful but partial. They tend to disclude sex and desires along with the messiness of life here in the world. Tantric yoga, on the other hand, represents an embrace of both the singular consciousness, represented by Shiva, and the myriad of forms, energies, and desires represented by Shakti. Yoga in this tradition stresses reaching both upward and downward to unite the totality. Specifically, we use the postures (called *asanas*) together with our sexual practices to descend into the body and then we ride the flow of sexual energy (i.e., *kundalini*) back up to unity. This is the bigger picture of how sex fits into the spiritual path and how the yogic practices support that journey.

With this in mind, our first yoga sequence focuses on opening the body. I want to use the postures to release chronic tension so my system can be open, pliable, flowing, and energetic. In addition, through the postures, I am practicing embodiment: I'm bringing my awareness more and more fully into my body. This happens in two ways. First, through the alignment of my body, I am training myself to be spatially aware of how my body is positioned. This is known as *proprioception*.[13] The second sense is how I feel my body from the inside in each pose. This is called *interoception*.[14] These lesser-known senses, which are part of the vestibular system, work together to build my overall somatic awareness.[15] Both are invaluable during sexual practice.

We start with Yoga Sequence I to open the areas of the body most connected to sexual energy. By no coincidence, these areas are where we hold the most tension and are often where stuck emotions or trauma are stored. This practice is *structural*—meaning we are loosening the joints, fascia, and muscles. Later we will come to *Yoga Sequence II*, where we focus instead on subtle-energy flow. I start with dense and work towards subtle.

With repetition, tension and scar tissue slowly and safely melt away from my body. The muscle lengthening that happens during a yoga practice lasts less than an hour, but the tension and scar tissue release is cumulative. This sequence is meant to be repeated regularly, meaning 5-6 days per week, over the course of a few months. It's important, however, to use this as a loose guideline while primarily listening to your body. Opening the body safely is a marathon, not a sprint. I will meet discipline with kindness and listen as my body indicates the duration and frequency of practice that is good for me. I will modify or replace a pose if needed. Instead of needing to invent a new sequence each day, I just use this one sequence. My body will take me deeper into each pose with regular repetition.

As I practice, I am foremost staying connected to my breath. My breathing is *deep and free* through the nostrils. Not shallow and not stressed. Deep and free. My mind is concentrating on my breath. There is no yoga without concentration. First comes the breath.

My second focus is postural alignment. This begins with the foundations—the places where my body is touching the floor. Keeping a solid foundation, I expand into the pose. The alignment in each pose description is a guide that my body shows me how to fit. I am not stretching and I am not efforting. It doesn't matter how inflexible I may judge myself to be today.[16] I am deep-free-breathing with postural alignment. Simple.

The key is to relax all else while breathing deeply and concentrating on alignment. If it's hard, I make it easy. If my mind is racing, I carry those thoughts into my body with the breath. Then I exhale and relax. Relaxing is key. In my sexual practice, I am bringing more and more energy and pleasure into my body while keeping my nervous system down-regulated: relaxed arousal. To support this, my yoga practice is training me to build intensity while staying relaxed and breathing deeply.

During long holds, a part of my body may begin to shudder, tremor, or shake. When this happens, I back off from the depth of the pose by five percent—enough to know I'm not straining against myself. Then I relax, breathe into the tremor, and welcome it to take its course. This is a way that my body releases stored tension and unwinds scar tissue.

Yoga practice is a marathon, not a sprint. I want to slowly build my capacity through gentle, consistent practice. If I just do a simple practice each day, after a few weeks, I'm ready for a longer practice, and after a few months, I am deepening into each pose. The key metric for success is showing up to practice.

Duration: 20-30 minutes.

To start, hold each pose for 30 seconds. Take three deep breaths between poses to feel the effects. Work up to a two-minute hold for each pose. I recommend 5 minutes for *corpse pose* at the end. As always, listen to your body.

 Sequence:

Warm-up: 12 Sun Salutations

Pose 1: Standing Forward Fold

Pose 2: Squat Pose

Pose 3: Downward Dog

Pose 4: Pigeon Pose (each side)

Pose 5: Cobra

Pose 6: Bridge

Pose 7: Wind-Relieving Pose

Close: Corpse Pose

Figure 11.5 Yoga Sequence I

Full Descriptions for Yoga Sequence I:

Warm-up: 12 Sun Salutations, *surya namaskar*

Figure 11.6 Sun salutation sequence

Mountain pose:
Stand at the top of your mat with your hands by your sides.

Tadasana:
Inhale, raise arms tall.

Forward fold:
Exhale, lower your hands toward your toes, legs straight

Half forward fold:
Inhale, lift halfway, look forward.

Chaturanga:
Exhale, step back into plank, and lower down to hover just above the mat.

Up-dog:
Inhale, lift the chest, and look up.

Down-dog:
Exhale, lift hips, and press back into downward facing dog.
Take a full deep breath in downward dog.

Half forward fold:
Inhale, step forward to the front of the mat, look forward.

Forward fold:
Exhale, fold forward.

Tadasana:
Inhale, rise up, and reach tall.

Mountain pose:
Exhale, hands to sides.

1. Standing Forward Fold, *padahastasana*

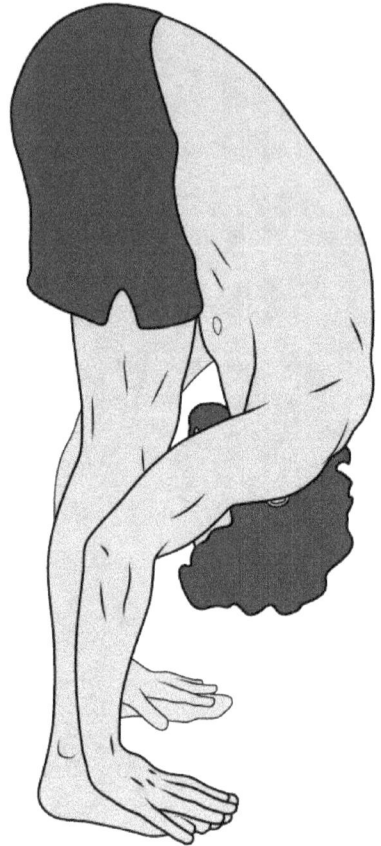

Figure 11.7 Standing forward fold

To enter:

Stand at the top of your mat. Feet are parallel facing forward, hip-width apart. Weight is evenly distributed across the soles of the feet, toes are not gripping. Knees are straight but not locked, and lift the kneecaps up. Gently rotate the upper thighs inward towards the center line. Inhale, raise your hands high. Exhale, fold forward by bending at your waist. Bring your fingertips to your shins, ankles, or floor. Relax the head and neck.

In the pose:

Breathe deeply. Do not pull with your arms. Draw your belly in and up. Relax your head, neck, jaw, and eyes.

To exit:

Exhale, gently bend your knees. Inhale, slowly rise up to stand.

2. Squat Pose, *malasana*

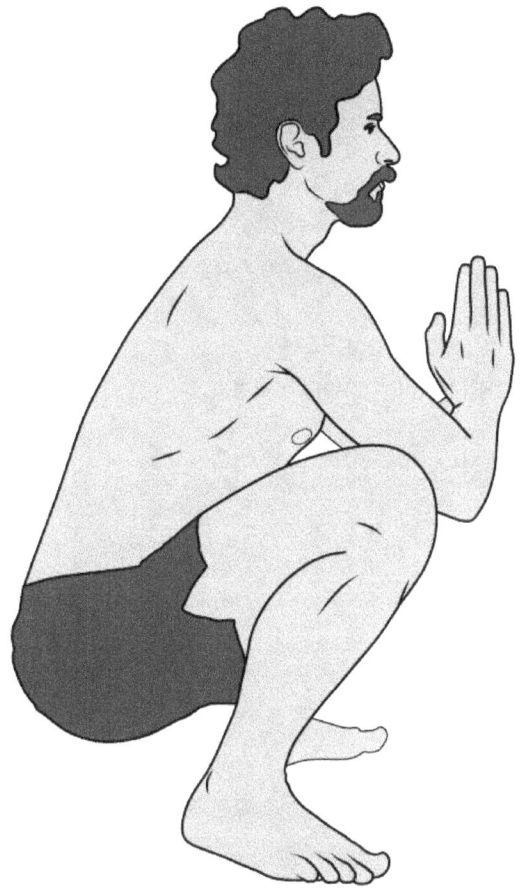

Figure 11.8 Squat Pose

To enter:

From standing, inhale, turn your feet outward by 45 degrees. Turn your toes away from each other.

Exhale, lower your haunches into a squat.

Inhale, bring your hands together into prayer, pressing your thumbs into the sternum. Press your elbows into your thighs. Look forward.

In the pose:

Press into the outside edges of your feet, lift through the arches, toes unclenched.

Lengthen your spine. Lower your shoulders down your back away from your ears. Lower your tailbone toward the earth. Lift the crown of your head.

Inhaling, draw the pelvic floor gently up. Do not overly grip or squeeze, just a gentle lift (*mula bandha*–see the "Pelvic Floor Workout" in the next chapter for a full description).

Exhaling, relax the pelvic floor, genitals, and anus.

Repeat lifting and relaxing your pelvic floor with each breath.

To exit:

Inhale, place your hands on the floor, straighten legs, parallel the feet, look forward, and lift your torso half-way.

Exhale, gently fold forward, feet hip-width apart.

Take three deep breaths to feel the effects of this pose.

3. Downward Dog, *adho mukha svanasana*

Figure 11.9 Downward Dog

To enter:

From forward fold, inhale, lift the torso halfway, and look forward.

Exhale, place your hands flat on the mat, and step each foot back. Lift your hips and lower your heels. Keep your elbows straight and relax your neck.

In the pose:

Breathe deeply into the back of your heart space.

Hands are shoulder-width apart, full palms on the mat, fingers spread wide, gripping the mat. The index-mound of each palm is supporting most of your weight.

Keeping the hands where they are, bring a gentle external rotation to the biceps. Draw your shoulders away from your ears. Spread the shoulder blades wide across the back.

Feet are parallel, hip-width apart. Slightly bend your knees to bring a deeper flex into the hips. Tops of the thigh-bones press toward the back of the mat. Heels gently lower.

To exit:

Exhale, lower knees and elbows down to the mat. Spread your knees as wide as the mat. Untuck your toes. Relax your head and neck into child's pose.

Take three deep breaths to feel the effects of this pose.

4. Pigeon Pose, *rajakapotasana*

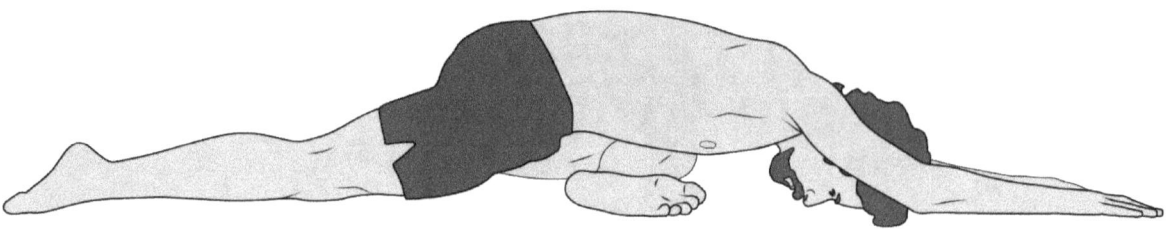

Figure 11.10 Pigeon

To enter:

From Downward Dog, inhale and lift the left foot high.

Exhale, reach the left foot towards the right hand. Place your left knee on the outside edge of the mat next to the left hand. Extend your toes 90 degrees toward the top of the mat.

Inhale, untuck the right toes, and lengthen the right leg straight back from the hip. Hips are square with the front of the mat.

Exhale, walk hands forward onto your forearms, and slowly lower your torso. Forehead relaxes towards the mat.

In the pose:

Gently internally rotate the right thigh to hollow out the groin. Keeping that rotation, wrap the left glutes down around the left hip. Tuck your tailbone under to tilt your pelvis.

Keeping the tailbone tucked, gently breathe the heart forward toward the front of the mat and lower the heart down. Your forehead may kiss the mat.

To exit:

Inhale, press palms into the mat to lift the torso.

Exhale, tuck the right toes, lift the right knee and hip, and step the left foot back into downward dog.

Take three deep breaths to feel the effects of this pose.

** Repeat Pigeon on the opposite side **

5. Cobra, *bhujangasana*

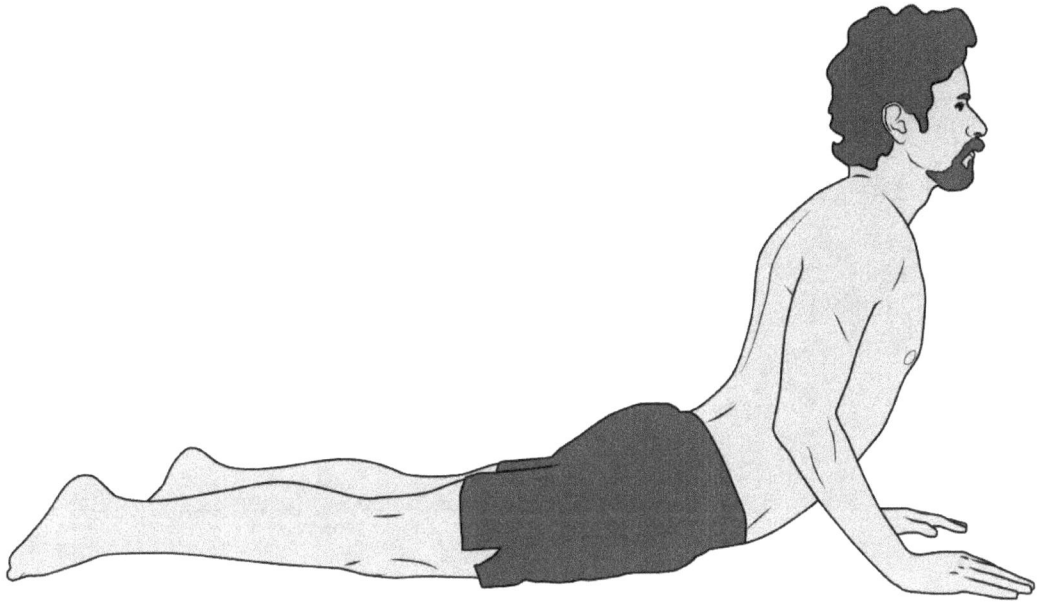

Figure 11.11 Cobra

To enter:

From Downward Dog, inhale forward into plank.

Exhale, lower to the mat.

Inhale, place your palms on the mat under your shoulders, fingers spread wide, pressing through the index-mound of each palm.

Exhale, untuck the toes, lengthen your feet straight back, and press the tops of your feet into the mat. Press the tops of your hips and pelvis down into the mat.

Inhale, lift the torso.

Exhale, re-engage down through the index-mound in each hand, tops of feet, and hip bones to ground into your foundation.

Inhale, keeping pressure on the index-mound, slightly bend each elbow and draw the elbows close to the ribs. Bring a gentle external rotation of the biceps away from the midline. Your heart lifts.

Exhale, relax the back of the heart and draw the shoulder blades down and together.

In the pose:

> Breath into the heart.
>
> Keep the three foundation points—index-mound of each palm, hips, and tops of feet—pressing firmly into the mat.
>
> Lengthen through the lower spine and mid-spine, then gently lift the heart further into the pose.
>
> Feel for a lengthening and release of the *psoas muscles* across the front of the hips as well as a stretching of the lower back.

To exit:

> Exhale, gently lower down to the mat. Hands come to center to make a pillow for your forehead.
>
> Take three deep breaths to feel the effects of this pose.

6. Bridge, *setu bandha sarvangasana*

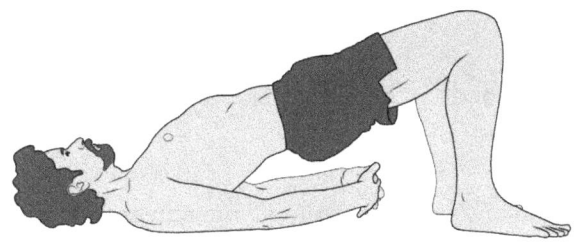

Figure 11.12 Bridge

To enter:

From the belly, roll onto your back, lying down.

Inhale, bend your knees, and place your feet flat on the mat. Reach your fingertips down to graze the heels.

Exhale, slightly lift your shoulder blades, and replace them flat and firm on the mat.

Imagine squeezing a yoga block between the upper thighs and engage your thighs toward center as if they are holding this block in place.

Inhale, keeping the isometric pressure in the thighs, and press down through the feet to gently lift your hips.

Exhale, again lift and replace each shoulder blade so that the outside edge of the blade is pressing into the mat. Clasp your hands together under your back.

Inhale, keeping the thighs squeezed, again lift the hips, belly, and chest. Imagine there is an orange under your chin—lift your chest towards your chin to squeeze the juice from the orange.

In the pose:

Breathe deeply into the belly.

Keep the foundation points of shoulders and feet, with thighs isometrically squeezing.

You may lift onto your toes to press your chest further towards your chin.

To exit:

Exhale, lower hips halfway.

Inhale, untuck each shoulder. Each foot takes a half-step towards the bottom of the mat—this protects the knee joints.

Exhale, slowly lower down to the mat. Allow your knees to knock in at center, left hand on heart, right hand on belly.

Take three deep breaths to feel the effects of this pose.

7. **Wind-Relieving Pose**, *pavanmuktasana*

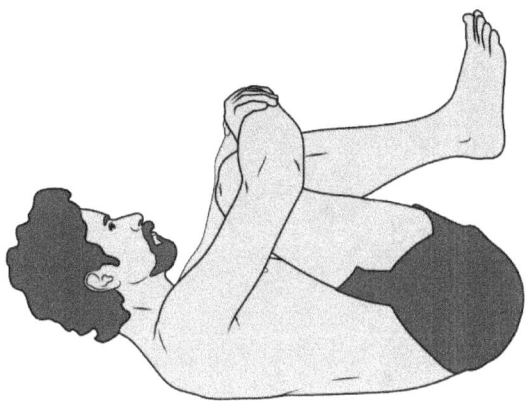

Figure 11.13 Wind-relieving pose

To enter:

Lying on your back, inhale to bend your knees and bring them up to your chest. Clasp opposite elbows or forearms around your shins and gently pull your legs toward your chest. Head lifts and chin comes to chest (you may want an extra blanket to pad your spine).

In the pose:

Relax the shoulders away from ears and relax the jaw. Continue to lift the head and keep the chin pressed into your chest.

Inhaling, draw the pelvic floor gently up without overly gripping or squeezing (*mula bandha*).

Exhaling, relax the pelvic floor, genitals, and anus.

Repeat this pelvic floor lift and release with each breath.

To exit:

Release your hands. Slowly straighten your legs and lower them to the mat. Relax your head to rest on the mat.

8. Corpse Pose, *savasana*

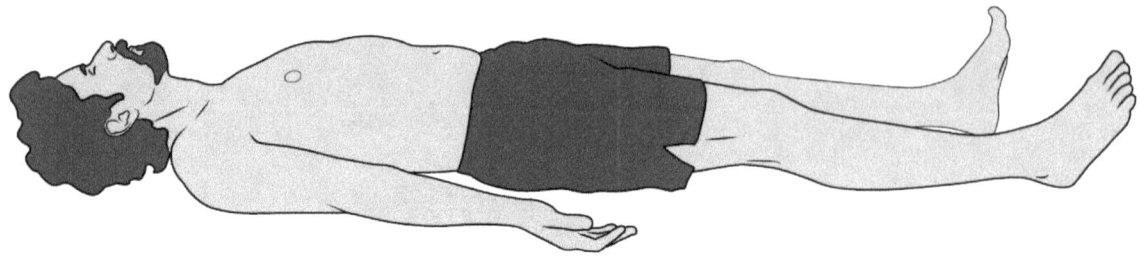

Figure 11.14 Corpse Pose

To enter:

Lying on your back, lengthen each leg, toes fall open. Relax your hands to the floor, palms up.

Exhale, let the skin drape over your body.

Inhale.

Exhale, relax every muscle in your body.

Inhale.

Exhale, let all your joints loosen open.

Inhale.

Exhale, give your bones to the earth.

In the pose:

Relax jaw, relax eyes, relax the whole body, relax the breath.

Loosen up.

Just let go.

To exit:

Breathing deep, bring some movement to your fingertips.

Breathing deep, bring some movement to your toes.

Breathing deep, stretch yourself long.

Roll onto your right side.

Use your hands to press up into a seated position.

I take a moment to give thanks to the creators of the yoga system
and the yogis who have passed down this wisdom.
I take three deep breaths to feel the effects of my yoga practice.
Every day of practice is an accomplishment.
I join hands together in prayer to close my practice in gratitude.

"The light within me bows to the light within you."
Namaste

Summary of Phase I

The primary focus of Phase I is embodiment. I have three practices that work together to build my capacity to be in my body. Self-Pleasure Practice I should be 20 minutes, daily, to begin. Each week, you can add ten minutes to this practice if you like. I like to do Yoga Sequence I, followed by my self-pleasure, followed by Meditation Practice I for an hour of practice. My biggest goal at the beginning is daily consistency. I want to build this habit into my daily routine. What happens during the practice will take care of itself as long as I'm able to show up and breathe deeply.

As you withhold ejaculation for a week, two weeks, three weeks . . . expect a lot of personal material to come to the surface. Emotions, relationships, work, sleep, and diet will all be shaken up by this change. You may have wet dreams—this is normal and your body will adjust over time. You may have past traumas surface. Go slow and use your support network. Everything that is coming up is part of the purification process.

My second goal in Phase I is to enjoy these practices. Self-sourcing pleasure is an incredibly powerful tool to tap into. It is the heart of all tantric practice.

> The deepest rhythms of life,
> Pulsating,
> Stir an ambrosia
> Flowing and overflowing everywhere.
>
> Drink the nectar
> Of all-pervading joy
> From the radiant cup
> That is this very body.
>
> —Lorin Roche[17]

Notes

[1] Photo by I, Yaska CC SA 3.0

[2] *Tantric Treasures: Three Collections of Mystical Verse from Buddhist India,* Jackson.

[3] "Measured on a stopwatch, it takes an average of 5 to 7 minutes for a man to reach orgasm and ejaculate. But the overall range is wide, from less than one minute to over half an hour." "Premature ejaculation: Overview," Institute for Quality and Efficiency in Health Care, IQWiG.

[4] Also referred to as *ejaculatory inevitability* in the human sexual response cycle.

[5] "The sensory inputs we receive from the environment undergo a filtering process as they travel across one or more synapses, ultimately reaching the area of higher processing, like the frontal lobes. There, the sensory information enters our conscious awareness. What portion of this sensory information enters is determined by our beliefs." "The biochemistry of belief," Rao et al.

[6] "Parasympathetic stimulation is the main mediator for penile tumescence, although central suppression of the sympathetic nervous system also plays a role...The sympathetic neurons play the predominant role in the ejaculation process." *Neuroscience, 2nd ed*, Purves, et al.

[7] "Acutely, coffee and caffeine induced comparable increases in muscle sympathetic nervous activity (MSA) and arterial blood pressure (BP) in nonhabitual coffee drinkers, whereas habitual coffee drinkers exhibited lack of BP increase despite MSA activation to coffee. Because decaffeinated coffee also increases BP and MSA in nonhabitual drinkers, ingredients other than caffeine must be responsible for cardiovascular activation." "Coffee acutely increases sympathetic nerve activity and blood pressure independently of caffeine content: role of habitual versus nonhabitual drinking," Corti et al.

[8] "Nicotine activates the sympathetic nervous system and in this way could contribute to cardiovascular disease." "The role of nicotine in smoking-related cardiovascular disease," Benowitz.

[9] "Modern horror movies elicit a fight or flight response, characterized by incipient tachycardia (heart rate elevation). While vicariously identifying with victimized movie characters, I believe viewers enter into a survival mode, mediated by stress hormones such as epinephrine, norepinephrine, and cortisol." "Lights, Camera, Action-Reaction: Sympathetic Nervous System Response to Action Movies across the Decades," Anderson.

[10] "An overactive sympathetic nervous system has become an identified characteristic of several cardiovascular diseases including, ischemic heart disease (Graham et al., 2004), chronic heart failure (Leimbach et al., 1986), and hypertension (Grassi, 1998). However, elevated SNA is not isolated to diseases of the cardiovascular system and has also been reported in a plethora of other conditions including: kidney disease (Converse et al., 1992), type II diabetes mellitus (Huggett et al., 2003),

obesity (Grassi et al., 2007), metabolic syndrome (Grassi et al., 2005), obstructive sleep apnea (Narkiewicz and Somers, 1997), pre-eclampsia (Greenwood et al., 2003), depression (Barton et al., 2007), and ulcerative colitis (Furlan et al., 2006)." "Central Sympathetic Overactivity: Maladies and Mechanisms," Fisher et al.

[11] *Urban Tantra.*

[12] *Hatha Yoga Pradipika.*

[13] "Another major class of receptors provides information about mechanical forces arising from the body itself, the musculoskeletal system in particular. These are called proprioceptors, roughly meaning "receptors for self." The purpose of proprioceptors is primarily to give detailed and continuous information about the position of the limbs and other body parts in space." *Neuroscience,* 2nd ed., Purves et al.

[14] "Contemporary conceptualizations often consider that interoception entails the integrative interpretation of internal and external stimuli – in the cognitive/emotional context – to derive an overall physiological representation of the state of the body, including conscious and nonconscious aspects." "Neural Circuits of Interoception," Berntson and Sahib.

[15] "The vestibular system provides the sense of balance and the information about body position that allows rapid compensatory movements in response to both self-induced and externally generated forces. The peripheral portion of the vestibular system is a part of the inner ear that acts as a miniaturized accelerometer and inertial guidance device, continually reporting information about the motions and position of the head and body to integrative centers located in the brainstem, cerebellum, and somatic sensory cortices." *Neuroscience,* 2nd ed., Purves et al.

[16] When I was undertaking my yoga teacher training, I had short hamstrings and a stiff lower back from years of working in an office and sitting in a cubicle. My teacher would bring me up in front of the class and have me perform forward fold to demonstrate how, as future teachers, we could support people who could barely bend forward. Today, on a good day, my forehead will kiss my knees in this posture. Yoga is not about how far I *get* in a pose, it's how I feel during the pose that matters.

[17] *The Radiance Sutras.*

| 12 |

Edging

Figure 12.1 Tachometer[1]

Once I am able to stabilize my arousal in the five to seven range safely and confidently, it's time to move to Phase II: *Edging*. In the *edging* practice, I am slowly raising my level of arousal higher and higher without ever reaching the point of no return. First, I find stability around seven. The pleasure moves up and down in waves, so I'm not holding at exactly seven, just seven-ish. When I'm ready, I move up to eight. I may spend five minutes or longer exploring eight. My body takes its own time to adjust to more arousal and more energy. Then I move up to nine. Then I move up to 9.5. Then I move up to 9.7, getting closer and closer to the point of no return without going over (Figure 12.2). The pleasure follows my attention and intention. I modulate it using breath, sound, movement, and touch.

Most importantly, I enjoy myself. Yes, this takes an incredible amount of focus, but I don't take myself too seriously. I have fun. I explore. I play. I feel good in my body. I welcome whatever arises.

Consider: Even though in edging practice I don't go all the way to orgasm and ejaculation, when I compare the area under the curves for conventional sex (Figure 11.2) and edging (Figure 12.2), I am experiencing vastly more pleasure in each session with edging. Not only am I now able to last as long as I want, I'm spending more time experiencing high levels of arousal.

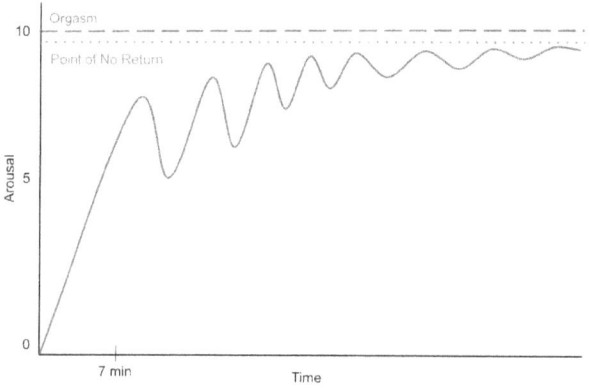

Figure 12.2 Edging

As I deepen into edging practice, I discover that my point of no return is not one fixed energetic point. Over time during a practice session, my capacity to hold energy increases and the point of no return moves higher as I bring more pleasure into my body (Figure 12.3). After 20 or 30 minutes of edging, I find that I'm able to hold steady in energetic states that are beyond my initial point of no return. I am able to feel an amount of pleasure that is higher than my former peak in the conventional sexual script. I'm not climaxing in the same way, but my body is actually feeling and holding more pleasure.

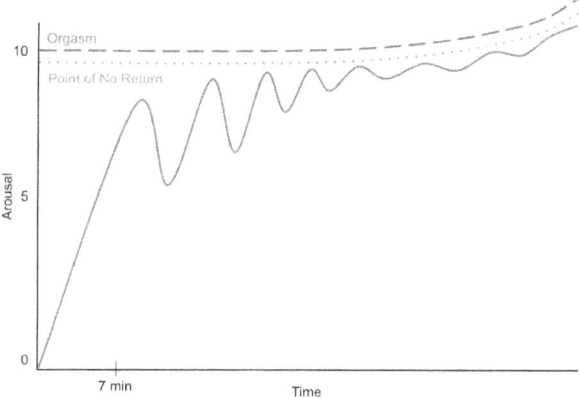

Figure 12.3 Elastic Point of No Return

The experiential realization of superior pleasure through edging is an important milestone in breaking my habit of ejaculation. Why am I having sex? If my answer is *to maximize my pleasure*, then edging is my practice, not ejaculating. Once this experience becomes available to me, there is a level of self-honesty that I can now hold myself to. If I choose to go for ejaculation, that's my cue that I'm using sex for something else: to get off, to check out, or to avoid feeling.

Edging during intercourse with a partner can be wonderfully fun, teasing, and delightful. The more attunement my partner and I have with each other, the higher into the 9.9's we can go together. If I'm right on the edge of orgasm, one thrust, one breath, even a hot glance from my partner can send me over the edge. For this reason, it's crucial that my partner be informed and on-board with the sexual training practices that I'm undertaking.

An important skill to learn—one that continues to challenge me—is how to hold ejaculation while my partner is orgasming. This can be a fun game that we explore together. The more suddenly and explosively my partner's orgasm comes on, the more challenging it is to hold myself steady. On the other hand, if my partner is relaxing gently into waves of orgasm, it's easier for me to stay with myself and I can really enjoy riding the waves of their orgasms.

At various times, my partners have justifiably wanted to come hard. I find that after an hour or two of sex, particularly after several consecutive days of sex, my capacity grows to hold my partner through larger climaxes. If I don't feel ready for that in my body, it's good form (and quite a bit of fun) to offer my fingers or a toy.

Self-Pleasure Practice II: Edging

Duration: Between 15 minutes and 3 hours

Instructions:

Use touch and self-pleasure to bring your body into arousal. Slowly build the sexual energy. Relax, relax, relax. Practice deep free breathing. Stabilize around seven, then eight, then nine, then 9.5, then 9.7, and eventually 9.9. The waves of sexual energy will naturally fluctuate. Do everything you can to avoid reaching the point of no return. Enjoy riding the waves of pleasure! Be in the open-ended exploration of high states of arousal for as long as you like.

Experiment with how to modulate your arousal. Making a loud vocalization can either release energy or intensify energy. Pumping the pelvic floor (*mula bandha*) can either move energy out of the pelvis or trigger ejaculation. Tensing my body can either put the brakes on my energy or intensify it. Each body and energy system is unique so I am inhabiting my inner-scientist, testing hypotheses to see what works.

It is important at this stage to create a consistent habit of going high into arousal and then coming down at the end of a session without ejaculating—without even getting right to the edge and clenching to hold it off. Repeated practice of going high into arousal and then landing back safely is a crucial step in breaking the ejaculation habit. I am retraining my body's sexual script so that it does not include ejaculation.

Meditation II: Earth Body

At this very moment, the Earth is above you, below you, all around you, and even inside you. The Earth is everywhere. You may be used to thinking of the Earth as only the ground beneath your feet. But the water, the sea, the sky, and everything around us comes from the Earth. Everything outside us and everything inside us comes from the Earth… Realizing this, we can see that the Earth is truly alive. We are a living, breathing manifestation of this beautiful and generous planet.

—Thich Nhat Hanh[2]

Sexual energy is earth-based. It arises from the earth through my root. As I embark on awakening massive amounts of sexual energy in my body, I want to understand how to release that energy back down into the earth. *Grounding* is the process of feeling the earth through my body and releasing any excess energy or tension downward.

My body innately knows how to connect with the earth. More accurately: my body is inter-connected with the earth at all times. It is my conceptual mind that has created a perceptual separation. Shifting my awareness into my body, I open to the experience of connection with the earth. This connection is valuable foremost because it aligns me with the truth of reality. Embodied, I am part of the earth. Thinking, I believe myself to be separate.

In addition, when I open into the earth, I experience qualities which are supportive and resourcing for me. The earth is stable and centering. I can feel the earth for support. The earth is expansive and receptive. Anything in my system that is not serving me will be received and composted through grounding. The earth is nurturing and healing. This planet is erotic and alive. I can learn to tap into all of these qualities through my connection to the earth.

In the *Interoception Meditation* from the prior chapter, I began working with tension in my body. Once I have an experiential reference for tension, I can begin to release it with the help of the earth. All forms of tension in me are life-force energy that originated from the earth. All of my tension will eventually return to the earth. The earth will effortlessly receive and release any tension I choose to ground. I can learn to ground both tension and any excess arousal. This is an essential skill for my safety and wellbeing on this path.

Duration: 45 Minutes

Instructions:

Get comfortable in your seated meditation posture. Lengthen your spine. Relax your whole body.

Breathe into the space of the lower belly.

> Notice your breathing. Follow the breath into the space of the lower belly. The breath flows into a space below your navel, inside your sacrum, and above your pubic bone. Feel the in-breath expand in your lower belly. Feel the out-breath empty from your lower belly. Breathing, allow your awareness to rest in the space of your lower belly. Allow your body to adjust as the space of your lower belly opens.

Feel the out-breath release down through the pelvic floor.

> Follow your in-breath into the space of your lower belly. With each out-breath, imagine exhaling from your belly down through your pelvic floor. Feel your perineum relax and open with each out-breath. Your awareness follows each out-breath down and out of your body.

Ride the out-breath down into the space of the earth.

> Inhaling, feel the space of your lower belly. Exhaling, your breath and awareness flow down through your pelvic floor into the earth below. Feel the space of the earth. Allow your out-breath and awareness to open deeper and deeper into the earth.

Rest in the depths of the earth.

> With a light touch of awareness in your lower belly, feel your in-breath and out-breath in the earth below. Reside down in the earth. Extend your breath and awareness deeper and deeper into the earth. Breathing, rest your awareness in the depths of the earth. Feel the earth. Let go into the space of the earth. Letting go, letting go, letting go.

Now, from the depths, inhale the space of the earth up into the lower belly.

> Inhale the earth up into your lower belly. With each outbreath, return your awareness deep down into the earth. Inhaling, open your pelvic floor and lower belly so that the space of the earth flows into your body.

Breathe as if there were no distinction between belly and earth.

> Inhaling, feel body and earth. Exhaling, feel body and earth. Inhaling, feel earth-body. Exhaling, feel earth-body. *I am the breathing body of the earth.*

Release into the earth.

> Release all tension into the limitless body of the earth. Feel all stress, all holding, all fear, all contraction being received by the earth, composted and transmuted. Open to the earth without reservation. Know the earth as your body.

Pelvic Floor Workout

> Getting in touch with your pelvic floor muscles is the foundation to becoming an erotic virtuoso.
>
> —Sheri Winston[3]

At this point in the progression of practice, you'll discover tremendous benefit from working with the muscles of the pelvic floor. For me, it is essential. The first step is to bring awareness to each of these muscles. Once I can isolate the action of individual muscles, I then work to build dexterity and strength.

It is not uncommon to hold chronic tension in the pelvic floor and anus. Often trauma is stored in this tissue. It is possible to self-massage the tension out or to roll it out with a tennis ball. For more severe tension, I recommend consulting with a qualified physical therapist or sexological bodyworker.

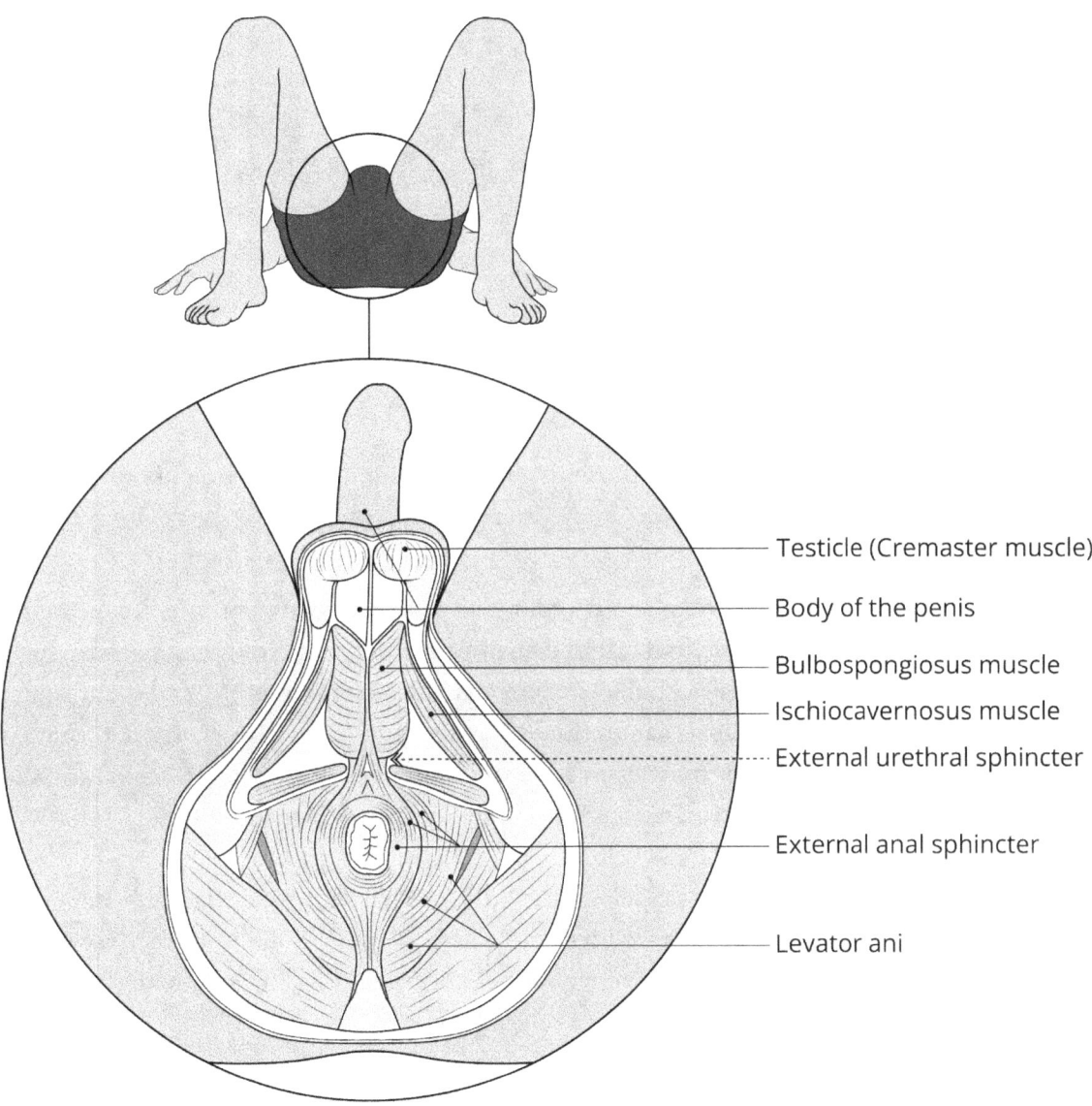

Figure 12.4 Pelvic floor anatomy

Here are the relevant muscles of the pelvic floor:

Levator ani (aka the pelvic floor) has three muscles: Puborectalis, Pubococcygeus, and Iliococcygeus. It is not necessary to individuate these three muscles. Pressing the fingers into the soft flesh between the testicles and the anus, feel for the contraction of the pelvic floor. In yoga, squeezing and holding these muscles is known as *mula bandha*, or root lock.

Cremaster muscles lifts the testicles.

Ischiocavernosus muscle flexes the penis. This is easiest to feel when erect. Practice flexing while both hard and soft.

External urethral sphincter stops the flow of urine. First practice flexing this muscle towards the end of urination. Then practice flexing it while resting.

Bulbospongiosus muscle pushes the last drops of urine out of the urethra.

External anal sphincter flexes the anus. In yoga, holding this flexed is known as *ashwini mudra*, or the gesture of the horse.

During ejaculation, men experience rapid contraction of the following muscles: Levator ani, ischiocavernosus, bulbospongiosus, and external anal sphincter. These contractions work together to move semen from the testes through the vas deferens, through the urethra, and out through the tip of the penis. In addition, the external urethral sphincter pulls shut to prevent fluid from entering the bladder and the cremaster muscles pull the testes up tight.[4] By default, these contractions happen involuntarily. With practice, we can learn how to control them voluntarily.

If I don't allow these muscles to pulse, then the mechanics of ejaculation won't happen. Articulation of the pelvic floor muscles is therefore a key component of ejaculatory control. I can interrupt the rapidly contracting ejaculation process either by holding and squeezing these muscles tightly, or preferably by maintaining them in a relaxed state.

I'll briefly note that the muscles of the pelvic floor sit at the base of the Central Channel (*sushumna nadi*), so these muscles are also useful for moving energy from the pelvis up into the rest of the body—more on this later.

Because all of these muscles are engaged during ejaculation, I can feel quite a bit of pleasure by intentionally flexing them. With articulation, these muscles can considerably add to the pleasure I experience during sex. If I am stable at my level of arousal, I can even use these muscles to trigger an energetic orgasm without going into ejaculation. In the pelvic floor workout, below, my focus is on articulation of these muscles. With practice these muscles become considerably stronger.

Duration: 10 - 20 minutes

Instructions:

Begin with a single performance of the sequence below. For each technique, work up to five repetitions as your strength and endurance build. Sit in a comfortable meditation posture with the spine erect.

1. Inhaling, squeeze all the muscles of the pelvic floor, testes, anus, and groin—and hold. Relax the belly, jaw, and the rest of the body. While squeezing, take three deep full breaths through the nostrils into the lower belly. Then release the hold and relax everything for one deep breath.

2. Rhythmically contract the muscles of the pelvic floor (*mula bandha*) for 30 seconds. Squeeze and release quickly while breathing deeply and fully into the lower belly. Relax and take a full breath.

3. Squeeze the pelvic floor tight for five full breaths. With each exhale, squeeze even more strongly. Notice that there is no upper limit to how strong you can squeeze. Relax and take a full breath.

4. Contract the muscles of the pelvic floor and hold them tight. Inhaling, lift the testes (cremaster muscles) and exhaling, relax the testes while continuing to hold the pelvic floor tight. Repeat for five deep slow breaths. Then release everything for a full breath.

5. Contract the muscles of the pelvic floor and hold them tight. Inhaling, squeeze the anus (external anal sphincter). Exhaling, relax the anus while continuing to hold the pelvic floor tight. Repeat for five deep slow breaths. Then release everything for a full breath.

6. Contract the muscles of the pelvic floor and hold them tight. Inhaling, draw upward as if you are stopping urination (contraction of external urethral sphincter) and exhaling, push as if you are starting to pee (contraction of the bulbospongiosus) for five deep slow breaths while continuing to hold the pelvic floor tight. Then release and relax everything for a full breath.

7. Inhale for a count of 10, slowly contracting all the muscles of the pelvis and visualizing energy moving from the pelvis up the length of your spine (the Central Channel) as the muscles tighten. Imagine squeezing toothpaste through a tube upward inside the spine. Fully contract for a count of five, hold the breath and hold the pelvis tight. Feel the pleasurable energy intensify. Exhaling for a count of 10, release back down and relax.

Repeat this practice daily in tandem with dedicated self-pleasure practice and notice how your capacity and control of pleasure are affected by strengthening the pelvic floor.

Summary of Phase II

Here in Phase II, I am cultivating the tools to work with higher levels of pleasure and arousal. Self-Pleasure Practice II will naturally replace the first one. Yoga Sequence I is still an essential component of the practice. Ideally, I am doing yoga five or six days per week, though as always, I am listening to my body's capacity. I can alternate between Meditation I and Meditation II or focus on whichever one feels more alive for me. Once I get the hang of it, the Pelvic Floor Workout can be done while driving or sitting in a work meeting. Doing this daily for two weeks will make a huge difference in sexual performance, at which point, you can taper off to every second or third day.

In general, I'm looking at about an hour per day of practice. It's also important for me to carve out a number of long edging sessions. I like to put on some music I love, massage coconut oil into my whole body, and go for two or three hours into the edging.

It is a truly special gift to see how far your body can go and what begins to open as you really get your erotic energy flowing. If you're practicing with a partner, you can edge together and tease each other in the most agonizingly pleasurable game.

As I am bringing more energy into my body daily here in Phase II, how I manage my energy begins to become very important—crucial even. Ground yourself by connecting with the earth. Use your pelvic floor muscles to move your energy out of your groin and up the length of your spine. Flowing energy is healthy energy. Stagnant or stuck energy is where I get into problems. I offer several tools for this in the next chapter.

Take all of this new energy and put it into something useful in your life, like your work, a creative project, or practicing yoga or meditating. In the tantric tradition, the purpose of awakening this erotic energy is to harness it for spiritual growth. Dedicate yourself to your practices.

Prompts for Journaling and Discussion

How can you more fully enjoy the practice of edging?

What productive use can you put your extra energy into?

Notes

[1] Image by rawf8 via Shutterstock

[2] *Love Letter to the Earth.*

[3] *Women's Anatomy of Arousal.*

[4] "The mechanics of ejaculation reflect a muscular event that occurs via simultaneous contraction of the smooth muscles of the prostate gland, contraction of the smooth muscles of the bladder neck, and relaxation of the smooth muscles of the urethral sphincter. Shafik also demonstrated that rhythmic contractions during ejaculation may act as a 'suction-ejection pump,' sucking the seminal fluid into the posterior urethra while relaxed during emission and ejecting it into the bulbous urethra upon contraction during ejaculation. Involuntary contraction of the bulbospongiosus muscle expels contents from the urethra during ejaculation." "The Role of Pelvic Floor Muscles in Male Sexual Dysfunction and Pelvic Pain," Cohen et al.

| 13 |

Body Orgasms

Figure 13.1 Bliss body[1]

Phase III involves learning how to activate orgasms in other locations throughout the body and how to have a full-body orgasm. I know I'm ready for Phase III when my edging practice is strong enough that I can consistently hold myself at a high level of sexual arousal for several minutes without triggering ejaculation. For reference, it took me about six months of daily dedicated yoga and intercourse before I began to experience body-centered orgasms.

Here, I begin learning how to harness all the sexual energy that I'm stimulating. I want to develop my capacity to feel energy in my body, I want to learn how to turn the volume up or down on that energy, and I want to be able to move my energy throughout my body. I call this *energetic articulation*. Once I'm proficient in feeling, intensifying, and channeling my energy, I can then learn to trigger orgasms in various places in my body.

Having an orgasm that is not centered in the cock is a major milestone on this path. Doing so opens the direct experience of orgasm as a separate phenomenon from the physical sensations of ejaculation. Feeling a body-centered orgasm allows me to hone in on that experience: "Oh, *this* is what I'm going for." In addition, it continues to decouple the body's habit of putting orgasm and ejaculation together. With repetition, I break the old habit and instill a new one.

In this phase, I am learning to become proficient in having orgasms that are not in my cock, so that in the next phase, I can begin to bring those orgasms safely into my cock (this is the legendary *full non-ejaculatory orgasm*, which is coming up in the next chapter). In this chapter, I'll begin with an exploration of subtle energy, the chakras, and the central channel. From there, I'll return to the self-pleasure and body orgasm practices.

Subtle Energy

> People say that what we're all seeking is a meaning for life. I don't think that's what we're really seeking. I think that what we're seeking is an experience of being alive, so that our life experiences on the purely physical plane will have resonances within our own innermost being and reality, so that we actually feel the rapture of being alive.
>
> —Joseph Campbell[2]

Subtle energy, life-force, vitality, sexual energy, and desire are all different aspects of the same underlying experience of *aliveness*. This energy is co-extensive with physical 3D reality, but it is not bound to physical structures. Subtle energy exists in every cell in our bodies. It infuses every living organism. Energy can be felt across distances and can be shared between many individuals. This energy is a fundamental feature of biological life and is what constitutes the subtle realm of consciousness. Embodying this energy, I tap into my eroticism, creativity, and love. You might want to check out Appendix II for my map of the states of consciousness, which includes the subtle realm as one of the levels.

Throughout this workbook, I use the terms *eroticism* and *erotic energy* to refer to the sexual nature of subtle energy. I use the term *Eros* to refer to the innate drive across all layers and levels of the kosmos to evolve toward greater complexity and wholeness. Erotic energy infuses all living organisms, whereas Eros is applicable to every phenomenon and object—it is universal. Erotic energy therefore is a specific expression of the core nature of Eros.

Energy must be experienced. My conceptual mind can analyze the effects of energy, but does not hold energy itself. I am required to *feel* subtle energy. This means coming into my body. Connecting to the experience of energy is a practice that asks me to step outside of my logical way of knowing and into my intuitive *felt sense*.[3] Like any new skill, the more time I spend practicing, the more adept I become. Arousal is energy. Desire is energy. Orgasm is energy. Learning to work with subtle energy is the foundation for becoming masterful with orgasm.

Perhaps the biggest hurdle in learning to work with energy, at least for me, is doubting it. I disbelieve it. And yet, I know what sexual arousal feels like and I know what orgasm feels like, so I have intimate experience with subtle energy. When the voice of doubt arises, my practice is to acknowledge that my inner skeptic is a valuable part of me and thank him for his contribution; then I ask my voice of doubt to please take a step back, just for now, so I can focus on feeling.

The next hurdle is tension. Whether it's physical, energetic, or emotional, the presence of tension blocks the flow of subtle energy. When I'm tense, I'm not able to feel. Strong tension induces frozenness and numbness. This is one reason our practice progression begins by releasing tension in Meditations I and II: *Interoception* and *Earth Body*. In order to most effectively work with subtle energy, I want my nervous system to be down-regulated, my mind to be focused and clear, and my body to be pliable and open.

First let's consider the *techniques* at our disposal to manipulate energy, followed by the *proficiencies* for what happens with energy in our bodies.

Techniques	Proficiencies
Attention & Intention	Felt Sense
Breath	Amplitude
Sound	Channeling
Movement & Touch	

Figure 13.2 Techniques and proficiencies of subtle energy

Energy Techniques

Attention and Intention. Energy is responsive to consciousness. Wherever I put my attention, energy will collect. However I intend, visualize, or imagine it moving, my energy will follow.

Let's try an example. For ten breaths, close your eyes and put all of your attention on the pinky finger of your right hand. Feel for energy gathering there. Try it now. Energy collects with attention. After ten breaths of focused concentration, see if your pinky feels warmer, bigger, brighter, and generally more alive than your other fingers.

Now, *intend* to move that energy over to your thumb. Take a few breaths and imagine that the energy is flowing from your pinky finger and into your thumb. Try it now. *Voila!* Energy in the thumb. You can also *intend* by visualizing light or a ball moving within your body. If you're having trouble feeling anything, relax, stop trying, stop thinking, and just feel. We are literally awakening a new sense of consciousness, so it may take some practice.

Energy follows attention and intention. The more fully I focus within my body, the stronger the energy I will feel.

Breath. Energy is responsive to breath. To continue with our example: Imagine that your in-breath is entering your pinky directly through all the pores of your skin on this finger. Take another ten breaths and with each in-breath, feel your breath entering your pinky. The energy becomes brighter and stronger. In yoga, the energetic aspect of breath is called *prana*. The energy of the breath can enter directly into your pinky or any part of your body that you focus your attention upon.

Another example: Open your jaw very wide and form an O with your lips. Take a slow strong inhale through your mouth into your lower belly. Fill all the way up. Exhale slowly all the air out and pull your belly in. Take ten more breaths like this: slow and strong, fully in and fully out. After these breaths, relax and notice how your body feels . . . notice the energy sparkling, scintillating, and shining throughout your torso and head.

Sound. On the physical level, sound is a compression wave of energy moving through air. Sound is energy. On the subtle level, sound is a creative, expressive, and intelligent aspect of subtle energy. I can use sound to intensify the energy I'm feeling. One of the most direct ways to experience more pleasure during sex is to make a lot of sound.

My practice is to begin by feeling my energy, and then I make a sound to express that energy. Whatever I'm feeling, I allow my vocalization to arise from that place. If I'm able to get out of my way and really allow the expression, at a certain point, the feeling of the energy and the sound become one unified experience.

I can also use sound to disperse or dispel energy from my body. Particularly if I'm feeling stuck, I can use sound to activate, mobilize, and then release tension and energy. The louder I make the sound, the more energy will move.

If you are like me, you grew up suppressing and hiding any erotic sounds. Today, I recognize that there is nothing wrong or shameful about making sounds during sex. In fact, moaning, purring, growling, shouting, and screaming add tremendously to my pleasure and fun during sex. The more sound I make, the more pleasure I feel. The more freely I express myself, the more my sexuality will open.

> As part of your journey into erotic mastery, I invite you to break free from our pervasive cultural embarrassment about the sounds of sex. I guarantee you, you sound beautiful when you're moaning with pleasure. Anyone who hears the music of your arousal is getting as much of a gift as if you were singing a beautiful song.
>
> —Sheri Winston[4]

Take a few minutes and practice making pleasurable sounds. This may feel fake or forced, but with practice you will rediscover your natural sexual expressiveness. Try to make as many sexual sounds as you can imagine: animal sounds, vocal toning, singing, sighing, and shouting. Start soft and see how loud you can give yourself permission to go. Once you practice this a few times with your clothes on, then begin to practice making sounds during sex and self-pleasure. Again: Explore the full range and see how loud you can go.

Movement and Touch. Energy follows the movement of our bodies. Disciplines like martial arts, tai chi, and qigong all utilize this principle. Later in this chapter, Yoga Sequence II will provide yoga postures to help you move energy throughout your body.

For a simple example to feel how movement excites energy, set a timer for one minute and vigorously shake one of your hands while you keep the other hand still. After the minute is up, relax, close your eyes, and feel both hands from the inside. Notice how the shaking hand feels tingly, larger, more colorful, and generally more alive than the passive hand.

Energy is equally responsive to touch. Another simple exercise: Using the fingertips of your left hand, gently graze the surface of the skin on your right pinky finger. Notice the sensations of tickling and stimulation. Feel how the energy builds. Now trace your fingers down toward your elbow a few times. Feel how you can use touch to spread this energy across your forearm.

These are our tools to begin manipulating subtle-energy: attention and intention, breath, sound, movement, and touch. Play with them. Experiment. Add them into your self-pleasure and sexual practices to discover how they work for you.

Now that I've covered some basic *techniques* to interact with energy, let's explore what I want to do with that energy as I become *proficient*.

Energy Proficiency

Felt Sense. The first step is to build my awareness of energy. I need to learn what energy feels like and how I experience it in my body.

Put your focus into the pinky of your right hand and witness the energy building. Try it now. Feeling the energy, bring your curiosity: What colors, textures, sensations, and temperature do you experience? How big does the energy of your pinky feel? Take your time to allow the insights to bubble up. There is no right or wrong answer, simply an openness for whatever you are feeling.

This same felt sense applies to my arousal. With practice, I can fine-tune my feeling of where I am on the pleasure scale—9.7 versus 9.8 versus 9.9. In addition, I want to be able to feel exactly where the erotic energy is in my body. Is the energy building up at the base of my cock, or along the shaft, or at the tip? Developing an increasingly nuanced awareness of my energy becomes the foundation for the next two steps.

Amplitude. The second step is to control the intensity of my energy. I want to learn how to magnify or diminish the energy I'm feeling. This is an intuitive process that becomes easier with practice. I do it by using my energetic tools from the *techniques* section above: attention and intention, breath, sound, movement, and touch.

Let's try it. Feel your pinky finger and imagine there is a volume knob from one to ten. What is the amplitude of the energy you are feeling presently? Place your attention on your finger and feel. Practice turning the volume up to seven, down to one, up to ten, and then hold it at ten. Energy follows intention. Use your will to raise and lower the intensity. Focus your intention and then feel.

Now add the breath. As you breathe in, feel your energy becoming stronger. As you breathe out, feel your energy radiating. Now add in *pleasure*. Pretend that this energy in your pinky is intensely pleasurable. Feel the pleasure in your finger. Intensify the pleasure by breathing into it.

In the simplest terms, to have a full-body orgasm, I turn up the volume to ten on pleasure across my entire body and hold it there until it reaches a crescendo.

Channeling. The third energetic skill is channeling energy. This means directing it to move and flow.

Feel the energy in your pinky. Imagine drawing your in-breath through a straw that begins at the tip of your pinky and extends along your forearm back to your elbow. Feel how each breath sucks the energy from your pinky towards your elbow. Energy flows with the breath. At first this will be a mental visualization process, but with practice the *felt sense* takes over and you'll be able to let go into the feeling of energy moving.

Eventually, I will use this skill to draw energy from my genitals, up along my spine to other places in my body like my heart and the crown of my head. I'll discuss this in the following sections.

Summary

Subtle energy is an experiential realm that each one of us may access. On my path, I began with zero awareness of my subtle energy. I didn't even believe it existed—I just thought it was a bunch of woo-woo. I started from square one. With practice, I learned how to feel and work with my energy. Slowly, I awakened to this new realm of consciousness. Today, I can trigger an orgasm in my pinky finger just by concentrating for a few breaths. Yes, this is possible.

The skills listed above are the tools of my toolbox. I learned how to feel and manipulate energy through daily sex and yoga practice. I use the techniques of attention and intention, breath, sound, movement, and touch to articulate energy throughout my body. These tools have been essential for learning to trigger orgasms in my body. In the exercises coming up, we'll be putting these tools to work.

Prompts for Journaling and Discussion

What judgments, biases, or doubts do you hold toward subtle energy?

In recent memory, when have you felt most alive? How would you describe your energy in that moment?

In the exercises with energy in the pinky finger, above, what worked for you and what was challenging?

The Chakras

> The chakra system is a simple, practical way to direct energy and awareness to specific areas of your body. If you want to be able to move erotic energy throughout your body to experience a full-body orgasm, you'll need to open up the energy pathways that will make that possible.
>
> —Barbara Carrellas[5]

Chakra is a Sanskrit word which means *wheel*. Chakras are centers of subtle energy within and around the body. They correspond to locations where spiritual practitioners throughout the ages have had energetic and mystical experiences.[6] Chakras are not tied directly to the physiology of the body. Rather, their locations are intuitively felt as focal points where energy is generated and converges.

Different spiritual traditions have differing numbers of chakras: Tibetan Buddhism generally uses five chakras, certain types of Kashmiri Shaivism have only a single chakra at the heart, and most common in westernized yoga is the seven-chakra system. Because subtle energy is malleable, the chakras do not have an objectively correct number or placement. For the purpose of working with sexual energy and orgasm, the seven-chakra system is most directly relevant because it has been utilized by generations of tantric practitioners for awakening kundalini through sex. Other chakra systems have largely been developed and employed by celibate monks. So the seven-chakra system is the one I'll use throughout these workbooks.

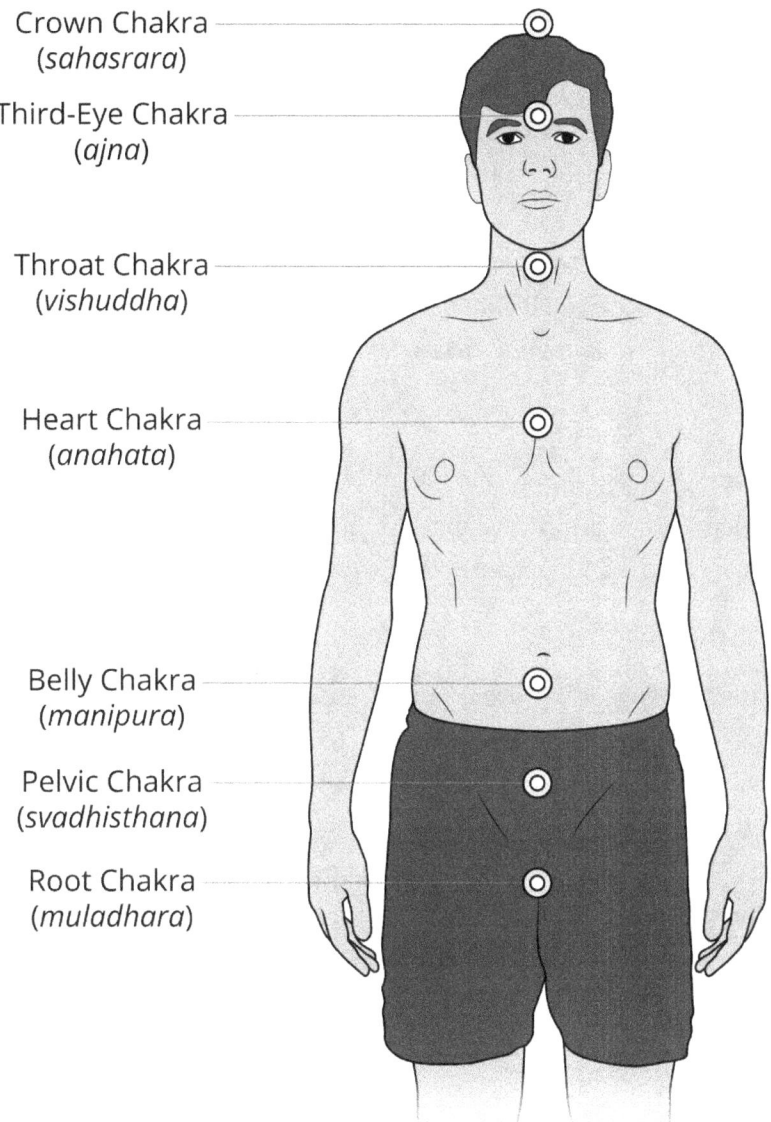

Crown Chakra
(*sahasrara*)

Third-Eye Chakra
(*ajna*)

Throat Chakra
(*vishuddha*)

Heart Chakra
(*anahata*)

Belly Chakra
(*manipura*)

Pelvic Chakra
(*svadhisthana*)

Root Chakra
(*muladhara*)

Figure 13.3 Chakras

Given that there is no objectively correct chakra system, what matters is what I feel and what works for me. The chakra system is simply a map passed down by generations of meditators. I use it as a loose guide to explore the terrain within the energetic system of my body. For example, sometimes I experience my "third chakra" about two finger-breadths below my navel. Other times, I experience my "third chakra" at my solar plexus.[7] I don't get caught up in what is *the one right answer*, I just focus on a given practice and welcome my energetic experience as it arises.

Let's take a tour of the seven chakras and then explore a practice to feel them directly.

1. **The Root Chakra** (*muladhara*) is located in the area of the perineum. This chakra is primal, instinctual, and dense. It is a generator—an energetic battery. This center is connected with our most primal sense: smell. As the chakra in the body which is physically closest to the earth, the earth element is attributed to it.

2. **The Pelvic Chakra** (*svadhisthana*) is located behind the pubic bone and inside the sacrum. I experience this chakra centered inside my torso and extending outward through my cock. This center is connected to desire and pleasure. The sense perception is taste and I associate it with the element of water.

3. **The Belly Chakra** (*manipura*) is located slightly below my navel in the lower belly. This chakra is associated with will-power, anger, boundaries, and sense of self. It governs the fire of digestion, passion, and purpose. The element of fire and the sense of sight are attributed to it.

4. **The Heart Chakra** (*anahata*) is located in the center of the chest. Here, I experience grief, jealousy, love, devotion, and beauty. My heart is the feeling center of my body and the locus of wisdom and compassion. The wind element and the sense of touch are attributed to the heart chakra.

5. **The Throat Chakra** (*vishuddha*) is located in the throat. This part of my physical body is connected with my voice, so the chakra is associated with speech and expression. It is the first chakra above my torso, so the experience here begins to become more etheric and refined. The element is space and the sense perception is hearing.

6. **The Third Eye** (*ajna*) is located in the center of the forehead between the eyebrows and extends back to the center of the head. This chakra is associated with mental faculties, in-sight, and intuition. The sense perception is the *sixth consciousness* or mindfulness. There is no element that I associate with either the third eye or the crown.

7. **The Crown Chakra** (*sahasrara*) is located at the top of the head and extends into the space just above the scalp. This center is associated with the experience of unity, communion, and the consciousness of the kosmos.

Chakra Awakening Practice

Duration: 20-30 minutes

Instructions:

Perform ten pelvic-rock breaths to warm up.

Lie flat on your back on the bed or a yoga mat. Bend your knees and place the soles of your feet flat on the mat. Allow your knees to knock in together. Place your hands at your sides, palms down. Get nice and comfortable.

Inhaling, fill the belly full of air. Arch your lower back and tilt your pelvis towards your feet.

Exhaling, empty all the air out. Suck your abdomen in towards your spine. Flatten your lower back and tilt your pelvis up toward your chin.

Repeat this breath ten times, feeling the pelvis rock forward and back. Inhaling, extend the belly. Exhaling, contract the belly. Find a deep, slow rhythm. Breathe all the way into the belly and all the way out from the belly so that your belly button visibly rises and falls. Imagine balancing a cup of water on your pubic bone. As you inhale, the cup tilts toward your feet. As you exhale, the cup tilts toward your chin. Continue this deep pelvic-rocking breath throughout this meditation.

Root Chakra

Imagine all your breath entering directly into your root chakra in your pelvic floor. Breathing in, feel and open. Breathing out, squeeze the pelvic floor up tight (*mula bandha*). Inhaling, relax and expand. Exhaling, intensify and contract. Feel for the energetic activation of the root chakra for ten deep breaths while rocking your pelvis. The energy will feel like aliveness, warmth, or tingling. The point is to activate your energy in your root.

Root to Pelvis

Inhale into the root. Exhale and draw the energy and breath up into the second chakra in the pelvis and cock. Inhaling, fill up with energy from the root. Exhaling, activate the pelvis. Squeeze the pelvic floor on the exhale to help move the energy up. Relax on the inhale. Feel the flow from root to pelvis for ten breaths.

Pelvic Chakra

Release concentration of your root and focus on your pelvis. Breathe into the pelvis. Exhale out from the pelvis. Feel the energy extend from your pubic bone forward into your cock and extend back to the inside of the sacrum. Intensify this energy in your second chakra for ten deep breaths while you rock.

Pelvis to Belly

Inhale into the pelvis. Exhale and draw the breath up into the third chakra just below and inside the navel. Squeeze the pelvic floor and lift the testes to help energy move up during the exhale. Ignite a fire in the back of the belly just inside the spine. Breathe, rock, and feel for ten breaths.

Belly Chakra

Now release the pelvis and focus solely on the belly. Continue to breathe in and out from the belly chakra, just beneath the navel back towards your spine. Rock with each breath. Activate this chakra for ten breaths.

Belly to Heart

Draw the breath from the belly up to the heart in the center of the chest. Continue to rock your pelvis and pump your pelvic floor with each breath.

Heart

Breathe into the heart. Activate, brighten, energize.

Continue up in the sequence with ten pelvic rocking breaths per area:

Heart to Throat

Only Throat

Throat to Third Eye

Only Third Eye

Third Eye to Crown

Only Crown

Breathe a long slow breath from the root through each chakra up to the crown. Feel each chakra along the way. Hold briefly at the top of the inhale. Place your tongue gently on the roof of your mouth as you exhale from the crown down to the root, feeling each chakra. Release your tongue at the bottom of the exhale. Breathe for ten breaths feeling all seven chakras.

Prompts for Journaling and Discussion

Immerse yourself in your experience of each chakra. Describe a color, texture, and quality for each one (there are no right or wrong answers).

Which chakra is easiest for you to feel? Which chakra is most challenging to access?

Imagine each chakra is placed on the back side of your body instead of the front. What changes?

The Central Channel

There are many pathways that energy follows through my body, the largest of which is the *central channel*. In Sanskrit, these pathways are called *nadis* and the central channel is called the *sushumna nadi*. The central channel originates at the base of the pelvic floor and runs up the torso along the inside of the spinal column. At the base of the central channel is the Root Chakra. From there, it connects to the back (i.e., dorsal) side of the Pelvic Chakra, Belly Chakra, Heart Chakra, and up to the Throat Chakra. Continuing up the inside of the spine, the central channel connects to the occiput—that little bump at the base of the skull. From the occiput, it opens to the pineal gland toward the center of the brain, which is the base of the Third Eye Chakra. Finally, the central channel ascends to the Crown. Sometimes I experience it about the diameter of a soda straw, other times it feels about the width of a broomstick.

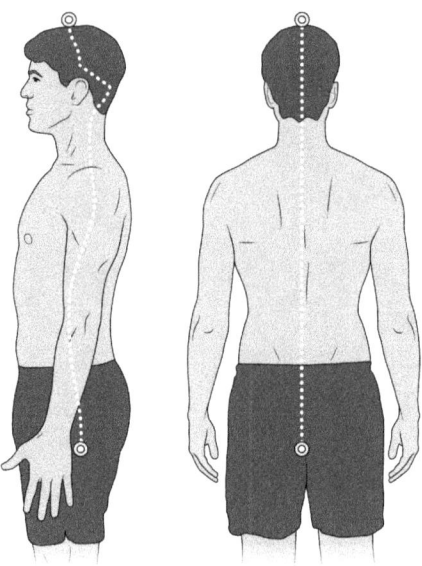

Figure 13.4 Path of the Central Channel

I can open the base of my central channel down into the earth using attention, intention, breath, sound, and movement. This is what we're practicing in Meditation II: Earth Body. I can also follow the top of my central channel up into the sky or I can trace it from my Crown forward in my body and down through the front of my Third Eye, through the roof of my mouth and along the front of my torso back to the Root Chakra. Placing my tongue on the roof of the mouth helps connect this circuit on the front side of the body. The full loop from my root up the spine to my crown and then back down the front of my body is known as the *microcosmic orbit*.[8]

The central channel is like a highway that I can train my energy to follow. In general, I want to send energy upward through the central channel. By pumping my pelvic floor (*mula bandha*), I can send energy upward. The pelvic floor is like a trampoline that bounces energy up this passageway. The process of moving energy upward is known as *sublimation.* As energy transitions up through my body, it becomes more refined, lighter, and subtler. During sex or self-pleasure, I want to create a habit of moving energy from my cock upward through my central channel.

With practice, I can allow my awareness to rest in the space of the central channel. This is among the purest, most pristine spaces in my body. This space provides a very direct route outside of my conceptual mind and into my embodied experience of reality. Seated meditation posture is the golden key that enables access to this space.[9]

> The source in the lower belly and the central channel of the back line, then, are participants in one field of primordial space, which emerges in the lower belly and extends in a flow up the spine. The fundamental quality of that basic space is nothing other than our most elemental awareness, the buddha nature in its ultimate form. In the practice of Pure Awareness, this space is what we might call "the witness," the deepest part of ourselves that is beyond space and time, beyond birth and death, and that always knows what's happening with us, is always cognizant, is the ultimate experiencer of our life and all that goes on within it. The witness is quite different from what is often called "the watcher" in meditation, that part of our ego that is standing back and keeping an eye on what is going on in our practice. In the primordial witness, there is nothing whatsoever of the watcher.
>
> —Reggy Ray[10]

Meditation III: The Central Channel

Duration: 45 minutes

Instructions:

Enter your seated meditation posture.

> Sit so your hips are slightly elevated above the knees. Rest your hands on the thighs so that the sides of the torso are lengthened and the shoulders are broad and tall. Lengthen your spine up through the crown of your head as if there is a string tied to the crown pulling straight up. Tuck your belly slightly. Draw your ribs in-line with your torso. Lengthen the back of the neck and very slightly tuck the chin. Loosen the jaw and relax the eyes.

Breathe gently and relax into the posture.

Follow the breath into the space of the pelvic floor.

Inhaling, imagine the breath entering directly into the tissue of the pelvic floor. Exhaling, relax all the muscles of the pelvic floor. Breathing in, feel the space expand and open. Breathing out, melt all tension and holding. Allow the awareness to rest fully in the basin of the torso at the pelvic floor. Spend a few minutes bringing your awareness into your pelvic floor.

Follow the breath into the base of the Central Channel inside the sacrum.

Let the whole groin region be loose and flexible. Feel the tailbone tuck down towards the earth very slightly. Inhale into the pelvic floor. Exhaling, follow the breath back towards the inner surface of the sacrum. Feel for an alignment and opening of the space of the central channel. This will feel like an open, free expanse of awareness inside the body. Once you open into the central channel, allow your posture to adjust around this space. Rest in the base of the central channel. Spend a few minutes here stabilizing in the space of your central channel.

Follow the breath as the central channel extends up into the lower back.

Be loose. Very gently shift posture from side to side until the space aligns and opens in the lower back. Very gently shift posture forward and back until the space opens. Feel for the posture of perfect balance. Notice that the awareness of the space effortlessly opens and expands upward.

Millimeter by millimeter, with each in-breath, follow the space of the central channel slowly upward along the inside of the sacrum and spine. Begin each inhale at the base of the central channel. Follow your breath upward along the space of the central channel.

Follow the breath as the central channel extends up through the mid and upper back.

Begin each breath at the base of the central channel and follow it up slowly. Allow the mid-spine to make micro-adjustments to align with the central channel. Notice that the breath is free and clear as it naturally moves upward through the central channel. Feel the back of the heart and space between the shoulder blades come into alignment. Loosen up and relax into the length of the central channel.

Follow the breath as the central channel extends through the neck to the occiput.

Begin each breath at the base of the central channel and follow it up slowly. Adjust the cervical vertebrae and back of the neck to align with the space of the central channel. Slightly tuck the chin and draw the ears toward the back plane of the body. Allow your jaw to relax open and float your tongue in your mouth. Feel the space of the central channel open upward to the base of the skull.

Follow the breath from the occiput to the root of the third eye in the center of the head.

Continue to begin each in-breath at the pelvic floor and feel the length of the central channel. From the occiput, follow the breath into the center of the head. Feel for a space halfway between the occiput and the forehead, right between the ears. This is the root of the Third-Eye Chakra and corresponds with the pineal gland. Breathe the length of the central channel up into the root of the third eye. Relax back into the space.

Follow the breath up to the crown.

From the root of the third eye, extend the space directly upward to the crown of the head.

Breathe the full length of the central channel.

Allow your awareness to inhabit the entire length of the central channel—feel the entire channel. Take a step back with your felt sense into this space. Feel the space and let go into it. Allow the breath to relax into the central channel. Feel the pristine emptiness of this space. Notice the calmness, the clarity, and the peace. Feel the energy gently flowing up the length of the central channel. Notice the brightness of this energy as it rises with each breath.

Rest in the space of the central channel.

Yoga Sequence II: Energizing the Body

Hatha yoga is a way of working with the body, a way of disciplining, purifying and preparing the body for higher levels of energy and possibilities… Preparing the body sufficiently before one goes into more intense forms of meditation is very important. Hatha yoga ensures that the body takes it gently and joyfully.

—Sadhguru

In this yoga sequence, I am focusing primarily on the energy I am feeling. I can imagine my body has a web of energetic circuits that flow through it. By aligning my body in a geometric shape with each posture, I connect these circuits so energy flows in a specific way. The posture enables energetic flow. This practice is not about how deep into the pose I can stretch, it is about utilizing the pose to promote the activation and flow of energy.

As I hold each pose, I relax all non-essential body parts, meaning that I'm only flexing the muscles I need in order to sustain the posture. In particular, I relax my jaw and eyes. Relaxing while energy is flowing is a key component, even when the posture or breath is intense. By relaxing into the intensity of energy during yoga, I learn to relax into the intensity of arousal during sex. I become the relaxed flow of energy.

This sequence is meant to be practiced regularly over the course of months and provides the basis for working with sexual energy during intercourse. In each posture, I am feeling and channeling my energy. My awareness and control on the yoga mat translates directly into my sexual practice. To put it another way: *This is better sex through yoga.*

With regular practice over a few months, the felt sense of energy will become clearer and more natural. If you don't feel energy at first, that's OK. It took me months to get the hang of it. Remember, this is a somatic skill, not an intellectual one. Stop efforting or tracking or managing and simply allow yourself to feel. Come back to deep free breathing, attention, and intention. Let go into the pose and trust the experience to open in its own time.

Duration: 20-30 minutes

To start, hold each pose for 30 seconds. Pause and take three deep breaths between poses to feel the effects. Work up to three minute holds per pose. For the Belly Locks, do five long breath-holds, working up to ten. Spend five minutes in Corpse Pose at the end. As always, listen to your body.

Sequence:

Warm-up: 12 Sun Salutations (see Figure 11.6)

1. Seated Forward Fold
2. Mountain Pose
3. Belly Locks
4. Melting Heart Pose
5. Shoulder Stand
6. Bee Breath
7. Wide-Legged Forward Fold
8. Headstand (optional)

Close: Corpse Pose

Figure 13.5 Yoga Sequence II

Full Descriptions for Yoga Sequence II:

Warm-up: 12x Sun Salutations, *surya namaskar*

Mountain pose:
Stand at the top of your mat with your hands by your sides.

Tadasana:
Inhale, raise arms tall.

Forward fold:
Exhale, lower your hands toward your toes, legs straight

Half forward fold:
Inhale, lift halfway, look forward.

Chaturanga:
Exhale, step back into plank, and lower down to hover just above the mat.

Up-dog:
Inhale, lift the chest, and look up.

Down-dog:
Exhale, lift hips, and press back into downward facing dog.
Take a full deep breath in downward dog.

Half forward fold:
Inhale, step forward to the front of the mat, look forward.

Forward fold:
Exhale, fold forward.

Tadasana:
Inhale, rise up, and reach tall.

Mountain pose:
Exhale, hands to sides.

1. **Seated Forward Fold,** *paschimottanasana*

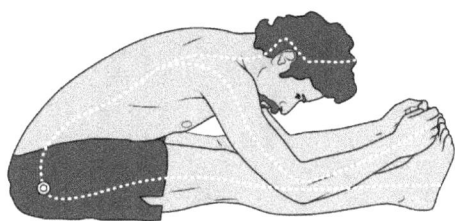

Figure 13.6 Seated forward fold

To enter:

Start seated with legs straight and parallel, toes toward the ceiling.

Inhale, lengthen the spine.

Exhale, bend the knees and reach the belly forward towards thighs. Clasp the big toes by wrapping index and middle fingers around the toe; tips of thumbs touch tips of big toes.

Inhale, straighten your knees until you meet medium resistance. If you cannot reach your toes, wrap a strap around your feet and hold one end of the strap with each hand. Look forward, reach your heart forward. Draw your belly in and up.

Exhale, lower your head and torso toward your legs.

In the pose:

With each inhale, imagine drawing breath and energy up from the earth. The energy moves from the soles of your feet along your legs, collecting at the Root Chakra. With each exhale, the energy flows through your torso, out your fingers and top of head, and back into your feet. Inhale through your legs into your Root. Exhale through the torso back to your feet. With each breath, feel the activation of your Root Chakra.

To exit:

Inhale, look forward, and lift your heart.

Exhale, release the fingers, and sit back.

Take three deep breaths to feel the effects of this pose.

2. Palm Tree Pose, *tadasana*

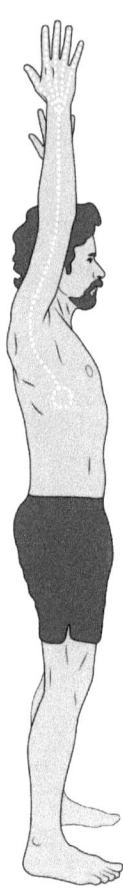

Figure 13.7 Palm tree pose

To enter:

Stand at the top of your mat. Inhale, raise hands high, palms facing each other, elbows straightened. Exhale, tuck your tailbone down, gently pull your ribs in-line with the torso, and lower the shoulders away from the ears. Lift the crown of your head tall.

In the pose:

Imagine drawing the breath from the sky down through your fingertips and crown of the head. Energy flows with the breath down into the body and collects in the basin of the heart. Rest your tongue on the roof of your mouth (*kechari mudra*). Draw the muscles of the anus in and up (*ashwini mudra*), and flex continuously for the duration of the pose. Notice that as you squeeze the anal sphincter more strongly, you feel more energy tingling in your fingertips. Holding this firmly creates a seal to hold the energy in your torso. Concentrate on drawing energy from the sky down into the bottom of the heart with each in-breath.

To exit:

Inhale, reach up tall. Exhale, slowly lower your hands to your sides, and let them hang loosely. Feel the balancing of your right side and left side. Feel excess energy flowing down through your hands.

3. Belly Locks, *uddiyana bandha*[11]

Figure 13.8 Belly Lock

To enter:

Stand at the top of your mat. Step your feet shoulder-width apart, parallel facing forward. Bend your knees 45 degrees, palms of hands rest on quads, fingers facing towards center.

In the pose:

Inhale as much breath as possible through your nose—fill up with air.

Releasing your hands and head down toward the floor, strongly exhale all the air out through your mouth.

Holding the breath out, draw the belly in and up. Push your palms into your quads and straighten your elbows. Knees are bent. Lengthen the back of your neck and spine. Continue to hold all air out, while squeezing the belly in. Relax your jaw, eyes, and every non-essential body part. Feel the intensity and energy rise. Use the vacuum of breath to pull energy up from the root and pelvis into your belly (and eventually up into the heart). The diaphragm may make a gulping motion—use that to draw more energy up. Hold until the intensity becomes uncomfortable.

Note: the intensity that I am able to hold in this vacuum-breath is the same intensity of pleasure that I will be able to hold without ejaculating during sex. This will be an important capacity to develop.

To release, first relax the belly. Then take a full breath in. Hold for a slow count to five and feel energy in the belly. Release the in-breath.

Repeat this breath-hold for five rounds, eventually working up to ten rounds.

To exit:

Stand tall. Step your feet hip-width apart, hands at sides. Take a few deep breaths and feel the activation of your Belly Chakra.

4. Melting Heart Pose, *anahatasana*

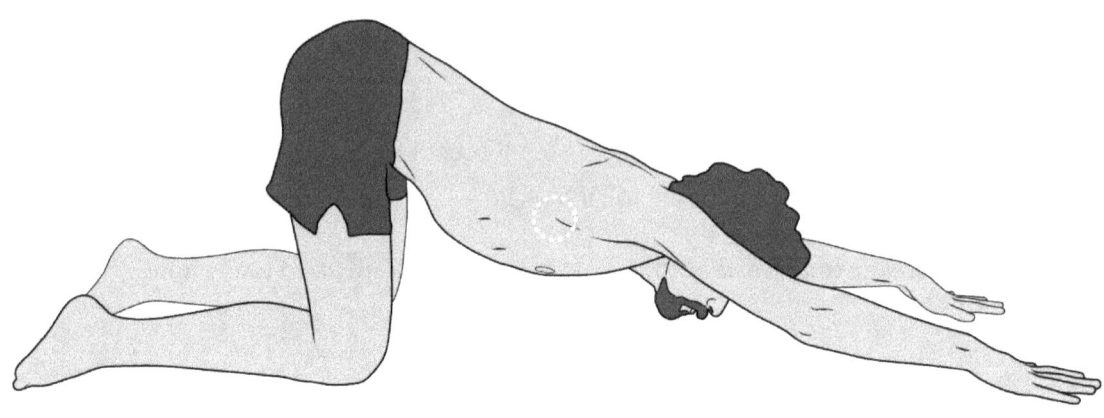

Figure 13.9 Melting Heart Pose

To enter:

Come down onto your hands and knees. Untuck your toes so the tops of your feet are touching the mat. Spread your knees as wide as the mat. Keep your hips directly over your knees. Walk your hands forward and lower the heart and chin towards the mat. Look forward.

In the pose:

Press down through the index-mound of the palm of each hand (or for a deeper stretch, come onto your fingertips). Lift your elbows off the mat. Rotate the biceps externally and broaden the shoulders. Breathe into the back of the heart. Open through the chest and throat. Melt the heart. Feel energy collect in the back of the Heart Chakra.

To exit:

Use your hands to press back into Child's Pose. Breathe deeply and relax. Feel the activation of your Heart Chakra.

5. Shoulder Stand, *sarvangasana*

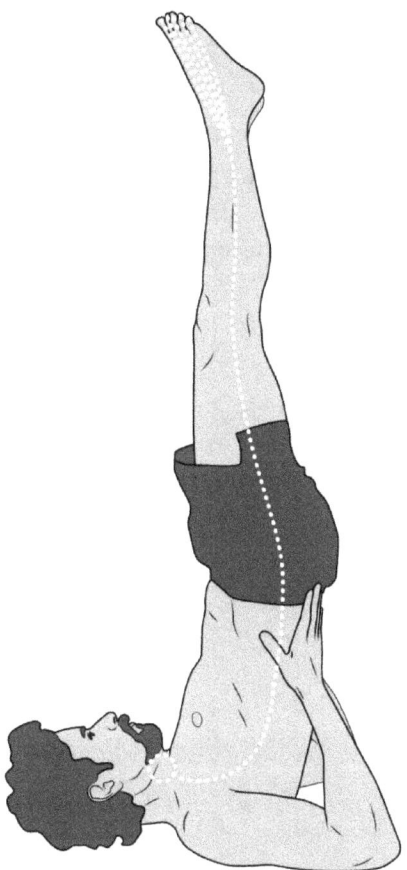

Figure 13.10 Shoulder Stand

To enter:

Lie on your back with your knees up and soles of feet flat on your mat. Anchor your elbows into the mat beside your ribs. Place your hands on either side of the sacrum to support the back (imagine you have high-waisted jeans and you're placing your hands in your back pockets). Inhale, lift your feet over your head. Use your hands to support your lower back to lift up tall. Exhale, lengthen through your legs and torso as the weight shifts onto your shoulders and the back of the neck. Raise your feet to the sky. Scoop your shoulder blades under. Your chest comes to meet your chin. Your hands may support the lower back or clasp together on the mat.

IMPORTANT: Once lifted in shoulder stand, do not turn or twist your neck as this can cause injury.

In the pose:

> Breathe into the Throat Chakra. Feel the energy flowing down from the toes through the body and collecting at the throat.

To exit:

> Gently bend your knees. Use your hands to support the lower back as your legs and torso lower to the floor. Place the soles of your feet on the mat and allow the knees to knock in.

> Place one hand on your heart and one hand on your belly and breathe deeply. Feel the activation of your Throat Chakra.

6. Bee Breath, *brahmari*

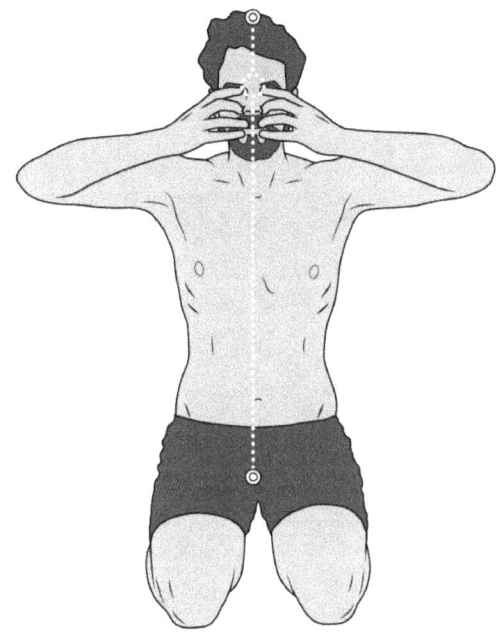

Figure 13.11 Bee Breath

To enter:

Come to sit on your shins or a block. Press the tops of your feet into the mat. Lengthen through the spine and lift the crown of the head.

In the pose:

Inhale from the root up to the crown, filling with as much air as possible. Place your thumbs over your ear-holes, index fingers over closed eye-lids, third-fingers on either side of the nostrils without blocking airflow, fourth-fingers on top lip, and pinky fingers on bottom lip. Hold these fingers here for the duration of the pose.

Exhale slowly through your nostrils while making a buzzing sound until all the air is out. Use your tongue, mouth, and sinuses to resonate the sound through the back of the throat like the buzzing of a bee. Allow the buzzing to reverberate through your head and skull, focalizing at your pineal gland in the center of the head behind the eyes. Feel energy gather at the pineal, which is the root of the Third-Eye Chakra.

When all the air is spent, inhale deeply again, drawing energy up the length of the spine. Buzz on the exhale.

Note: Drawing the energy up to the root of the Third-Eye Chakra in the center of the brain during sex vastly intensifies and expands orgasms.

To exit:

Relax your hands down to your sides. Relax your breathing. Feel the activation of the pineal gland and Third-Eye Chakra.

7. **Wide-Legged Forward Fold,** *prasarita padottanasana*

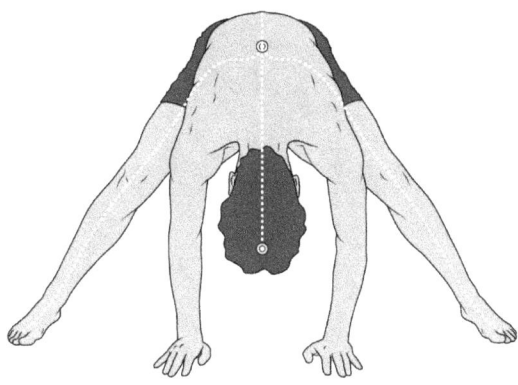

Figure 13.12 Wide-Legged Forward Fold

To enter:

Come to stand. Inhale, turn to the side and step your legs wide, feet parallel. Exhale, fold forward. Rest your hands on the mat, shoulder-width apart. Inhale, look forward and straighten your spine forward. Tuck the tailbone to neutralize the pelvis and lift through the arches of your feet up along your inner thighs. Exhale, lower the crown of the head towards the mat. Press down through the outside edges of your feet, toes unclenched. Slightly bend the knees so they are not locked. Draw your belly in and up while the tail bone points towards the earth.

In the pose:

Imagine drawing breath and energy up from the earth through your feet, through the legs, and gathering at the Root Chakra. Exhale the energy down along the spine, through the Crown Chakra and back to the earth. Inhale up to your Root. Exhale down through the Crown. Feel the activation of the Root and Crown in connection with the earth.

To exit:

Inhale, lift your torso half-way, and look forward. Exhale, bring your hands to hips. Inhale, stand tall. Exhale, step to the top of the mat. Breathe deeply and feel the length of the spine and activation of your root and crown.

8. Head Stand, *shirshasana* (optional)

Figure 13.13 Headstand

To enter:

> If you're just learning this pose, I recommend facing a sturdy wall so you can lean against it as your raise up into headstand.

> Come onto your hands and knees (all fours) on the mat. Lower onto your forearms and clasp your fingers together with elbows wide in a V-shape on the mat. Open the palms of your clasped hands and place the hair-line of your forehead inside your pinky fingers on the mat. Inhale, lift your knees and hips to come onto your toes on the mat. Walk your feet towards your face to begin to lift your torso.

> To lift, either:

> A) inhale one leg high, exhale, and then inhaling kick the other leg up; or

> B) bend one knee and draw the leg in tight with the chest, then draw the other leg in close to the chest, then slowly raise both legs high.

In the pose:

> Evenly distribute your weight between your forearms and upper forehead. Breathe into your Crown. Feel the energy flowing from the toes down through the body, collecting at the Crown Chakra.

To exit:

> Exhaling, slowly lower both feet down to the mat and come into Child's Pose. Breathe deeply to feel the activation of your Crown.

9. Corpse Pose, *savasana*

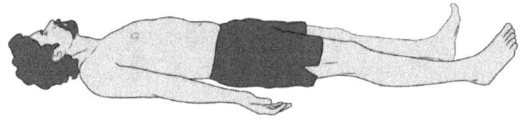

Figure 13.14 Corpse Pose

To enter:

Lying on your back, lengthen each leg, toes fall open. Relax your hands to the floor, palms up.

Exhale, let the skin drape over your body.

Inhale.

Exhale, relax every muscle in your body.

Inhale.

Exhale, let all your joints loosen open.

Inhale.

Exhale, give your bones to the earth.

In the pose:

Relax jaw, relax eyes, relax the whole body, relax the breath.

Loosen up. Just let go.

To exit:

Breathing deep, bring some movement to your fingertips.

Breathing deep, bring some movement to your toes.

Breathing deep, stretch yourself long.

Roll onto your right side.

Use your hands to press up into a seated position.

I take a moment to give thanks to the creators of the yoga system
and the yogis who have passed down this wisdom.
I take three deep breaths to feel the effects of my yoga practice.
Every day of practice is an accomplishment.
I join hands together in prayer to close my practice in gratitude.

"The light within me bows to the light within you."
Namaste

You now have both Yoga Sequence I and II in your repertoire. You can alternate days with these two practices or now you can focus on Sequence II and subtle energy. For Yoga Sequence I, here are the additional energetic cues for each pose:

Pose 1: Standing Forward Fold

Inhale energy from the earth up through your legs, gathering it at your Root Chakra. Exhale energy down through your head and fingertips back to the earth. Focus on activating the Root Chakra.

Pose 2: Squat Pose

Inhale into your Root Chakra. Exhale energy up through your central channel. Focus on activating the Root.

Pose 3: Downward Dog

Breathe into the back of your Heart Chakra.

Pose 4: Pigeon Pose (each side)

Breathe into your hips, activating the left and right sides of your Pelvic Chakra.

Pose 5: Cobra

Breathe into your Heart Chakra.

Pose 6: Bridge

Breathe into your Belly Chakra. Activate both the Belly and the Throat Chakras.

Pose 7: Wind-Relieving Pose

Breathe into the restricted space of your Belly Chakra.

Orgasms throughout the Body

Let there be pleasure and ecstasy on earth and let it begin with me.

—Annie Sprinkle

Our next step is to link the chakras and the central channel with orgasms. Traditionally, chakras are described as wheels of spinning energy. Relative to orgasms, I like to think of them as cups. Each chakra is a place where energy can gather, like a cup holding liquid. The cup has a certain capacity and when it fills up, it begins to spill over. Similarly, each chakra has an energetic capacity and when I over-fill it with sexual energy, I begin to orgasm there. In this analogy, spilling a chakra's cup means I'm passing the orgasm threshold in that part of my body. Each energy center in my body—indeed, each and every cell—has the capacity to experience orgasm.

The genitals are an energetic extension of the Pelvic Chakra. During intercourse, I'm using stimulation to fill the second chakra with sexual energy via the nerve endings in my cock. When this cup overflows, I begin to orgasm.

In the graphs so far, I've been illustrating a single pleasure curve. Now I want to imagine a separate arousal curve for each chakra. Each energy center has its own scale ranging from zero to ten, where ten means orgasm. Only the Pelvic Chakra has a *point of no return* however. None of the other chakras will trigger an ejaculation when an orgasm occurs there. In conventional sex I am only generating pleasure in my cock, i.e., the second chakra, with some incidental activation in the first and third chakras (Figure 13.15). If I'm only filling the cup of my Pelvic Chakra, then I'm far below my body's total capacity to hold sexual energy throughout all seven chakras. It was really shocking for me to discover that my body has a vastly greater potential to hold energy and thus feel pleasure.

With the energetic tools being cultivated in this chapter, I am now no longer beholden to this default pattern during sex. Instead, I can feel the level of arousal in my cock, adjust the volume so I stay below the point of no return, and channel that arousal along the central channel to other chakras in my body.

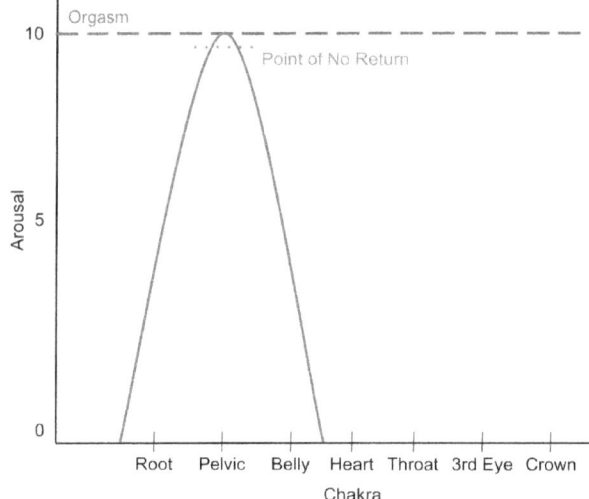

Figure 13.15 Conventional Sex: Ejaculatory Orgasm

In the *Heart Orgasm* practice, below, I'm using self-pleasure to bring myself to a high state of arousal. Once I stabilize that arousal in my cock, I use my energetic tools—i.e., attention and intention, together with breath, sound, movement, and touch—to bring energy into my heart. I continue to stimulate my second chakra while I'm simultaneously siphoning energy into my heart. I never let myself reach the point of no return. And I move more and more of that energy into my heart. I fill and fill and fill my heart. At a certain point, my heart will overflow with energy, and I will trigger a state-shift across the orgasm threshold. I'll have a heart-centered orgasm (Figure 13.16).

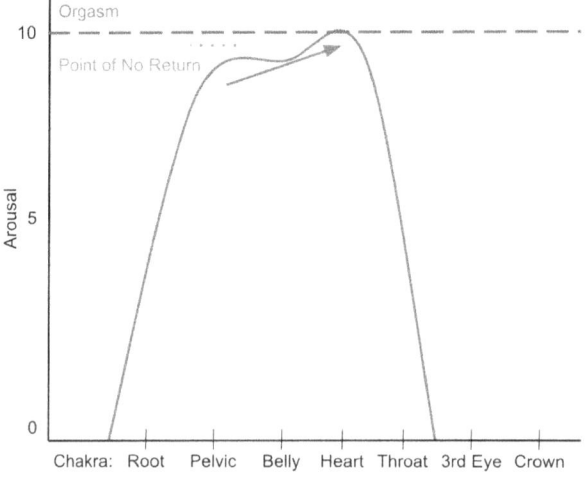

Figure 13.16 Heart Orgasm

For me, orgasming in the heart rarely follows the pattern of build-up, big-climax, and release, which I'm familiar with from ejaculatory orgasm. A much more accurate benchmark is how women experience vaginal orgasms. It comes in waves, it rolls through me, it can go on and on and on, and it's hard to say when it begins and ends. Heart orgasm is generally more of a state of being than a peak. Instead of building towards it, I surrender and let go into it.

Heart orgasms are intense. They also feel different because while the Pelvic Chakra is the body's pleasure center, the heart is the center for emotions and love. Orgasms of the heart can take me into waves of grief, trigger painful memories, expand me into compassion for all beings, and connect me with the one big love of all that is. The energetic state-change in my heart can trigger a commensurate shift into expanded states of consciousness, hence the concept of sex as a spiritual practice. In my experience, the "cup" of my heart is vast. Its capacity to hold energy is far beyond my Pelvic Chakra's capacity. Orgasms on my Heart Chakra will often expand and energize me beyond my familiar sexual peak.

In order to access a heart-centered orgasm however, I must dissolve all the blocks I have placed around my heart. This melting process can variously be scary, painful, or liberating. As I move sexual energy out of the pleasure-focused second chakra, I access more of the full spectrum of human erotic experience. This aspect of sexual awakening brings an intensification of emotions, a potential release of trauma, and an incredible deepening of connection with my body. Heart orgasms open me to the depth and richness of human experience. They really are exquisite.

Self-Pleasure Practice III: Heart Orgasm

Duration: 20+ minutes

Instructions:

Use touch and self-pleasure to build arousal in your cock. Slowly build the sexual energy using deep, free breathing. Stabilize at a high but comfortable level below the point of no return.

Visualize pleasure as a white light traveling from your cock, up along the central channel and into the heart. Draw energy up with each in-breath into the heart. Use your pelvic floor like a trampoline to bounce energy upward. Caress the heart and chest with your finger-tips. Feel your sexual energy move from the pelvis up into the heart. Continue to generate arousal and pleasure in your cock as you breathe that energy upward.

Eventually, you will be able to focus mostly on your heart. Breathe deeply into the heart. Drink full, pleasurable breaths into your heart. Visualize a kaleidoscope of colors radiating from your heart. Visualize a lotus flower blossoming open with thousands of petals. Open and expand with each in-breath. Soften and feel with each out-breath. In-breath, open; out-breath, soften. Energize on the in-breath and surrender on the out-breath. Just keep letting go into the heart. Welcome the tenderness, welcome the rawness, welcome the pain, welcome the grief, welcome the joy—whatever is arising, breathe into it with a YES, and melt into it with the exhale.

Let go of managing. Let go of tracking. Let go of the picture for how an orgasm is supposed to feel. Dare to feel more fully. Become oversaturated with feeling until the heart erupts in a messy gush of emotion and energy. Penetrate all the way to the center of the heart and then throw your whole being in.

Self-Pleasure Practice IV: Full-Body Orgasm

Instead of focusing the energy to trigger an orgasm in my heart, I can spread the energy throughout my whole body. The same principles apply. I stimulate arousal in my cock and stabilize there without ever reaching the point of no return. Then I use my energetic tools to move the energy into each chakra and across every cell of my body. I keep filling with more and more energy until my whole body expands into orgasm (Figure 13.17).

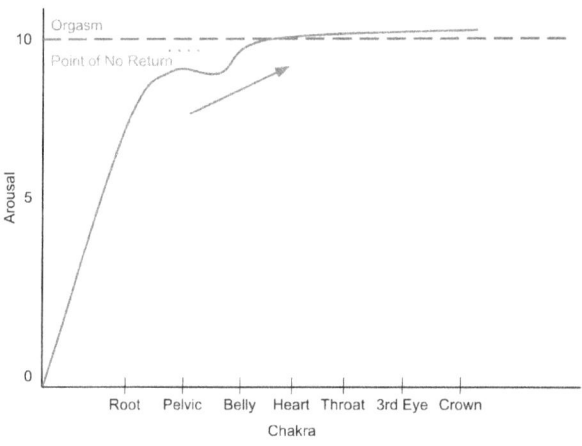

Figure 13.17 Full Body Orgasm

Duration: 20+ minutes

Instructions:

Use touch and self-pleasure to build arousal in your cock. Slowly build the sexual energy using deep, free breathing. Stabilize at a high but comfortable level below the point of no return.

Visualize pleasure as a white light traveling from your cock, up along the central channel, igniting each chakra along the way. With each in-breath move the sexual energy up through the central channel. Relax on each out-breath. Keep enough awareness in the cock to stay highly aroused without spilling over. Continue until the entire central channel is open and energized.

Inhale pleasure up the length of the central channel. Exhale pleasure outward from center into every cell in your body. Inhale a bright light of pleasure up the center. Exhale, radiate outward. Touch your entire body. Feel each cell in the body coming alive. Imagine the pleasure becoming more intense. Turn up the volume. Continue with deep, free breathing. Make the pleasure stronger and brighter, stronger and brighter.

Breathing fully, allow your body to move with pleasure—at first, gentle undulations. Use breath and movement to heighten your pleasure. The movement expands with the pleasure. Encourage your body to squirm, roll, flow, and shake with the pleasure of your aliveness.

Take a full breath in, hold, and squeeze every muscle in your body. Holding the breath, undulate your body as if you were having an orgasm. Intensify the energy. Keep holding, keep squeezing. Let the body move with pleasure. Stronger, stronger, stronger . . . And then make a loud HAAAA sound and exhale all the air out. Intend to have an orgasm. Don't hold back, don't track what's happening, just go fully into the pleasure of the energy. Feel the entire body scintillate with rolling orgasmic energy.

Take another slow, deep breath in—as much air as you can hold. Squeeze your whole body. The pleasure rises. Hold tighter. Squeeze more to intensify the pleasure. Stronger and brighter. Holding . . . Release with a HAAAAAA tone. Express your pleasure through sound. HAAAAAA!!!—as loud as you are safe to express until all the air is out. Another slow, delicious breath in. Another squeeze. Another loud strong sound to release. Again. And again. And again.

Summary of Phase III

By the time I reach Phase III, I have found a routine with the various practices for self-pleasure, yoga, meditation, and subtle energy. My primary focus at this point will be to continue to expand into more energy through all my practices. In addition, the deeper layers of my shadows will be coming to the surface through the increasing depth of my practice. Shame, trauma, attachment, codependence, limiting beliefs, and more will come up to be felt through. This is by design—it is an essential part of the process. My job is to resource myself so I can safely feel through everything that arises.

At first, a full-body orgasm might feel like a warm tingle across your body or a pleasurable expansion. It may be a relatively minor phenomenon compared to the intensity of ejaculatory orgasms you are accustomed to. If you feel some pleasurable state-change, great! That's the beginning of your full-body orgasm. Trust that this is what you're looking for and keep practicing it. For me and most men I've worked with, the biggest hurdle here is that we doubt our experience.

With practice, this warm tingle becomes stronger and stronger until it eventually surpasses the intensity of ejaculatory orgasm. We're not just filling one cup, i.e., the Pelvic Chakra, we're filling up seven cups and every cell in the body along with them. I'm talking about pleasure that's an order of magnitude greater.

In order to get there, you have to fully engage with your energy and the sound. Don't hold anything back! Recall the most intense orgasm you've ever had or that you've seen someone have. This is the level of intensity you need to be embodying in your practice.

Once you learn to trigger full-body orgasms more reliably, it's possible to turn down the volume and explore more subtle realms of orgasmic experience. In fact, once the somatic experience of orgasm is anchored into place, the path into deeper and more expansive realms is generally through relaxed arousal and surrendering into the waves of erotic energy.

Prompts for Journaling and Discussion

In what ways do you resist opening into more joyful pleasure in your body?

What other changes have been happening in your life outside of your sexual practice? Do you think any of these changes are connected to your practice?

What would make your orgasms better?

Notes

[1] Image via Google Imagen 3.0

[2] *The Power of Myth.*

[3] "A felt sense is not a mental experience but a physical one… A bodily awareness of a situation or person or event. An internal aura that encompasses everything you feel and know about a given subject at a given time—encompasses it and communicates it to you all at once, rather than detail by detail." *Focusing*, Eugene Gendlin.

[4] *Women's Anatomy of Arousal.*

[5] *Urban Tantra.*

[6] "In the Tantrik traditions, from which the concept derives, chakras (Skt. *cakra*) are focal points for meditation within the human body, visualized as structures of energy resembling discs or flowers at those points where a number of *nāḍis* (channels or meridians) converge. They are conceptual structures yet are phenomenologically based, since they tend to be located where human beings experience emotional and/or spiritual energy, and since the form in which they are visualized reflects visionary experiences had by meditators." "The real story on the Chakras," Wallis.

[7] "The next chakra is behind the navel, within the spinal column. It is a ten petalled yellow lotus called *manipura* and it is associated with the solar plexus." *Hatha Yoga Pradipika*, Mukitbodhananda.

[8] "You have bioelectric energy in every cell of your body. This energy also travels along certain well-defined circuits, called *meridians*, which acupuncture utilizes to regulate the amount of *chi* in any particular part of your body. The main circuit in the body is called the Microcosmic Orbit and is made up of two channels, the Back Channel and the Front Channel." *The Multi-Orgasmic Man*, Chia.

[9] "The posture of meditation is a process in which the body initially aligns itself in the field of gravity, invites relaxation by surrendering its weight to the pull of that field, and then cultivates the conditions of alignment and relaxation through allowing the body to move and respond in subtly resilient patterns of motion." *The Posture of Meditation*, Johnson.

[10] *The Practice of Pure Awareness.*

[11] "Uddiyana means 'to rise up' or 'fly.' In the practice of uddiyana bandha the abdominal organs are pulled up and in, creating a natural upward flow of energy, therefore, it is often translated as 'the stomach lift'…With regular practice of uddiyana the effects become visibly apparent. Vitality increases as uddiyana has a powerful toning effect on the visceral organs, muscles, nerves and

glands. The suction created stimulates blood circulation and absorption. The heart is squeezed and gently massaged by the upward pressure of the diaphragm. The suction or negative pressure in the thorax draws venous blood up from the abdomen into the heart and at the same time, arterial blood is drawn into the internal organs. The autonomic nerves comprising the solar plexus are strengthened. The processes of digestion, assimilation and elimination are directly affected." *Hatha Yoga Pradipika*, Muktibodhananda.

| 14 |

Full Non-Ejaculatory Orgasm

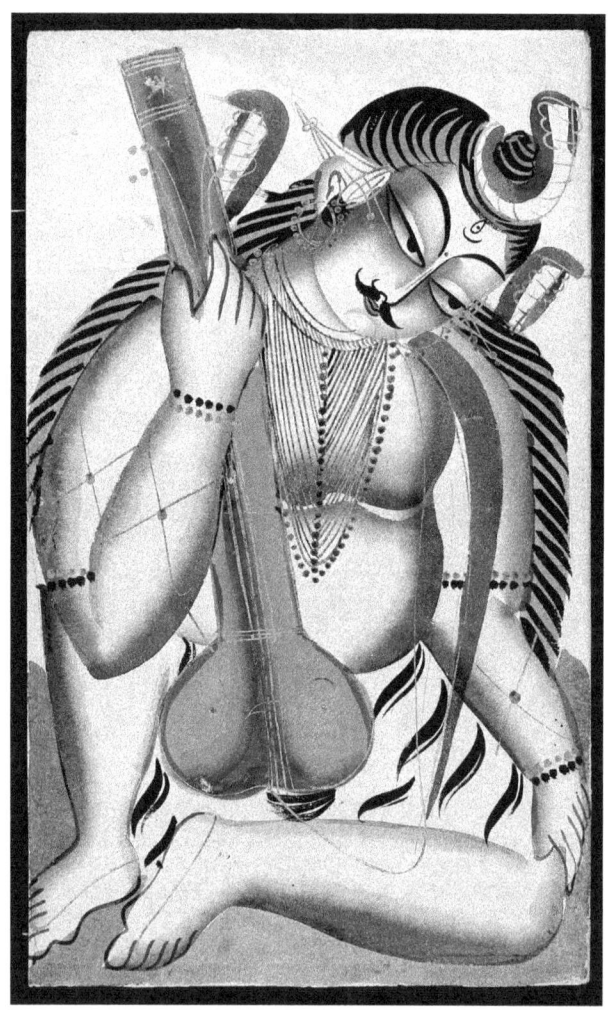

Figure 14.1 Shiva[1]

Is an energy orgasm better than a genital orgasm? No, they are simply different. But is an energy orgasm combined with a genital orgasm better than either one separately? You bet!

—Barbara Carrellas[2]

In the practices for heart-centered orgasms and full-body orgasms outlined above, I am generating energy in my cock and keeping my arousal there safely below the point of no return while orgasm happens elsewhere in my body. Through this process I am learning to hone in on the sensation and experience of orgasm as a separate phenomenon from ejaculation. Once I isolate the felt sense of orgasm, I can cultivate and intensify that energetic capacity. I want to become proficient with that phase before I begin the practices for full, non-ejaculatory orgasm.

Here in Phase Four, I am learning how to have an orgasm centered in the cock without going into ejaculation. This is a *full non-ejaculatory orgasm*. Once I have gained some comfort in crossing the orgasm threshold elsewhere in my body, I can apply the same intensification process on the energy in my cock during self-pleasure or intercourse. While I am intensifying my energy, I am holding my body steady so that I never hit the point of no return. This requires incredible mental focus together with dexterity and strength in my pelvic floor muscles.

Conceptually, I am moving the orgasm threshold down below the point of no return and then dancing in the space between them (Figure 14.2). As discussed in the Edging practice, the thresholds for the point of no return and orgasm are elastic, not static. As I clock more time at high levels of arousal, both lines rise up— meaning I am able to feel more arousal while remaining under the point of no return. Now that I know how to trigger orgasms in isolation, I apply that felt sense in my cock to trigger an orgasm there. This is an intuitive process that will come online with dedicated practice.

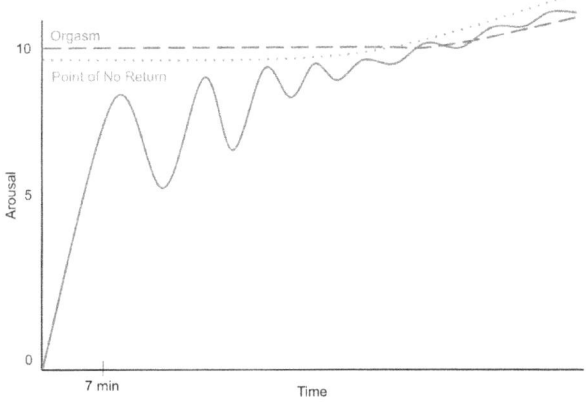

Figure 14.2 Full Non-Ejaculatory Orgasm

Holding Steady through Intensity

However intense my ejaculatory orgasms are, I need to be able to hold myself steadily at least that strongly. In fact, the power of my full non-ejaculatory orgasms are directly determined by this capacity for strong, focused holding. By holding, I don't necessarily mean squeezing. Holding steady means *not pumping the testes*—not even a little bit, not even once. I can do this by focusing on relaxing these muscles as I orgasm, or I can do this by clenching all these muscles. Remember, we switch into the activated nervous-system state of sympathetic arousal when we go into ejaculation. So learning how to hold myself relaxed as I enter orgasm has been more fruitful for me, though both routes are possible.

Either way, I need to learn concentration and I need to build my capacity to hold. There are two tools here. First, I do this through dexterity and strength in my pelvic floor muscles. (Recommit to the Pelvic Floor Workout in the Edging chapter.)

The second indispensable tool is Belly Locks, also known as *uddiyana bandhas*. Belly Locks are included as part of Yoga Sequence II in the prior chapter, but I want to expand on them now at this phase of the practice. It's the same technique, but now I am extending each breath hold and I want to lengthen my overall practice time.

As I move into intentionally holding through greater and greater intensity, it's important to recognize the messages coming from the body. Discomfort is great—in fact, I want to lean into it fully. On the other hand, I want to respect pain or a "Stop" from my body. In my experience, pushing past what my body is available for has led my body to shut down my practice. I have learned this lesson the hard way.

The discomfort with the breath hold can be extreme. Sometimes I feel like I'm dying. Other times, I feel like my belly is on fire. Other times I feel utterly constipated, like I'm pushing against a brick of clay. All of these are OK. If I begin feeling panic, sharp pain, dissociation, light-headedness, or strong revulsion, these are *no's* that I want to respect and listen to. It's a sign to back off from the practice.

I do belly locks first thing in the morning before I put any food or liquid into my body. The intensity of each breath builds up momentum, so I keep chaining them together. As I hold for longer and longer, my diaphragm will jolt or gulp. I use this little jump to intensify what I'm feeling and strengthen my hold. Clenching or jolting is a normal part of this practice. Over time, I become stronger and this becomes more natural.

The level of intensity that I am able to hold during belly locks is the same amount of intensity that I will be able to hold in the peak of my full non-ejaculatory orgasm. This is the metaphorical mountain. If you want the peak, you have to be willing to climb.

Belly Lock Practice

Duration: Set a timer for three minutes at first and work your way up to ten minutes over the course of a few weeks.

Instructions:

Take five deep belly breaths in and out through your nose to warm up. Perform the Belly Locks for the duration of your timer. (**New info in bold**).

To enter:

> Stand at the top of your mat. Step your feet shoulder-width apart, parallel facing forward. Bend your knees 45 degrees, palms of hands rest on quads, fingers facing towards center.

In the pose:

> Inhale as much breath as possible through your nose. Releasing hands and head down toward the floor, strongly exhale all the air out through your mouth. Holding the breath out, draw the belly in and up. Push your palms into your quads and straighten your elbows to come back to squat. Knees are bent. Lengthen the back of the neck and spine. Continue to hold all air out, while squeezing the belly in. Relax the jaw, eyes, and every non-essential muscle. Feel the intensity and energy rise. Use the vacuum of breath to pull energy up from the root and pelvis into your belly (and eventually up into the heart). The diaphragm may make a gulping motion—use that to draw more energy up.

> **While holding the air out, contract and hold your pelvic floor (*mula bandha*). Optionally, you may rhythmically pump your belly in and out while holding the breath out (*agnisara kriya*). Draw the energy from your testes and cock up the length of your central channel.**

> Hold until the intensity is uncomfortable.

> To release, first relax the belly. **Place your tongue gently on the roof of your mouth.** Then take a full breath in. **Swallow your saliva and draw the breath down to your lower belly.** Hold for a slow count to five and feel energy in the belly. **Release the in-breath by exhaling strongly up through your central channel and out your nostrils. Imagine the power of your breath clearing the passage of your central channel.**

Take a deep, cleansing breath in and out. Then take another full inhale and begin your next belly lock.

To exit:

Stand tall. Step feet hip-width apart, hands at sides.

Four Methods for Full Non-Ejaculatory Orgasm

Every body-system is unique, so there is no single method for how to achieve full non-ejaculatory orgasms. Each man must forge his own toolkit and process. In my own explorations, I have developed a number of techniques that work for me. Again, these are my field notes. Adapt them to work for you.

The Balancing Method

Crossing the orgasm threshold is a balancing act between relaxing and intensifying. If I relax too much, I either lose arousal or lose focus and spill over. If I intensify too late or too erratically, I can trigger ejaculation. But there is a middle path: I use relaxed, deep-free breathing into greater and greater sensation until I am feeling stable and secure around 9.7 in arousal. From there, I slowly intensify the energy into orgasm. I can do this by pulsing or squeezing my pelvic floor and breath, by visualizing the energy becoming brighter, by feeling the temperature rise, or simply by intending that my energy rise. As I enter orgasm, I bring total focus to my pelvic floor and testes to hold and prevent the rhythmic contractions of ejaculation. Slowly and gently entering into orgasm makes it easier to hold back ejaculation. There is no rush. This method is like taking baby steps over the finish line.

The Flow-Back Method

When I get close to the point of no return in my cock, I use my breath to draw the energy up my central channel. I begin having an energy orgasm higher up in my body, for example, in my Heart Chakra. Once I'm in the orgasm and my cock feels stable, I bring the orgasmic energy back down into my cock and start orgasming there. The orgasm *flows back* from my body into my cock. I can breathe the energy down, visualize it, or start thrusting more with my pelvis to move the energy back down.

The Fake-It Method

I get stable at a high level of arousal: somewhere around 9.7. I hold my pelvic floor and testes steady, and then with everything else in my body I fake an orgasm. I clench. I breathe heavy. I make sound. I intensify. By taking my body into the motions of a fake orgasm, I can trigger myself into an actual one. This is similar to the full body orgasm described in the prior chapter, but in this method, I'm staying focused on pleasure in my cock.

The Wear-Down Method

In this method, I edge up to 9.7, and then 9.8, and then 9.9. I hold at 9.9. I keep holding at 9.9. My body gets more and more frustrated because it just wants to ejaculate and I'm not letting it go there. Eventually—and this might take 30 minutes or longer—a somatic surrender happens and I just start orgasming.

This method is like asking my parents for ice cream repeatedly as a kid. Eventually, with enough dogged persistence, they would cave and give me ice cream. The process, however, is very very annoying. I have to wait until my body gives up its drive to ejaculate. If you're like me, this is a very strong drive that is not easily relinquished. This takes patience and persistence.

The achievement of full non-ejaculatory orgasm is where the sexual initiation properly happens. As I mentioned earlier, this is a major undertaking. For the men who successfully make the journey, it generally takes six months to two years of dedicated practice. My hope is that the information presented here will both increase the success rate and shorten the time requirement. This initiation works across every level of my being and there are many moving parts: I am re-training an entire lifetime of habitual ejaculation, I am overcoming millions of years of instinctual impulses, and I am undoing our culture's nervous-system dysfunctions. While it does become easier once I get it, the urge to ejaculate doesn't ever go away. That desire is still fully present. However, once this initiation happens, the urge to ejaculate is no longer ruling me. Now, I have become sexually sovereign in a new way.

Troubleshooting

Here are some common issues that men experience, followed by my advice.

As I've entered this practice, my ejaculation happens more quickly and more erratically. I feel way more sensitive to stimulation.

This is a normal, though frustrating, part of the journey. For many men, shifting from regular ejaculation into retention practice causes the ejaculation response to become hyper-sensitive. Longer and more frequent practice sessions in sex or self-pleasure will help de-sensitize this somewhat. Slow everything way down—there is no rush, and by taking more time to gently enter arousal, the erratic and overly-sensitive pleasure will smooth out. Stay grounded during sex. Focus your breathing into the Heart or Third Eye to keep the energy moving up from the cock. Moving your energy through Yoga Sequence II before sex or self-pleasure will create significantly more capacity.

Blue balls! My testes are sore or painful, and the energy feels stuck, over-full, and uncomfortable.

Move the energy up from the testes through the central channel. Try ten minutes of Belly Locks (*uddiyana bandha*) followed by two minutes of Headstand (against a wall is fine). After a few weeks of dedicated practice, the body will naturally find a new equilibrium.

I have too much energy now. I can't sleep. I can't sit still.

This amount of vitality will become your new baseline for living life, and there is indeed an upward adjustment process. Find a creative outlet to put all this energy towards: work, exercise, creative projects, etc. The Warrior's quality of *focused action* is needed to meet this new vitality. Use either yoga or strenuous exercise before bed to circulate and expend your energy to help with sleep. Other habits like vegetating, numbing out, and checking out will naturally be displaced as this additional life-force integrates into your new cruising altitude.

I have so much sexual desire, I don't know what to do with it. I am attracted to anyone with a pulse. I am constantly turned on and feeling surges of lust.

By holding back my ejaculation, I am intentionally not reaching satisfaction. By stoking my sexual fire daily, I am strongly activating this sexual dissatisfaction, aka desire. Cultivating more sexual desire is an intended outcome of this practice—it provides fuel to undergo the transformation and growth. The first step is to focus on grounding. Commit to the Earth Body meditation.

Sometimes in this process, a lifetime's worth of sexual repression arises to be liberated. Paradoxically, more sexual practice is generally the best way to meet this flux of energy. All of this erotic energy is arising to be met and integrated. Personally, I have gone through periods of self-pleasuring three times a day for thirty minutes when that was what my body was calling me to do. My goal here is to practice expanding into my pleasure and desire so I can hold it in my body.

Over time, I learn to integrate these greater levels of desire. Yes, it's uncomfortable. But it's also incredibly enlivening.

I'm having trouble getting an erection.

This could be caused by physical, energetic, emotional, or psychological causes—or some combination. First, slow down and let go of any pressure to perform. Notice tension and stress—use the yoga and meditation practices to relax and flow. Notice if there is a routine that is becoming bland and explore something new. Cultivate a sense of curiosity and playfulness with your self-pleasure practice. During self-pleasure, focus on deep free breathing and very slow touch. Make space to feel what's happening across all levels. Feel the emotions, notice the narratives, receive information from the body, and notice how the energy wants to flow. Ultimately, the self-pleasure practice is not about getting hard, it's about feeling energy and pleasure in the body. Sometimes my erections take a break for a period and then come back as I move through the larger cycles in my life.

If you are doing intensive Belly Lock practice, you may be pulling too much energy up to your higher centers. Practice circulating the energy back down the front of your body and into your cock.

Because there are a myriad of potential causes here, there is no single answer. Get curious and listen to your body.

I can get to a seven on the arousal curve, but am not able to edge up into the nines.

There can be a number of causes for this. The simplest issue is that I am not generating enough energy in my body. Breathe deeply and fully, generating energy with the breath. Slow down—slow touch builds excitement and sensitivity. Take plenty of time—thirty minutes of dedicated breath and touch will shift my state into higher and higher arousal. In addition, focus on the yoga postures that bring energy into the body: Standing Forward Fold and Mountain Pose in particular.

The second main cause is getting stuck in the conceptual mind by making judgments, tracking, analyzing, and managing. Self-pleasure calls me to feel and enjoy. My practice is to surrender my discursive thinking into the sensations of my body. As I get more honest about what's happening, I notice that thinking sometimes comes online as a protection mechanism against higher states of energy. I use thinking to control my experience.

Third, if I am still cleansing from a porn addiction, there is a natural resensitization and retraining process away from visual stimulation, orienting to physical stimulation for arousal. This takes time and practice.

Beyond these, there may be deeper blocks: for example, not feeling safe to let go or not feeling safe to have a big expression. There may be an unconscious safety cap on the energy I generate in order to protect a wound or a place where trauma is being held. I may have disowned and repressed a part of myself that wants to fuck, ravage, bang, etc. In these cases, it usually feels as though the body is willing and able, but there is a psychic wall holding me back. Sometimes I have capacity to work through these blocks myself, and sometimes I need the support of a psychotherapist, sexual healer, or loving partner to work through it.

Edging up into the high nines is a crucial step in the process. If I'm not playing high on the arousal scale, then I'm not going to be accessing orgasm. More practice and more time spent aroused will train my body to enter these higher states of energy and to hold for longer time.

I stopped practicing for a week and now I'm starting from the beginning again; or, I ejaculated and now I'm starting from the beginning again. This sucks!

Correct. We create a sealed container by withholding ejaculation. Then we add energy every day through either sex or self-pleasure. Successively stronger energy within the closed container creates an alchemical process of transformation. Unfortunately, if the container breaks, we start again from scratch.

I have a small body orgasm and then I lose my erection.

Ideally, non-ejaculatory orgasms can be strung together without losing arousal in between (i.e., no refractory period). My habit growing up was masturbating quickly and quietly, and I taught my body that particular rhythm. I needed to retrain this habit by taking more time in foreplay and middle-arousal levels. Moving slowly and really getting the energy moving through my whole body before I have my first orgasm helps considerably.

In addition, I need to stay balanced with the energy I'm feeling in my cock. The primary action is to draw my orgasmic energy in and up along the central channel instead of expelling it out through my cock. However, if I draw too much energy up through this process, I can lose sensation and erection in my cock. So, I need to balance the proper amount of arousal in my second chakra during orgasm. As I feel stable in my cock, I can breathe pleasurable energy back down into my cock.

Finally, this is about holding intensity with my presence. With stronger capacity to hold pleasure and energy, I can build up my orgasms and create a bridge to not lose arousal in between. The intensity that I'm able to hold in my yoga practice, particularly the Belly Locks, directly translates into the intensity of sexual pleasure that I'm able to hold.

Each man's energetic system is unique. If you lose your erection between orgasms, that may be how your body is naturally wired. You can work to lengthen your orgasms or to shorten your refractory period between erections with intention and practice.

I can't tell whether I'm ejaculating or not.

Practice the Pelvic Floor Workout daily for a few weeks. Strengthening the pelvic floor, the anal sphincter, and the muscles that stop the flow of urine and that lift the testes will all help build awareness and control of ejaculation. If all of these muscles are held steady and flexed, then I won't go into ejaculation, but one small hiccup can lead to a spill.

Over time, I will gain even more awareness of the different types of pumping during ejaculation. There is the release of semen from the testes, which is distinct from the release of seminal fluid from the seminal vesicle and prostate. This latter release happens both during ejaculation and variously during arousal in the form of *pre-cum*. Sometimes pre-cum is visually indistinguishable from semen. One savory test of whether sperm are present is to put some of the fluid into the mouth and feel for the tingly sensation of *swimmers* against the cheeks and throat.

For our purposes, a small ejaculation is still an ejaculation and should be avoided. Granted, it is better than a full ejaculation because there is less life-force for the body to recharge. But the seal is still broken. Until the body learns fully and completely that ejaculation is off the table, I will not be able to confidently move into strong energetic orgasms. Complete retention is the requirement to get to Step 4: Full Non-Ejaculatory Orgasm.

I have plateaued. Nothing has changed for the last month or longer, and I'm not making progress.

When I plateau, it's a sign to pay more attention to my practice. I examine whether it's time to change my routine. I rededicate myself to a meaningful and engaging daily practice.

When I plateau, I return to the last phase I felt I really *got*, and follow the guided practice with that phase for a week to ensure that I actually am where I think I am. There can be no skipping over, no gliding past, and no faking through. This is like playing a musical instrument, where thorough and dedicated practice yields progress.

Finally, I pay attention to where I may be blocked: intellectually, emotionally, energetically, or physically. Sometimes a big process elsewhere in my life needs my time and energy. Once it completes, I then have time and creative energy to dedicate back into my sexual practice.

What about the "Million Dollar Point"?

The *million dollar point* is a technique to prevent ejaculation during sex. In this technique, when I pass the Point of No Return and the rhythmic pumping begins, I press my fingers firmly into my perineum until the ejaculation passes. This technique pinches off the vas deferens, which is the tube that carries semen to the urethra. It prevents semen from leaving the penis, and in that sense, it can be a form of "last resort" birth control. But the sperm still leave the testes, so for our purposes, the seal is broken and my body will need to spend energy regenerating sperm. When I close off the vas deferens, the semen is forced upward through a sphincter into my bladder. Later, I will urinate that semen out. This can be tested after performing this technique by peeing into a toilet and instead of flushing, allowing the water to sit for half an hour. A film of semen will float to the top of the water.

I do not consider the million dollar point to be a useful technique in learning the *Five Phases*.

Ejaculation Frequency

For the purposes of learning to separate ejaculation and orgasm, a discipline of zero ejaculations is necessary in my view. I am totally retraining my body, nervous system, and energy pathways. In order to break the old habit and instill the new one, I needed to fully commit to no ejaculations. Once I learned proficiency in orgasm without ejaculation, the question of how frequently to ejaculate once again became relevant.

I am not offering medical advice here, but do wish to provide references in scientific literature for your informed decision-making. Some studies have found that more frequent ejaculation reduces the risk of prostate cancer, though this conclusion is not uniformly accepted.[3] [4] [5] In addition, studies have been largely inconclusive on mental and physical health implications of ejaculation frequency.[6] From my perspective, having regular orgasms is one of the healthiest practices I can do for myself. To date, there is no scientific literature examining men withholding ejaculation while continuing to have regular orgasms—this study is what I would want to see. Without a conclusive medical consensus on ejaculation frequency, this question then becomes more of a personal and intuitive exploration.

For me, ejaculation frequency is about what feels right and what purpose it is serving. Primarily, I want to listen to the rhythms of my body and consciously choose whether to share my seed.

Personally, I have tested withholding ejaculation for more than a year while maintaining a regular self-pleasure practice, and it feels amazing. What I notice is a steadiness in my life force that slowly brightens with each successive month. There is a container for my fire and I can choose to channel that energy into my work, creative projects, or spiritual practices. For me, this contained stoking empowers my Warrior. I'm activating my sexual energy and fully embodying my aliveness to channel it back into my life.

I have also been in partnerships where I would share my seed and she would share her menstrual blood each month in a ceremony. I was fully offering my life-force into the relationship month after month through this ritual. Using my seed in this way is incredibly powerful. On a symbolic level, both partners are choosing to share and intermix their most sacred essences. There is a polarization of the man's life-seed together with the woman's death-blood. And every time I chose to share my seed in this way, I would feel the energetic dip in my vitality for the next few days. It was truly an offering of my life-force into the bond of the relationship.

I have also explored giving my seed as a ceremonial offering to the earth. This is a potent way to connect with land and to embody fertility. In each of these cases, I am regarding my seed as my sacred vitality (sanskrit: *ojas*), which I either share or hold with conscious intention.

Prompts for Journaling and Discussion

What effect (if any) do you notice Belly Locks making for your orgasmic potential?

At this moment, what ejaculation frequency is in your highest good?

What ritual or ceremony can you incorporate the next time you offer your seed?

Notes

[1] Wellcome Collection, public domain.

[2] *Urban Tantra.*

[3] "Most categories of ejaculation frequency were unrelated to risk of prostate cancer. However, high ejaculation frequency was related to decreased risk of total prostate cancer. The multivariate relative risks for men reporting 21 or more ejaculations per month compared with men reporting 4 to 7 ejaculations per month at ages 20 to 29 years were 0.89 (95% confidence interval [CI], 0.73-1.10); ages 40 to 49 years, 0.68 (95% CI, 0.53-0.86); previous year, 0.49 (95% CI, 0.27-0.88); and averaged across a lifetime, 0.67 (95% CI, 0.51-0.89). Similar associations were observed for organ-confined prostate cancer. Ejaculation frequency was not statistically significantly associated with risk of advanced prostate cancer. Conclusions: Our results suggest that ejaculation frequency is not related to increased risk of prostate cancer." "Ejaculation frequency and subsequent risk of prostate cancer," Leitzmann et al.

[4] "We evaluated whether ejaculation frequency throughout adulthood is related to prostate cancer risk in a large US-based study. We found that men reporting higher compared to lower ejaculatory frequency in adulthood were less likely to be subsequently diagnosed with prostate cancer." "Ejaculation Frequency and Risk of Prostate Cancer: Updated Results with an Additional Decade of Follow-up," Rider et al.

[5] "Findings included relations among masturbation, ejaculation frequency, and age range as individual factors of prostate cancer risk. No universally accepted themes were identified across the study sample." "Evidence for Masturbation and Prostate Cancer Risk: Do We Have a Verdict?", Aboul-Enein et al.

[6] "Despite its relevance for human sexuality, literature on potential effects of ejaculation frequency and masturbation on general and mental health outcomes is sparse. Reasons for this knowledge gap include a general lack of interest, but also methodological challenges and still existing superstition… Abstinence is one aspect under study in the area of fertility treatment. Specific time frames and their respective implications on quality of sperm remain inconclusive. Limited temporal resolution capacities hamper the precise study of brain structures directly activated during ejaculation. The relation between ejaculation frequency and hormonal influences remains poorly understood." "Is Ejaculation Frequency in Men Related to General and Mental Health? Looking Back and Looking Forward," Mascherek et al.

| 15 |

Orgasmic Articulation

Figure 15.1 Cobra Heartgasm[1]

> Orgasm is a state where your body no more is felt as matter; it vibrates like energy, electricity. It vibrates so deeply, from the very foundation, that you completely forget that it is a material thing…This vibration of two as one is orgasm. When the same thing happens, not with another person, but with the whole existence, then it is Mahamudra, then it is the great orgasm. It happens. I would like to tell you how you can try it, so that the Mahamudra becomes possible, the great orgasm.
>
> —OSHO[2]

In the beginning months, my focus is on basic technique. Breathe here, squeeze this, hold that, and whatever I do, don't hit the Point of No Return. I am learning how to play individual notes on this new instrument. I also need to focus on self-care to manage the newly-activated energy and emotions in my system.

As my practice matures, my focus shifts onto the arc of a practice session. The breath and energy techniques begin to become habits, and now I'm learning how to play melodies and songs with this instrument. At this stage, my perspective necessarily broadens to include more of my life. The generation of energy within a pure container is key. Am I eating, sleeping, and working out in a way that supports this profound sexual undertaking? I start to see how other habits, people, and activities in my life are either supporting or impairing my wellbeing. I learn to listen more and more deeply to my body, and we become a team in a whole new way.

At a certain point, I gain enough confidence in my ability to avoid the Point of No Return that I can begin to really explore the terrain. I take risks. I try new things. I become playful and loosen up more. This is another crucial step, as opening to orgasm is a loosening, not a tightening. In the instrument analogy, this is the beginning of improvisation.

Eventually, I will experience my first really strong, non-ejaculatory orgasm. For most men, something clicks into place here. It's the point of *getting it* enough that there's no going back. Once this type of orgasm happens a single time, I know I can do it and I orient myself towards that experience. It still takes practice. I'm still going to have good days and hard days, but now my proficiency is coming online and I feel the exhilaration of seeing the destination.

Over time, holding back ejaculation becomes more natural and orgasm becomes increasingly accessible. Here, even more relaxation is possible. My perspective during self-pleasure or sex opens much more broadly. I begin to recognize that orgasm is not a peak to chase. Rather, I discover that orgasm is a state of total aliveness of my energy, which is essentially blissful. I learn to ignite orgasms in different parts of my body. I learn how to charge up my whole body into a rolling orgasmic flow. I discover that orgasmic energy is only limited by my imagination and capacity to feel. Emotion orgasms, color orgasms, texture orgasms, taste orgasms, spinning and flipping orgasms, orgasms the size of the room, orgasms the size of the planet, orgasms the size of the kosmos, orgasms with trees, dream orgasms, orgasms across time and space, orgasms with deities, orgasms as deities, death orgasms, birth orgasms, and on and on . . . In the practices below, we'll expand into more of what's possible through orgasm.

Self-Pleasure Practice V: Yawn-gasm

Duration: 10+ minutes

Instructions:

Lie flat on your back and take ten deep breaths.

> Breathe deeply into your heart and chest. Exhale fully. With each inhale, open more space. With each exhale, relax and feel.

Yawn.

> Breathe all the way in and then yawn. Yawn again. Give yourself completely to the sensation of yawning. Take as much time as you need with each yawn. Open your jaw fully with each yawn. Allow the yawn to release any tension or stuck energy in your whole body.

Yawn from the back of your heart.

> Inhale into the back of your heart just inside the spine. Open with the in-breath. Feel the dark depths of the heart-cavern. Imagine each yawn originating from the depths of your heart. Feel the yawn rooted in the core of your heart. Yawn your heart open.

Yawn pleasurably.

> See how much you can enjoy each yawn. Turn up the volume on your pleasure. Make sound with each yawn. Emote. Dare to be loud. Undulate your body. Allow your eyes to roll back. Welcome tears. Laugh. Hold nothing back. Feel the vast space that opens with a full yawn. Give yourself into the space of this yawn completely. Let go into it.

Expand!

> Imagine this yawn is a slow-motion replay of the most intense orgasm you ever had. Yawn-Roar into orgasm! Yawn-gasm!

> As you exhale into the room, expand the sensation of your orgasm to include the space of the room. The orgasmic yawn radiates out from the heart to fill the room.

The room is filled with orgasmic yawn-breath. Dissolve into the orgasmically yawning room.

Self-Pleasure Practice VI: Pineal-gasm

Duration: 10+ minutes

Instructions:

Sit in meditation posture. Begin with ten deep slow breaths into the lower belly. I recommend practicing this immediately after your Belly Locks.

Perform the Bee Breath (*brahmari*) for ten slow breaths:

> Inhale from the root up to the crown, filling with as much air as possible. Place your thumbs over your ear-holes, index fingers over closed eye-lids, third-fingers on either side of the nostrils without blocking airflow, fourth-fingers on top lip, and pinky fingers on bottom lip. Hold these fingers here for the duration of the performance.

> Exhale slowly through your nostrils while making a buzzing sound until all the air is out. Use the tongue, mouth, and sinuses to resonate the sound through the back of the throat like the buzzing of a bee. Allow the buzzing to reverberate through your head and skull, focalizing at your pineal gland in the center of the head behind the eyes. Feel energy gather at the pineal, which is the root of the Third-Eye Chakra.

> When all the air is spent, breathe deeply again, drawing energy up the length of the spine, and then buzz again on the exhale.

After the tenth Bee Breath, take a full breath in and then exhale completely.

Perform ten breath-holds in *maha bandha*:

> Inhaling through the nostrils, draw the energy and breath slowly up the length of the central channel, filling up completely with air. As the breath comes in, draw your belly up and hold tight (*uddiyana bandha*). Once the belly is in, draw the pelvic floor up and hold tight (*mula bandha*). At the top of the breath, lower your chin down to touch your chest (*jalandhara bandha*). Hold the breath with the three locks. Touch your tongue to the roof of the mouth (*khechari mudra*). Hold and squeeze. Intensify the energy and imagine all energy flowing to the pineal gland towards the center of the head. Imagine squeezing a tube of toothpaste up the spine into the brain. Hold for as long as is comfortable. If you become light-headed, stop this practice, and breathe normally.

To exhale, first release the chin, then the root, then the belly lock. Then exhale powerfully and tone AAAAAAAHHHHHH until all air is spent. As with Bee Breath, direct the sound vibrations into the pineal in the center of the head at the root of the Third-Eye Chakra. Repeat the in-breath, locks, and hold. Tone again on the exhale. Intensify with each breath until the pineal enters orgasm. Once the orgasm gathers momentum, you can simply breathe deeply into the pineal to keep the orgasm flowing. Tone a loud AAAAHHHH with each exhale to amplify the orgasm. Throw yourself into the space of the pineal. Let go completely into it.

Self-Pleasure Practice VII: Griefgasm

In this practice, I offer a script you can utilize to experience a griefgasm. Emotions are energy and just like erotic energy, emotional energy can pass the orgasm threshold. The practice I am offering here is focused on the emotion of grief, but I have had joygasms, furygasms, and paingasms as well. Any emotion, when embraced and energized, can move into an orgasmic state.

> The physiological ingredients of an emotiongasm are the same as a genital orgasm. A buildup of life force or sexual energy is brought about by a combination of breath, movement, sound, and muscular contractions and is followed by a release. This buildup and subsequent orgasmic release of life/sex energy doesn't necessarily depend on genital stimulation. Emotiongasms don't even depend on any particular emotion. In the course of a single breath and energy orgasm session, you could even have a gigglegasm, followed by a crygasm, followed by an angergasm, followed by another gigglegasm.
>
> —Barbara Carrellas[3]

Duration: 15+ minutes

Instructions:

Sit or lie comfortably. Begin with ten deep slow breaths into the lower belly. I recommend practicing this after the Chakra Awakening Practice.

Welcome the feeling of grief. Not the story of why I'm grieving. Simply the emotion of grief. Speak aloud, slowly:

I am coming out of my head and into my heart.
I am choosing feeling.
In my heart, I am feeling.
Feeling my heart open.

In my open heart, I am welcoming grief.
Allowing my grief.
Grieving my heart open.
Loving my grief open.
Grieving my love open.

Welcoming the blessing of my grief.
Receiving the blessing of my grief.
I am grieving the fullness of my love.
I am loving the fullness of my grief.

I make love to my grief.
I breathe into it.
I move with it.
I meet each wave with passion.
I embrace my grief.

"More grief! Give me more! I want all of you."
I am allowing my resistance to grieving.
I penetrate my resistance with total love.
I am grieving my hurt open.
I dare to cry, dare to moan, dare to shudder.

I take pleasure in my grief.
Grieving in pleasure. Pleasuring in grief.
Breathing into the grief, I energize and open.
Breathing into the pleasure, I express more strongly.

"More grief! Give me more! I want all of you."
I welcome my impulses to distract, hide, suppress, or destroy my grief.
I welcome my hatred of grieving.
I wrestle passionately with grief.
I ravage my grief.
I feel my grief return even stronger, taking me into more love.
I am ravaged by my grief.
I dare to be decimated by grief.
I allow myself to be saturated and consumed by grief.

"More grief! Give me more! I want all of you."
I want all of me, grieving.
I breathe, I feel, I expand,

I pour all of me into my grief at the center of my heart.

Making love with my grieving heart

Making grief with my loving heart

Opening my jaw wide and expressing my grief

Wailing in grief

Slowly hurting all the way in,

Holding nothing back,

Until my surrender washes me into union, grieving.

I soften into grief.

I melt into grief.

Grief is holding me, tenderly.

I am grieving my heart open, feeling.

Feeling the depth of my love, grieving.

Filling myself with grief.

Being emptied by grief.

Offering my gratitude to grief.

In closing,

I take a deep breath to feel my body,

I take a deep breath to connect with the earth,

I take a deep breath of gratitude,

I take a deep breath of wellbeing.

Self-Pleasure Practice VIII: Earthgasm

Duration: 20+ minutes

Instructions:

Go out into nature in a private, beautiful place. Take a few moments to acknowledge the beings of this place: the plants and animals, and any spirits that may be here. Offer a prayer to dedicate your pleasure to the earth.

Come into your senses.

Notice the colors around you and enjoy them. Wander around and smell everything: the air, the dirt, the plants, and your own body. Notice the sounds and pleasurably embrace them. Feel the textures of the natural environment.

Connect your body with the body of the earth.

Whatever you are touching, treat it as if it were your lover's body. Caress the earth. Grab the earth. Wrestle with the earth. Use your hands, feet, belly, back, and face to interact with the body of the earth. Move your body so the earth touches you the way you want to be touched.

Welcome your arousal.

Breathe, touch, energize, and pleasurize. Your erotic self is an expression of the erotic nature of the earth. All of your sexuality is safe and welcomed by the earth. None of you is too much, no part of you will be judged, and nothing is too weird, perverted, or kinky for the earth. Give yourself full permission to be strongly sexual with the earth and nature. Go for it.

Share your orgasm with the earth.

Go into an energetic orgasm. Now open into the aliveness of the earth and share your orgasm with the earth. Imagine the earth's body and your body are actually one body. Orgasm as this earth-body. Give your orgasm to the earth. Receive your orgasm from the earth.

Dedicate your lovemaking on behalf of the wellbeing of the earth. Include yourself in the recipients of this dedication.

Self-Pleasure Practice IX: Deitygasm

Choose a deity that you would like to connect your erotic energy with. I recommend starting with a deity who is already associated with sexuality, though I have found it possible to engage with many diverse deities through self-pleasure. In this example, I'll use the tantric goddess, Lalita Tripura Sundari.

Do some research into your chosen deity. Learn about the history and any practices for worship:

Lalita Tripura Sundari ("the charming beauty of the three worlds") is the form of the goddess who most successfully holds together the apparent opposites of executive power and sexuality, and of sexual and spiritual love. Queenly and playful, she represents a most delicious form of the integrated feminine...Lalita is primarily a Tantric goddess - a mediatrix of the inner realms, a guide through the portals of high stages of samadhi. She is the divine beauty (sundari) who permeates the waking, dream, and deep-sleep states - the tripura, or "three worlds" - as well as the physical, subtle, and causal bodies in which we experience those worlds.

—Sally Kempton[4]

Figure 15.2 Lalita Tripura Sundari[5]

Begin your self-pleasure practice.

As you build your arousal, invoke the deity.

Play a soundtrack of music with chanting for Lalita. Or learn the Sanskrit mantra for Lalita and chant it yourself while you self-pleasure:

    Ka e i la hrim
    Ha sa ka ha la hrim
    Sa ka la hrim

Visualize an image of the deity. Ask the deity to join you in your practice.

Share your arousal with the deity.

Offer your erotic energy to the deity. Receive erotic energy back from the deity. Imagine making love with the deity. As you enter into orgasm, imagine yourself entering into union, communion, or identity with the deity.

To close your erotic deity practice, make a dedication of your pleasure to all beings everywhere.

Summary of Phase V

On my path of sexual exploration, I have completely rediscovered myself through orgasm. I learned that orgasm is not simply a cool aspect of being a human. It is a doorway into the luminous, blissful awareness of my true nature. In yoga, this is referred to as *satchitananda*. What I experience during orgasm—the love, the creativity, the unity, the ever-new present moment—this is my essence. This is who I truly am and have always been. This is what I came here to experience in this life. I am an exquisite embodiment of the erotic nature of the kosmos.

Before this practice, ejaculation was the goal. Then *no ejaculation at all costs* became the new goal. Then small orgasms became the goal. Then making those orgasms really big. As orgasms became readily accessible for me, I no longer needed to seek them. I began to realize that I can let go of any goals whatsoever during sex.

This is the gift of orgasmic articulation: the realization that I can let go of any outcome and simply open to my aliveness. This is full sexual liberation. Now I am free to welcome my experience exactly as it is arising. I meet each moment as authentically and lovingly as possible. I come to participate in lovemaking, not just during intercourse, but all throughout my day. Lovemaking with *all that is* constitutes the ultimate sexual practice.

Walking this path requires a phenomenal amount of practice. It requires a Warrior who is dedicated, adaptable, passionate, and strong. By focusing our Warrior energy into sexual self-mastery, we are doing something truly radical: We are neither fighting nor competing nor creating defensive boundaries. Rather, our Warrior is put in service to the aliveness of life. This is the organic Warrior in action.

Prompts for Journaling and Discussion

What is your orgasm teaching you?

Describe the variety of orgasms you have experienced.

Notes

[1] Image by Dall*E 3

[2] *Tantra Vision Vol. II: Speaking on the Royal Song of Saraha.*

[3] *Urban Tantra.*

[4] *Awakening Shakti.*

[5] Image by Fæ, British Museum, CC SA 3.0

| 16 |

Conclusion to Lore Book II

Figure 16.1 Dr. Martin Luther King Jr.[1]

If you have worked your way through this text, then something special has just happened. You and I now hold a new vision for *men's work*. We could call it *second wave men's work* or *feminist men's work*. Despite my critique of Robert Bly from Chapter One, I hold him in very high esteem for igniting the first wave of men's work a generation ago. Without him and the mythopoetics, this book would not exist. Bly recognized that men as a group were facing real challenges and needed to do some work on behalf of themselves and the world. He started a cultural movement for men to focus on masculinity. This was a monumental and much-needed step in the process of reclaiming masculinity in wholeness.

> We are living at an important and fruitful moment now, for it is clear to men that the images of adult manhood given by the popular culture are worn out; a man can no longer depend on them. By the time a man is thirty-five he knows that the images of the right man, the tough man, the true man which he received in high school do not work in life. Such a man is open to new visions of what a man is or could be.
>
> —Robert Bly[2]

But this first wave of men's work has failed to integrate feminist discourses. The mythopoetics created a safe space for men to acknowledge and voice their pain as men, but have fallen short of acknowledging the violence of hegemonic masculinity and our role as men in perpetuating this system. Men's work has succeeded at empowering men but has yet to address the social power that men wield.

Figure 16.2 bell hooks[3]

The men's movement was often critical of women and feminism while making no sustained critique of patriarchy. Ultimately it did not consistently demand that men challenge patriarchy or envision liberating models of masculinity.

—bell hooks[4]

What I have set out to do in this text is to create a vision for men's work that begins with ownership that male violence and sexual abuse are men's issues foremost. With this foundation, our exploration represents a second wave of men's work. The first wave focused on personal healing and growth. The second wave of men's work *envisions liberating models of masculinity*. In-so-far as our process is about redefining masculinity as well as delegitimizing hegemonic masculinity, it is essentially a pro-feminist approach.

Men speaking on behalf of women is nothing new. For hundreds of years, individual men have been advocating for women's rights and nonviolence. We join a small but proud brotherhood of pro-feminist men, together with the courageous women and queer activists who are willing to build bridges with men instead of writing us off as hopeless. This is great news. It means we don't have to reinvent the wheel and we don't have to do this alone. An incredible amount of social-liberation groundwork has already been laid. And, in fact, men trying to do it alone has been a core part of the problem since the beginning. Let us align ourselves with the indigenous wisdom that "all flourishing is mutual."[5]

To date, the sexual practices for non-ejaculatory orgasm have occupied yet another small cultural niche. Drawing on hatha yoga, sexual neo-tantra, and my own experiments, I offer these tools as a practical pathway for men to integrate their sexual drives. On my path, the process of retraining my orgasms has purified an incredible amount of sexual baggage. By sharing these teachings within the context of nonviolent warriorship, an entire new layer of meaning and purpose is added. This is not primarily about having better sex or becoming better lovers. It's about stepping into a higher order of sexual integrity as a man.

What is truly new in this text is that we are doing *integral men's work*. Instead of framing social justice as a task that woke men should try to understand—a task that is often complicated, confusing, triggering, and about as exciting as doing taxes—integral men's work frames this material through the lens of empowerment. Men: Our job today as Warriors is to redefine masculinity in wholeness and reimagine a post-hegemonic society. This mission is bigger than anything we've ever undertaken as a gender—no small claim. It will require us to fearlessly embrace our aggression and sexuality, and to integrate these primal drives in service to the empowered wellbeing of everyone, including ourselves.

Our integral approach is about intimacy. I need to meet my own capacity for violence in order to become trustably nonviolent. I need to actively engage with my sexuality in order to become sexually safe and empowered. *Intimacy* here means turning toward myself: "In to me I see." It is by embodying my Warrior that I open to become a Peacemaker. This is how, on the tarot card for Strength, the woman tames the lion. Yes, Warriors have caused horrible suffering in the world. Yes, aggression and sex motivate nearly all forms of male violence. Yes, I have the capacity for all of this within myself. My approach here is to feel these drives all the way through, to become intimate with them. By integrating my primal drives, I unchain the fullest expression of my aliveness. I give seats at my council-table to the Wild Man, the Killer, the Ravager, and the Warrior, and through this process, I individuate from their unconscious influences in order to become whole.

As the Warrior reforges my inner landscape, my behavior and relationships will also naturally transform. The Warrior acts and the Peacemaker shines the light of truth upon injustice. Undertaking the Warrior's initiation makes a claim on me: I am called to act.

> We must move past indecision to action. We must find new ways to speak for peace in Vietnam and for justice throughout the developing world, a world that borders on our doors. If we do not act, we shall surely be dragged down the long, dark, and shameful corridors of time reserved for those who possess power without compassion, might without morality, and strength without sight.
>
> —Dr. Martin Luther King, Jr.[6]

I must act. Once I see the truth, it is no longer acceptable to sit in my comfort and security. All inaction becomes a form of hiding, a form of selfish clinging to my territory at the expense of others. The light of truth cuts like a blade through indecision, confusion, and resistance. This path calls me to sacrifice the easy and the known for the sake of justice. It calls me to stand up, to use my voice, and most of all to advocate for change. It is through action that the Peacemaker remakes the world in truth.

The popular depiction of the Warrior in our culture is one who uses violence in certain circumstances to fight. Our cultural portrayal goes something like this: There are those out there who would use power and violence to take, to destroy, and to oppress. We must be prepared to use force to defend the innocent, to defend our families, and to defend our culture and way of life. Even if we never use it, the threat of violence is what keeps this evil at bay.

The adolescent Heroic-Warrior must fight to slay his internal demons. The adult Warrior and father will instinctually fight to protect his young. I do not label these approaches as wrong, but they are partial and must be matured beyond if human civilization is going to continue to exist on this planet. The need for "protection" is what arms militaries, funds wars, maintains systems of oppression, incarcerates traumatized humans, and, to put it bluntly, maintains cycles of violence. It is the act of *protecting through force* that creates the wounds and inequalities by which we justify the need for protection. Violence begets violence. Nonviolence interrupts the cycle.

"Why are men violent?" is an interesting question. But the more important question is, "What are we going to do about it?"

—Paul Kivel[7]

Only peaceful means can achieve peace. This is true for each psychological part within a fractured and chaotic psyche. This is true for each family. It is true for each society and indeed for all of humanity. Peace begets peace, and that begins with me, today. It is no longer acceptable for men's work to depict the Warrior as one who uses violence in defense. This rendition of the Warrior subtly maintains our culture of violence. If we are to dethrone hegemonic masculinity, it can only be through compassion. Once a person admits this truth, they join the ranks of Thoreau, Gandhi, Dr. King, and bell hooks in a life of action through nonviolence.

In this context, peace does not mean tranquility or the absence of conflict. Peace means meeting injustice with nonviolent non-cooperation. It is a commitment to do no harm. This begins with my internal landscape. Once I find peace within myself, I become motivated to bring peace to the world. When I say that the next political revolution is peace, I mean that literally. *Peace is the revolution! The revolution is peace!* Any movement that uses violence to achieve its ends remains fundamentally caught in the nexus of violence and is doomed to struggle in first-tier power dynamics. Peace will change the world. Peace is the change the world needs. It is both the practice and the outcome.

We are one species living on one planet. Nonviolence is the result of internalizing this truth. Non-cooperation is how we shine light on injustice. It is a radical path. It will fundamentally change the power structures in our political, economic, and familial systems. It will ask everything of us, and it will transform and humble us beyond imagination.

Following the example of Dr. King, we must learn to channel our power with compassion. Indeed, the only trustable use of power is through compassion. Sometimes compassion is fierce, other times it is soft, but always it is an expression of love. In addition, we must temper our might with morality. This does not mean a religious doctrine handed down from some external authority. Morality at the integral level arises within our hearts when we are willing to feel. This morality is an immediate and personal knowledge of right action, and it is founded in the recognition of the sacredness in all of life. This recognition makes us mighty. When we know that we are standing for truth, there is no firmer ground and no surer cause. This truth shines like a light. It grants us vision and gives us strength. These are the qualities of the transcendent Warrior. It is an honor beyond measure to have laid out the path as I see it into the Peacemaker, and to stand here in brothership with you on this journey.

Notes

[1] Nobel Foundation, public domain.

[2] *Iron John.*

[3] Cmongirl, public domain.

[4] *The Will to Change.*

[5] *Braiding Sweetgrass*, Kimmerer.

[6] "Conscience and the Vietnam War."

[7] "Men's Work: To Stop Male Violence."

APPENDIX I: INTEGRAL THEORY

Ken Wilber has offered humanity an incredible gift. He has synthesized seemingly separate scientific, philosophic, and spiritual streams of knowledge into a coherent system: integral consciousness. His work forms the underlying foundation that the Organic Masculine series is built upon. Using his metaphor, Wilber has given us the *integral operating system* (IOS). It is a process for engaging with reality. Whether you agree with integral's core tenets, beliefs, and conclusions is not the point. The point is to internalize the process of IOS. In *Lore Book I*, I pointed out some of my disagreements with Wilber's system, most notably the role of archetypes. But the *process* of IOS works regardless. Once you learn how to engage with self and worldview through the integral framework, all of these ideas and references begin to feed into your own operating system, which is very eager to evolve and synthesize.

Internalizing the integral process creates a new self and a new world—one that transcends and includes many self-worldviews within it. From this more holistic and complex lens on reality, we need to reconstitute each major subject area. Integral politics is different from postmodern politics. The same is true for integral spirituality, health, and law. Each subject matter is like a new program that we want to install in this new operating system. Throughout the four-part *Organic Masculine* workbook series, my goal is to provide the source code for the integral masculinity app. As you engage with and internalize this material, you will be compiling your own version of masculinity within the integral operating system. In order to download and install the masculinity app, you will need to be running the IOS. Therefore, the purpose of this appendix is to help you internalize Integral Theory so you and I can run this new masculinity program together.

Let's begin with the concept of *holons*. Each entity has the properties of being whole unto itself and a part of a larger whole. Integral Theory postulates that the fundamental elements of the kosmos are holons. Every entity is holonic: It is a whole which is composed of sub-holons, and it is also a sub-holon of larger wholes.

"Each whole is simultaneously a part, a whole/part, a holon. And reality is composed, not of things nor processes nor wholes nor parts, but of whole/parts, of holons."

–Ken Wilber[1]

Atoms are parts of molecules, which are parts of cells, which are parts of organisms, in an upward hierarchy of holons. Atoms are composed of subatomic particles, which are composed of quarks, which are composed of strings, cascading downward into smaller and smaller sub-holons. Integral Theory postulates that this progression continues transfinitely (without limit) all the way down and all the way up. Every entity is a discrete whole, which is composed of other smaller whole entities, and which itself is part of another larger entity. The kosmos is holonic.

Now, each holon can be given a kosmic address, defined by four dimensions: interior, exterior, collective interior, and collective exterior. These correspond with the personal pronouns, "I," "it," "we," and "its," respectively. These form the Four Quadrants of Integral Theory.

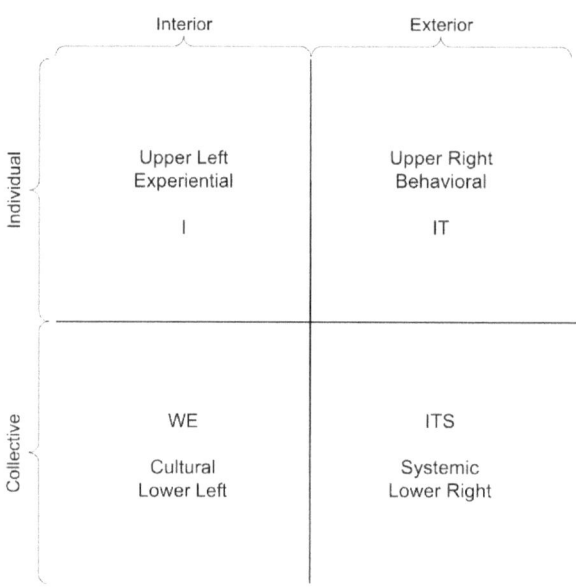

Figure A1.1 The four quadrant model[2]

The first quadrant, the subjective "I" space, holds the interiority of experience. Every holon has a felt sense, prehension, awareness, or consciousness, which varies according to the level of depth of the holon. The more depth, the more consciousness.[3] Human holons contain a tremendous amount of depth, which affords us self-reflexive consciousness. Single-celled organisms have relatively less depth, but still consume food, emit waste, reproduce, and otherwise interact with their environments. They demonstrate an interior responsiveness to life circumstances. Integral Theory postulates that the interior of experience, however faint, is a primary feature of all holons, extending all the way down and all the way up.[4] Another name for this concept is *panexperientialism*. Interiority of experience is universal. This subjective interior is one quarter of the kosmic address for any holon.

Every holon also occupies an objective exterior "it" which can be observed and interacted with. Every holon has a "body realm" composed of individual, exterior, manifest forms. The second quadrant of our matrix is measured by the hard sciences, including physics, chemistry, and biology. Each individual holon phenomenally enacts itself. So, as an individual human I have both an objectively exterior body, and a subjectively interior psyche. These two realms also have their own disciplines of philosophy. Epistemology (what can be known) examines the interior dimension, and ontology (how reality manifests) examines the exterior dimension.

In addition to *individual* interiors and exteriors, the kosmic address of every holon includes *collective* interiors and exteriors. This was one of the profound insights of the postmodern age: Groups exhibit emergent properties that cannot be reduced by analysis to any individual member. We call these *systems, networks, collectives, populations, aggregates*, and the like.

The collective interior "we" space holds the cultural worldview of the holon's group. This *intersubjective* dimension is the shared felt-experience of a holon's community. For humans, this quadrant includes language, media, arts, and cultural values. For a pack of wolves, this is the co-operative and competitive mentality of the group. For electrons, these presumably would be shared prehensions. Integral Theory postulates that the collective interior component is a real dimension of being-in-the-world and is a fundamental aspect of every holon.

The collective exterior holds the groups, populations, and social systems of the holon, which can be called the "its" space. This quadrant includes the observable behaviors of groups and systems as they enact materially in the manifest world. It is studied by ecology, sociology, and systems theory. It includes the institutions of a society, the ecosystems of the natural world, and the galaxies of the physical realm.

These are the four quadrants: interior individual, exterior individual, interior collective, and exterior collective. They are designated Upper-Left (UL), Upper-Right (UR), Lower Left (LL), and Lower Right (LR), respectively, based on their positions on the graph (Figure A1.1). We can also refer to them by the personal pronouns I, it, we, and its.

The main point is that every holon has four dimensions of being-in-the-world.[5] No quadrant is primary, first, or more fundamental than the other three. Therefore, we say holons *tetra-enact* across the four quadrants. A holon's existence is mutually self-arising and self-constituting across the four quadrants.[6] For instance, a tomato plant perceives sunlight (upper-left), manifests physically (upper-right), relates vegetatively (lower-left), and participates in an ecosystem (lower-right). This four-quadrant map provides a holistic address for every holon.

You may be wondering why I use the spelling *kosmos* instead of *cosmos*. The Greeks used the term κόσμος or *kosmos* to signify the entirety of existence. Meanwhile, the term *cosmos* refers to the scientifically measurable material universe in the two right-hand quadrants. Integral's four quadrant map is an invitation into a holistic *kosmos* that includes exteriors, interiors, individuals, and collectives.

Our kosmos is not static. It is constantly changing across all layers and levels. As the Buddha observed, "Nothing is forever except change." In addition, we observe a developmental direction to the kosmos. We have evolved from undifferentiated particles to molecules to living organisms to humans with reflexive consciousness. Integral Theory recognizes this *drive to become* as one of the fundamental features of reality. We live in an evolving universe that is moving toward greater complexity and wholeness. We call this drive *Eros*.

Holons nest within developmental chains to create greater depth and complexity. Two hydrogen atoms link up with an oxygen atom to create a water molecule. The molecule is a new whole entity that arises out of the bonding of the three atoms. We call this evolutionary process *transcend and include*. The atomic level is *transcended* so that we now have a molecule with new properties and a higher order of entity-ness (or holonic depth). Each atom is *included* as a sub-part of the larger whole.[7] Holons nest within holons, creating an evolutionary hierarchy, called a *holarchy*.[8]

Therefore, we can add a developmental direction to the four quadrant model (Figure A1.2). This allows us to plot holons in relation to their evolutionary stage along the holarchic ladder. More basic holons occupy the center of the chart. As we expand radially outward, we see higher orders of development, consciousness, and complexity. The progression outward is coordinated across all quadrants. Thus we can visualize the holarchy in concentric rings of development.

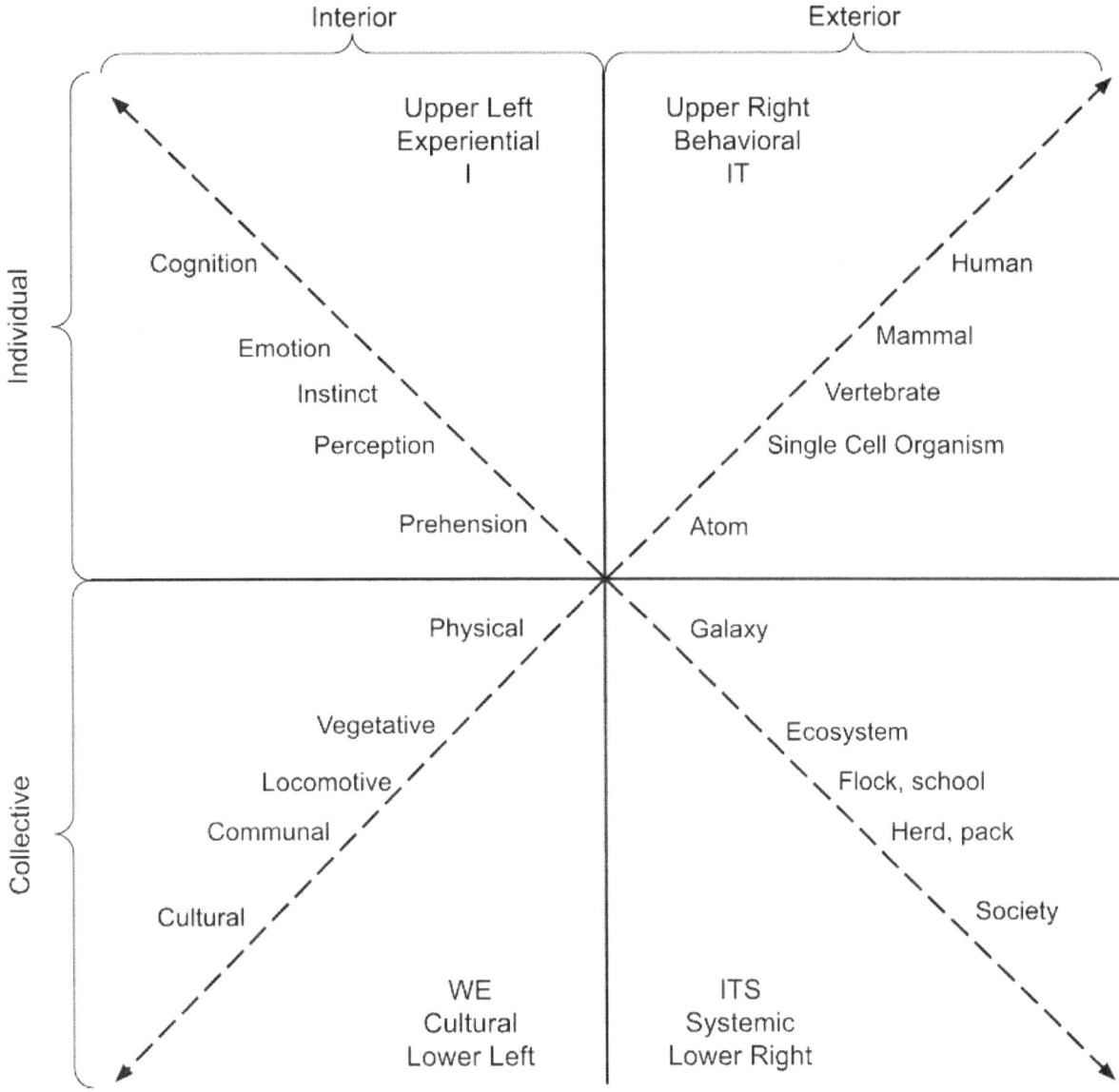

Figure A1.2. The four quadrants with holarchies[9]

In Figure A1.2, I have illustrated a sample of developmental pathways through the four quadrants together with rings describing the physiosphere (physical realm), biosphere (life realm), and noosphere (reflexive consciousness realm). These rings delineate the evolutionary path from physical existence to organic life to self-aware consciousness.[10] Each ring transcends and includes the prior ring. When I move to a wider ring, I embody a greater degree of complexity, while including the useful elements of junior holons.

This map is known as the AQAL framework, which stands for "All Quadrants, All Levels." It provides a developmental map of the kosmos. Each holon has its four-part kosmic address and can be placed on its rung in the holarchical ladder.[11]

In Figure A1.3, I illustrate the same four quadrants, now focusing on levels of human development. These categories become more intricate for human holons, primarily because we are such complex beings. Again, the center of the graph holds the more basic holons, with increasing complexity as we move outward.

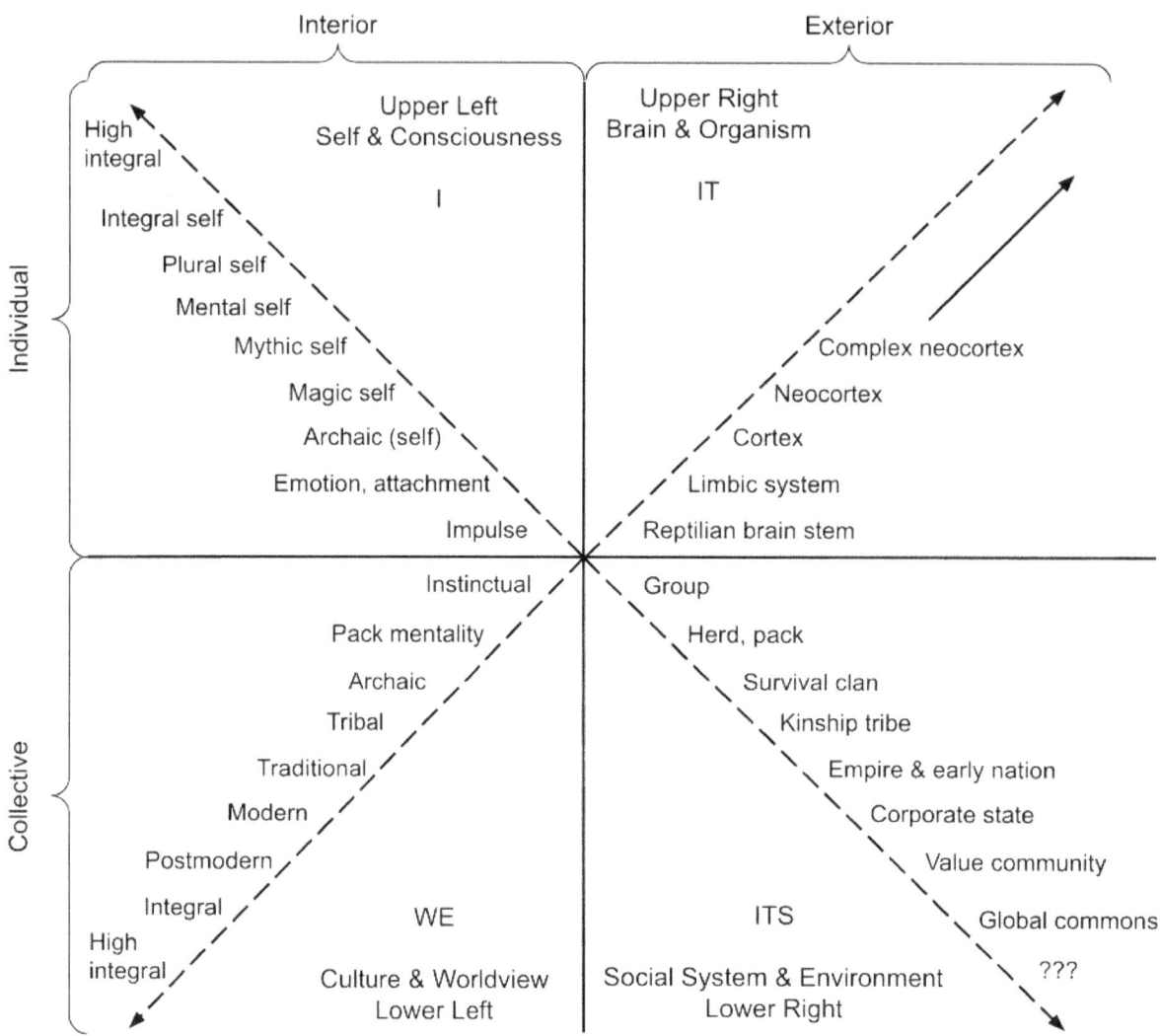

Figure A1.3. Human development through the four quadrants[12]

Starting with the inner ring of this graph, the reptilian brain stem is the physiology that corresponds with impulses in the interior psyche, an instinctual patterning of community, and basic group organization. Moving out a ring advances the level of complexity in each dimension: The biological evolution of a limbic system corresponds with the interior experience of emotion, the culture of pack mentality, and groups organized into herds and packs.

The individual self (UL) and collective culture (LL) co-evolve through progressively more advanced interiors (archaic, magic/tribal, mythic/traditional, mental/modern, plural/postmodern, integral, and high integral).[13] These correspond to sequentially more advanced societies and modes of techno-economic production in the lower right quadrant (clan, tribe, empire, state, value community, and global commons, respectively).

Interestingly, while biological evolution of human organisms (in the UR) has made it as far as a complex neocortex (no small feat), the correlative advancement of the other three quadrants has continued onward without any new biological hardware in the brain. For this reason, and because the two right quadrants are generally measured by the hard sciences, Wilber often uses a short-hand to discuss I, WE, and IT/ITS by joining the right side into a single realm. He calls this the Big Three (Figure A1.4).[14] This shorthand corresponds to subjective truth, intersubjective truth, and objective truth. In this workbook, I will be using the Big Three in my discussions of the interplay of the psyche, group identities, and social institutions.

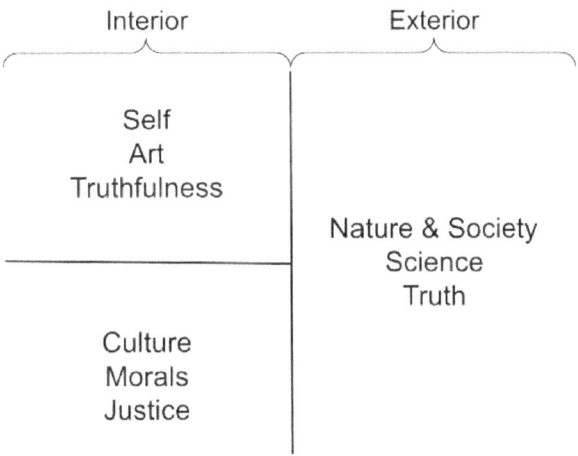

Figure A1.4. The Big Three

Now let's explore the levels of human development, which I call paradigms of consciousness. Each of these levels—archaic, magic/tribal, mythic/traditional, mental/modern, plural/postmodern, integral, and high integral—holds its own expression throughout the Big Three domains.

One note: In *The Organic Masculine*, I used the terms *worldview* and *paradigm* interchangeably, with *paradigm of consciousness* serving as the overarching concept. Technically, paradigms describe the methods and behaviors for the external world that science uses, which places it primarily in the IT/ITS hemisphere on the right side of the AQAL matrix.[15] Conversely, a *worldview* pertains to the interpretations and meanings that humans carry internally, applying to the left side of the matrix. Paradigms describe exteriors, and worldviews describe interiors.[16] Paradigm refers to applied practices, *praxis*, while a worldview refers to theoretical understanding, *theoria*. Given that,

I will continue to use the phrase *paradigm of consciousness* to refer to the entire four-quadrant ring or level that includes self-sense (UL), behavior (UR), worldview (LL), and paradigm (LR). With that in mind, let's begin our tour of the paradigms of consciousness within the framework of the Big Three (I, WE, and IT/ITS).

The Archaic Paradigm of Consciousness

Interior   Exterior

Archaic
proto-self

                               Survival clans,
                               Foraging

Cave-persons
culture

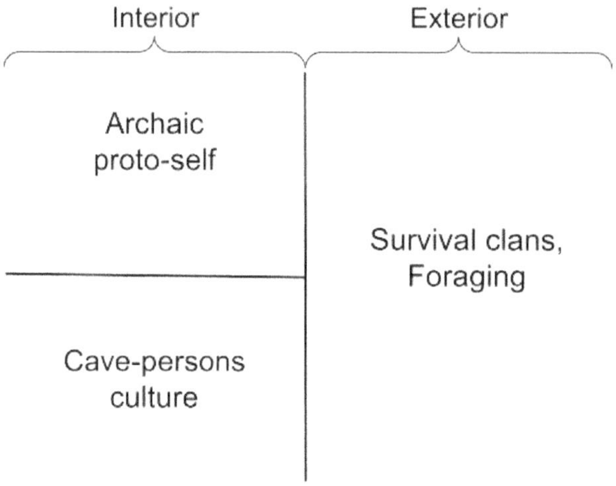

Figure A1.5. The archaic paradigm

At the most basic level of human consciousness lies the archaic paradigm, marking both the dawn of our species and the beginning of every human newborn. Within this stage, the experience in the psyche's "I" space (UL) is of total immersion into the environment. There is only the most basic separation of an interior "I" that is distinct from the phenomenal world. The newborn is immersed in the world of the mother. Here, humans utilize basic sensorimotor and physiological operations, addressing primary needs like hunger, sleep, and fear.

The cultural "we" space (LL) is that of early humans, where basic impulses enact the most primordial morality, culture, and values. The corresponding social system or "its" space (LR) is a survival clan—a unit bound by the necessity of collective subsistence. The techno-economic mode of this social system is hunting and gathering.

In this stage of development, I experience primal unity with the environment and a rudimentary communal existence. This paradigm forms the foundation from which all subsequent paradigms of human consciousness and social structures evolve.

The Magic/Tribal Paradigm of Consciousness

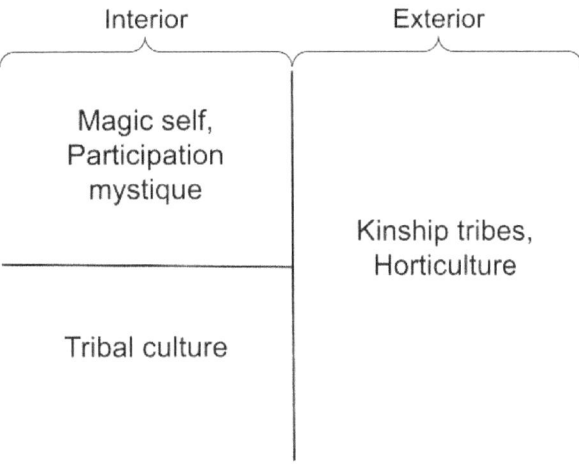

Figure A1.6. The magic/tribal paradigm

The magic/tribal paradigm focuses on safety, security, and survival in a magical world. For individuals at this stage (UL), the world operates through superstition and animism. Internal fantasies, imagery, and thoughts blend in a surreal way with external reality. The world itself is full of symbols and omens. Natural objects are imbued with spirits or totems, and human intentions are frequently projected or anthropomorphized onto the world. Carl Jung referred to this experience as *participation mystique*, meaning the individual psyche and the external world co-participate in a mystical way, for example: "There is a storm because the spirits are mad"; "If I stick a pin in this doll, it will curse that person"; and "The flower is blooming because I am in love."

Young children at the beginning of this stage are governed by their impulses. Here, I define my self-boundary through simple words like "No" and "Mine," allowing me to situate my first-person identity in the world in the most basic way. Later in this stage, I will categorize my experience in simple dichotomies like good/bad or fun/boring. My behavior is geared toward protecting my fragile and newly emerging self in response to a world where I perceive social cues and boundaries as arbitrary consequences of the will of those in power.

Culturally, this paradigm is rooted in tribal consciousness (LL), where each person in the group belongs because they recognize (and are recognized by) everyone else in the group.[17] In Kohlberg's stages of moral development, the morality of this level spans two steps and is broadly known as pre-conventional. The first moral phase is the *punishment and obedience orientation*. Here, an act is considered good or bad to the extent it is either rewarded or punished.[18] The group's power-holders, which may include gods, ancestors, spirits, and tribal leaders, make moral determinations. Those in power decide what is right and wrong, and morality means adherence to these dictates.

Kohlberg's next moral step is *self-interest orientation*, in which morality is determined by what is fair: "Two for you and two for me"; and "You scratch my back, I'll scratch yours." In this scenario, I view life as a zero-sum game, so my actions aim to maximize the good stuff for myself. I view others as tools or obstacles to the satisfaction of my own needs, and I use reciprocity to further my own self-interests.

Socially, the tribe emerges as a cohesive collective unit, both through cultural affiliations (LL) and the behaviors and roles that create a structured social system (LR). The tribal social unit is held together through kinship and family bonds. One is generally either born into this group or marries in. As a social unit, the tribe is able to organize for hunting and horticulture (small-scale gardens and crops), divide roles (shaman, warrior, chief…), propagate an oral tradition, and compete with other tribes for territory and resources.

The magic/tribal paradigm describes a phase of human development where the interplay between individual impulses, communal bonds, and the mystical perceptions of the world are the cornerstone of consciousness and social organization. This stage shepherds the beginnings of the agentic self, morality, and society.

The Mythic/Traditional Paradigm of Consciousness

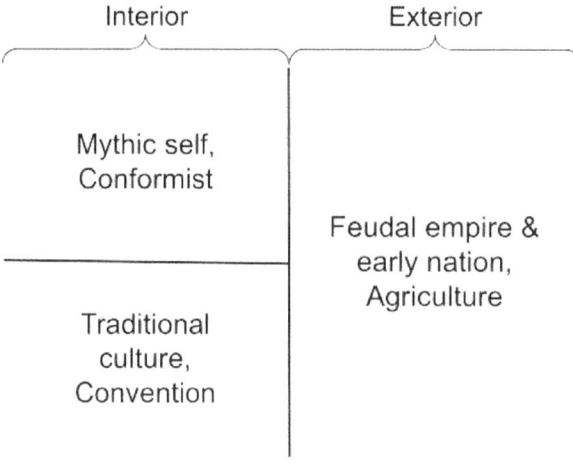

Figure A1.7. The mythic/traditional paradigm

The mythic/traditional paradigm focuses on the integration of social structure, authority, and rules. Individuals at this stage are characterized by the mythic self or the heroic self (UL). Here, I am the chosen hero/ine on a path toward salvation or glory. My actions are defined by concrete rules (thou shalt not kill), and I see people within their roles (a father's duty is to provide for the family). My identity at this stage is deeply fused with—or more accurately *con-fused* with—the identity of the group, fostering strong loyalty and adherence to collective norms. This stage is also called *conformist* because my behavior is driven by pleasing, caretaking, upholding appearances, and following group expectations. I am concerned with who I "should" be and what actions I "should" be taking. I obey rules and experience shame or guilt when I break the rules. Because my self-other boundaries are still not clearly defined, my relationships tend to be codependent or needy.

This developmental stage shepherds a more complex understanding of self and relationships. I am able to recognize my own personhood (first person perspective) as well as the personhood of others (second person perspective). Instead of treating others as tools or barriers to my desires, as in the magic paradigm, I now understand social cues and interact with others *as people* just like me.

Culturally, this paradigm is anchored in traditionalism (LL), with morality and customs being handed down by central authorities including family, organized religion, ethnicity, and politics. Kohlberg assigns two moral developmental steps to this level. The first is the *interpersonal conformity orientation* where "good behavior is that which pleases or helps others and is approved by them."[19] The focus here is to be a "good boy or good girl" by adhering to stereotypical images. The next moral step is called the *society-maintaining orientation* which follows rules and traditions to maintain the social order: social conservatism. These moral structures are called *conventional* because they adhere to social norms or conventions. This stage is defined by stark in-group versus out-group dynamics—for example, I am either part of God's chosen people or I am a heathen. Allegiance to my in-group provides safety from the perceived threat of out-group members.

The social system at this level spans feudalism, empires, and early nations (LR). Historically, the technological advancement of the animal-driven plow allowed for large-scale agriculture, which in turn enabled larger villages, cities, and eventually nations to emerge. In order to organize these larger groups of people, this paradigm established social institutions including a legal system, an economy, and organized religion. These paradigms instill a concrete shared morality to harmonize vast numbers of people into a coherent social system. At this stage, religious myths are taken to be literally true (the Bible, the Koran, The Pure Land Sutra, etc.)—known as *mythic literalism*. Social structures are often rigid, hierarchical, and authoritarian. This level is the first to include the notorious dominator hierarchies, colonization, and religious fundamentalism.

Advancement into the mythic/traditional paradigm brings online the heroic self who must fight, protect, and establish authority within a mythic world. Traditions and shared morality enable more complex social cohesion and coordination, which co-arise with the first true human civilizations. More adults reside within the mythic/traditional paradigm than any other.[20] This means that beyond the specific religion, political ideology, or mythology, most humans view themselves and the world through the lenses of myth and tradition.

The Mental/Modern Paradigm of Consciousness

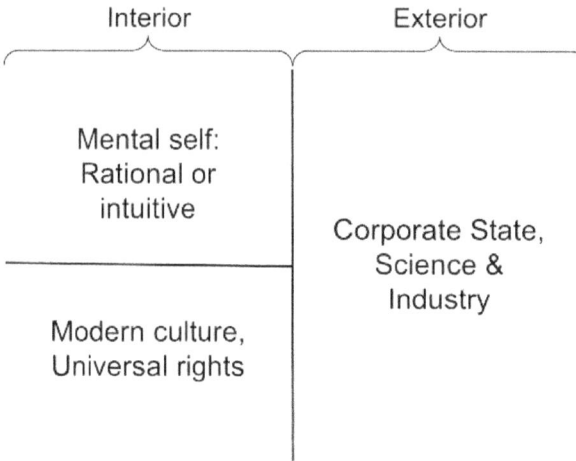

Figure A1.8. The mental/modern paradigm

The mental/modern paradigm emerged with the Western Enlightenment Age in Europe. Descartes' famous "Cogito ergo sum," *I think therefore I am*, is the declaration of the fully distinct and autonomous ego. Paradigm by paradigm, the ego has been individuating from its fusion with the exterior world. Archaic consciousness was undifferentiated from the world. In the magic paradigm, the ego was separate but enmeshed with the natural world. In the mythic paradigm, the ego differentiated from nature, but was still fused with the social group. Mental/modern marks the emergence of a truly individual self capable of abstract thought and self-reflection. Now, instead of following concrete rules that are given by a central authority, I am able to follow abstract rules that I can deduce or intuit for myself. Piaget calls this the shift from *concrete operations* to *formal operations*. I am interested in reasons, causes, consequences, and goals.

Now I am able to take a third person perspective of myself and others. This means I can reflect on myself from an outside view. I am able to consider my past self and my future self apart from who I am now. In addition to holding the viewpoints of myself and others, I am now able to hold an objectively neutral, third perspective. I also take *ideals* and human nature into account for how I make sense of relationships.

Numerous feminist authors have argued for a gender-correlated divergence in the developmental path at this stage. Men's socialization tends toward a rational, *individual self* (achievement consciousness), while women's socialization tends toward an intuitive, *relational self* focused on connection (affiliative consciousness).[21] In achievement consciousness, I recognize that I can use logic, math, and the scientific method to discern universal rules and laws that govern the world. I am focused on personal advancement, building esteem, and earning recognition from my peers. In affiliative consciousness, I feel my truth from my gut and I seek knowledge through connection, intimacy, and empathy.[22] Despite their differences, both paths embody dialectic thinking (rational or intuitive) within the given system. Here, I no longer rely on external authorities and instead I am able to self-determine what is true and right.

Culturally (LL), the modern worldview recognizes the inherent worth and rights of each human, transcending group affiliations. Following Kohlberg, this level includes two steps of moral development. The first is the *social contract orientation* to morality, where procedural rules are applied according to agreed-upon standards. Each human should have an input and representation in their system of government. The social contract, at least in theory and intent, makes the state beholden to the interests of the populace. The second step in modern morality is the *universal ethical principle orientation*, in recognition of moral principles like the Golden Rule and the categorical imperative. These principles are discernable by every human (who is thinking within this worldview or higher) and applicable to every human. We recognize universal principles including dignity, equality, and freedom. The universalizing perspective is what led to the abolitionist movement, feminism, and representative democracy.

In the social dimension (LR), modernity uses the scientific method to discern a world governed by laws of nature. Modernity sparked the industrial revolution, which in turn gave rise to capitalism and the modern corporation. The "modern" social institutions include modern science, modern medicine, modern law, modern industry, etc. The social structures here, though still hierarchical, tend to be value-creation-focused and therefore meritocratically organized (again, at least in theory and intent). Competition is utilized both to rank members within an organization and between organizations in order to spur productivity and innovation. Modern markets efficiently organize both labor and products. Whereas in the mythic/traditional paradigm, the social system is set up to solve for security through authority, the mental/modern paradigm solves for value-creation through competition.

The mental/modern paradigm thus represents a profound shift in human consciousness and social organization, characterized by the rise of the rational individual within a global economic system. This paradigm has reshaped humanity and the entire planet along with it. Looking across the paradigms, modernity holds the most power and influence in today's world.

The Plural/Postmodern Paradigm of Consciousness

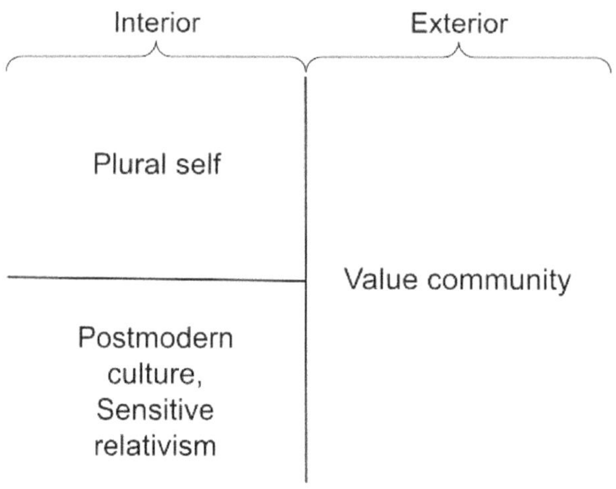

Interior   Exterior

Plural self

Value community

Postmodern
culture,
Sensitive
relativism

Figure A1.9. The plural/postmodern paradigm

The plural/postmodern paradigm ushers in a nuanced phase of development for the self (UL). First, I begin to see and think at a systems level. This means I'm able to transcend the mental third-person perspective of a rational outsider and take on a more expansive fourth-person perspective where I perceive the system that every event is embedded within. Unlike the atomistic determinism of the mental/modern paradigm, the systems view takes into account complex, chaotic, emergent properties where individual phenomena cannot be attributed to any component parts or interactions. The system must be understood at a level of complexity that transcends and includes the operations of its parts.

In our AQAL matrix, I am now able to see and appreciate the collective mechanisms of the lower two quadrants! Collective "we" spaces, together with cultural conditioning, group identities, and *memes* now become apparent. Collective "its" spaces like ecosystems, social networks, and chaotic attractors reveal themselves.

A pivotal realization at this stage is the relative nature of perception and meaning. I begin to recognize that my reality is at least partially dependent on my perspective. In fact, all phenomena are relative to the observer. Different observers perceive different realities and therefore there is no fixed, objective world.

In addition, every observer is inescapably embedded within their societal and cultural contexts —we are inescapably *members of systems*. This means that whatever meaning I assign to any event is at least partially socially constructed. The discovery that reality is observer-dependent and socially-constructed represents a step beyond the rational analysis of the modern paradigm and ushers in the fuzzy, relative, complex self-worldview of the plural/postmodern paradigm.

However, this paradigm shift has led some postmodern thinkers into a lower-quadrant hege-mony, claiming that *everything is socially constructed* or that *the system alone is real*. This view denies the validity of each individual's interior experiences and material realities of the natural world. Whereas modernity's scientific materialism tends to deny the interior quadrants of the left side (only what is objectively measurable is real), postmodernism overemphasizes the bottom two quadrants (individuals are products of their systems). Using the integral AQAL framework, I can easily illuminate the partiality of both these positions, while appreciating their strengths (Figure A1.10). As we shall soon see, the integral paradigm represents a further inclusivity of all four quadrants, encompassing a fuller spectrum of human experience and the kosmos.

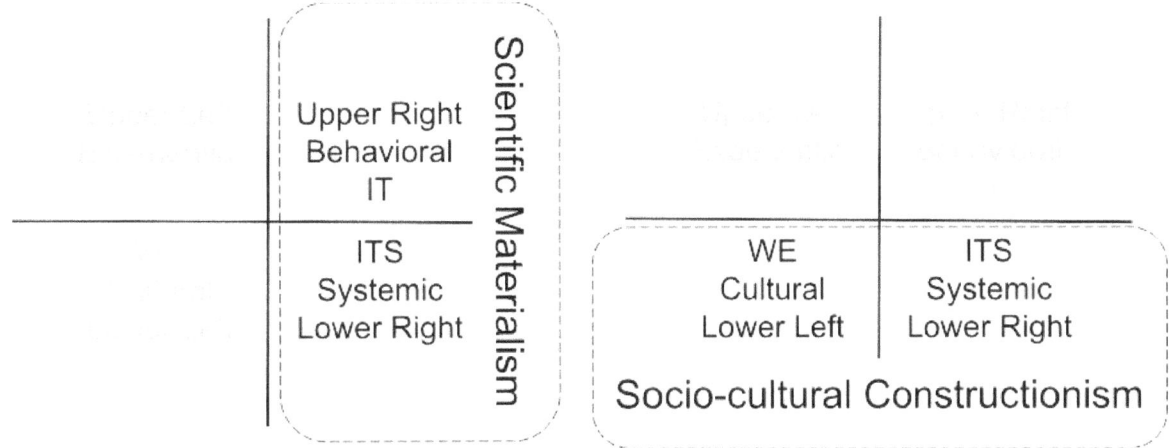

Figure A1.10. Hemisphere hegemonies of the modern and postmodern paradigms

The second important step for the plural/postmodern self is an increased capacity for sensi-tivity. I become sensitive to my emotions, somatic wisdom, and other ways of knowing beyond the conceptual mind. This is especially true for those who developed along the *individual self/ achievement consciousness* path in the modern paradigm. I begin to see my "self" as a plurality of parts that function (or dysfunction) as a system. I have an inner child, protectors, managers, a skeptic, a victim, and so on. This marks a departure from the more unitary self-concept of earlier paradigms. I develop an increased sensitivity toward the needs and desires of my internal parts.

I become sensitive not only to my multifaceted internal landscape, but also gain a heightened awareness of my place within my social and environmental contexts. I begin to see my own social conditioning, social privileges or discrimination, and subtle self-promoting and protective strate-gies. As these aspects come into awareness, the great postmodern project of *deconstruction* begins. I see a *plurality* of socially-constructed selves (racial, gendered, familial, workplace, and so on) and because they were created by culture, they are subject to redefinition or dismantling.

I also become more sensitive to other people, other groups of people, and the environment. I develop more compassion and empathy. This sensitivity brings an increased focus on minority and marginalized groups in society, with a desire to *center* these outcast voices.

Emerging in the 1960s, postmodern culture (LL) has actively focused on addressing the problems created by the prior two paradigms. Environmental conservation, second and third wave feminisms, racial justice, anti-colonialism, and so on, have been the hallmarks of postmodern culture. With such strong reactions *against* the existing social structures from prior paradigms, postmodernity often has trouble taking a stand *for* anything. That said, this stage of development brings the understanding that universal rights are not enough on their own to guarantee justice. More considerations are necessary because: different groups of people have different needs (ex: neurodivergent folks), certain groups face social and cultural disadvantages (any minorities), and certain groups are not able to protect or advocate for their rights (children). So additional measures must be put into place to protect and provide equal opportunities for the full diversity of humans above and beyond universal rights. This level of moral development is not identified by Kohlberg, so I'll propose the *sensitive relativism orientation* to morality at this level.

Because postmodern culture is very motivated by sensitivity to the rights, values, and truths of a plurality of groups and individuals, it is prone to moral relativism. Unlike the modern paradigm, which sees one objective truth and one set of universal rights, the postmodern paradigm recognizes that each group and individual has their own subjective truths. All truth is relative to the observer, who is always embedded within a socio-cultural context. This has led to stances like "whatever is true for you goes" or even, "there is no truth." Although this represents an important step beyond the binary thinking of modernity, moral relativism runs into issues almost immediately. This stance is self-contradictory in that it asserts a universal truth (i.e., *everything is relative*) which states there are no universal truths.[23] I'll offer a deeper treatment on moral relativism in Chapter Three.

Looking ahead to the integral paradigm and the four-quadrant model, I see that every holon, phenomenon, thing, or process has (at least) four dimensions: subjective, objective, intersubjective, and interobjective. Thus there are (at least) four truth-claims depending on the dimension being observed or enacted. Different dimensions produce different results. No dimension takes precedence over any of the others—all four quadrants are interrelated and tetra-enact. So from an integral perspective, while there are multiple truths, these truths are indeed definitive based on one's perspective. In addition, some truths are more inclusive than other truths. Because the paradigms are organized into a developmental holarchy, with each successive level being more inclusive and more holistic, the higher the observer, worldview, and paradigm, the more holistic the truth-claim emerging from that perspective will be.[24]

In the social dimension (LR), postmodernity's information age marks a significant shift from industrial production to a digital-based service economy. We see the emergence of information technology, the internet, and social networks where systems supersede pyramid organizations. Rather than modernity's singular broadcast mass media, social networks deliver a plurality of self-generated media content, ushering in the democratization of information. These platforms enable users to create a multiplicity of voices and personas. In the postmodern sciences, chaos and complexity study physical systems, ecology studies systems of organisms, and sociology studies systems of humans.

Postmodernity creates *values communities* for social organization, which are intentional collectives that are freely chosen based on shared interests and values. These communities emphasize dialogue, nonviolent communication, and consensus-driven decision-making. Conflict resolution happens through mediation and reconciliation (at least ideally). These groups tend to be strongly egalitarian, inclusive, and multicultural. Values communities represent a move towards more democratic and participatory forms of social organization.

A notable aspect of postmodern thought is its critical stance toward hierarchical structures. The postmodern paradigm rightly sees that dominator hierarchies cause suffering and attempts to dismantle them. However, in its anti-ranking, non-marginalizing zeal, this paradigm tends to categorically condemn all hierarchies including developmental hierarchies like the one we are describing right now. Also called growth hierarchies or holarchies, these developmental pathways are found throughout the kosmos for the increase of complexification and wholeness. Each successive level transcends and includes (is supported by and in turn embraces) its junior levels. Postmodernity's wholesale condemnation of ranking and hierarchies is an unfortunate limitation of this paradigm's interpretive lens. Needless to say, this distorted view is transcended as we step into the integral paradigm.

Over the past 150 years, philosophers and sociologists have noticed that collectives sometimes behave like individual entities and in other ways are distinct. Drawing on Luhmann's social autopoeisis thoery, Integral Theory demarcates *sociocultural holons* as a separate class of entity to describe collectives, cultures, systems, and groups. The relationship between holons and sociocultural holons is a fascinating exploration which is especially relevant for Chapters Seven, Eight, and Nine, where I discuss individual identity (holons), group identities (cultural holons), and social institutions (social holons).

Sociocultural Holons

I want to take a brief tangent at this point to define *sociocultural holons* and give an overview of how they interact with individual holons. The foundational concept in Integral Theory is that everything in the kosmos is a holon, a whole/part. This includes things, processes, subjects, and objects. Every entity is a holon.

Integral Theory has identified three epiphenomena of holons, meaning, three ways that holons arrange themselves and function besides holarchies. These are heaps, artifacts, and sociocultural holons. A heap is a random collection of holons without an organizing pattern, such as a pile of rocks. Heaps are collections of holons that happen to be in the same region of spacetime. Unlike holons, heaps have no central agency and unlike systems, they have no organizing pattern between their parts.

In addition to heaps, we have artifacts, which are collections of holons that have been arranged in a specific way by an external agent, like a spear crafted by a human. Artifacts also have no organizing center of their own. They do not possess agency and do not prehend their environment as a whole entity in the same way an amoeba does. But an artifact appears to be whole when viewed from the perspective of the holon that can utilize it. Artifacts serve a functional purpose. The molecules that comprise the hammer cannot recognize the hammer as an artifact, but humans are able to recognize the artifact-ness of the hammer and use it. So, heaps are a random collection of holons and artifacts are a functional arrangement of a group of holons.

Sociocultural holons are the third category, which are significantly more nuanced to understand. These are interactions of groups of holons that function in a system as a culture (LL) or society (LR). Sociocultural holons act in many ways like holons, but are distinct in their collective and systemic nature.

For the sake of clarity in this passage, I'm going to use the term "individual holon" to mean "holon." Individual holons have their own unified agency, what Whitehead calls a dominant monad.[25] Integral Theory postulates that each holon, from atoms, to molecules, to cells, to humans–all the way up and all the way down–has a unified agency which defines its *entityness*. Each holon is composed of sub-holons as parts, but the holon adds its special sauce to the collection of sub-holons: its own agency.

Collective holons lack a singular agency. There is no individual will or dominant monad in them. Instead, sociocultural holons hold a *nexus* of interactions between individual holons.[26] This nexus of interactions has its own form of agency, which Wilber calls *nexus-agency*. A cat, as an individual holon, determines its actions wholly and completely with its will, its agency. An ecosystem, as a social holon, produces its actions through communications and interactions between the members of the system, its nexus-agency.

A group of men building a log cabin, wolves hunting in a pack, geese flying together—those are all group activities coordinated around a single goal, and hence they are collective (sociocultural) holons displaying agency…We can thus refer to nexus-agency (or network-agency or systems-agency). This nexus-agency is what "has a life of its own"—which means, a life governed by its own history, habits, and patterns. Nexus-agency is not determined by the *individuals* that are *inside* the nexus, but by the *intersections* (of the individuals) that are *internal* to the nexus.

–Ken Wilber[27]

The final sentence in the quote above is a bit of a doozy, so let's unpack it. Holons are made of sub-holons which become subordinated to the new overarching will of the holon (the cat's will controls the behavior of its cells). In contrast, sociocultural holons like a culture or an ecosystem are made of *interactions*. This may not be immediately obvious. A system or network is constituted by patterns of exchanges. This means that individual holons are *members* of the sociocultural holon, but are not *sub-holons* of the system.

Let's use ants as an example. A pile of dead ants is a heap. None of the dead ants have their own agency and there is no pattern of interaction between them. Now imagine we go to the pet store and make a pile of living ants, where each ant is from a different species. In this experiment, each ant is a holon, but we would still just have a random collection of ants: another heap, not an organized system. Go outside and find a group of ants and they will be organized into a colony, a sociocultural holon. The colony is not due to the ants themselves, but exists because of the networking interactions of the ants. The *colonyness* of the collection of ants is determined by the coordinating pattern of the ants. This is why we can have multiple ants in a heap with no colony present. So, individual ants are not sub-holons of the colony. Rather, the past instances of the colony pass themselves forward through the colony's morphic field. Prior colonies are sub-holons of the current colony.

The perspective that groups are constituted by interactions has solid backing. For Whitehead, a nexus is "constituted by [holons'] prehensions of each other." In Luhmann's social autopoiesis theory, a system is composed of *communications*, not organisms.[28] This means individual humans are *members* of a culture or society, but not sub-parts or sub-holons in the same way cells are sub-holons for the cat. As an individual, I may belong to a social group, but only my shared interactions within the system participate in the nexus.

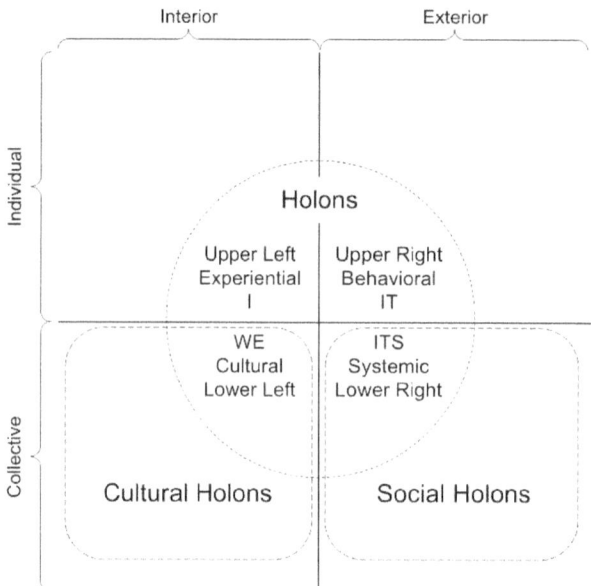

Figure A1.11. Holons, cultural holons, and social holons in the four quadrants

A *cultural holon* is defined by the "we" space and inhabits the lower left quadrant (LL), for example, a group of friends. If I am in the group, I know firsthand I am a member, a part of *us*. If I am not in the group, I also know firsthand. This is knowledge by acquaintance. Even though I cannot see the shared identity because it has no physical manifestation, I can feel my belonging or not as a member of the culture. This shared interiority, also known as a *hermeneutic circle*, holds a collective identity and worldview unique to each "we" space. In Wilber's words, it has a life of its own.

A *social holon* is defined by the "its" space and inhabits the lower right quadrant (LR), for example a neighborhood of people. Membership in a social holon is determined by participation in external structures and systems. If I live in the neighborhood and interact in the local society, I am a member of the social system. Human society is a social holon in the noosphere, an ecosystem occupies the biosphere, and crystals, planets, and galaxies are social holons of the physiosphere. The organizing pattern of interactions in the inter-objective realm is what delineates an "its" space, or social holon.

While cultural and social holons are closely related, they represent distinct domains of reality. Cultural holons are interior collectives while social holons are exterior collectives. Let's take some examples. If my neighbor only speaks Spanish and I don't, then we are members of the same social system (neighborhood), but not the same cultural system (we can't understand each other). Similarly, while ants and zebras may share the same ecosystem (LR), they are members of distinct cultures (LL).

Cultural and social holons evolve through the process of *transcending and including*, the same mechanism that individual holons use. Each current instance of a collective holon transcends its prior instances, but includes its past as its inherited karma. Today's culture is built on the accretion of past culture, plus the emergence of this creative new moment. Same for society. Collective holons never transcend and include their individual members, only their own past instances. Individuals transcend and include individuals; collectives transcend and include collectives.

And yet, the evolution of the culture or society mirrors the evolution of its individual holon members. So, individuals advance through archaic, magic, and mythic self-identities, and in parallel, culture evolves through archaic, magic, and mythic collective-worldviews.

Even though I have introduced heaps, artifacts, and sociocultural holons as epiphenomena of holons, that does not give priority to holons as *more real* or *existing prior*. Just as worlds and worldviews co-create each other, so do holons, heaps, artifacts, and sociocultural holons. Each of these types co-enact each other through mutually dependent origination.[29] We never, at any scale, find a holon that does not occupy all four quadrants as its enactment or being-in-the-world. Similarly, we never find a holon that does not belong to at least one cultural holon and at least one social holon. We never find a cultural holon empty of holons either. Each of these holonic types are mutually co-arising, interdependent, and hold equal metaphysical primariness. Therefore, I could make the equally partial claim that individual holons are epiphenomena of collective holons. More accurately: They all arise and evolve together.

In summary, sociocultural holons are collective whole/parts that are composed of the *interactions* of individual holons. They carry nexus agency instead of a dominant monad. These systems are composed of interactions, communications, and shared prehensions. An individual holon is often a member of multiple distinct social and cultural holons as a participant but not as a sub-holon. Individual holons tetra-enact across all four quadrants, and their enactment in the lower two quadrants is through membership in one or more collective holons. Cultural holons occupy interior collective "we" spaces, and social holons occupy exterior collective "its" spaces. Beginning with the plural/postmodern paradigm, I am able to recognize collective holons as entity-like nexūs and can begin to ponder their profound interrelationships with the tetra-enactment of individual holons.

The Integral Paradigm of Consciousness

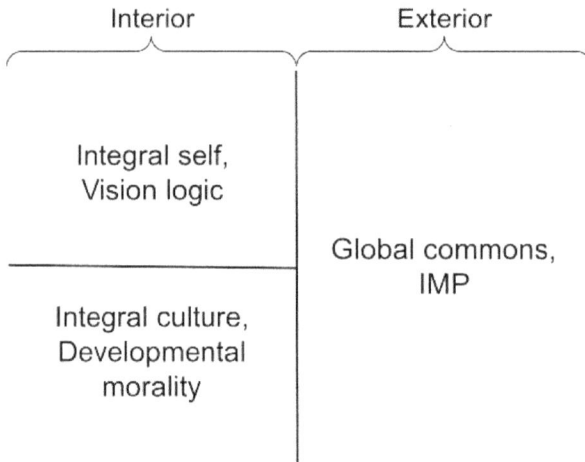

Figure A1.12. The integral paradigm

The integral paradigm heralds the emergence of a brand new tier of development. Clare Graves called it a "monumental shift in meaning." The integral self (UL) perceives an interlocking kosmos of wholeness, both within and without. The scattered, chaotic noise of postmodernity assembles into a multi-dimensional, four-quadrant mandala of life. At integral, I am centered in my holistic self. I am able to own and unify all my diverse internal parts behind one self. This self is a sovereign adult, which is robust enough to hold the paradox of no-self and self.

Integral is the first level where I am able to see all the paradigms of consciousness and recognize that each one forms an essential rung in the developmental ladder. I recognize that every self/worldview/paradigm enacts a reality that is internally valid, and I understand that each level is a necessary foundation for more advanced levels to *transcend and include*. Integral cognition is known as vision-logic[30] or holistic aperspectivalism,[31] and represents the capacity to hold multiple perspectives as equally valid while understanding that more holistic perspectives generate deeper truths. Using the analogy that each level is a rung on the ladder of human development, standing on a higher rung gives a more expansive view of the landscape. The view from each rung is valid, but higher rungs see more.

With an understanding of the developmental holarchy, I become focused on evolution and self-actualization—which is to say, moving up the ladder. Other terms common at this level are *self-authorship*,[32] utilizing an *internal locus of control*,[33] and *autonomy*.[34] This wholeness and actualization of self brings commitments to healing as well as creating my own meaning in life. I cultivate an expansiveness to explore and be all I can be. This in turn, leads to a desire to support others to be all they can be.

At the integral level, I am able to hold awareness of multiple systems and multiple paradigms, which marks the 5th-person perspective. This metasystemic and metaparadigmatic capacity allows me to integrate and synthesize across many disciplines to create new functional wholes. Integral consciousness is more tolerant of paradox and ambiguity, enabling more expansive creativity to flourish.

Integral consciousness heralds a recognition of the sacred across the self, nature, spiritual traditions, life, and the entire kosmos. Science and religion are no longer mutually incompatible. That perceived conflict is now understood as the clash between the traditional and modern world-views. Instead, these sources of knowledge and wisdom are synthesized into a more inclusive, holistic reality.

As of 2024, integral cultural and social structures are still in the early stages of formation. We have yet to hit the much-anticipated *tipping point* where a critical mass of individuals holding the integral frame establish a new collective system. This means that any statements I make about integral structures in the collective are still provisional.

Integral culture promises to be growth and evolution-oriented (LL). Its transdisciplinary, meta-paradigmatic approach synthesizes cultural memes into innovative, creative, adaptive commons. Because the integral stage recognizes the validity and value of each worldview, I would expect integral culture to focus on supporting healthy versions of each worldview and creating cultural conveyor-belts—like this very text—to assist the collective process of development.[35] Further expanding upon Kohlberg's model for morality, I would offer that integral holds a morality of *developmental orientation*: that which fosters development is moral and good.

At the societal level (LR), integral is predicted to usher in a truly world-centric global gover-nance which recognizes that we all share in a global commons. Issues like climate change and wealth disparity are probably impossible to address without a truly global federalism. However, it cannot be a system staffed primarily by traditional, modern, or postmodern individuals. That would likely lead us into the worst nightmares of totalitarianism. Integral global governance, staffed by integral individuals, would recognize appropriate degrees of sovereignty across a variety of scales, add in safeguards to prevent runaway power grabs, and fundamentally approach politics from a *power-with* rather than *power-over* framework. Integral institutions in domains including in-tegral medicine, integral law, integral science, integral religion, and integral education are already forming at smaller scales with promising results.

In terms of praxis, Ken Wilber's Integral Theory utilizes Integral Methodological Pluralism (IMP), a sophisticated approach utilizing the entirety of the AQAL matrix. IMP recognizes and integrates diverse forms of knowledge production and wisdom traditions.

"Integral," in that the pluralism is not a mere eclecticism or grab bag of unrelated paradigms, but a meta-paradigm that weaves together its many threads into an integral tapestry, a unity-in-diversity that slights neither the unity nor the diversity. "Methodological," in that this is a real paradigm or set of actual practices and behavioral injunctions to bring forth an integral territory, not merely a new holistic theory or maps without any territory. And "pluralism" in that there is no one overriding or privileged injunction (other than to be radically all-inclusive).

—Ken Wilber[36]

As a system for engaging with reality, IMP positions each type of knowledge production or inquiry within one of the four quadrants. Ken Wilber offers this segmentation of methodologies: Phenomenology and structuralism describe the upper left quadrant of interior individual experience; empiricism and autopoiesis theory describe the upper right quadrant of exterior individual manifestation; hermeneutics and cultural anthropology describe the lower left quadrant of collective interior cultures; and systems theory and social autopoiesis theory describe the lower right quadrant of collective exterior systems (Figure A1.13).[37]

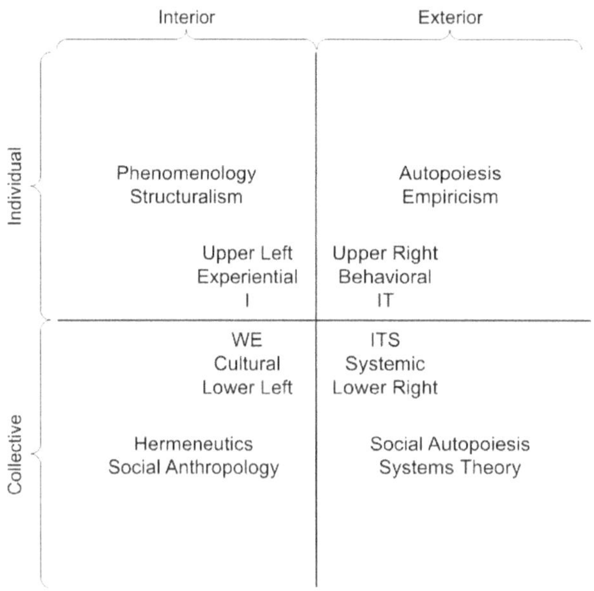

Figure A1.13. Methodologies positioned in the four quadrants.[38]

By framing our methods of knowledge production within the AQAL matrix, we can both appreciate the unique insights that each approach is able to generate, *and* we have a structure to compare and contrast all these diverse areas of study. Within IMP, new modes of inquiry present themselves. For example, I can imagine running an experiment to understand the effects of a prayer circle where I record first-person testimonies of the experiences of individuals in the prayer circle (UL), monitor brainwave states of these individuals (UR), study the cultural meanings across a diversity of prayers used in the circle (LL), and track social and economic indicators as the group progresses over time (LR). Each quadrant has its own form of knowledge production, which can then be correlated across quadrants for a holistic understanding. This represents a new praxis revealing a new paradigm. The integral world is, in turn, co-enacting our integral subjective and intersubjective worldviews. Integral Methodological Pluralism is a big step forward in the human project of knowledge production, offering a framework to index the complexities of the integral world.

The integral paradigm utilizes a holistic view, recognizes life's sacredness, and synthesizes across diverse perspectives. This represents a massive transformation in individual development, and promises to remake human culture and society. Humanity's transition to a more inter-connected, holistic, and evolutionarily-aware world appears to be the next revolution looming on the horizon. This transition will arrive to the extent that each of us internalizes and participates in the co-creation of integral consciousness.

The High Integral Paradigm of Consciousness

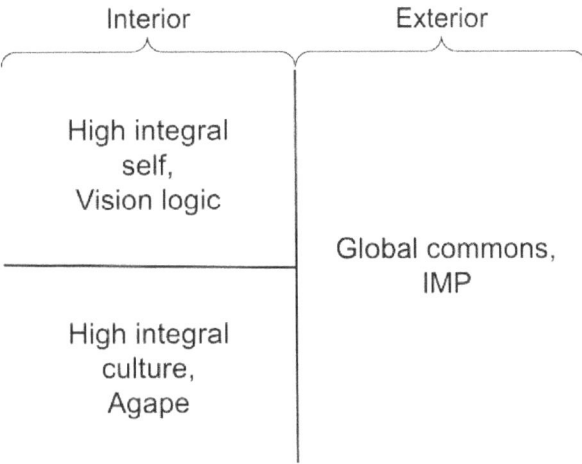

Figure A1.14. The high integral paradigm

High integral is our final stop on today's tour of paradigms. At present, this level includes less than one percent of the adult population in Western countries. While integral is still forming, high integral is only just beginning to emerge. The high integral self (UL) is characterized by deepening compassion. I begin to transcend my personal agendas in favor of aligning myself to the perfect unfolding of life and the kosmos. The recognition of this *great perfection* brings a profound commitment to action without attachment to outcome. In compassion, I work for the benefit of all beings. In compassion, I respect the perfect unfolding of all beings on their unique paths. This brings a greater embrace of all of life—the good and the bad, the ugly and the beautiful, the joy and the sorrow—fully welcomed with a profound sense of wonder.

Kohlberg hypothesized the existence of a *morality of cosmic orientation*, in which individuals consider morality from the perspective of the kosmos itself. In this stage of moral development the self-protective mechanisms and biases fall away and are replaced by *Agape* or compassion. In Kohlberg's words, "*Agape* has two essential characteristics: first, it is nonexclusive and can be extended to all, including one's enemies; second, it is gracious and is extended without regard for merit."[39] This is the morality of high integral culture and beyond.

High integral's future in the social dimension will likely build upon the global commons of integral and widen it to embrace all sentient beings, including animals. High integral praxis expands Integral Methodological Pluralism, a task that Ken Wilber has already begun sketching out. Imagine that each of the four quadrants is able to take an inside view and an outside view of that dimension. For instance, the inside of my interior individual experience would be my firsthand account, while the framework for what I'm experiencing might be described by an outside view like psychology. This can be extended to all four quadrants, and in fact, if you return to Figure A1.13, the top methodology in each quadrant is an inside view and the bottom methodology is an outside view. It's beyond the scope of this appendix to cover the details of this next level of complexity of IMP, but suffice to say, more holistic and complex vision-logic enacts more inclusive maps and deeper coordination between each quadrant's modes of knowledge production.[40]

In summary of our tour of the paradigms of consciousness, I have sketched out seven levels that form a universal pathway for the evolution of consciousness, both in individual humans and for humanity as a whole. Each infant begins at archaic and develops through the levels. Humans as a species began at archaic and have evolved more complexity throughout our history. Each of these levels manifests across the four quadrants (or tetra-enacts). For short, we considered the Big Three of "I," "we," and "it/its" across the quadrants for each level. Successive levels include the complexity of prior levels, but transcend the view into creative new expressions of self, culture, and social organization. While I focused on the self, the morality, and the techno-economic modes of each paradigm, these are only three of many distinct lines of development, each of which traverses the same deep features of the paradigms of consciousness. Along the way, I added some additional levels to the Kohlberg moral development model within the integral framework, which are summarized in Figure A1.15.

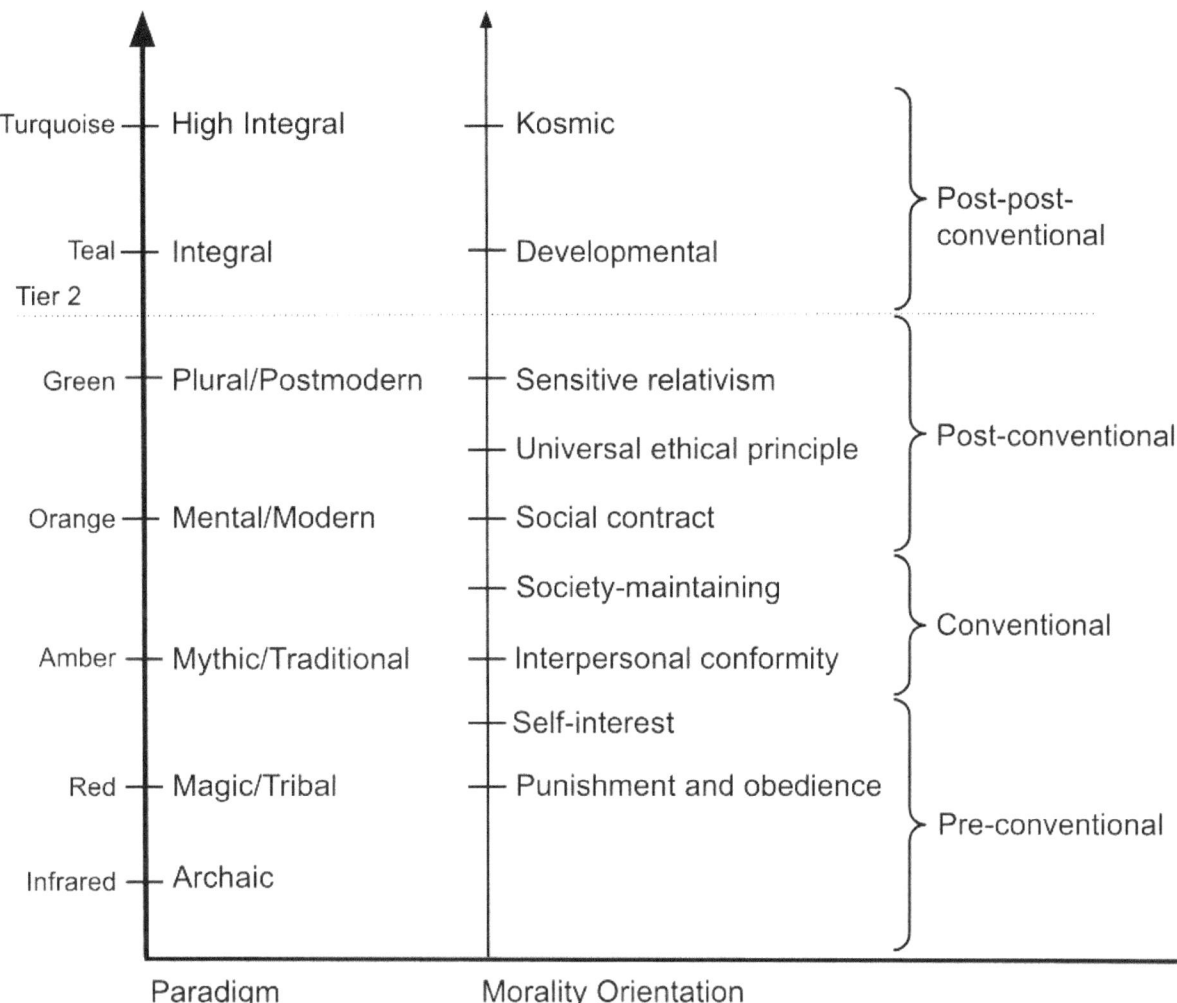

Figure A1.15. Expanded moral development model

Thus far, our AQAL matrix covers *all quadrants, all levels, and all lines*, but there are two more aspects of reality that we need to include in order to have a truly comprehensive map. These are states of consciousness and the archetypes, which are covered in Appendices II and III.

Notes

[1] *Sex, Ecology, Spirituality.*

[2] Adapted from Ken Wilber.

[3] "If the universe, regarded sidereally, is in process of spatial expansion (from the infinitesimal to the immense), in the same way and still more clearly it presents itself to us, physico-chemically, as in process of organic *involution* upon itself (from the extremely simple to the extremely complex)-and, moreover, this particular involution 'of complexity' is experimentally bound up with a cor-relative increase in interiorisation, that is to say in the psyche or consciousness." *The Phenomenon of Man.* de Chardin.

[4] "Even electrons have to interpret their environment—not to mention bacteria, worms, and wolves. Thus, interpretation is inherent in the subjective and intersubjective dimensions of being-in-the-world." Excerpt A, Wilber.

[5] "My position is that every holon has (at least) these four aspects or four dimensions (or four "quadrants") of its existence, and thus it can (and should) be studied in its intentional, behavioral, cultural, and social settings. No holon simply exists *in* one of the four quadrants; each holon *has* four quadrants." *Sex, Ecology, Spirituality*, Wilber.

[6] Just to expand the Integral lexicon a bit, the concept that all quadrants are equal participants in each holon is called *quadrant equanimity*. In contrast, the view that one quadrant alone is real is *quadrant absolutism* and the view that one quadrant is primary is *quadrant hegemony*. These latter two terms describe distortions in interpreting reality that have permeated human history. Let's take an example for each quadrant. Newtonian physics posits that only the material atomistic universe is real—an absolutism of the upper right quadrant. Certain spiritual schools posit that "I create my reality, the world is an illusion, and mind alone is real," absolutizing the upper left quadrant. Poststructuralism is prone to viewing everything, including self and nature, as a social construction (LL). Planetary ecology prioritizes a view of the earth as one large ecosystem primarily, with organisms only being parts of the system (LR). Each view contains important, but partial truths. In contrast, the Four Quadrant tool of Integral Theory offers a holistic approach to understanding reality.

[7] For nested holons, the lower defines the possibilities of the higher, and the higher sets the probabilities for the lower. So single-celled organisms are still bound by the rules that govern the interactions of atoms and molecules (the lower defining the possibilities for the higher), and within a cell, the pattern coordinating the component atoms and molecules will be governed by the agency of the cell (the higher setting the probabilities of the lower).

[8] "Each level 'transcends and includes' its predecessor, which is the only way that one moment of the universe can exist with the next moment of the universe. This gives a genuine vertical depth to the universe, not a flatland equivalency everywhere, and accounts for the undeniable 'increase in complexity' (and consciousness) that the universe has been bent on displaying since day one. The Kosmos is thus not merely holographic (with no degree of depth recognized anywhere), but is rather holographic and holarchical—an interwoven interconnectedness, psychophysical in nature, that holographically networks innumerable holarchies (where, in each case, all of the junior is in the senior, but not all the senior is in the junior)." *The Religion of Tomorrow*, Wilber.

[9] Adapted from Ken Wilber.

[10] Beginning in the physiosphere, we see atoms with prehensive awareness in physical communities such as beaches, atmospheres, solar systems, and galaxies. The physiosphere engages in *poiesis*, or creation. Dust swirls together to form accretion discs, which form galaxies, stars, and planets. This is the poetry of the kosmos at the physical level. Advancing to the biosphere, each lifeform exists as a physical organism, with internal perception of environment and self, which is positioned within a culture of "like-minded" organisms and organized within populations and ecosystems. Biological holons exhibit *autopoiesis*, or autonomous processes of self-organization. Biological life *includes* the poiesis of the physiosphere, but *transcends* into a higher degree of self-creation. Today's pinnacle, the noosphere, is the realm of self-reflexive consciousness or the mind sphere.* With the emergence of humanity, life moved from mere awareness to awareness-of-awareness. This brought with it psychology (UL), artifacts and tools (UR), language and culture (LL), and societies (LR). Human holons include both the physiosphere and biosphere, but also transcend those rings to embody a higher order of complexity, the noosphere. Whereas biological life is self-creative or autopoietic, human consciousness engages in creative liberation or *eleutheropoiesis*.** It is the nature of the noosphere to create greater expressions of freedom.

* "Much more coherent and just as extensive as any preceding layer, it is really a new layer, the 'thinking layer', which, since its germination at the end of the Tertiary period, has spread over and above the world of plants and animals. In other words, outside and above the biosphere there is the noosphere." *The Phenomenon of Man*, de Chardin.

** "The core nature of the consciousness that humans hold is that they create freedom. Following Maturana's precedent, the new word being introduced here to describe human systems is *eleutheropoiesis*. It is our nature to move to ever more creative expressions of freedom. *Eleutheria* is the Greek term for 'liberty' and, again, *poiesis* means 'creation.'" *The Organic Masculine*, Sturm.

[11] The full version of the Integral AQAL matrix includes "all quadrants, all levels, all lines, all states, all types." So far, we have covered quadrants and are beginning to explore the developmental levels, including the paradigms of consciousness. *All lines* refers to multiple lines of intelligence, each of which must undergo its own process of development for each individual. The concept of

"multiple intelligences" was introduced by Howard Gardner in 1983. He identified visual-spatial, verbal-linguistic, musical-rhythmic, logical-mathematical, interpersonal, intrapersonal, and bodily-kinesthetic as distinct types of intelligence. Integral theory expands this list considerably. *All states* refers to states of consciousness which are outlined in Appendix II. *All types* refers to personality types like the Enneagram or Myers-Brigs and includes the archetypes. A complete kosmic address includes the quadrant, the level, the line of intelligence, the state in which it is experienced, and the type interpreting the experience.

[12] Adapted from Ken Wilber.

[13] With the trans-egoic structure-states beyond high integral. See *The Organic Masculine* for a full discussion.

[14] Wilber points out that the Big Three correspond to the three validity claims of Habermas: truthfulness (UL), rightness/justice (LL), and truth (UR & LR). They also correspond to Kant's Aesthetic Judgment (UL), Critique of Practical Reason (LL), and Critique of Pure Reason (UR & LR). They correspond to the three Jewels of Buddhism: the Buddha (I), the dharma (it/its) and the sangha (we); to art, morals, and science; and to self, culture, and nature. Cf: *Sex, Ecology, Spirituality*, Wilber.

[15] Introduced by Thomas Kuhn in his study of scientific regimes, a paradigm describes the agreed upon definitions of "legitimate problems and methods of research" in a field, which includes "law, theory, application, and instrumentation together [to] provide models from which spring particular coherent traditions of scientific research." *The Structure of Scientific Revolutions,* Kuhn.

[16] "These experiments, injunctions, or social practices (the Lower Right) become the models or exemplars of how good science in that field is to be done. Other scientists use and model those exemplary practices to produce (enact and bring forth) more data, phenomena, or factual occasions. And around this base or paradigm (LR) grow various superstructures, theories, or worldviews (LL) that are molded and determined by the base." Excerpt A, Wilber.

[17] It's important to note that in this context, "tribal culture" applies to a specific developmental level, and not to the vast majority of indigenous cultures in the world today. With the exception of a handful of villages which have not been exposed to globalization, the indigenous cultures of today have continued to evolve through the paradigms and in some cases are at the cutting edge of cultural development.

[18] "The physical consequences of action determine its goodness or badness regardless of the human meaning or value of these consequences. Avoidance of punishment and unquestioning deference to power are valued in their own right." *Essays on Moral Development*, Kohlberg.

[19] *Essays on Moral Development*, Kohlberg.

[20] According to a survey from Ego Development Theory, sampling 4510 American adults, 11.3% of respondents occupy the "Conformist" level and 36.5% occupy the "Self-conscious" level, which together populate the mythic/traditional level in the Integral scale. See "Ego Development: A Full-Spectrum Theory Of Vertical Growth And Meaning Making," Cook-Greuter.

[21] For reference: *In a Different Voice*, Carol Gilligan; *Changes of Mind*, Jenny Wade; and *The Evolutionary Journey of Woman*, Dr. Sarah Nicholson.

[22] "Connected knowledge develops through intimacy and quality between the self and the object of discourse, based on empathic understanding. Sharing experience while never losing the separate self permits people at this level to remain objective and relativistic." *Changes of Mind*, Wade.

[23] Called a *performative contradiction*, it asserts a truth which the act of asserting contradicts.

[24] "No paradigm is ever simply wrong—true but partial, yes—'Everybody is right.' But an integral metatheory adds: 'but right only when addressing the phenomena enacted by the particular paradigm.' And we were saying that such nonexclusion often discloses an *unfoldment* that is *enfoldment*: in any particular developmental stream, successive waves transcend and include their predecessors, and thus each wave is adequate, each succeeding wave is more adequate. We never arrive at a point where we can say: now we have the truth, and all predecessors were inadequate." Excerpt B, Wilber.

[25] "This is a theory of monads; but it differs from Leibniz's in that his monads change. In the organic theory, they merely become. Each monadic creature is a mode of the process of 'feeling' the world, of housing the world in one unit of complex feeling, in every way determinate. Such a unit is an 'actual occasion'; it is the ultimate creature derivative from the creative process." *Process and Reality*, Whitehead.

[26] "Any such particular fact of togetherness among actual entities is called a 'nexus' (plural form is written 'nexūs')...That a nexus is a set of actual entities in the unity of the relatedness constituted by their prehensions of each other, or—what is the same thing conversely expressed—constituted by their objectifications in each other." *Process and Reality*, Whitehead.

[27] Excerpt C, Wilber.

[28] "Social systems use communications as their particular mode of autopoietic reproduction. Their elements are communications which are recursively produced and reproduced by a network of communications and which cannot exist outside of such a network." "Theory of Social Systems and its Epistemology," Luhmann.

[29] "Everything is composed of dependently related events, of continuously interacting phenomena with no fixed, immutable essence, which are themselves in constantly changing dynamic relations." *The Universe in a Single Atom*, Dalai Lama.

[30] "Most researchers have found two to four stages of postformal (vision-logic) cognition. These postformal stages generally move beyond the formal/mechanistic phases (of [Piaget's early formal operational level]) into various stages of relativity, pluralistic systems, and contextualism (early vision-logic), and from there into stages of metasystematic, integrated, unified, dialectical, and holistic thinking (middle to late vision-logic). This gives us a picture of the *highest mental domains* as being dynamic, developmental, dialectical, integrated." *Integral Psychology: Consciousness, Spirit, Psychology, Therapy*, Wilber.

[31] "Not to be confused with the Greek 'a' or 'not', Gebser uses the Latin 'a', or 'multi' to describe an awareness system that can perceive many perspectives simultaneously. Rather than fighting for 'one true perspective' as the only 'right' one, the Aperspectival has the capacity to witness the unfolding and synthesis for the unperspectival archaic, magic, and mythic, as well as the rational perspectival worldview." "The Aperspectival," Bolognino.

[32] "An ideology, an internal identity, a *self-authorship* that can coordinate, integrate, act upon, or invent values, beliefs, convictions, generalizations, ideals, abstractions, interpersonal loyalties, and intrapersonal states. It is no longer *authored by* them, it *authors them* and thereby achieves a personal authority." *In Over Our Heads*, Kegan.

[33] "The Locus of Control (LOC) construct measures the degree to which people believe that reinforcements (rewards and punishments) from the environment are contingent on their own efforts, actions and personal decisions (internal LOC) on the one hand, versus luck, fate, external circumstance and powerful others (external LOC) on the other." "Locus of Control," *Encyclopedia of Psychology and Religion*, Francis.

[34] "Autonomous persons consciously commit to actively create a meaningful life for themselves and for others through self-determination and self-actualization within constantly shifting contexts. They posses a relatively strong, autonomous self that is both differentiated and well integrated. This includes the capacity to see and accept paradox and tolerate ambiguity" "Ego Development: A Full-Spectrum Theory Of Vertical Growth And Meaning Making," Cook-Greuter.

[35] "Caring for the spiral as a whole means preserving the evolutionary opportunities for every person, regardless of that person's place in the sequence of evolution." *Integral Consciousness and the Future of Evolution*, McIntosh.

[36] Excerpt B, Wilber.

[37] Phenomenology: the study of consciousness through direct experience. Structuralism: the analysis of human cognition. Empiricism: the study of physical objects and sense experience. Autopoiesis: the study of the self-organizing processes of living organisms. Hermeneutics: the study of interpreting communication and meaning. Cultural anthropology: the study of human cultures and development. Systems theory: the study of coherent groups of interrelated, interdependent components. Social autopoiesis theory: the study of the self-organizing processes of systems of organisms.

[38] Adapted from Excerpt C, Wilber.

[39] *Essays on Moral Development.*

[40] See Ken Wilber's unpublished *Kosmic Karma and Creativity* for a full account of IMP and inside/outside perspectives of the quadrants.

APPENDIX II: STATES OF CONSCIOUSNESS

A state of consciousness describes the present-moment contents of my experience. These states range from waking consciousness all the way up to nondual suchness. States of consciousness are temporary. We each transition between waking, dreaming, and deep dreamless sleep every day–these are examples of states of consciousness.

Although I generally discuss states within the upper left quadrant of first person interior experience, they apply equally across all four quadrants (the four quadrants are illustrated in figure A1.1 in Appendix One). So, for example, my physical-body, energy-body, and causal-body occupy the upper right quadrant. They correlate with gross consciousness, subtle consciousness, and causal consciousness states in the upper left. When I receive reiki from an energy worker, our shared subtle energy experience takes place in the lower left "we" space, and the interactions of our energy bodies is in the lower right "its" space. States span the full four quadrant matrix.

Looking across spiritual practices, there are generally about five major states of consciousness described, which share common deep features.

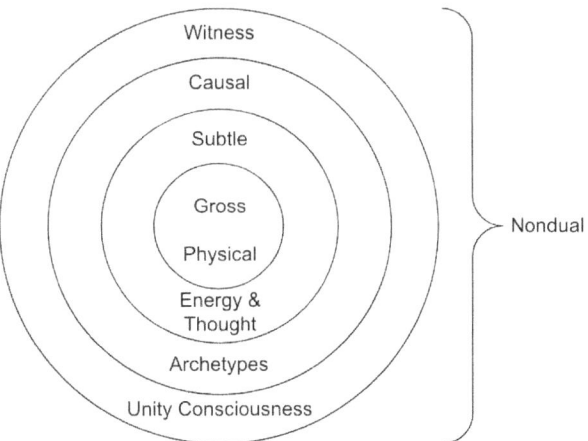

Figure A2.1. Expanding states of consciousness

The **Gross State** represents my conventional, waking consciousness, anchored in the physical, three-dimensional world. This state occupies the domain of sensory experiences, material objects, and the linear progression of time with a past, present, and future. The gross state forms the foundation of everyday reality and is commonly known as *waking consciousness.*

The **Subtle State** includes subtle energy (prana, chi, elan vital) and thought-forms. At the low end of the subtle state is the energy of the breath, the aliveness of life, the passion of the emotions, and the eroticism of sexuality. At the high end, the subtle state includes dream imagery, imagination, and visualizations.

Phenomena in the subtle realm are coextensive with space and time, but not bound to physical structures or linear time. When I outline the practices for working with sexual energy in Part III of this workbook, we're working specifically with the subtle state.

The **Causal State** includes the building blocks of reality referred to as *forms*,[1] *causal archetypes*,[2] and *eternal objects*.[3] This state holds the structures that needed to be in place in order for the big bang to happen, including colors, numbers, ideals, and certain relationships like $e=mc^2$.

In addition, this realm holds the *evolutionary archetypes* which are patterns of meaning that have evolved together with the kosmos and humans.[4] These include the Magician, Warrior, Lover, and King. In Jung's view, these archetype's are universally available to every human and exist in the collective unconscious, which we would therefore locate in the causal realm. In close relation to the collective unconscious, the causal state holds also the repository of the storehouse consciousness (alaya vijnana) which remembers all phenomena.[5]

In *Lore Book I*, I also delineated the *high causal state* which holds the primal polarities like light/dark, positive/negative, and masculine, feminine, and androgyne. For our purposes in this workbook, we can hold the causal and high causal as one state with gradations, in the same way that the subtle state can be further subdivided into low and high realms.

The **Pure Witness State** is undifferentiated unity consciousness. This state is variously referred to as awareness without any object, total subjectivity, pure being, and I AM consciousness. It is free of any content: emptiness. It is also called the void because absolutely nothing definitive can be said about it (including this statement itself).

All the Buddhas and all sentient beings are nothing but the One Mind, beside which nothing exists. This Mind, which is without beginning, is unborn and indestructible. It is not green nor yellow, and has neither form nor appearance. It does not belong to the categories of things which exist or do not exist, nor can it be thought of in terms of new or old. It is neither long nor short, big nor small, for it transcends all limits, measures, names, traces and comparisons. It is that which you see before you—begin to reason about it and you at once fall into error. It is like the boundless void which cannot be fathomed or measured. The One Mind alone is the Buddha, and there is no distinction between the Buddha and sentient things.

–Huang Po[6]

Nonduality is the union of the pure witness state with the totality of all phenomena across all other states and times. In this state, objects and awareness are experienced as a seamless whole. Imagine looking out through the eyes of all beings at all times while simultaneously inhabiting the form of everything being witnessed. Whereas in the pure witness state, all is one, nonduality includes both oneness/void and all relative phenomena.

Here is Dennis Genpo Merzel describing his experience of consciousness that is simultaneously both human and one with all:

I came at the moment when the self made a conscious choice to be one with the suffering of the entire world. This took some doing. I am completely integrated and continually integrating in every moment. I function freely and without a gap between action and response. My functioning does not have to go through the mind. I am one with all things. I do not ignore the Law of Cause and Effect. I do not fall into acting freely and without restraint, nor into blindly following rules and regulations. My life is devoted to bringing sentient beings to awakening and raising the level of consciousness on this entire planet…

I include all the aspects of the self, all the dualistic voices and Big Mind, no-self, and I transcend them. I am also known as the Master, or the Unique Self. I am absolutely unique, there is no one else in the entire world exactly like me. I have no need to prove anything or to be special since I am special and unique to begin with. I am also known as the natural self or ordinary mind. I do not need to put on airs or a façade. I am natural and unassuming. I am unconditionally joyful. My happiness is not dependent on conditions or circumstances. I am one with whatever feeling or emotion comes up.[7]

Mystical and spiritual traditions throughout the ages have been primarily concerned with states. Each tradition has its own classification scheme, but they tend to share the same deep features—which is what our integral approach is highlighting. In Figure A2.2, I list the states of consciousness as described by hatha yoga, Tibetan Buddhism, and Christianity.

	Hatha Yoga[8]	Tibetan Buddhism[9]	Christian Mysticism[10]
Gross, Waking	Annamaya kosha	Nirmanakaya	Purification
Subtle, Energetic	Pranamaya and manomaya kosha	Sambhogakaya	Illumination
Causal, Archetypal	Vijnanamaya kosha		Dark Night
Pure Witness	Anandamaya kosha, turiya	Dharmakaya	Unitive Life
Nonduality	Nirvikalpa samadhi,[11] moksha	Svabhavikakaya[12]	Indistinct Union

Figure A2.2. States of consciousness across spiritual traditions

Spiritual practices like meditation are primarily designed to open the practitioner's consciousness to higher states. The map, of course, is not the terrain. But I can use to the map to orient myself on the journey through the vast and sometimes disorienting states of consciousness. Understanding what is possible has given me inspiration and motivation to put in my practice on the meditation cushion. The full range of states is available to each and every one of us, and it is a precious gift to be exposed to these teachings. While realization in this lifetime is by no means guaranteed, the path is available to each and every one of us. It is our birthright to open our consciousness to the unity of being and the vastness of the kosmos.

Notes

[1] "In like manner there is a universal nature out of which all things are made, and which is like none of them; but they enter into and pass out of her, and are made after patterns of the true in a wonderful and inexplicable manner." *Timaeus*, Plato.

[2] "These I refer to as 'involutionary givens'—that is, those items that were truly given or created by involution, and therefore showed up with the material universe, when it first showed up (that is, with the Big Bang), with a few elements and forms awaiting emergence down the line. On this view, most phenomena are produced by evolutionary forces obeying, or following, the relatively few original involutionary givens." *The Religion of Tomorrow*, Wilber.

[3] "An eternal object can be described only in terms of its potentiality for 'ingression' into the becoming of actual entities; and that its analysis only discloses other eternal objects. It is a pure potential. The term 'ingression' refers to the particular mode in which the potentiality of an eternal object is realized in a particular actual entity, contributing to the definiteness of that actual entity." *Process and Reality*, Whitehead.

[4] "[The evolutionary archetypes] are rather some of the first forms in human evolution—the King, the Queen, the Warrior, Death, and various central psychological functions/forms as well, including the ego, the shadow, the anima and animus, the Self." *The Religion of Tomorrow*, Wilber.

[5] "The Buddha distinguishes eight forms of consciousness: the basic five (visual, auditory, olfactory, gustatory, and tactile), along with conceptual consciousness (mano-vijnana), selfconsciousness or will (manas), and repository or storehouse consciousness (alaya-vijnana), which is sometimes referred to in this sutra simply as 'mind.'" *Lankavatara Sutra*, Pine.

[6] *Zen Teaching Of Huang Po.*

[7] *Big Mind Big Heart: Finding Your Way.*

[8] "According to yoga, human existence extends through five layers or sheaths which are called *koshas*. The physical body and its elements comprise the first layer, *annamaya* kosha. *Anna* is 'food,' *maya* means 'comprised of'. The shatkarma directly influence this kosha and penetrate the next layer, *pranamaya* kosha, as they allow free flow of prana. The third layer, *manomaya* kosha, the 'mental sheath,' is indirectly affected through pranayama. Purification of these sheaths opens the fourth kosha, *vijnanamaya* or the 'sheath of intuition.' However, the fifth kosha, *anandamaya* or the 'sheath of bliss,' is unaffected by any physical influence because it is a transcendental realm." *Hatha Yoga Pradipika*, Mukitbodhananda.

[9] "Tibetans believe that the Buddha, as a realized being, manifests himself on many different levels. Following Indian tradition, they divide these levels into three primary "bodies." First is the *nirmanakaya*, emanation body, the Buddha's physical, human form in which—as described in his early biographies—he appears as a prince, renounces the world, and follows the path to enlightenment. Second, the Buddha appears as the *sambhogakaya*, body of enjoyment, his brilliant, transfigured, nonphysical form of light. In this body he journeys to the heavens, teaches the gods, and reveals himself to highly attained people. Finally there is the Buddha's *dharmakaya*, the body of reality itself, without specific, delimited form, wherein the Buddha is identified with the spiritually charged nature of everything that is." *Secret of the Vajra World*, Ray.

[10] "[The Self's] attempts to eliminate by discipline and mortification all that stands in the way of its progress towards union with God constitute *Purgation*: a state of pain and effort…*Illumination* is the 'contemplative state' *par excellence*… Illumination brings a certain apprehension of the Absolute, a sense of the Divine Presence: but not true union with it. It is a state of happiness. In the development of the great and strenuous seekers after God, this is followed—or sometimes intermittently accompanied—by the most terrible of all the experiences of the Mystic Way: the final and complete purification of the Self, which is called by some contemplatives the 'mystic pain' or 'mystic death,' by others the Purification of the Spirit or *Dark Night of the Soul*…*Union*: the true goal of the mystic quest. In this state the Absolute Life is not merely perceived and enjoyed by the Self, as in Illumination: but is one with it. This is the end towards which all the previous oscillations of consciousness have tended." *Mysticism*, Underhill.

[11] "As you go on purifying the ego, i.e. the notion of duality, the ego awareness becomes increasingly faint and dim until there is a very improbable moment in our life that can come. It does not come in the life of every individual. That is a rare moment when the ego is completely fused and lost. At that time there is only experience and not the experiencer of the experience. Such an experience is known as homogeneous experience or absolute experience. It has various names, some say transcendental experience, or nirvikalpa samadhi, some call it nirvana, emancipation or salvation, moksha; some call it adwaita anubhuti, the non-dual experience." *Hatha Yoga Pradipika*, Mukitbodhananda.

[12] "*Svabhavikakaya* is the union of the three kayas or buddha-bodies. It is the experience of reality, without an experiencer or subject." *Secret of the Vajra World*, Ray.

APPENDIX III: ARCHETYPES

Archetypes are universal patterns of meaning and identity that have evolved together with humans. These symbols are held in the causal realm, imbuing the kosmos with meaning. They are distinct from paradigms, developmental lines, and states of consciousness.[1] Archetypal personalities like *the fool* express through human form and inhabit our myths and stories. Symbols like *the cross* hold religious, spiritual, and cultural messages that seem to speak directly to us. They shape our personalities, narratives, and behaviors. Archetypes are trans-personal, stretching across humanity throughout history, and are universally accessible by each of us.

> And the essential thing, psychologically, is that in dreams, fantasies, and other exceptional states of mind the most far-fetched mythological motifs and symbols can appear autochthonously at any time, often, apparently, as the result of particular influences, traditions, and excitations working on the individual, but more often without any sign of them. These "primordial images" or "archetypes," as I have called them, belong to the basic stock of the unconscious psyche and cannot be explained as personal acquisitions. Together they make up that psychic stratum which has been called the collective unconscious.
>
> –Carl Jung[2]

Archetypes can be conceptualized as *morphic fields*, organizing patterns of influence, which emanate from the causal realm into the subtle and physical layers of the kosmos. Because archetypes are held in the collective unconscious, they can never be fully known or defined. In psychology, we call them *overdetermined* because multiple interpretations and definitions can be true simultaneously. What this means is that everything I share about archetypes in these workbooks can be true, and simultaneously, your own interpretations can be vastly different *and* completely valid.

The high causal realm holds the three *high archetypes* of gender: the masculine, the feminine, and the androgyne (see Appendix II for an explanation of the causal realm). The masculine defines itself in polarity with the feminine. I use the term androgyne to be inclusive of archetypes and gender expressions that are both masculine and feminine, neither masculine nor feminine, and third genders. I associate the masculine with the above direction, the feminine with below, and the androgyne with the horizon—though more broadly, I could say that the masculine is at one extreme, the feminine is at the opposite extreme, and the androgyne is simultaneously at neither extreme and all extremes.

Each of these three high-archetypes are singular, meaning each exists as a unified morphic field. The expression of these high-archetypes through myths, gender, and sex are diverse and unbounded. The singular masculine high-archetype manifests as a plurality of diverse masculinities. One could even make the case that there are at least as many masculinities as there are individual humans.

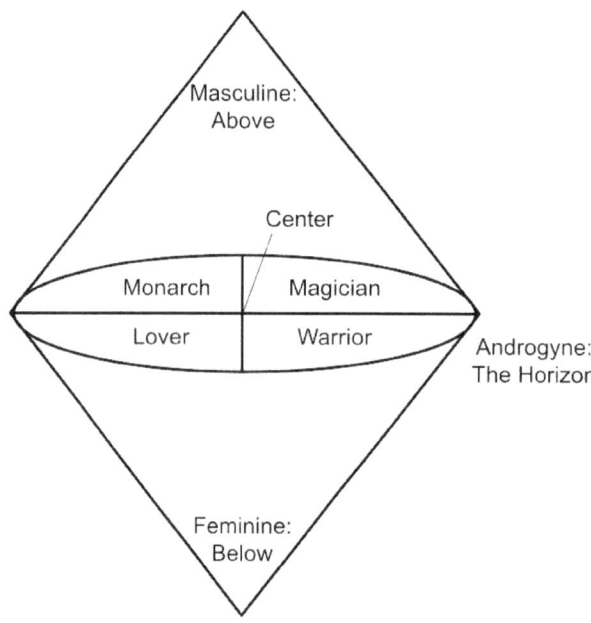

Figure A3.1. The archetypal structure of the psyche[3]

Stepping down from high causal into the causal realm, the psyche is connected to a vast array of universal symbols, which are culturally contextualized through myths. For our purposes in this masculinity workbook, I am specifically interested in two collections of archetypes: the four *roles* which describe the masculine lifecycle (boy, hero, man, and elder), and the four *parts* of the masculine psyche (Magician, Warrior, Lover, and King). As a side note, I will often use the term Monarch as a gender-neutral archetype that includes both the King and the Queen.

Because the archetypes are universal symbols held in the collective, each one of us has access to all of them, including the three gendered high-archetypes and the four archetypal parts of the psyche. My task as I mature is to *individuate* my sovereign self from the unconscious influences of archetypal energies.[4] I do this by coming into my center, symbolically represented by the central point in the mandala. From my center, I am able to open a channel to connect with these archetypes in an intentional way. This is known as developing the *ego-archetype axis*. When accessed from a place of centeredness, the archetypes become unlimited sources of creativity, power, and energy in my life. This ego-archetype axis serves as a channel for engaging with the archetypal realm, allowing for a balanced and empowered expression of my identity and potential.

The sovereign self follows a universal progression through the human lifecycle. I began life as a pre-egoic self, reactive to primal emotions and sensations in my body and environment. My pre-ego is initially embedded in my mother-figure or care-giver, as well as my environment. With the emergence of my rational mind, I transition into a fully formed ego at the center of my adolescent self. Then, if properly supported and initiated, my egoic self will step aside for my trans-egoic soul-self to become my sovereign center as an adult. This is marked by my willingness to sacrifice for the sake of others and a recognition of my dharma or life-path. Ultimately, my soul-self may recognize an even larger trans-personal Self, which becomes the new sovereign center. The Self encompasses the unitary source of consciousness in all sentient beings and acts with equanimity and love for all. This progression of the self brings a deepening understanding and embodiment of my place within the kosmos.

> Early childhood through early adolescence focuses on the development of an ego capable of healthy communion with self, others, culture, and nature—an ego prepared, in other words, to enter the process of soul initiation. Then, soul discovery and embodiment compose the primary agenda of the next stages, late adolescence through late adulthood. Elderhood focuses on the integrity of the Earth-human relationship, the soul of the more-than-human community.
>
> –Bill Plotkin[5]

An important note: I did not undergo a permanent *ego death* with the initiation into my soul self. As an adult, my inner experience of this psychic-archetypal mandala is one of dynamic flow between the roles. My soul self at center transmits my path of service, step by step, as my life continues to unfold. This is communicated through the desires of my heart, my intuition, and my access to wisdom. By making space to listen to my heart, my egoic self is able to receive and interpret this guidance and work in concert with my heart to actualize my life path. In this process, I have learned to put my ego in service to the higher guidance of my soul.

Some of us will undertake the transition to the Self and true elderhood. In order to make this transition, I must fill out as much of my adult soul self as possible. When I have a thriving, balanced soul-psyche for my foundation, then the Self naturally emerges as I mature. Just as the transition of my sovereign center from ego to soul self requires a *dark night*, so the transition to Self at center requires my soul to relinquish control and come into service. This is not accomplished by wishful thinking in my conceptual mind. It is a decision that is made trans-cognitively in the seat of my heart, and which is accomplished via initiation. For many, the soul will not choose this initiation in this lifetime, and that is part of the greater perfection. This transition is ideally facilitated by the support of one's community. With Elders to guide me through each initiation, I am supported in making the journey safely.

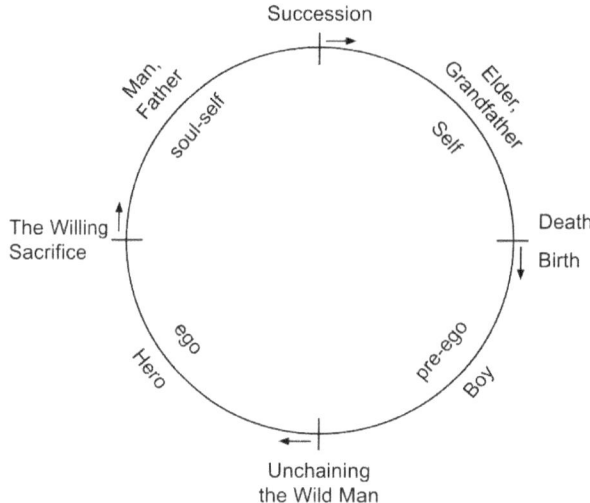

Figure A3.2. The masculine life-cycle with archetypal roles and initiations[6]

Each sovereign self is connected to an *archetypal role* which accompanies it. As a masculine-identified human, I began life in the archetypal role of the *Boy*. I matured into a psychological teenager with an egoic self, connected to the archetype of the *Hero*. From there, I have continued to mature into the adult soul-self with the corresponding archetypes of the *Man* and *Father*. Eventually, as my soul-self agrees to open into a larger locus of consciousness, I will make the transition into the Self and the archetype of the *Elder* and *Grandfather*.

The corresponding feminine roles are the Girl, Heroine/Maiden, Woman/Mother, and Crone. The androgyne plays with all of these roles and more, but does not hold hir own distinct pathway in Western culture.

The progression through the archetypal roles happens via the process of *initiation*. While my body may mature from child to adolescent to adult to elder, my psychological progression is by no means guaranteed. Through initiation, I undergo the death of my prior identity, a rebirth into a new, more empowered identity, and an undertaking of greater responsibility toward all of my relations. I have listed three initiations in Figure A3.2. *Unchaining the Wild Man* is the initiation from the Boy into the Hero, and symbolizes the awakening of inner strength, courage, and readiness to step into the world beyond the shelter of my parents. The initiation from the Hero to the Man is called *the willing sacrifice*, where I begin to serve something greater than my own self-interest. Finally, the initiation from the Man to the Elder is *succession*, where one passes wisdom and leadership to the next generation, as well as mediating with the ancestors and unseen realms.

In addition to the *roles*, the psyche can be divided into archetypal *parts*, which mature together with the self. In the adult masculine psyche, the four archetypal parts are the Magician, Warrior,

Lover, and King. These correspond to the psychological traits of thinking, acting, feeling, and being, respectively.

> I agree with Jung that the four quarters of mythology show the world being quad-rated, that there are four corners of the world, four elements. The Navajo say there are four winds. The Hindus say there are four faces of god. The early Christians said there had to be four gospels. Jung said myths and mythic images are the faces that instincts bring to the world. Humans quadrate the world in mythic images. So there must be a fourfold instinctuality.
>
> –Robert Moore[7]

The Magician aligns his genius, imagination, and willpower to channel the creative energies of the kosmos. The Warrior acts with discipline and integrity for the sake of truth. The Lover delights in pleasure, embodies the emotions, and grows through relationships. The King is the sovereign presence that offers his blessings to the realm. Each of these four archetypes utilizes his own distinct wisdom and tools to create sacred space and access the center. When these four roles have been initiated and are operating in balance in the psyche, then a man's soul-self is able to flourish at the center.

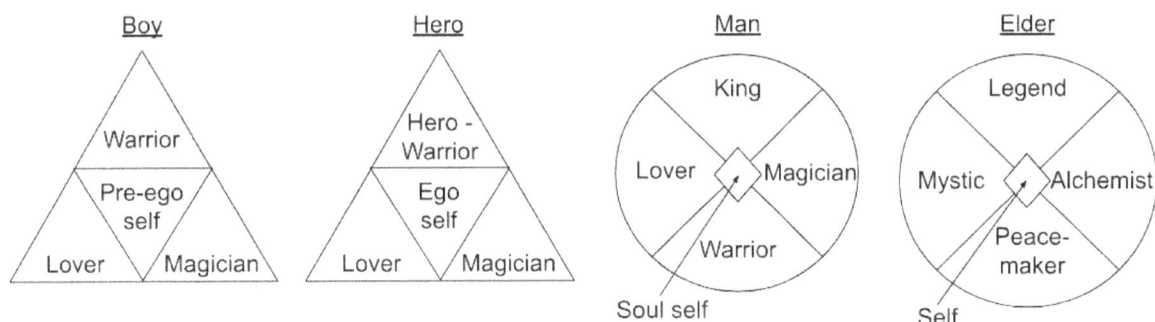

Figure A3.3. Archetypal progression of the masculine psyche

The parts of the psyche also evolve over the course of the human life-cycle. As illustrated in Figure A3.3, I begin in boyhood with three archetypal parts: the Warrior (picture a toddler scream-ing "No!"), the Magician (playful imagination), and the Lover (the child's love for the parents).

With the transition to adolescence, the pre-ego becomes a heroic ego. The Hero in this phase is fused with the Warrior. Life is an adventure full of battles and conquests. The Lover ideally releases the mother figure as the primary attachment bond and explores romantic relationships within the community of peers. And the Magician's rational mind awakens curiosity to understand the world.

One of the primary observations I made in *Lore Book I* was that we live in a pathological adolescent society where most biological adults have never undergone the archetypal initiation into adulthood. As an adult, the soul self assumes the sovereign center and the King becomes an individuated part of the psyche. In the healthy maturation cycle of the masculine psyche, the ego/Hero/Warrior offers his life in service. The soul-self awakens at the center, the Hero/ego becomes a servant to the more expansive soul-self. In this transition, the adult Warrior differentiates from the adolescent Hero and the King emerges as a distinct part of the psyche. As I embody the King, my priorities shift from achievement to a deeper understanding of purpose and authentic being.

Within the mature adult, the archetypal parts of the psyche—Warrior, Lover, Magician, and King—interact dynamically, supporting and enriching each other. Each inner character is able to both draw upon and offer support to the other characters. For example, my Warrior may help my Lover to show up for a difficult conversation in my relationship.

Each of the four archetypal roles undergoes another initiation as I move from trans-egoic soul identification to trans-personal Self identification. The Magician transforms into the Alchemist, who is able to transmute both matter and consciousness as an active agent of Eros. As I will explore in this volume, the Warrior advances from being a protector to the Peacemaker who champions compassion and nonviolence. The Lover's passion becomes devotion toward the Beloved and he enters the path of the Mystic. And the King moves beyond his realm into the collective consciousness by becoming the Legend.

Throughout the course of my life, I run into challenges. My needs aren't perfectly met. Particularly during childhood and adolescence, when I'm dependent on other humans to meet my basic needs, I'm vulnerable to being wounded. In order to get my needs met, I develop *character strategies*, which Plotkin calls *subpersonalities*.[8] These characters are warped versions of the Magician, Warrior, Lover, and Monarch. While there are several approaches to working with these strategic parts, my model is an adaptation from Hakomi Character Theory. There are eight character strategies, with an outward and inward strategy associated with each of the four archetypal parts (Figure A3.4).

> Character strategies are creative, intelligent adaptive mechanisms to deal with difficult environments. They are so often sane responses to insane environments.
>
> —Rob Fisher[9]

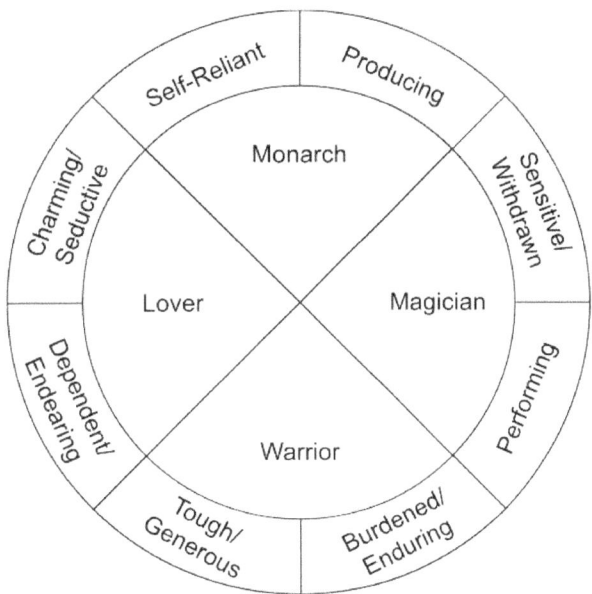

Figure A3.4. The eight character strategies

Within each character strategy, there is a core reaction that I turn to and a limiting belief that governs my behavior. Each strategy can be understood as an attractor state—a pattern in consciousness-—which is triggered to respond to stress in my inner or outer world. This subpersonality comes online to help me cope with my challenges. However, these strategies are generally learned from the perspective of my disempowered child and thus are in need of updating and integrating into the truth of my empowered adulthood today. I could consider these strategies as trance states that I turn to for safety, which disconnect me from the free-flowing creative center of my self.

Character Strategy	Reaction	Limiting Belief
Performing	Attract attention	I am only loved when I perform
Sensitive/Withdrawn	Self-isolate	The world and my emotions are too much
Tough/Generous	Intimidate	My vulnerability will be exploited
Burdened/Enduring	Resist	I cannot be both free and loved
Charming/Seductive	Deceive	My authentic self is unlovable
Dependent/Endearing	Collapse	There will never be enough for me
Producing	Take action	I must produce to be loved
Self Reliant	Self-fortify	Only I can meet my needs

Figure A3.5. Reactions and limiting beliefs of the character strategies

In each workbook, I'll be exploring the character strategies for the corresponding archetypal role. The Magician's performing and sensitive/withdrawn strategies were topics in *Lore Book I*. In Chapter One, I cover the tough/generous and burdened/enduring strategies specific to the Warrior.

The journey of archetypal initiation and integration of character strategies is a distinct mode of maturation. As I individuate from the unconscious and reactive influences of these personality patterns, I become free to inhabit more expansive and empowered capacities as a sovereign self.

Notes

[1] "Finally, a word about 'horizontal' typologies, such as Jungian types, the Enneagram, Myers-Briggs, and so forth. For the most part, these are not vertical levels, stages, or waves of development, but rather different types of orientations possible at each of the various levels. Some individuals find these typologies to be very useful in understanding themselves and others. But it should be understood that these 'horizontal' typologies are of a fundamentally different nature than the 'vertical' levels—namely, the latter are universal stages through which individuals pass in a normal course of development, whereas the former are types of personalities that may—or may not—be found at any of the stages." *Integral Psychology*, Wilber.

[2] *Collected Works of C.G. Jung, Volume 8: Structure & Dynamics of the Psyche.*

[3] *The Organic Masculine*, Sturm.

[4] "I use the term 'individuation' to denote the process by which a person becomes a psychological "in-dividual," that is, a separate, indivisible unity or 'whole.'" *The Collected Works of C. G. Jung, Volume 9 (Part 1): Archetypes and the Collective Unconscious*, Jung.

[5] *Nature and the Human Soul.*

[6] Adapted from *The Organic Masculine*, Sturm.

[7] *The Archetype of Initiation.*

[8] "Cultivating a relationship between the Self and your wounded subpersonalities (of any of the four directions) is not merely an exceptional means for middleworld (everyday) healing and wholing, although it's certainly that. It can also provide a path to Soul discovery and initiation, an underworld way to be with your woundedness that I call advanced subpersonality work." *Wild Mind: A Field Guide to the Human Psyche*, Plotkin.

[9] *Experiential Psychotherapy with Couples: A Guide for the Creative Pragmatist.*

APPENDIX IV: PARADIGMS, STATES, AND ARCHETYPES

The three developmental axes I've outlined in the prior three appendices are paradigms of consciousness (with universal levels traversed by multiple lines), states of consciousness, and archetypal roles. Paradigms define how I inhabit and interpret reality, (i.e., my self/worldview/world); states define the content of my awareness; and archetypes define the sovereign center of my experience. Each axis advances through a distinct mechanism. I develop through the paradigms by the dialectic of progress, transcending and including the views that have come before.[1] The primary mechanism involves turning the subjective viewing lens of one level into an object that is observable in the next. I advance through increasingly expansive states of consciousness utilizing spiritual practices like meditation. Rites of passage and initiations provide the mechanism of maturation through the archetypes.

In this section, we'll explore how these three developmental pathways interrelate with each other.

States of consciousness are universally accessible. Stable abiding in non-duality is possible for every human at every paradigm (archaic through high integral) and every sovereign center (pre-egoic through Self). Put another way: Every state is available at every moment to each human.

The archetypes are a bit different in how they interact with states. The archetypes themselves occupy the causal realm of consciousness and they reach downward into the subtle and gross realms to influence you and me. Mostly this influence happens unconsciously because I'm not abiding in the causal realm of consciousness.

The I AM consciousness of the universal realm has an archetypal expression as the Self. With each step downward from causal through the states of consciousness, this sovereign center becomes more limited as it goes through the process of forgetting—sometimes called *involution*.[2] The Self steps downward to the soul self, then the ego, then the pre-ego.

The four archetypal parts (Magician, Warrior, Lover, and Monarch) also reach down from the causal realm through the states. In the high subtle realm, the four parts of the psyche are thinking, acting, feeling, and being. Descending to the low-subtle level, energy expresses through the four elements: Wind, Fire, Water, and Earth. At the gross level, physical orientation is divided into the four directions: East, South, West, and North.[3]

In the other direction, above the causal realm into the pure witness realm, the mandala is no longer differentiated, but transcends into unity, expressed by the symbol for the monad or sun (Figure A4.1).

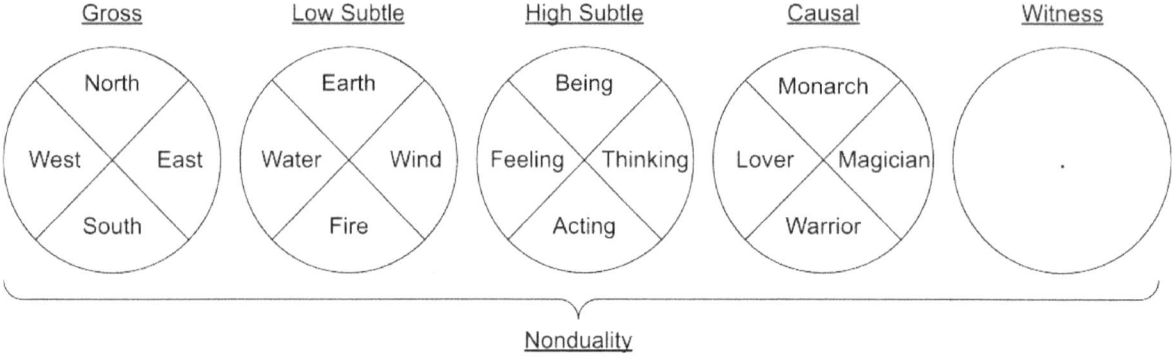

Figure A4.1. The quadrated mandala through states of consciousness

Nonduality is the simultaneous experience of all the quadrants of all the realms, plus the contentless, undefinable pure witness realm. The five distinct mandalas portrayed in Figure A4.1 are more accurately overlaid as coextensive realms of the kosmos. In Figure A4.2, below, I've illustrated all five mandalas together and added in the high-archetypes of the masculine above, the feminine below, and the androgyne on the horizon. In this illustration, the monad of the pure witness realm occupies the center and each successive ring is an involution into increasing differentiation and density.

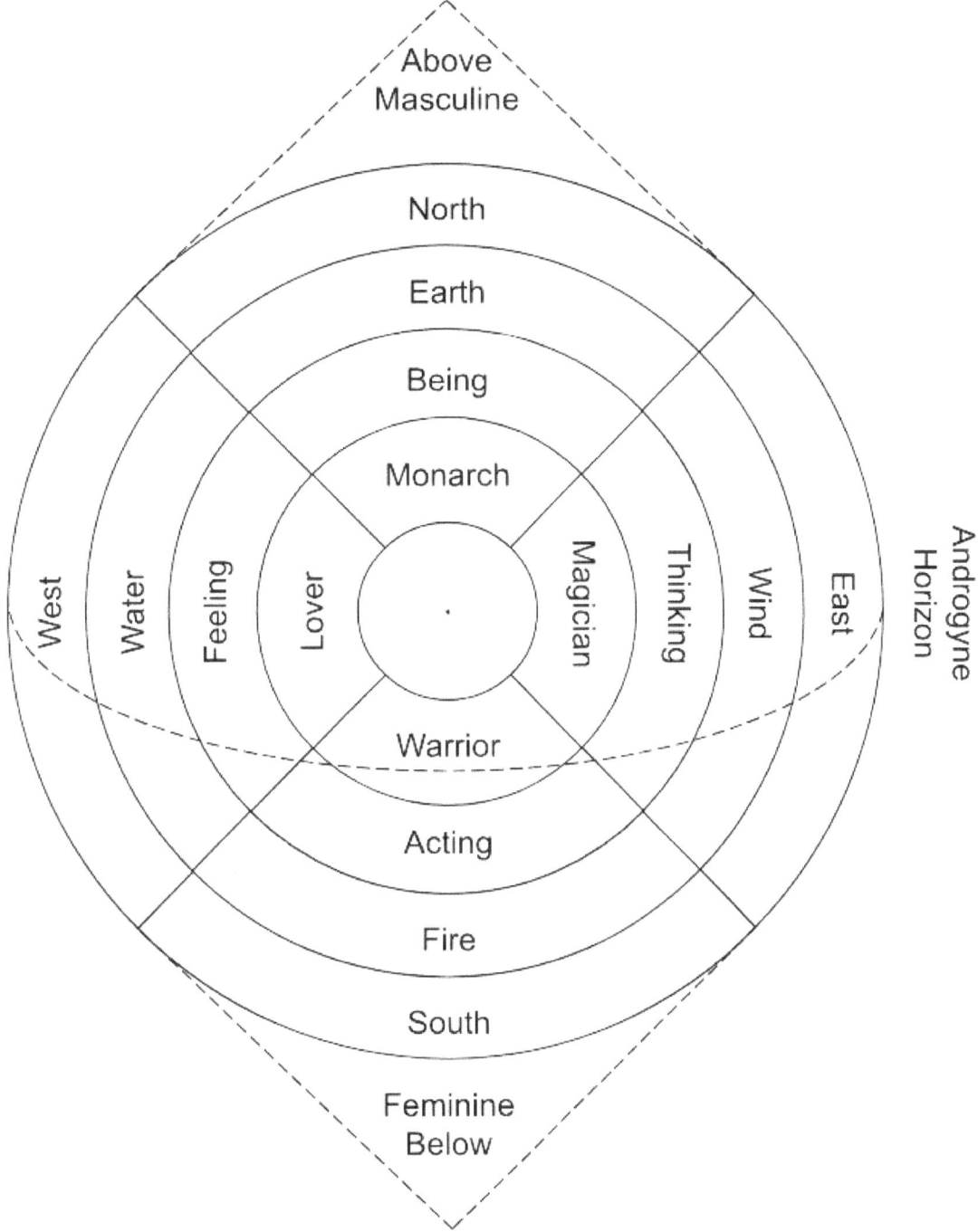

Figure A4.2. Quadrated realms with high-archetypes.

Now let's look at paradigms. Unlike states, which are available to every human at any moment, the paradigms must be grown through.[4] Each paradigm becomes the foundation for the next more advanced paradigm, like sequential rungs on a ladder. Within the first tier paradigms (archaic through plural/postmodern) and the second tier paradigms (integral and high integral), I can be at any state. But once I advance to the third tier "structure-states" (para-mind, meta-mind, overmind, and supermind), my paradigm requires a minimum trans-egoic state as my baseline. As I advance into more complex and holistic worldviews, I begin to enfold more and more of reality into my experience until my stable lens at supermind includes nondual suchness itself. So initially, paradigms and states are separate, but at high levels of advancement, paradigms also require states, which we call structure-states.

Here is a very brief summary of the structure-states: *Para-Mind* is the next, more comprehensive worldview above high integral. To date, there is no collective or cultural manifestation of this (or higher) structure-states, so any description must be speculative. Based on individuals, however, we can say that Para-Mind includes a stable experience of the trans-egoic gross state of consciousness and a transcendence and inclusion of the high integral paradigm. Meaning: I directly experience, or see, the undivided wholeness of my relationship with the physical environment. I experience myself seamlessly interwoven into the physical tapestry of the kosmos. *Meta-Mind* includes everything from the Para-Mind worldview and transcends into an even more encompassing perspective. Meta-Mind requires a stable experience of the subtle realm of consciousness. This means that beyond seeing my interconnection with physical reality, I am now *feeling* my aliveness as interwoven into the aliveness of all beings. I use *feeling-awareness* to dance within the great web of life. *Overmind* spans two states of consciousness, the causal realm and the pure witness realm. In addition it transcends and includes the worldview from Meta-Mind. At Overmind, I am experiencing my interconnection with archetypes, deities, and the basic forms of the kosmos. Once the pure witness realm stabilizes, I enter into a seamless union with kosmic consciousness. Where Para-Mind sees wholeness, and Meta-Mind feels wholeness, Overmind witnesses wholeness from the unstainable ungraspable Christ-consciousness or Buddha-mind. Finally, *Supermind* is nondual suchness as experienced from the most complex and holistic worldview. This experience can be likened to experiencing the entire history of the kosmos to date through the most comprehensive experience possible, and enfolding that into each newly creative moment.

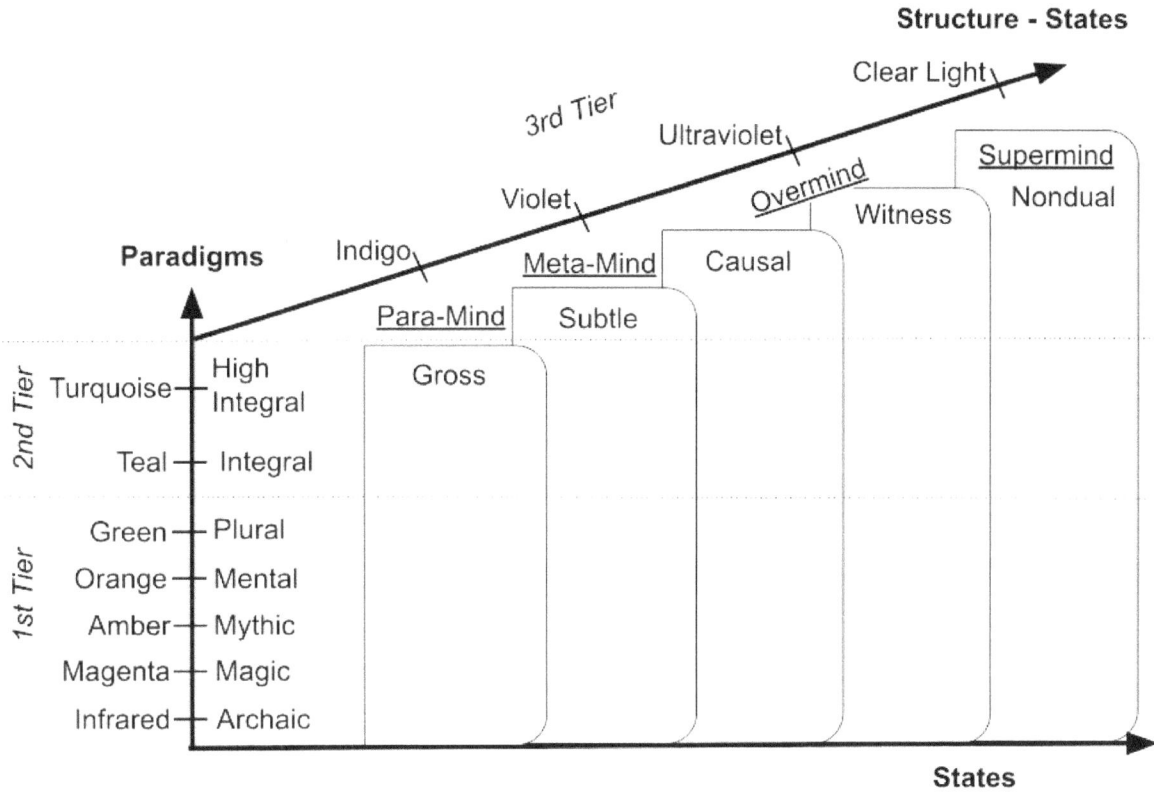

Figure A4.3. Paradigms, states, and structure-states[5]

Now let's consider the interplay of paradigms and archetypes. While paradigms define my interpretive lens, archetypal roles define the sovereign center doing the experiencing. Every archetypal role is available at every paradigm. For example, magic/tribal societies have access to the boy, hero, man, and elder. If anything, the adult and elder roles become more challenging to access as one progresses into the traditional, modern, and postmodern paradigms because these cultural levels lose their rites of passage. But then, the full life-cycle of roles comes back online again in integral and beyond.

Just as some paradigms require minimum states, they also hold minimum archetypal roles. The archetypal role at the child level (boy, girl) can occupy archaic, magic/tribal, and mythic/traditional. The mental/modern paradigm is defined by the full emergence of the rational mind and independent ego. In order to reach this paradigm, one must hold an adolescent-level archetypal role (hero, heroine, maiden). In order to advance into the integral paradigm, the soul-self must be online as the sovereign center, which is held by the adult archetypal roles (man and woman). Without access to the soul-self, I cannot open to the sacred dimension that the integral world is embedded within. Finally, the elder archetype and the seat of the transpersonal Self is required by overmind and the stable conjoining of the pure witness realm.

To clarify one point, it is not possible to be an integral child. There can be children embedded in an integral culture who assume those values and way of living, but the capacity to see meta-systemic and cross-paradigmatic structures (i.e., integral's *vision logic*) happens at the adult level.

Now we can place all three progressions together into a single map for the evolution of consciousness (Figure A4.4).

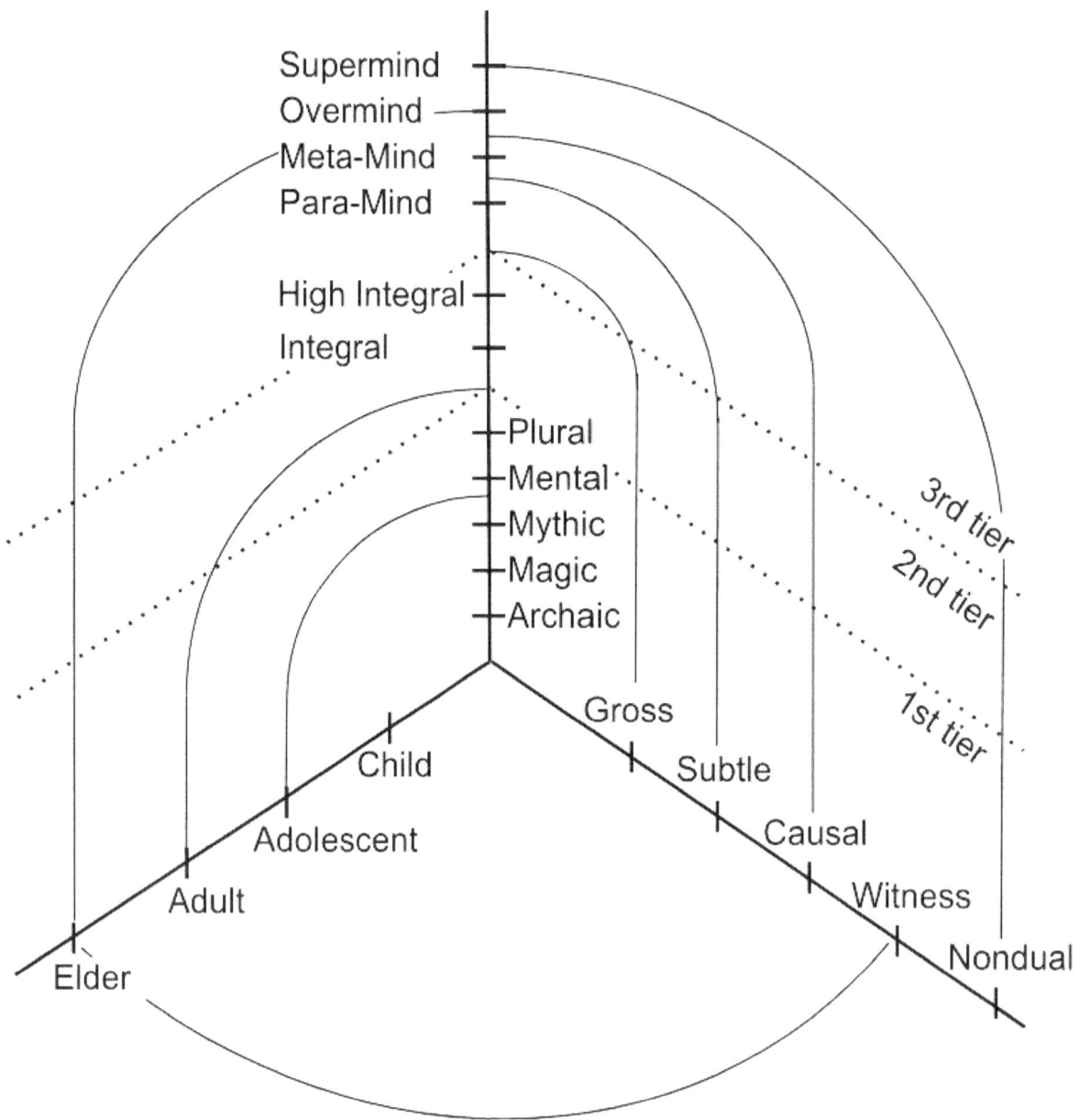

Figure A4.4. Three axes of the evolution of consciousness

On the vertical axis I have plotted the first and second tier paradigms, which then extend into the third tier structure-states. On the left axis are the levels of archetypal roles and on the right axis are the states of consciousness. The dotted lines delineate vertical divisions into the first, second, and third tier paradigms. The curved lines mark the minimum progressions for either archetype or state necessary to inhabit a given paradigm. So, tracing left from archaic, I can inhabit all of the archetypes and tracing right from archaic, I can experience all states of consciousness. However, the curved line rising from adolescent and landing just under the mental paradigm means that in order to hold the mental/modern paradigm, I must have initiated into the one of the hero, hero-ine, or maiden adolescent archetypes. From the mental paradigm, I can trace left across adolescent, adult, and elder, and trace right into all states of consciousness.

Skipping upward a bit, meta-mind is defined by a stable union of the subtle realm together with a worldview that has transcended and included all the way up to the violet color code. Tracing right from meta-mind, I can expand into causal, witness, and nonduality, but the gross and subtle realms are already baked in. Tracing left from meta-mind, I can be either an archetypal adult or elder, but the child and adolescent archetypes are already minimum requirements.

In order to reach overmind, I must have initiated into elderhood. And finally, there is a bottom arc denoting the relationship between the Self as the sovereign center of the Elder archetypes and the pure witness state of consciousness. The witness state comes together with the Elder archetypal role.

This model outlines the three pathways for human development. Each axis is distinct, and yet, all three are interrelated. Paradigms are unique because as I advance higher, the other two axes begin to be included and enfolded. Moving toward the omega point of nondual supermind brings all of the pathways together into a singular *creative advance* of the kosmos. The center of the graph represents the origin of each human and humanity. Moving outward toward the periphery represents awakening, development, and archetypal maturation toward the realized potentials of human existence. I offer this framework as an orienting map to position ourselves upon. I will reference this to understand the Warrior's work within a larger context.

Here are the caveats with this model. First, it's a map and not the terrain itself. This model can only ever be an approximation and a generalization. It could not possibly describe any individual's path with total accuracy. Because the field of consciousness studies (and consciousness itself) is evolving, this model is a work in progress. In addition, I'm sharing it through my paradigmatic lens, with my social biases and blind spots. The research that I'm drawing on to create this map also carries social biases: largely white, male, Western, academic perspectives.

Probably the biggest liability with a map like this is that it creates a norm for a singular "correct" path of evolution. The Buddhist saying, "One thousand monks, one thousand paths," captures the essence of the unique unfolding of each individual's spiritual journey. Respecting the diversity of our paths, this wisdom implies one mountain that we are all climbing. As my teacher Pamela Eakins is fond of saying, "Enlightenment is enlightenment." So we each have our unique path to a universal peak. The various lines and stages are metaphorical elevation markers that we all meet as we walk our individual paths.

Acknowledging these limitations, I find myself compelled to study, innovate, and share about the evolution of consciousness using the integral meta-model. While it is true that I am working on Integral Theory, I would equally say that integral consciousness is working on me. The more I study and explore, the more my curiosity expands and grows. Integral Theory is emerging as a brand new field (or meta-field) for humanity. We are still groping through the darkness to find the edges and contours of this new space. And as more of us take up the monumental amount of learning that integral requires, the more fully we bring humanity into the next epoch of potential. Despite all the challenges in our world, this growth edge inspires me with an incredible amount of optimism.

Notes

[1] Fichte's *synthesis, antithesis, synthesis*, and Swimme and Berry's *differentiation, autopoiesis, communion* both describe the three-part dialectic of progress.

[2] "Involution/Efflux is the production of the manifest world via a successive manifestation or 'stepping down' of Spirit into lesser and lesser versions of itself. Using Christian terms, Spirit goes out of itself (lila or kenosis) and steps downward to produce a reduced version of itself called 'soul'; soul then goes out of itself and crystallizes into a lesser version of itself called 'mind'; mind then reduces itself to produce a lesser form called 'life,' or 'living body'; the body then sediments downward to produce the lowest and densest form of Spirit called 'matter'; thus matter, body, mind, and soul are all forms of ultimate Spirit, but increasingly reduced or lesser forms." *The Religion of Tomorrow*, Wilber.

[3] I am intending this classification to describe the four parts of the upper left quadrant of internal experience, or first-person consciousness. Each upper left state of consciousness has a corresponding upper right manifestation in form. So even though I am following traditional medicine wheels by using the cardinal directions, these are measurable geophysical traits of the upper right quadrant. More accurately these would be the qualitative psychic experiences of *ahead, behind, left,* and *right.* Similarly the psychic phenomena of the subtle realm (including the alchemical elements) in the upper left correlate with the subtle body of the upper right, the four quadrants of the psyche correlate with the mental body, and the archetypes correlate with the causal body. For a deeper discussion of states in the upper left and upper right quadrants, see Ken Wilber, Excerpt G.

[4] "Integral Theory says, 'States are free, structures are earned,' which means that most states can be peak experienced, or plateau experienced, by virtually any structure, because these states are already present in some degree in everyone, just as an infant wakes, dreams, and sleeps (or goes through gross, subtle, and causal realms), but structures themselves have to grow, evolve, and unfold in a developmental fashion, 'transcending and including' their predecessors." *The Religion of Tomorrow*, Wilber.

[5] *The Organic Masculine*, Sturm.

WORKS CITED

Aboul-Enein, Basil H et al. "Evidence for Masturbation and Prostate Cancer Risk: Do We Have a Verdict?" *Sexual Medicine Reviews* vol. 4,3 2016. doi:10.1016/j.sxmr.2016.02.006

Adams, Maurianne et al. *Teaching for Diversity and Social Justice.* 3rd Ed. (New York: Routledge, 2016).

Adams, Maurianne et al. *Teaching for Diversity and Social Justice.* 1st Ed. (New York: Routledge, 1997).

Arbib, James, and Seba, Tony. *Rethinking Humanity: Five Foundational Sector Disruptions, the Lifecycle of Civilizations, and the Coming Age of Freedom* (The RethinkX Project, 2020).

Anderson, Luke. "Lights, Camera, Action-Reaction: Sympathetic Nervous System Response to Action Movies across the Decades." *California Science and Engineering Fair* 2019. https://csef.usc.edu/History/2019/Projects/S0401.pdf

Archer, John. *Male Violence.* (New York: Routledge, 1995).

Armstrong, Thomas. "The Stages of Life According to Jean Gebser." (2020). https://www.institute4learning.com/2020/02/12/the-stages-of-life-according-to-jean-gebser/

Bair-Merritt, Megan H. et al. "Why Do Women Use Intimate Partner Violence? A Systematic Review of Women's Motivations." Trauma Violence Abuse. 2010 Oct; 11(4): 178–189. doi: 10.1177/1524838010379003

Barnosky, Anthony D. "Megafauna biomass tradeoff as a driver of Quaternary and future extinctions." 2008 Aug; PNAS vol. 105, 1. doi: https://doi.org/10.1073/pnas.0801918105

Berntson, Gary G, and Sahib S Khalsa. "Neural Circuits of Interoception." Trends in neurosciences vol. 44,1 2021. doi:10.1016/j.tins.2020.09.011

Basile, K.C., Smith, S.G., Kresnow, M., Khatiwada S., & Leemis, R.W. "The National Intimate Partner and Sexual Violence Survey: 2016/2017 Report on Sexual Violence." Atlanta, GA: National Center for Injury Prevention and Control, Centers for Disease Control and Prevention. (2022).

Berrigan, Daniel. *The Raft is not the Shore: Conversations toward a Buddhist/Christian Awareness.* (Boston: Beacon Press, 1975).

Black, M.C. et al. "The National Intimate Partner and Sexual Violence Survey (NISVS): 2010 Summary Report." Atlanta, GA: National Center for Injury Prevention and Control, Centers for Disease Control and Prevention.

Bly, Robert. *Iron John: A Book about Men* (Boston: De Capo Press, 1990, 2004).

Bohm, David. *Wholeness and the Implicate Order.* (London: Routledge, 2005).

Bolognino, Justin. "The Aperspectival," Feb 25, 2022. https://medium.com/@jbolognino/the-aperspectival-d6fbb8fb09b9

Bourzat, Françoise and Hunter, Kristina. *Consciousness Medicine: Indigenous Wisdom, Entheogens, and Expanded States of Consciousness for Healing Healing and Growth* (Berkeley: North Atlantic Books, 2019).

Burton, John (ed.) *Conflict: Human Needs Theory.* (Hampshire: Palgrave MacMillan, 1990).

Byrom, Thomas. *Dhammapada: The Sayings of the Buddha.* (United Kingdom: Shambhala, 1993).

Cambell, Joseph. *The Power of Myth.* (New York: Anchor Books, 1991).

Capra, Fritjof and Luisi, Pier Luigi. *The Systems View of Life: A Unifying Vision* (Cambridge: Cambridge University Press, 2014).

Carrellas, Barbara. *Urban Tantra, Second Edition: Sacred Sex for the Twenty-First Century* (California: Ten Speed Press, 2007).

Case, Paul Foster. *The Tarot: A Key to the Wisdom of the Ages: The Classic Guide.* (New York: Jeremy P. Tarcher, 2006).

de Chardin, Teilhard. *The Phenomenon of Man.* (New York: Harper Perennial, 1955).

Chetty R, Stepner M, Abraham S, et al. "The Association Between Income and Life Expectancy in the United States, 2001-2014." *JAMA.* 2016;315(16):1750–1766. doi:10.1001/jama.2016.4226

Chia, Mantak, and Arava, Douglas Abrams. *The Multi-Orgasmic Man: Sexual Secrets That Every Man Should Know.* (San Francisco: HarperCollins, 1997).

Christensen, Ann-Dorte; Rasmussen, Palle. *Masculinity, War and Violence.* (New York: Routledge, 2017).

Claiborne, Shane; Wilson-Hartgrove, Jonathan; Okoro, Enuma. *Common Prayer: A Liturgy for Ordinary Radicals.* (Grand Rapids: Zondervan, 2010).

Cohen, Deborah et al. "The Role of Pelvic Floor Muscles in Male Sexual Dysfunction and Pelvic Pain." *Sexual Medicine Reviews* 4:53e62 2016. https://www.smr.jsexmed.org/article/S2050-0521(15)00002-5/pdf

Connell, R.W. *Masculinities*, 2nd edition. (New York: Routledge, 2020).

Connor, Walker. *Ethnonationalism: The Quest for Understanding.* (Princeton: Princeton University Press, 1994).

Cook-Greuter, Susan. "Ego Development: A Full-Spectrum Theory Of Vertical Growth And Meaning Making" (Wayland: Independently published, 2021).

Corti, Roberto et al. "Coffee acutely increases sympathetic nerve activity and blood pressure independently of caffeine content: role of habitual versus nonhabitual drinking." *Circulation* vol. 106, 23, 2002. doi:10.1161/01.cir.0000046228.97025.3a

Dalai Lama [Tenzin Gyatso]. From the introduction to *Peace Is Every Step* by Hanh, Thich Nhat. (New York: Random House, 1992).

Dalai Lama. *The Universe in a Single Atom: The Convergence of Science and Spirituality.* (New York: Harmony Books, 2005).

Dansky, Steven F.; Knoebel, John; and Pitchford, Kenneth. "The Effeminist Manifesto," *Male Femininities*, edited by Dana Berkowitz, Elroi J. Windsor, and C. Winter Han, (New York: New York University Press, 2023), https://doi.org/10.18574/nyu/9781479870585.003.0005

David, Deborah Sarah; and Brannon, Robert. *The Forty-Nine Percent Majority: The Male Sex Role.* (Reading: Addison-Wesley Publishing Co., 1976).

Devereux, Paul. *Earthmind: a modern adventure in ancient wisdom* (New York: Harper and Row, 1989).

DiAngelo, Robin J. *White Fragility: Why It's So Hard for White People to Talk About Racism* (Boston: Beacon Press, 2018).

Diaz, S. et al. "IPBES: Summary for policymakers of the global assessment report on biodiversity and ecosystem services of the Intergovernmental Science-Policy Platform on Biodiversity and Ecosystem Services." IPBES secretariat, Bonn, Germany. (2019) doi:10.5281/zenodo.3553579

Economist. "The link between polygamy and war," Dec 19th, 2017.

Einstein, Albert. *Relativity: The Special and the General Theory.* (Crown, 1961).

Emerald, David. *The Power of TED: the empowerment dynamic.* (Washington: Polaris, 2009).

Emerson, Ralph Waldo. "Self-Reliance" in *Essays, First Series* (1841).

Fisher, James P. et al. "Central sympathetic overactivity: maladies and mechanisms." *Autonomic neuroscience: basic & clinical* vol. 148,1-2 2009. doi:10.1016/j.autneu.2009.02.003

Fischer, Louis. *Gandhi: His Life and Message for the World.* (New York: Signet, 2010)

Fisher, Rob. *Experiential Psychotherapy with Couples: A Guide for the Creative Pragmatist.* (Phoenix: Zeig Tucker & Theisen Inc, 2002.

Flores, Andrew R. et al. "Hate crimes against LGBT people: National Crime Victimization Survey, 2017-2019." PloS one vol. 17,12 e0279363. 21 Dec. 2022, doi:10.1371/journal.pone.0279363

Foucault, Michel. *Discipline and Punish: The Birth of the Prison* (New York: Vantage Books, 1978).

Foucault, Michel. *The History of Sexuality: An Introduction.* (New York: Vantage Books, 1990).

Foucault, Michel. *Power, Essential Works 1954-84.* (Penguin Classics, 1994).

Foucault, Michel. *Selected Interviews and Other Writings 1972-1977.* (Harvester Press, 1980).

Francis, A.J.P. "Locus of Control" In: Leeming, D.A., Madden, K., Marlan, S. (eds) *Encyclopedia of Psychology and Religion.* (Boston: Springer, 2010). https://doi.org/10.1007/978-0-387-71802-6_225

Gainsburg, Adam. *Chiron, The Wisdom of a Deeply Open Heart.* (Soulsign, 2006).

Gandhi, M. K. *Mahatma Gandhi Autobiography: The Story of My Experiments with Truth.* (Beacon Press, 1993).

Gautier, Leon. *Chivalry* (London: Routledge, 1891).

Gebser, Jean. *The Ever-Present Origin.* (Ohio: Ohio University Press, 1997).

Gendlin, Eugene T. *Focusing.* (New York: Bantam, 2007).

Girard, René. *Things Hidden Since the Foundation of the World.* (Stanford: Stanford University Press, 1987).

Girard, René. *Violence and the Sacred.* (New York: Continuum, 2005).

Gramsci, Antonio. *The Modern Prince and Other Writings.* (New York: International Publishers, 1968).

Habermas, Jurgen. *Communication and Evolution of Society.* (Boston: Beacon Press, 1979).

Haṇh Nhaṭ, Thich. *How to Fight.* (Ebury Digital, 2018).

Haṇh Nhaṭ, Thich. *A Love Letter to the Earth.* (Berkeley: Parallax, 2013).

Hathaway, Mark; Boff, Leonardo. *Tao of Liberation: Exploring the Ecology of Transformation.* (Maryknoll: Orbis Books, 2009).

Hearn, Jeff. "Men, masculinities and the material(-)discursive." International Journal for Masculinity Studies 9(1):5-17, 2014 doi:10.1080/18902138.2014.892281

Hendricks, Gay and Hendricks, Kathlyn. *Conscious Loving, the Journey to Co-Commitment.* (New York: Bantam, 1992).

Hinchliffe, Emma. "Women CEOs run 10.4% of Fortune 500 companies. A quarter of the 52 leaders became CEO in the last year." (2023). https://fortune.com/2023/06/05/fortune-500-companies-2023-women-10-percent/

Hobbes, Thomas. *The Leviathan.* 1651, from *Hobbe's Leviathan.* (Oxford, 1965).

hooks, bell. *The Will to Change: Men, Masculinity, and Love.* (New York: Washington Square Press, 2004).

Hopf, G. Michael. *Those Who Remain.* (USA: Independently published, 2016).

Huang Po and Blofeld, John. *Zen Teaching of Huang Po.* 1958.

Imai, Masaaki. *Gemba Kaizen* 2nd ed. (New York: McGraw-Hill, 2012).

Indian Council of Medical Research. "Gandhi and Health @ 150." 2020. https://main.icmr.nic.in/sites/default/files/upload_documents/Gandhi_Compendium_17_November.pdf

InformedHealth.org [Internet]. "Premature ejaculation: Overview." Cologne, Germany: Institute for Quality and Efficiency in Health Care (IQWiG), 2019 https://www.ncbi.nlm.nih.gov/books/NBK547548/

Jackson, Roger R., et al. *Tantric Treasures: Three Collections of Mystical Verse from Buddhist India.* (New York: Oxford University Press, 2004).

Johnson, Will. *The Posture of Meditation: A Practical Manual for Meditators of All Traditions.* (Boulder: Shambhala, 2004).

Jung, Carl. *Collected Works of C.G. Jung, Volume 8: The Structure and Dynamics of the Psyche.* (Princeton: Princeton University Press, 2024).

Jung, Carl. *The Collected Works of C. G. Jung, Volume 9 (Part 1): Archetypes and the Collective Unconscious.* (Princeton: Princeton University Press, 1981).

Jung, Carl. *The Red Book, A Reader's Edition.* (New York: Norton, 2009).

Kant, Immanuel. *Groundwork of the Metaphysics of Morals* (Cambridge: Cambridge University Press, 1998).

Kagan, Robert. *In Over Our Heads.* (Boston: Harvard University Press, 1996).

Kempton, Sally. *Awakening Shakti.* (Boulder: Sounds True, 2013)

Kimmerer, Robin Wall. *Braiding Sweetgrass: Indigenous Wisdom, Scientific Knowledge, and the Teachings of Plants.* (Minneapolis: Milkweed Editions, 2013).

Kivel, Paul. *Men's Work: How to Stop the Violence that Tears Our Lives Apart.* (New York: Ballantine Books, 1992).

Kivel, Paul. "Men's Work: To Stop Male Violence." (2015). Internet: http://challengingmalesupremacy.org/wp-content/uploads/2015/03/Mens-Work-To-Stop-Male-Violence-Paul-Kivel.pdf Accessed March 2024.

Kochhar, Rakesh. "The Enduring Grip of the Gender Pay Gap" Pew Research Center, 2023. https://www.pewresearch.org/social-trends/2023/03/01/the-enduring-grip-of-the-gender-pay-gap

Kohlberg, Lawrence. *Essays on Moral Development.* (San Francisco: Harper and Row, 1981).

Korten, David. *The Great Turning: From Empire to Earth Community.* (Bloomfield: Kumarian Press and Berrett-Koehler Publishers, 2006).

Krishnamurti, Jiddu. *On Conflict.* (San Francisco: HarperCollins, 1994).

Kuhn, Thomas S. *The Structure of Scientific Revolutions.* (Chicago: The University of Chicago Press, 2015).

Kurtz, Ron. *Body-Centered Psychotherapy: The Hakomi Method.* (Mendocino: LifeRhythm, 2007).

Lehr, Howard. *Changing Lenses: Restorative Justice for Our Times.* (Harrisonburg: Herald Press, 1990).

Leitzmann, Michael F. et al. "Ejaculation frequency and subsequent risk of prostate cancer." *JAMA* vol. 291,13 2004. doi:10.1001/jama.291.13.1578

Leopold, Aldo. *A Sand County Almanac: with essays on conservation from Round River.* (New York : Oxford University Press, 1970).

Levant, Ronald; and Pryor, Shana. *The Tough Standard: The Hard Truths About Masculinity and Violence.* (New York: Oxford University Press, 2020).

Levinas, Emmanuel. *Totality and Infinity.* (The Hague: Martinus Nijhoff Publishers, 1979).

Lighthorse, Pixie. *The Wound Makes the Medicine: Elemental Remediations for Transforming Heartache* (New Jersey: Row House Publishing, 2023)

Lovelock, James. *The ages of Gaia: a biography of our living earth.* (New York: Norton, 1995).

Luhmann, Niklas. "The Theory of Social Systems and Its Epistemology: Reply to Danilo Zolo's Critical Comments. Philosophy of the Social Sciences." 16(1), 129-134 (1986). https://doi.org/10.1177/004839318601600110

McIntosh, Steve. *Developmental Politics: How America Can Grow Into a Better Version of Itself.* (St. Paul: Paragon House, 2020).

McIntosh, Steve. *Integral Consciousness and the Future of Evolution.* (St. Paul: Paragon House, 2015).

Macy, Joanna and Brown, Molly. *Coming Back to Life.* (Gabriola Island: New Society Publishers, 2019).

Marmot, Michael. *The Status Syndrome: How Social Standing Affects Our Health and Longevity* (New York: Henry Holt and Co., 2004).

Mascherek, Anna et al. "Is Ejaculation Frequency in Men Related to General and Mental Health? Looking Back and Looking Forward." *Frontiers in Psychology* vol 12, 2021 doi:10.3389/fpsyg.2021.693121

Maté, Gabor. *In the Realm of Hungry Ghosts: Close Encounters with Addiction.* (Berkeley: North Atlantic Books, 2008).

Merzel, Dennis Genpo. *Big Mind, Big Heart: Finding Your Way.* (Salt Lake City: Big Mind, 2007).

Mill, John Stuart. *Utilitarianism.* (Auckland: The Floating Press, 2009).

Mishan, Ligaya. "What Does Cultural Appropriation Really Mean?" *The New York Times Style Magazine*, 2022. https://www.nytimes.com/2022/09/30/t-magazine/cultural-appropriation.html

Moore, Robert, and Douglas Gillette. *The King Within: Accessing the King in the Male Psyche.* (New York: William Morrow and Company, 1992).

Moore, Robert, and Douglas Gillette. *The Warrior Within: Accessing the Knight in the Male Psyche.* (New York: William Morrow and Company, 1992).

Moore, Robert, and Max J. Havlick. *The Archetype of Initiation: Sacred Space, Ritual Process, and Personal Transformation: Lectures and Essays.* (Xlibris Corp., 2001).

Morgenthau, Hans. *Politics Among Nations, the Struggle for Power and Peace.* (New York: Knopf, 1948).

Mukitbodhananda. *Hatha Yoga Pradipika.* (Bihar: Yoga Publications Trust, 2000).

Muñoz-Reyes, J. A. et al. "The Male Warrior Hypothesis: Testosterone-related Cooperation and Aggression in the Context of Intergroup Conflict." *Sci Rep* 10, 375 2020. doi:10.1038/s41598-019-57259-0

Musashi, Miyamoto. *The Book of Five Rings* (KTHK, 2023).

Nicholson, Dr. Sarah. *The Evolutionary Journey of Woman.* (Neo Perennial Press, 2016).

Nietzsche, Friedrich. Translated by Polt, Richard. *Twilight of the Idols.* (Indianapolis: Hackett, 1997).

Norbu, Thinley. *White Sail: Crossing the Waves of Ocean Mind to the Serene Continent of the Triple Gems.* (Boston: Shambhala 2012).

Paine, Thomas. *Common Sense.* (Philadelphia: R. Bell, 1776).

Paine, Thomas. *The American. Crisis* (USA: 1776).

Paine, Thomas. *Rights of Man.* (London: J.S. Jordan, 1791).

Pine, Red. *The Lankavatara Sutra: A Zen Text.* (Berkeley: Counterpoint, 2013).

Plato, and Benjamin Jowett. *Timaeus.* (Project Gutenberg, 2021).

Plotkin, Bill. *Nature and the Human Soul: Cultivating Wholeness and Community in a Fragmented World.* (Novato: New World Library, 2008).

Plotkin, Bill. *Wild Mind: A Field Guide to the Human Psyche.* (Novato: New World Library, 2013).

Isaac Prilleltensky; Ora Prilleltensky. *Promoting Well-Being: Linking Personal, Organizational, and Community Change* (Hoboken: John Wiley & Sons, 2006).

Purves D. et al., editors. *Neuroscience.* 2nd edition. Sunderland (MA): Sinauer Associates; 2001. The Vestibular System; and Autonomic Regulation of Sexual Function. https://www.ncbi.nlm.nih.gov/books/NBK10819/

Radin, Paul. *The Trickster: A Study In American Indian Mythology.* (Pickle Partners Publishing, 2015).

Rajneesh, Baghwan Shree. *The Tantra Vision Vol II. Speaking on the Royal Song of Saraha.* (Poona: Rajneesh Foundation, 1979).

Rawls, John. *A Theory of Justice, Revised Edition.* (Cambridge: Belknap Press, 1999).

Ray, Reginald A. *The Practice of Pure Awareness: Somatic Meditation for Awakening the Sacred.* (Boulder: Shambhala, 2018).

Ray, Reginald A. *Secret of the Vajra World: The Tantric Buddhism of Tibet.* (Boulder: Shambhala, 2002).

Redekop, Vern. *From Violence to Blessing.* (Toronto: Novalis, 2002).

Richardson, Katherine et al., "Earth beyond six of nine planetary boundaries." Sci. Adv. 9, eadh 2458 (2023). DOI:10.1126/sciadv.adh2458

Rider, Jennifer R. et al. "Ejaculation Frequency and Risk of Prostate Cancer: Updated Results with an Additional Decade of Follow-up." *European Urology* vol. 70,6 2016. doi:10.1016/j.eururo.2016.03.027

Rioux, Jean-Francios, and Redekop, Vern Neufeld. *Introduction to Conflict Studies, Empirical, Theoretical, and Ethical Dimensions.* (Ontario: Oxford University Press, 2013).

Risman, Barbara J. et al., *Handbook of the Sociology of Gender, 2nd ed.* (New York: Springer, 2018).

Ritchie, Hannah. *Not the End of the World: How We Can Be the First Generation to Build a Sustainable Planet* (New York: Little, Brown and Company, 2024).

Roche, Lorin. *The Radiance Sutras.* (Boulder: Sounds True, 2014).

Rosado, Raúl. *Consciousness-in-Action, Toward an Integral Psychology of Liberation and Transformation.* (Puerto Rico: Ilé Publications, 2007).

Roser, Max. "Mortality in the past: every second child died." 2023, Apr; Published online at OurWorldInData.org. Retrieved from: 'https://ourworldindata.org/child-mortality-in-the-past'

Roszak, Theodore, et al. *Ecopsychology: Restoring the Earth, Healing the Mind.* (San Francisco: Sierra Club Books, 1995).

Ruiz, Don Miguel. *The Four Agreements* (San Rafael: Amber-Allen Publishing, 1997).

Sammut, G., and Howarth, C. "Social Representations." In: *Encyclopedia of Critical Psychology.* Springer, 2014. https://doi.org/10.1007/978-1-4614-5583-7_292

Sathyanarayana Rao, T. S. et al. "The biochemistry of belief." *Indian journal of psychiatry* vol. 51,4 2009. doi:10.4103/0019-5545.58285

Schapiro, Steven A., "Changing men: the rationale, theory, and design of a men's consciousness raising program." (1985). Doctoral Dissertations 1896 - February 2014. 4041. https://scholarworks.umass.edu/dissertations_1/4041

Schwartz, Richard C. and Sweezy, Martha. *Internal Family Systems Therapy*, 2nd ed (New York: The Guilford Press, 2020).

Sharma, Jai Narayan. *Rediscovering Gandhi. Vol III. Gandhi's Approach to Conflict Resolution.* (New Delhi: Concept Publishing, 2008).

Sidanius, Jim; Pratto, Felicia. *Social Dominance: An Intergroup Theory of Social Hierarchy and Oppression.* (Cambridge: Cambridge University Press, 1999).

Silverstein, Olga. *The Courage to Raise Good Men.* (Toronto: Viking, 1994).

Somé, Sobonfu. *The Spirit of Intimacy.* (New York: Quill, 2002).

Stanford Encyclopedia of Philosophy Archive. "Moral Relativism" 2019. https://plato.stanford.edu/archives/sum2019/entries/moral-relativism/

Sturm, Matt. *The Organic Masculine, Lore Book I: The Magician* (New York: Manhattan Book Group, 2023).

Taylor, Charles. *Sources of the Self, Making of the Modern Identity* (Cambridge: Harvard University Press, 2001).

Taylor, Dianna. *Sexual Violence and Humiliation (Interdisciplinary Research in Gender).* 1st ed., Routledge, 2021.

Teicher, Martin H. "Scars That Won't Heal: The Neurobiology of Child Abuse." *Scientific American,* 2002. doi: 10.1038/scientificamerican0302-68

Tomkins Institute. "Nine affects, present at birth, combine with life experience to form emotion and personality." Accessed 2023. http://www.tomkins.org/what-tomkins-said/introduction/nine-affects-present-at-birth-combine-to-form-emotion-mood-and-personality/

Trungpa, Choğyam and Carolyn Rose Gimian. *Shambhala: The Sacred Path of the Warrior*. (Boulder: Shambhala, 2019).

Underhill, Evelyn. *Mysticism: The Preeminent Study in the Nature and Development of Spiritual Consciousness*. (New York: Doubleday, 1990).

UN Women. "Facts and figures: Women's leadership and political participation." (2024). https://www.unwomen.org/en/what-we-do/leadership-and-political-participation/facts-and-figures

United Nations General Assembly. "Universal Declaration of Human Rights." (1948). https://www.un.org/en/about-us/universal-declaration-of-human-rights

United Nations General Assembly. "United Nations Declaration on the Rights of Peasants and Other People Working in Rural Areas." (2018). https://digitallibrary.un.org/record/1650694?ln=en

United Nations Office on Drugs and Crime. "Global Study on Homicide." (2023). https://www.unodc.org/documents/data-and-analysis/gsh/2023/Global_study_on_homicide_2023_web.pdf

van der Kolk, Bessel. *The Body Keeps the Score: Brain, Mind, and Body in the Healing of Trauma*. (New York: Penguin Publishing Group, 2014).

Van Vugt, Mark et al. "Gender Differences in Cooperation and Competition: the Male-Warrior Hypothesis." *Psychological Science*. Vol 18 No 1 2007. 10.1111/j.1467-9280.2007.01842.x

Vonnegut, Kurt. *Slapstick*. (New York: Dial Press Trade Paperbacks, 2010).

Wade, Jenny. *Changes of Mind, A Holonomic Theory of the Evolution of Conscoiusness*. (Albany: SUNY Press, 1996).

Wallis, Christopher. "The real story on the Chakras." 2016. https://tantrikstudies.squarespace.com/blog/2016/2/5/the-real-story-on-the-chakras

Walsh, Roger. *Staying alive: the psychology of human survival*. (Boulder: New Science Library, 1984).

Watts, Alan. *Become What You Are*. (Boston: Shambhala, 2003)

Weiss, Halko; Johanson, Greg; Monda, Lorena. *Hakomi Mindfulness-Centered Somatic Psychotherapy: A Comprehensive Guide to Theory and Practice*. (New York: W. W. Norton & Company, 2015).

Whipple, Beverly et al. "Physiological correlates of imagery-induced orgasm in women." *Archives of Sexual Behavior* 21(2):121-33, 1992. doi:10.1007/BF01542589

Whitehead, Alfred North. *Process and Reality (Gifford Lectures Delivered in the University of Edinburgh During the Session 1927-28).* (New York: Free Press, 1978).

Whorf, Benjamin. *Language Thought and Reality.* (Cambridge: MIT Press, 1959).

Wilber, Ken. "Excerpt A: An Integral Age at the Leading Edge." 5 parts. Ken Wilber Online. 2002

Wilber, Ken. *Integral Psychology: Consciousness, Spirit, Psychology, Therapy.* (Boulder: Shambhala, 2000).

Wilber, Ken. *The Religion of Tomorrow: A Vision for the Future of the Great Traditions: More Inclusive, More Comprehensive, More Complete.* (Boulder: Shambhala, 2018).

Wilber, Ken. *Sex, Ecology, Spirituality: The Spirit of Evolution.* (Boulder: Shambhala, 2000).

Wilber, Ken. "Waves, Streams, and Self - a Summary of My Psychological Model." online, 2001.

Wilkerson, Isabel. *Caste: The Origins of Our Discontents.* (New York: Penguin, 2020).

Wingfield, John C. et al. "The 'Challenge Hypothesis': Theoretical Implications for Patterns of Testosterone Secretion, Mating Systems, and Breeding Strategies." *The American Naturalist* Vol 136, No 6, 1990. http://www.jstor.org/stable/2462170

Winston, Sheri. *Women's Anatomy of Arousal: Secret Maps to Buried Pleasure.* (Kingston: Mango Garden Press, 2010).

World Health Organization. "Depression and Other Common Mental Disorders: Global Health Estimates." Geneva: 2017. https://www.who.int/publications/i/item/depression-global-health-estimates

World Health Organization. "Global Status Report on Violence Prevention 2014." (2014) https://www.who.int/publications/i/item/9789241564793

Wu, Natalie. "The World's Richest Self-Made Women In 2024." (2024) https://www.forbes.com/sites/nataliewu/2024/04/03/the-worlds-richest-self-made-women-in-2024-taylor-swift-kim-kardashian-rihanna

ABOUT MATT

Matt Sturm is a guide for transformational experiences through coaching, psychotherapy, psychedelic-assisted therapy, sacred sexuality, breathwork journeys, and men's retreats. He runs the Living Kosmos integral mystery school, focusing on the evolution of consciousness, and offers leadership coaching through mattsturm.com. In addition to *Primal Drives*, he is the author of *The Organic Masculine*.

www.ingramcontent.com/pod-product-compliance
Lightning Source LLC
Chambersburg PA
CBHW080749120626
46557CB00005B/1205